CRIMINAL &
BEHAVIORAL
PROFILING

*One more for Kai, Maddie, Darya, and Shannon,
each one a profile in goodness, intelligence, wit, and beauty.*

CRIMINAL & BEHAVIORAL PROFILING

Curt R. Bartol

Anne M. Bartol

Los Angeles | London | New Delhi
Singapore | Washington DC

Los Angeles | London | New Delhi
Singapore | Washington DC

FOR INFORMATION:

SAGE Publications, Inc.
2455 Teller Road
Thousand Oaks, California 91320
E-mail: order@sagepub.com

SAGE Publications Ltd.
1 Oliver's Yard
55 City Road
London EC1Y 1SP
United Kingdom

SAGE Publications India Pvt. Ltd.
B 1/I 1 Mohan Cooperative Industrial Area
Mathura Road, New Delhi 110 044
India

SAGE Publications Asia-Pacific Pte. Ltd.
3 Church Street
#10-04 Samsung Hub
Singapore 049483

Publisher: Jerry Westby
Publishing Associate: MaryAnn Vail
Production Editor: Libby Larson
Copy Editor: Teresa Herlinger
Typesetter: C&M Digitals (P) Ltd
Proofreader: Theresa Kay
Indexer: Judy Hunt
Cover Designer: Anupama Krishnan
Marketing Manager: Terra Schultz
Permissions Editor: Karen Ehrmann

Printed in the United States of America

Library of Congress Cataloging-in-Publication Data

Bartol, Curt R.

Criminal & behavioral profiling / Curt R. Bartol.

p. cm.
Includes bibliographical references and index.

ISBN 978-1-4129-8308-2 (pbk.)

1. Criminal behavior, Prediction of. 2. Criminal profilers
3. Criminal investigation. I. Bartol, Anne M. II. Title.

HV8073.5.B368 2013
364.3—dc23   2012019296

This book is printed on acid-free paper.

12 13 14 15 10 9 8 7 6 5 4 3 2 1

Brief Contents

Detailed Contents

Preface

Profiling can be broadly defined as a technique that identifies behavioral, cognitive, emotional, and demographic characteristics of known and unknown individuals, based on clues gleaned from a wide range of information. That information includes but is not limited to crime scenes, databases, documents, published research, interviews, and even suicide notes. When we first proposed writing a profiling book, some people were skeptical. After all, what can you say about profiling? It works or it doesn't work; it's an art or it's a science; it's helpful or it's harmful. These statements are relevant, but they do not begin to touch upon the content of this book.

Most readers will be familiar with profiling in its criminal context. They have read books, watched fictional profilers in the entertainment media, heard about profiling related to sensational crimes, and perhaps visited the websites of both self-proclaimed and well-recognized profilers. However, these sources rarely address theory and research on profiling, which is a main mission in the present book. In addition, they rarely mention the psychological concepts that lead us to be cautious about the profiling endeavor and help identify the many pitfalls in the process. Furthermore, many readers may not think of profiling as it applies to civil cases. We have titled the book *Criminal & Behavioral Profiling* to make these points.

We use the generic term *profiling* throughout the book for consistency, but other terms are used both in practice and in the research literature. These include behavioral analysis, psychological profiling, criminal profiling, offender profiling, and behavioral investigative analysis, among others. "Profilers" are given comparable titles, such as behavioral analyst. As we note in the book, profiling is regarded with so much suspicion in some quarters that the same techniques by a different name are considered more acceptable.

To organize the material, we have divided profiling into five types: crime scene profiling, geographic profiling, psychological profiling, suspect-based profiling, and equivalent death analysis (or psychological autopsies). These types are not mutually exclusive—they often overlap—but the division is helpful in understanding profiling in its broad context. The content of the book has largely been dictated by the research currently being conducted in these five subdivisions.

The first efforts at profiling—covered in Chapter 1—were attempts to speculate about a possible offender based on clues from the crime scene, typically involving sensational or serial crimes. Investigators, stymied in their efforts to identify the perpetrator, turned to early profilers for assistance. Over the years, particularly in association with the FBI, profiling developed in both its training and techniques to the point where it is now generally accepted in law enforcement practice. Nevertheless, there are very few individuals who are "certified" as behavioral analysts, and the profession still has a long way to go before being accepted as a valid scientific enterprise.

In the early chapters, we contrast rather sharply the crime scene profiling methods promoted by the FBI with those promoted by profilers in the United Kingdom, Canada, Australia, and other countries. While all of these profilers now prefer to be called "analysts," the FBI methods were more clinical or subjectively based; early profilers, many of whom still work as consultants today, preferred to see their work as a craft rather than a science, and their conclusions were arrived at through hunches and "gut feelings" based on extensive experience at crime investigation. Throughout the book, we refer often to the work of FBI profilers. By contrast, analysts in the United Kingdom, Canada, Australia, and some other countries depend upon the actuarial method, which involves developing large databases for statistical analyses of crimes. In recent years, the database approach has gained more favor internationally, although it is still regarded with suspicion, and its methods and databases need validation.

Geographic profiling—the work done by geoprofilers—is relatively unknown to many people. Geoprofilers try to hone in on the place of residence of an offender based on the location of crimes. Geographic profiling is the modern-day equivalent of placing pins in a map to try to determine where a serial offender may live and where he or she may strike next. It is, of course, far more technologically advanced, and the reader may be surprised to learn about some of the techniques that are available to investigators. Psychological profiling is typically performed on a known individual, but another form of psychological profiling involves examining research-based typologies and deciding whether someone matches them. This is a controversial topic, because many typologies have been proposed but few have been validated. We discuss various typologies in the middle chapters of the book. Suspect-based profiling—also a controversial area—is often used by government agents to interdict drug trafficking, prevent terrorist activities, or identify those with other forms of malicious intent. Finally, psychological autopsies are gaining considerable attention in both criminal and civil contexts. Here, the psychologist gathers information about a deceased person in an attempt to understand the manner of death, particularly in cases where a suicide may be a homicide, or vice versa.

This book is distinct from other profiling books in several ways. First, the five-part division—which we have made in an effort to improve readability—is unique. Second, the book has an international flavor, integrating research, theory, practice, and examples from not only the United States but also Great Britain, Canada, and Australia, among other areas. Third, we emphasize the ongoing importance—for profiling purposes—of gathering information about the victim and how serial offenders treat their victims. In addition, we are skeptical—although not dismissive—of profiling approaches that rely too heavily on typologies of crimes and offenders, and we are supportive of approaches that promote *both* actuarial and clinical methods.

By way of acknowledgments, we are greatly indebted to publisher Jerry Westby, a long-time supporter of our work. Throughout this project, from providing the first very helpful reviews of our proposal to waiting patiently while we completed the project, Jerry has been a good friend and a steady presence. Dina Allen, editorial assistant, found valuable resources for us and gave incisive comments on various chapters of the book. We appreciate the input of professors who reviewed the book's original prospectus and outline and provided suggestions for what might be added or deleted. To our efficient and perceptive copy editor, Teresa Herlinger, we say once again: thank you for leading us to the *real* finish line; you're the best. We also thank MaryAnn Vail and Libby Larson. Finally, and as always, we are grateful for the continuing love and laughter provided by our immediate family: Shannon, Darya, Maddie, Kai, Jim, Soraya, Ian, and Gina—listed this time in reverse order of when they came into our lives! We'd be lost without you.

1

Introduction

In the late 20th century and into the 21st, criminal "profiling" became ubiquitous. Profilers, some but not all lacking professional credentials, appeared on media talk shows, wrote books, or offered their services to police to help identify and apprehend suspects. At times, the profilers were law enforcement agents or former agents; at other times, they were individuals with academic backgrounds in psychology, psychiatry, criminology, or even literature. Occasionally, the profilers held dubious degrees from questionable correspondence schools. This range of backgrounds—from the person who has extensive experience in criminal investigation or psychological research to the person with minimal credentials seeking the media spotlight—continues today.

In crime news, the media sometimes cover stories in which profilers help solve crimes, while other stories indicate they were not accurate in their predictions. Among the most notable in the latter category is the Beltway Sniper case in the fall of 2002, when 10 people were killed and 3 were critically wounded in shootings in Maryland and Virginia and the general Washington, D.C., area over a 3-week period. In that case, profilers told police the sniper probably was white, lived in the vicinity, and acted alone. Because white panel trucks were seen at the site of many of the shootings, attention was placed on these vehicles. The snipers were apprehended without resistance at a rest stop as they slept in their blue Chevrolet Caprice sedan with a shooting hole cut out of its trunk. They were identified as 41-year-old John Allen Muhammad and his 17-year-old companion, Lee Boyd Malvo. Both were African American, unemployed, with no permanent ties to the area. The car had attracted police attention at least 10 times, once when they were sleeping overnight in their car, but as D.C. Police Chief Charles Ramsey stated, based on the profile, police were on the lookout for a white van driven by a white male. When the case was solved, the profilers were widely derided for their inaccurate predictions. Muhammad has since been executed, and Malvo is serving a life sentence without the possibility of parole.

In popular literature and the entertainment media, though, profilers are more often glorified than criticized. In 1991, the film *The Silence of the Lambs*, based on the book by Thomas Harris, introduced the public to the exciting role of the profiler in police work. A number of additional films of the genre followed, including *Slaughter of the*

Innocents, When the Bough Breaks, The Bone Collector, Kiss the Girls, Se7en, Copycat, Postmortem, Resurrection, The Watcher, Murder by Numbers, and television series such as *Prime Suspect, Criminal Minds, Cracker,* and *Profiler.* As noted by Canter, Alison, Alison, and Wentink (2004), information about profiling is most often disseminated in the form of popular books intended for a nontechnical and inexpert audience, rather than in peer-reviewed professional or scholarly journals. When loosely formulated and often unsubstantiated theories and methods are featured in movies and television shows, this is sometimes referred to as the "Hollywood effect" (Canter & Youngs, 2003). However, as one detective told researchers investigating the usefulness of profiling to law enforcement, "There is no Cracker" (Gekoski & Gray, 2011). In other words, the perfect profiler does not exist.

Nonetheless, crime shows and films typically extol the competence and worth of profilers. Their lives are often portrayed as charmed, frenetic, and/or controversial. They are witty and perceptive, occasionally gruff, and they sometimes skirt the law to gain access to information. Their cases are riveting, with no shortage of grisly detail, and these fictional profilers invariably solve them. "The resulting popular image of a profiler is a quasi-mythical being with special abilities and intuition that always help him to successfully target wanted criminals" (Bourque, LeBlanc, Utzschneider, & Wright, 2009, p. 15).

More controversial forms of profiling also have emerged. Specifically, law enforcement agents have sometimes used characteristics such as race, religion, or ethnicity to detain individuals who might fit the "profile" of a drug dealer or a ter-rorist. More recently, partly in response to criticisms about focusing on factors like race or ethnicity, law enforcement agents look for behavioral indicators. As just one illustration, some Transportation Safety Agents are now trained as "behavioral detection officers" who passively observe passengers in airports for signs of charac-teristics that deviate from those of the average passenger (U.S. Department of Homeland Security, 2008). We will discuss this again in Chapter 7. In addition, some criminologists maintain that they can identify a rapist profile, or a batterer profile, or a child sex abuser profile—and to some extent this is possible. That is— as we shall cover in later chapters—rapists, batterers, and child sex abusers often (but not always) have characteristics in common. In more recent years, a form of profiling called geographic profiling has been gaining attention in the research lit-erature as well as among law enforcement agencies worldwide. These various forms of profiling will be addressed in this book.

Early Accounts of Profiling

Although profiling captured the public interest relatively recently, it actually has a long history, perhaps as far back as 500 years. According to Woodworth and Porter (1999), the documented history of profiling dates back to the publication of the *Malleus Maleficarum (The Hammer of Witches),* written during the late 1400s by two Dominican monks who were commissioned by the Catholic Church to produce a document for the purpose of accurately identifying, interrogating, and eradicating witches. That text may represent the first systematic approach for "profiling" individuals who were supposedly guilty of horrific crimes, such as the killing of children and the torture of animals. The book, which was published in 28 editions between 1486 and 1600, became the handbook for witch hunters and inquisitors throughout medieval Europe. Witches were said to make diabolic compacts with evil, to be transported in the sky at night, to have sexual relations with the devil, and to stir up hailstorms, among other unusual and outrageous acts. To help identify witches, witch hunters were advised to look for persons who had visible marks (scars, moles, birthmarks) on their body, who chanted incantations over the sick, or used herbal remedies to alleviate suffering. The *Malleus Malificarum* also prescribed numerous methods of eliciting confessions, such as hanging suspected witches by their thumbs or placing them naked in cold cells with thumbscrews attached to their fingers.

Profilers today obviously do not take such drastic and primitive approaches. Quite possibly, the idea for *modern* profiling emerged from early literary works, including detective novels (Bourque et al., 2009). Bourque and his colleagues suggest that the first "profiler" may have appeared in Edgar Allan Poe's *The Murders in the Rue Morgue*, published in 1841. Poe created the fictional detective C. Auguste Dupin, a somewhat eccentric French police officer who pieced together clues based on newspaper reports and a single visit to the crime scene. Eventually, he solved the crime through the process of "ratiocination," meaning he was able to put himself into the mind of the criminal through rational thought and a vivid imagination. The character Dupin solved more crime mysteries in Poe's next two detective novels, *The Mystery of Marie Rogêt* (1842) and *The Purloined Letter* (1844). In addition, the fictional detective Sherlock Holmes, created by Sir Arthur Conan Doyle in 1887, consistently employed a form of criminal profiling in his intriguing search for the offender. Since then, the main characters in many detective or mystery novels engage in criminal profiling or seek profiling assistance.

In real life, and closer in time to the present, profiling can be traced back to Jack the Ripper, the serial killer who brutally murdered five prostitutes in separate incidents in London's East End in 1888. Although the case was never solved, the chief forensic pathologist, Dr. George Baxter Phillips, tried to help police investigators by inferring personality characteristics based on the nature of the wounds inflicted on the victims (Turvey, 2012). Phillips reconstructed various crime scenes and described the wounds of victims to gain a greater insight into the offender's psychological makeup. Phillips believed that an examination of the wound patterns of murder victims could provide clues about both the behavior and personality of the offender. That is, he noticed that the wounds were inflicted with considerable skill and knowledge, suggesting that the killer had a sophisticated understanding of human anatomy. "In particular, he was referring to the postmortem removal of . . . organs, and what he felt was the cleanliness and preciseness of the incisions involved" (Turvey, 2002, p. 10).

The profiling of *known* individuals—and not necessarily those suspected of crimes—is also not a new undertaking. For example, during World War II, an intelligence officer in the U.S. Office of Strategic Services (OSS) named William Langer created a profile of Adolf Hitler, based upon all material about Hitler he could assemble from various reports (Ault & Reese, 1980). This form of profiling will be discussed in Chapter 6.

Origins of Modern Profiling

In the United States, profiling in its modern form was publicly acknowledged during a police manhunt in New York during the 1940s and 1950s, a hunt that ended with the arrest of George Metesky, called the "Mad Bomber." Metesky apparently planted about 47 homemade bombs during a 16-year reign of terror. Police at one point contacted Dr. James Brussel, a psychiatrist who offered clues to the possible identity of the bomber. There is debate over the extent to which Brussel's profile was actually helpful—one police officer indicated that the profile could fit most men within a certain age range—but there is no debate that Brussel brought profiling to the forefront. As a result, he is often considered the "father of profiling" in the United States. Brussel also served as a consultant to the Behavioral Science Unit (BSU) of the FBI when it established its profiling unit in 1972. We discuss the history of the BSU in Chapter 2. In the present chapter, we cover the **Mad Bomber case** in some detail because of its historical significance, and also because Brussel's work illustrates both the benefits and the costs of crime scene profiling.

In England, interest in profiling soared in the mid-1980s, in two different directions. First, some psychologists, such as Paul Britton, began offering advice to police that was similar to that provided by James Brussel in the United States. Britton's star began to fade after he was involved in a very controversial undercover operation to persuade a suspect to confess to a brutal murder, which it was later learned the suspect did not commit. A judge freed the suspect, noted that profiling was far too unscientific to be admitted into criminal trials, and even questioned its use by police in investigating a crime. The case (*Regina v. Stagg, 1994*), along with the specific comments made by the judge, will be discussed in Chapter 9. In the other direction British profiling took, psychologist David Canter contributed to the investigation leading to the arrest of the railway rapists, John Duffy and David Mulcahy (Hicks & Sales, 2006). Canter's approach to profiling was more statistically oriented, and he eventually established the first university program in investigative psychology at the University of Liverpool in 1994—a center that continues today and is highlighted in Chapter 3.

As you will see throughout this book, profiling can be regarded as both an art and a science. Some see it as a sham; others are guarded and cautious, but are willing to acknowledge its potential; still others are avidly supportive of its use. In recent years, particularly because profiling evidence is sometimes introduced in criminal and civil courts, there are more calls for careful research on profiling techniques. As we will note, the courts have set criteria for allowing the testimony of experts in court hearings and trials; profilers who want to testify—particularly if they are not law enforcement agents—must justify the scientific basis of their approach. However, many professional profilers are not prepared to reveal their methods, for fear of being criticized or copied

(Hicks & Sales, 2006). James Brussel called his "method" his own private blend of science, intuition, and hope (Ramsland, 2009), and did not tell how he arrived at this blend. We turn now to a discussion of the case that brought Brussel considerable fame.

THE MAD BOMBER CASE

"Con Edison Crooks. This is for you."

So read the note attached to a bomb left on a windowsill in a toolbox at the Consolidated Edison Building in New York City in November 1940. The bomb consisted of a short brass pipe filled with gunpowder that police believed was from rifle bullets, but either by design or faulty technique, it did not detonate. The release, or triggering, mechanism contained sugar, which is linked with dry-cell batteries. Nearly a year later, a similar bomb was found lying in the street about four blocks from Con Ed headquarters. There was no note, and that crude bomb, which was wrapped in a red sock, also did not detonate. Neither bomb drew much attention, but New York detectives speculated that the person who made them probably was someone on the company payroll with easy access to the building—possibly a former employee who had been fired and harbored bitter resentment (Meagher, 1956).

After the United States entered World War II in December of 1941, police received a letter from the bomber. He wrote that he would no longer make bombs for the duration of the war, indicating that his patriotic feelings led him to stop temporarily. However, once the war had ended, the bomber sent a letter that said, "I WILL BRING THE CON EDISON TO JUSTICE—THEY WILL PAY FOR THEIR DASTARDLY DEEDS . . . F. P." It would later be revealed that these initials stood for "fair play."

During his hiatus, however, the bomber continued to send letters and postcards to the police, newspapers, theaters, hotels, private citizens, and Con Edison executives, many letters containing the words and phrases "dastardly deeds" or "acts" and signed with the initials F. P. (See Focus 1.1 for a discussion of the relationship between the bomber and New York newspapers.)

The gunpowder-filled pipe bombs began to reappear in 1951, the first one detonating in Grand Central Terminal. Some bombs were discovered before they detonated, others did not detonate, and some detonated but caused no injuries. The Grand Central bomb was followed by other bombs at Con Ed, the Paramount Theatre, subway stations, Radio City Music Hall, telephone booths, and other theaters. The first injury occurred in December of 1952, when a bomb exploded at the Lexington Theatre (Greenburg, 2011). In 1953, the bomber placed bombs at Radio City Music Hall, Penn Station and Grand Central Station, and the Capitol Theatre. Three more bombs were placed in 1954, and another in 1955.

Altogether, over his 16-year history, the bomber had targeted numerous locations, including the New York Public Library, Radio City Music Hall, Macy's, the Port Authority Bus Terminal, train stations, and several phone booths (Greenburg, 2011). The seemingly random placement of the bombs was baffling to the police, who concluded that the bomber was probably an eccentric and possibly "mad." Hence, the perpetrator was soon dubbed the "Mad Bomber of New York City."

Focus 1.1

Metesky and the Media

An interesting aspect of the "Mad Bomber" case was Metesky's relationship with the news media. During his bombing spree period, he wrote to the *New York Herald Tribune*, the *Journal American,* and the *New York Times,* warning that he planned to continue planting bombs until justice was done. The writing appeared to be fairly literate, and it was always in heavy pencil in printed letters. The letters G and Y were rather peculiar, and the detectives thought that this indicated the person was educated in a European country (Meagher, 1956). Sometimes, the bomber would send notes that were created from pasted block letters from newspapers or magazines rather than hand printed.

The *Journal American* in particular established an ongoing correspondence with the bomber. The newspaper agreed to publish his letters and even promised to investigate his injury case against Con Edison (Considine, 1957). The *Journal American* kept this promise, as Greenburg (2011) noted: Within hours of his arrest, the paper retained the services of a prominent attorney to represent him in his compensation claim. After his capture, Metesky revealed that he had come very close to walking into the *Journal American* editorial office to get some "first-hand advice" (Considine, 1957, p. 25). He told investigators that he appreciated what the newspaper had done for him and said, "I felt I had to talk to someone" (p. 25).

After the bomber was captured, many credited the *Journal American* with helping solve the case. On the other hand, media scholars and critics have argued that the press in the Mad Bomber case often skirted ethical boundaries and allowed itself to be manipulated by Metesky. Greenburg (2011) notes that the newspaper took full advantage of the acclaim it received; its representatives allowed themselves to be interviewed, and the paper published virtually every accolade that came across its editorial desks.

Greenburg (2011) has written an extensive and well-documented account of the years of terror inflicted on New York by the bomber. The unpredictable appearance of the bombs produced intense public anxiety and taxed the resources of the New York City Police Department. When bombs were found under seats of movie theaters, parents understandably began to forbid their children to attend movies. Often, the bomb placements were accompanied by warning phone calls to police or the media, but the caller did not provide an exact location of the bomb. Some bombs were timed to detonate precisely at the start of rush hour (Greenburg, 2011). No one died from bombs that detonated, but many were injured, some seriously.

The police were quite certain that the bomber had been in the armed service because the postwar bombs were of semi-military design. Furthermore, they identified and investigated 9,750 persons with a history of mental illness in the New York metropolitan area, focusing on those with mechanical skills, such as toolmakers, machinists, electricians, and plumbers. The police even believed that they had identified a time pattern in that the bombs had been planted within 3 days of a full moon. This hypothesis led some detectives to refer to the bomber as a "mooner" or "the moon bomber." At one point during the investigation, a person was arrested as a suspect and was sent to Bellevue Hospital for psychiatric evaluation; during his 37-day evaluation period, another bomb was placed, and authorities realized they had arrested the wrong man.

In December 1956, after a bomb went off under a seat in the Paramount Movie Theatre in Brooklyn, New York Police Commissioner Stephen P. Kennedy ordered the department to undertake the greatest manhunt in the history of the department ("Suspect Is Held as 'Mad Bomber,'" 1957). Note that by that time, numerous bombs had been placed, many had exploded, and some had caused injuries. The New York Bomb Investigation Unit, the Police Bureau of Technical Service, handwriting experts, fingerprint technicians, demolition engineers, and machinists all worked on the case. A reward of $26,000 was offered for the apprehension of the mysterious "F. P." by the Board of Estimate and the Patrolmen's Benevolent Association.

Interestingly, police investigators had apparently contacted several psychiatrists and possibly psychologists during their 16-year search for the bomber. However, none of their names was revealed to the press except for that of Dr. James A. Brussel, Assistant Commissioner of the New York State Department of Mental Hygiene. By all accounts, Brussel offered the most interesting and perhaps the most comprehensive "profile" of the bomber during the investigation. He was given access to the bomber's postcards and every scrap of information police considered significant to the investigation, including crime scene photographs. Brussel then provided an oral profile within hours of reviewing the information. The profile was eventually published in the *New York Times* on Christmas Day, 1956:

> Single man, between 40 and 50 years old, introvert. Unsocial but not anti-social. Skilled mechanic. Cunning. Neat with tools. Egotistical of mechanical skill. Contemptuous of other people. Resentful of criticism of his work but probably conceals resentment. Moral. Honest. [Not] interested in women. High school graduate. Expert in civil or military ordnance. Religious. Might flare up violent at work when criticized. Possible motive: discharge or reprimand. Feels superior to critics. Resentment keeps growing. Present or former Consolidated Edison worker. Probably case of progressive paranoia. (quoted in Meagher, 1956, p. 31)

In his memoirs, *Casebook of a Crime Psychiatrist*, Brussel (1968) refers to the profile quoted above and stated it included his essential and major predictions (p. 47). The profile really did not add much information beyond what the police detectives had theorized or already knew, but to some extent it validated their suspicions. The police had surmised, long before consulting Brussel, that the bomber had a grudge against Con Ed, and they strongly suspected he was either a current or past employee of the utility company.

A different version of the profile appeared in newspapers across the country a week later, in January 1957, shortly before the bomber was captured:

> He believes he has a pact with God to right some wrong done to him by the Consolidated Edison Company, the first victim of his bombing attempts 16 years ago. He feels he is persecuted and has no qualms or conscience about destroying lives or property in "getting back" at instituted authorities who have "done him wrong." (Winship, 1957, p. 9)

On that same date, the Associated Press (Winship, 1957) further reported that Dr. Brussel believed the bomber was of German descent and might live in Manhattan's East Side "Yorkville" district. Brussel further thought he was a skilled mechanic and might have worked for Con Ed at some time during the 1930s. In addition, Brussel predicted that the bomber led the life of a lone wolf and would probably have the appearance of a quiet, scholarly, middle-aged man.

Several weeks later, 53-year-old George Metesky was arrested in Waterbury, Connecticut. When detectives closed in on the three-family apartment house shortly after midnight, Metesky was in bed. As the police officers entered the house, they told a barely awake Metesky that they were investigating an accident. Metesky greeted them cordially (in his robe and pajamas) and said to the police, "You're looking for more than an accident," and then, "I guess it's because you suspect that I am the mad bomber" (quoted in Sheehan & Butler, 1957, p. 12). He smiled frequently and appeared to be in a state of high self-satisfaction at being captured. When the police ordered Metesky to get dressed, he reappeared wearing a double-breasted suit, buttoned. Photos of him surrounded by arresting officers show a bespectacled man smiling broadly (see Photo 1.1). It was only after extensive questioning through the night that Metesky eventually confessed. Due to the statute of limitations in effect at that time, he could only be charged with crimes that occurred from March 1952 forward (Greenburg, 2011).

Photo 1.1: George Metesky, the "Mad Bomber," flashes a smile as he is led by police into the station in Waterbury, Connecticut, for booking.

After his arrest, details about Metesky's motivation for his 16-year bombing mission began to emerge. On September 5, 1931, he was working on a generator wiper at the company's plant when a broiler produced a blast of hot gases, knocking him to the ground. The hot gasses filled his lungs, causing serious and extensive lung damage. The accident left him disabled; after collecting 26 weeks of sick pay, he lost his job. Eventually, he developed a disabling case of pulmonary tuberculosis, which he believed was directly linked to the Con Ed accident. According to his two older sisters, he was in bed much of the time, coughing blood after the accident, and unable to eat. After receiving hospital treatment for months, he was told he would have to go to Arizona for relief for his lungs, which he did. However, while in Arizona, financial support from his sisters and parents began to run out. He returned to Connecticut and sought monetary compensation from Con Ed for his injury. Unfortunately, his claim for workers' compensation was denied because he had waited too long to file it. Metesky was angry and resentful about the injury and the fact that he had never been justifiably compensated—thus his habit of signing his notes F. P., for fair play.

Metesky was the youngest child and only son of Lithuanian immigrant parents. A resident of Waterbury, Connecticut, all his life, he lived with his unmarried sisters who supported him during his 20 years of unemployment. Additional background information revealed that Metesky did not complete high school, but did serve in the military as a Marine Corps specialist electrician at the United States Consulate in Shanghai (Berger, 1957). When he returned home, he worked as a machinist for a subsidiary of Con Ed for 2 years (1929–1931). Metesky was interested in women and had a steady girlfriend at the time of his arrest, but refused to name her. Although he considered himself a devout Catholic, he could not bring himself to confess his bombing "sins."

Interestingly, Metesky was never put on trial for the offenses. He was arraigned and then sent to Matteawan State Hospital for observation and assessment of whether he was competent to stand trial. Following this initial examination period, he returned to court where a judge in 1957 declared that he lacked the sufficient ability to understand the charges against him and help his attorney in his own defense—in other words, he was found incompetent to stand trial. Throughout these early court appearances, Metesky beamed and seemed to be enjoying the attention he was gaining in the press. Metesky remained at Matteawan, but his lawyers continually challenged the state's authority to keep him there (Greenburg, 2011). Approximately 15 years later, in the case *Jackson v. Indiana* (1972), the U.S. Supreme Court ruled that a defendant found incompetent to stand trial could not be committed to a mental hospital indefinitely unless he was making progress toward competency—"treat me or release me," Jackson had told his doctors. However, if he was considered dangerous to the public, an incompetent defendant could be committed to a mental institution under civil commitment laws. In the wake of the *Jackson* decision, doctors determined that Metesky was not dangerous, and apparently they could not demonstrate that he was making progress toward competency. He was released on December 13, 1973, having been institutionalized for about 16 years. He went back to Waterbury, Connecticut, and—defying all predictions based on his ill health—he lived another 20 years, dying at the age of 90.

THE BRUSSEL LEGACY

We have described the Mad Bomber case in considerable detail because it was the first documented case in the United States where a criminal profile was sought by police investigators and widely reported in the news media. The public was fascinated with this new approach to crime investigation. Moreover, Dr. James Brussel became highly recognized as the first profiling expert in U.S. history and—as noted earlier—he is sometimes called the father of criminal profiling (Gladwell, 2009; Ramsland, 2009). But an examination of the profiles Brussel provided the police before Metesky's arrest do not closely fit the description of the man arrested. Brussel's original profiles—as printed in the newspapers during the 1950s—were often "Barnum-like" statements that could be descriptive of many men during the 1940s and 1950s. (See Focus 1.2 for illustrations of **Barnum statements**.) Moreover, large portions of the profiles provided by Brussel included much of the information the police had revealed to the news media during their extensive and widely publicized investigations. It is likely that Brussel himself had followed the news accounts.

Focus 1.2

Barnum Statements

In social psychology, Barnum statements refer to very general terms or comments that could apply to many different people. The term is said to originate from a quote by the showman P. T. Barnum, who claimed with regard to his stage offerings, "We've got something for everyone." Given a list of Barnum-like statements, almost anyone would say, "Sure, that describes me well." Following are some examples:

- There are occasions when you do not make full use of your potential.
- You have a strong need to have other people like you.
- Disciplined and self-controlled outside, you tend to be worrisome and somewhat insecure inside.
- At times you will put things off, but you are generally compulsive about getting work done.
- You have found it unwise to be too frank in revealing yourself to others.
- You are relatively open-minded.
- You prefer a certain amount of change and variety, and you become dissatisfied when hemmed in by restrictions and limitations.

In addition, Brussel's profiles did not necessarily lead to the discovery of the bomber. As we shall see shortly, they missed the mark in many important aspects. One of the true heroes in this case was Alice G. Kelly, a filing clerk at Consolidated Edison, who was struck by phrases used in the letters to the *New York Journal American*. According to Greenburg (2011), Kelly had been instructed to review employment compensation cases at Con Ed labeled "troublesome." Other sources indicate that she did this on her own initiative ("Who Gets 'Mad Bomber' Reward?" 1957). Regardless, it is undisputed that she uncovered the dusty file of George P. Metesky, a machinist and electrician, who had been seriously injured at work at Con Ed in 1931. The file also contained his photographs, work record, and address, and letters with the phrases "injustices," and "take justice in my own hands." Greenburg reports that there was a scramble for the reward money when Metesky was arrested (even the *Journal American* sought some of the cash), but there was great sympathy for Kelly and her discovery. She, however, declined the reward on the grounds that she had only been doing her job.

Forensic literary scholar Donald Foster (2000) and noted author Malcolm Gladwell (2009) point out that the actual profiles Brussel gave the police during the Mad Bomber investigation were nothing like the one he described in his book, *Casebook of a Crime Psychiatrist* (1968). Brussel's *Casebook* reads like a detective novel, full of elaborate and embellished accounts of how he skillfully developed various profiles, including one of the Boston Strangler, another case in which he was involved and which will be discussed below. Interestingly, the profile that most writers and experts cite as being a highly accurate one of the Mad Bomber comes exclusively from Brussel's memoirs—published nearly 12 years after Metesky was arrested—and not from those published in newspapers and other accounts prior to Metesky's arrest.

Essentially, it appears that Brussel—as reflected in this profile—may have had a serious case of hindsight bias. **Hindsight bias** is the tendency to change a previous judgment in the direction of newly provided information (Mazzoni & Vannucci, 2007). It is one of the most pervasive errors in everyday human judgment and prediction. Brussel used hindsight bias by reconstructing his original prediction and using the knowledge of the arrested offender as a guide in his memoirs. Hindsight bias is especially likely to occur when an individual strives to protect his or her professional skill, knowledge, and reputation. The motive to present oneself favorably may encourage experts to demonstrate hindsight bias (Musch & Wagner, 2007). Hindsight bias is most likely to occur in situations where experts are uncertain or just plain wrong about the outcome (Ash, 2009). Nonetheless, we should note that anyone writing memoirs may be subject to hindsight bias, and this does not necessarily imply something devious or a deliberate attempt to mislead readers. Without the benefit of documentation on one's past life, one is apt to see past events in a very subjective light. In the profiling world, there is no shortage of such memoirs.

In Brussel's book, and true to his psychiatric profession, he writes that he was convinced the bomber suffered from chronic and progressive paranoia, which was accompanied by persistent delusions. It appears, however, that Metesky was basically suffering from an angry, long-term, and misguided grudge toward a major utility company that he felt had done him wrong. An incentive that likely spurred him on was the attention the random bombings were receiving from the media, the public, and the New York Police Department (NYPD). Whether Metesky's grudge against Con Ed would qualify as paranoia, a relatively rare disorder, is highly debatable. Today, the term "delusional disorder" has replaced "paranoid disorder," and it is possible that Metesky would have more likely met the criteria for that disorder. One of the essential features of delusional disorder is non-bizarre delusions that are not due to schizophrenia (American Psychiatric Association, 2000).

In the *Casebook*, Brussel also elaborates on what went into his thinking in the development of the profile. Brussel was thoroughly Freudian in his orientation, which was a very popular approach in psychiatry (and to some extent psychology) during that time. For example, as mentioned, Metesky had a distinctive way of forming certain letters, including W, G, and Y. In explaining why Metesky made rounded W's or why he slashed the bottom of the seat at the Paramount Movie Theater, Brussel concluded that Metesky was fixated at the Oedipal stage of psychosexual development and felt antagonism toward his father and sexual attraction toward his mother. Brussel believed that the curved W found in Metesky's letters resembled a pair of female breasts as seen from the front, or it could symbolize a scrotum. After examining a police photograph of the slashed seat at the Paramount Theatre, Brussel surmised that the bomber lashed the underside of the seat because the seat symbolized the pelvic region of a human body. Brussel further deduced that, in the act of slashing the seat, the bomber gave expression to a submerged wish to penetrate his mother and castrate his father. These speculations could have been made by anyone and are beyond scientific scrutiny.

Moreover, the extent to which they contribute to criminal investigation of the case is highly questionable.

In his *Casebook*, Brussel writes that he had further predicted the bomber was likely a Slav, and therefore was most likely Roman Catholic. Interestingly, however, no profile or description *prior to the arrest* mentions the bomber being a Slav. Since his letters were usually postmarked from New York or Westchester County, Connecticut, where the largest population of Slavs resided, Brussel assumed that the bomber lived in or near Westchester. Even though it was unlikely that the bomber would mail his letters from his hometown, there were enough Slavs living in nearby areas to suggest the region. Brussel (1968) writes, "For a long while, as ... police officers sat and waited in silence, I studied the Mad Bomber's letters. I lost all sense of time. I tried to immerse myself in the man's mind" (p. 33).

Brussel adds that, as detectives prepared to leave his office, he said,

> "One more thing. When you catch him—and I have no doubt you will—he'll be wearing a double-breasted suit."
>
> "Jesus!" one of the detectives whispered.
>
> "And it will be buttoned," I said. I opened my eyes. Finney [the lead detective] and his men were looking at each other. (p. 46)

Although the above dialogue may have been exactly what happened that afternoon, we have only Brussel's account of the conversation, written after the fact. Nothing written prior to Metesky's arrest mentioned the double-breasted suit, buttoned. However, many today believe the most impressive part of the profile was the prediction concerning the offender's preference for clothing. When the police told Metesky to get dressed at the time of his arrest, he did proudly appear with the double-breasted suit, buttoned. The description of what the bomber would be wearing at the time of his arrest prompted many modern writers to extol the accuracy of the profile.

Furthermore, even assuming Brussel *did* make this oft-cited prediction of clothing, it is not that astonishing. Double-breasted suits were very popular between the mid-1930s and the early 1950s (Bryan, 2006; Nolan, 2011). In fact, over 50% of the suit jackets sold during the 1940s and early 1950s were double-breasted (Chenoune, 1993). Consequently, it was not hard to predict that a middle-aged man during the 1950s would be wearing one. Furthermore, it was also highly fashionable and culturally expected to have it buttoned, especially for someone ready to meet the press.

Another strategy that Brussel used in optimizing his profile was that he made more incorrect predictions than correct ones. Gladwell (2009) writes,

> Brussel did not really understand the mind of the Mad Bomber. He seems to have understood only that, if you make a great number of predictions, the ones that were wrong will soon be forgotten, and the ones that turn out to be true will make you famous. (p. 354)

Making more incorrect predictions than correct ones is not unusual, say some profilers (Finn, 2008). One well-known profiler quoted in Finn (p. 36) recently confessed, "You make hundreds of mistakes, but you get a couple of things right. ... It helps lead the investigation in a new direction." The problem with this, however, is that the many mistakes can lead officers in inconsequential directions (the prototypical "wild goose chase") and may prove costly in terms of wasted investigation time.

To be fair to Brussel, he was indeed a pioneer in the uncharted and murky waters of criminal or offender profiling. He was able to bring this new technique of crime investigation—using psychological or psychiatric knowledge to assist law enforcement agents—to the forefront. In fact, the director of the Behavioral Science Unit of the FBI, Howard Teten, sought his advice and knowledge for the training of FBI agents during the early 1970s, a topic to be discussed in more detail in the next chapter. Interestingly, Brussel reported, again in his *Casebook* (1968), that he lost favor with the NYPD after he insisted in a later case that two men they had arrested, at separate times, were not responsible for the brutal deaths of two young women. Charges were eventually dropped against the first man, but the second—Richard Robles—was tried, convicted, and sentenced to life imprisonment. Brussel provided police with a list of characteristics, few of which fit Robles. Brussel believed the real killer had fled to Europe, and that the wrong man had been imprisoned. "Richard Robles did not murder anybody," Brussel said in his memoirs (p. 135). Nonetheless, Robles confessed to the murders, was repeatedly denied parole, and remains imprisoned as of 2012.

If the NYPD became disenchanted with Brussel, the Boston Police Department was more welcoming, as we see below.

THE BOSTON STRANGLER

Between June 14, 1962, and January 4, 1964, a total of 13 single women in the Boston area were murdered by a single serial killer or possibly several killers. At least 11 of these women were considered victims of the Boston Strangler. All the women were murdered in their apartments, had been sexually assaulted—sometimes with objects—and their bodies were positioned in a degrading manner. The women were all strangled with articles of their own clothing, such as stockings or belts. With no indications of forced entry, police believed the women may have known their killer. These horrific incidents were later encapsulated in a movie in which the actor Tony Curtis played the lead role; to this day, some movie aficionados see Curtis's face when they are reminded of the Boston Strangler.

The first five women were advanced in age, ranging from 55 to 85. After a short hiatus, a 21-year-old woman was found, followed by both young and older women. Police were not sure that the murders were the work of a single individual, and a group of behavioral scientists (psychologists, criminologists, psychiatrists) tended to agree that they probably were not. The victims varied widely in age, occupations, education, and interests, and the sexual assault method was often different. Brussel, however, felt there was only one strangler. As described in his *Casebook*, he believed the strangler was first striking out at his mother, symbolized by the older women. Once he came to terms with his Oedipal complex, he was able to respond sexually to young women, as evidenced by semen left at the scene. Brussel (1968) indicated that, with his last victim, a 19-year-old named Mary Sullivan, the stranger had "suddenly grown, psychosexually, from infancy to puberty to manhood," which he termed "instant maturity" (p. 152).

Photo 1.2: Albert DeSalvo in custody after being charged with multiple rapes. He was convicted and imprisoned for the "Green Man" crimes, but it was never established that he was responsible for the crimes committed by the Boston Strangler.

Brussel also suggested that the strangler was a paranoid schizophrenic, of muscular build, in his late twenties or thirties, of average height, with no noticeable distinguishing features. He was clean-shaven, with clean fingernails, and a neat dresser. "I see him as a man who tends his hair lovingly. He probably has a mane of hair the average girl would envy" (Brussel, 1968, p. 157). He also predicted that he would be unmarried. Brussel's profile of the strangler included a considerable amount of Freudian concepts, including the Oedipal conflict, but police made little headway in finding a suspect.

Then, in the summer and fall of 1964, a number of women in the Boston area were sexually assaulted, but not killed, in their homes. The rapist became known as the Green Man because he wore green coveralls, sunglasses, and work gloves. The man eventually arrested for these offenses was Albert DeSalvo (see Photo 1.2). He was sent to Bridgewater State Hospital, where he apparently hinted to fellow patients that he was also the Boston Strangler and bragged of many conquests. DeSalvo met many of the broad demographic and descriptive characteristics outlined by Brussel, with the exception of the fact that he was married. Brussel would later say that he was wrong in that prediction, but that it was the only mistake he made.

Critics like Ramsland (2009) have indicated that Brussel's profile of the Boston Strangler was unsophisticated and largely off-base, and it has never been established that DeSalvo was indeed the Boston Strangler. He was tried in 1967 for the Green Man crimes, convicted, and sentenced to life imprisonment. His defense lawyer, the noted attorney F. Lee Bailey, hired Brussel to testify that DeSalvo met the criteria for insanity and therefore should not be held responsible for the crimes but was not successful. After his conviction, DeSalvo was first sent to Bridgewater, from which he escaped for a brief period, and ultimately to Walpole State Prison. On November 25, 1973, he was stabbed to death by another inmate.

An interesting postscript to the Boston Strangler story is the fact that DeSalvo—due to DNA and other forensic evidence—was eventually cleared of the death of at least one of his supposed victims, the young Mary Sullivan (Sherman, 2003). Brussel had highlighted the significance of Mary Sullivan's death, telling police the murders would then stop because the Strangler had finally achieved sexual intimacy. Indeed, Brussel indicated that killings that occurred after Sullivan's death were not attributed to the Strangler. Because DeSalvo was eventually cleared of that murder, a key aspect of Brussel's theory about the Strangler was negated.

The Mad Bomber and Boston Strangler cases are undoubtedly the two most sensational involving Brussel, whom we have used as the linchpin in our discussion of the early history of profiling in the United States. In later chapters, we will discuss more contemporary cases in which today's profilers or behavioral analysts are involved. For now, we turn our attention to the various forms of profiling and to concepts that are central to material in the remaining chapters.

The Five Areas of Behavioral Profiling

The very general term *profiling* encompasses an enormous range of investigations, methods, and assessments. As practiced, there are many models and classification systems primarily based on the analysis of homicide and sexual assault—these are the crimes that are most likely to attract the attention of profilers. However, as we have seen in the historical material above, "profiling" is not necessarily scientifically based. Brussel himself, for example, commented that his "method" was part science, but also part intuition and hope, and that he had "images" of the perpetrators in his mind. In addition, what was first called simply "profiling" now goes by various overlapping names, in both the scholarly and popular literature. These include offender profiling, investigative analysis, behavioral analysis, crime scene profiling, and criminal investigative analysis, to name just a few. Law enforcement agencies now often prefer the more respectable term "behavioral analysis," presumably to divert attention away from the negative publicity "profiling" has sometimes garnered. In England, the term "behavioural investigative analyst" (BIA) is used rather than "profiler." It should also be emphasized that profiling may involve a variety of investigative tasks, including providing advice for interviewing suspects, offering media strategies, prioritizing resources, and conducting statement validity analysis (Snook, Taylor, Gendreau, & Bennell, 2009). This text, however, will focus on one of the central processes of profiling, making inferences about an offender or potential offender.

Perhaps as a way of raising its credibility, supporters stress that profiling is an activity, but only one of several under the umbrella of behavioral analysis. For example, according to Bourque et al. (2009), "behavioral analysis units" in Canada perform the following duties:

- Develop profiles of unidentified offenders;
- Analyze crime scenes;
- Reconstruct crime scenes;
- Conduct indirect personality assessments;
- Provide advice on investigations and interrogations;
- Assist in the execution of search warrants;
- Analyze statements or testimony;
- Analyze suspicious deaths;
- Conduct threat assessments.

Likewise, the Behavioral Analysis Units of the FBI list "profiling" as one of many different activities in which it engages. This will be addressed in more detail in Chapter 2.

In order to present the material in this book in a meaningful and manageable way, we use profiling as a general term, and then divide it into five somewhat overlapping categories:

(1) Crime scene profiling

(2) Geographic profiling

(3) Psychological profiling

(4) Suspect-based profiling

(5) Equivocal death analysis (psychological autopsy)

Because each of the above focuses on individual behavior, we have included the phrase "behavioral profiling" in the title of our book. We devote one or two chapters to each of these categories, which are introduced very briefly below.

CRIME SCENE PROFILING

Crime scene profiling is the process of identifying cognitive tendencies, behavioral patterns, motivation, emotional dispositions, and demographic variables of an *unknown offender*, based on characteristics and evidence gathered at the scene of the crime. Some researchers (e.g., Knight, Warren, Reboussin, & Soley, 1998) have introduced the term "crime scene analysis," or the more technical term "criminal investigative analysis," to describe the practice of developing offender descriptions based on the analysis of the crime scene. Others use the term "offender profiling." This latter term can also apply to suspect-based profiling, however. To avoid confusion, we use the phrase "crime scene profiling."

Crime scene profiling—even in its most sophisticated form—rarely can point *directly* to the person who committed the crime. Instead, the process helps develop a reasonable set of hypotheses for determining who may have been responsible for the crime. A crime scene profiler may employ research-based typologies, such as rapist or batterer typologies, to offer investigative leads. If done correctly, a profile will provide some subjective descriptions of the demographic, motivational, behavioral patterns, and psychological features of the offender and the probabilities that the offender or offenders will commit the crime again. If done incorrectly (consider the D.C.-area sniper case), it can lead investigators far astray. In recent years, much attention has been paid to common elements observed across different crime scenes, suggesting that the crimes may have been committed by the same person. Known as "linkage analysis," this procedure has both supporters and critics but is often used in crime scene profiling, especially in the investigation of violent crimes. Crime scene profiling is currently regarded as art by some, and science by others. One mission of this book is to examine its *scientific* aspects and accuracy.

GEOGRAPHIC PROFILING

Geographic profiling is a method of identifying the area of probable residence or the probable area of the next crime of an unknown offender, based on the location of and the spatial relationships among various crime sites (Guerette, 2002). Geographic profiling, therefore, can help in any criminal investigation by locating the approximate area in which an offender lives, or by narrowing the surveillance and stakeouts to places where the next crime is most likely to occur. This type of profiling basically tries to identify the geographic territory the offender knows well, feels most comfortable in, and prefers to find or take victims in (Rossmo, 1997). Whereas a crime scene profiler hypothesizes about the demographic, motivational, and psychological features of the crime and offender, a geoprofiler focuses on the location of the crime and how it relates to the residence or base of operations of the offender. Nevertheless, behavioral aspects are important. For example, geoprofilers will pay attention to perpetrators' selection of body disposal sites or the zones in which they are comfortable in carrying out their crimes. Geographic profiling is useful not only in the search for serial violent offenders, but also in the search for property offenders, such as serial burglars.

Investigators have long used maps to help them identify "hot spots" of criminal activity or to follow the trail of crimes presumably committed by the same offender. Even agencies with few officers and resources may display a wall map with pushpins inserted in problem locations. Today, though, geographic profiling, particularly in urban areas, is sophisticated and computerized, as we will see in Chapter 4.

PSYCHOLOGICAL PROFILING

Psychological profiling is most often used to identify and predict dangerous individuals in society—though it may also be used to identify positive traits. In most cases, the identity of the person being assessed and predicted is already known. There are two highly similar procedures for accomplishing the former task: **threat assessment** and **risk assessment**. Threat assessment is a process to determine the credibility and seriousness of a threat being carried out. In some cases, the identity of the person or persons making the threat may not be known. Risk assessment comes in many forms and is often used to evaluate "individuals who have violated social norms or displayed bizarre behavior, particularly when they appear menacing or unpredictable" (Hanson, 2009, p. 172). The goal is to assess the probability that someone will harm himself or herself or others. Both of these assessments are accomplished through various kinds of psychological measures, observations, and interviews. In most instances, the agency or parties requesting the threat or risk assessment report want more than a statistical statement about the chances of a damaging or violent act occurring. They usually desire an estimate of the potential consequences, and what can be done to reduce or mitigate those consequences (Hanson, 2009). David Canter, the British psychologist who is credited with developing the field of investigative psychology, and his colleague Laurence Alison (2000) point out that psychological profiling is basically an offshoot of psychological testing and assessment procedures.

SUSPECT-BASED PROFILING

Suspect-based profiling—some researchers prefer the term "prospective profiling"—refers to identifying the psychological or behavioral features of persons who may commit a particular crime, such as drug trafficking, school shooting, stalking, shoplifting, bombing, skyjacking, or terrorist activities. Whereas crime scene profiling examines features of the crime scene and tries to link a potential offender to that crime, suspect-based profiling is derived from the systematic collection of behavioral, personality, cognitive, and demographic data on previous offenders. Its basic principle "is to develop correlations between specific criminal activity and certain group-based traits in order to help the police identify potential suspects for investigation" (Harcourt, 2003, p. 109).

Suspect-based profiling is generally developed from statistical links between group membership defined by certain traits and the prevalence of criminal activities (Bourque et al., 2009; Harcourt, 2007). In other words, it assumes that the rate of criminality of the members of certain groups is proportionately higher than that found in the general population. Suspect-based profiling is largely actuarial in that it uses statistical rather than clinical methods to determine different levels of criminal offending associated with one or more groups.

The end product of suspect-based profiling should describe people from various offending groups. "For example, someone driving at a certain speed, at a certain time of day, in a certain type of car, and of a certain general appearance may fit the profile of a drug courier and be stopped for a search" (Homant & Kennedy, 1998, p. 325). "General appearance," as used in the above quote, may refer to suspicious behavior, age, gender, or manner of dress, but it also has referred to race, religion, or ethnicity. Racial profiling, sometimes called race-based profiling and encompassing ethnicity as well as race, continues to be a major problem in modern society. In late 2011, the FBI arrested officers of the East Haven (Connecticut) Police Department for terrorizing residents of Hispanic neighborhoods, and the Justice Department announced its investigation of the department for wide-ranging illegal activities, including violations of constitutional rights, use of excessive force, and racial profiling. The recent move by the Transportation Safety Administration to train behavioral detection officers (BDOs) is another example of using suspect-based profiling. Although the use of BDOs has not been determined to be illegal, their training and the methods they employ merit continuing oversight.

EQUIVOCAL DEATH ANALYSIS

Equivocal death analysis, also called **reconstructive psychological evaluation,** is the reconstruction of the emotional life, behavioral patterns, and cognitive features of a deceased person. In this sense, it is a postmortem psychological analysis, and therefore is frequently referred to simply as a **psychological autopsy** (Brent, 1989; Ebert, 1987; Selkin, 1987). Most often, equivocal death analysis or the psychological autopsy is done to determine whether the death was a suicide, and if it was a suicide, the reasons why the person did it. Psychological autopsies may be performed in insurance claims cases. At times, however, they are used to determine if the death was the result of homicide or foul play rather than suicide. Interestingly, many psychological autopsies today are conducted by military psychologists; this is because suicide rates among military personnel have been rising in recent years. The U.S. Army, for example, recently reported a record 32 suicides for July of 2011 (Jaffe, 2011). Although the military suicide rates are not disproportionate to those for the general population when controlling for age, race, and sex, they are cause for concern in the context of military life. In many if not all of these cases, psychological autopsies are conducted to assure that self-inflicted harm—and not homicide—was the cause of the death. We will discuss this issue in more detail in Chapter 8.

To some extent, the above five categories are overlapping, and one case can involve more than one form. Nevertheless, it is helpful to keep the categories conceptually distinct as we discuss them throughout the book, because they involve different techniques and research strategies. As you will learn in the book, effective profiling requires an integration of experience and judgment with theory, research, and professional consensus (including ethical standards). Ultimately, progress in the field demands well-executed empirical research.

Summary and Conclusions

Profiling—which is essentially looking for characteristics that "fit" a particular individual—is not a new enterprise. Scientifically based profiling, however, is of recent origin. Some scholars have traced profiling back at least 500 years, to an era when religious officials were given guidelines for hunting and eradicating witches. Examples of more modern profiling are found in literary works, particularly detective novels, as well as in accounts of actual law enforcement investigations.

We covered in some detail the profiling efforts of James Brussel, a psychiatrist who is sometimes considered the father of profiling. Brussel's work on the Mad Bomber case is the first documented illustration of someone called in to assist law enforcement officers in their search for a serial offender. Brussel is often credited with helping investigators uncover the identity of the bomber, but evidence suggests he may not have been as influential as first believed. Police were already aware of many of the characteristics displayed by George Metesky, the bomber, and many of Brussel's assertions either applied to many individuals or were so psychoanalytically oriented that they could not be proven. Furthermore, in recounting his own successes in his memoirs, Brussel likely experienced some hindsight bias.

Brussel consulted with police on a number of other cases, including the Boston Strangler case, with less impressive results. However, it is clear that Brussel deserves some credit for raising awareness that psychological characteristics of offenders were relevant to criminal investigations. Furthermore, he was called as a consultant when the FBI established its Behavioral Science Unit in the early 1970s.

In addition to providing a brief early history of profiling, we delineated five categories of criminal and behavioral profiling that will be covered in the book: crime scene profiling, geographic profiling, psychological profiling, suspect-based profiling, and equivocal death analysis. It is important to stress that these are not the only terms that are encountered in the literature, and that "profilers" may be proficient in more than one of these categories. In addition, some profilers prefer to call themselves by other titles, such as behavioral analysts. As will become clear in the following two chapters, though, there is no universally accepted method of profiling, despite the fact that various programs are now available for the training of profilers or behavioral analysts. In addition, although certification is now available to those who complete these programs, they are not equivalent in their approach or in the extent to which they are based on research findings.

KEY CONCEPTS

Barnum statements	Geographic profiling	Reconstructive psychological evaluation
Behavioral analysis	Hindsight bias	Risk assessment
Boston Strangler case	Mad Bomber case	Suspect-based profiling
Crime scene profiling	Psychological autopsy	Threat assessment
Equivocal death analysis	Psychological profiling	

2

Crime Scene Profiling

Her boyfriend found her body lying inside a large-diameter concrete sewer or drainage pipe along a roadway.... She was wearing a shirt, but no bra. Her shorts, with her underwear still inside them, were found on a nearby shrub. The assailant had brutally beaten [the victim] about her face and head, and her nose was broken. She had been killed by manual strangulation. The autopsy revealed rectal tearing and bite marks on [the victim's] left breast, left nipple, and the left side of her chin.

—New Jersey v. Fortin (2000)

Descriptions of crime scenes are sobering and often agonizing, but the crime scene like the one described above is atypical. Sexual murders are very rare, constituting from 1 to 3% of all homicides (Alison, West, & Goodwill, 2004), and homicides themselves are rare compared with other crimes. Nevertheless, we open with the above description from an actual case because it relates to concepts that will be discussed throughout the chapter. Steven Fortin was charged with the 1994 murder of Melissa Padilla. At the time of the charges, Fortin was serving a 20-year sentence for the aggravated sexual assault of a Maine state trooper, which occurred 8 months after the Padilla murder in New Jersey. Some of the details of the two crimes were similar. The Maine trooper—who survived the crime—was sexually assaulted and bitten, and her uniform pants were found with her underwear still inside them. Prosecutors in the New Jersey case wanted to introduce the expert testimony of a former special agent with the FBI, a well-known profiler, to testify on the similarities between the two cases—the process called **linkage analysis** that was mentioned in Chapter 1. We will return to that case and its subsequent developments in Chapter 9.

In the present chapter, you will learn more about the history of crime scene profiling, terminology associated with it, the research on its accuracy and usefulness, and the psychological concepts that are relevant to understanding why crime scene profilers sometimes miss their mark. However, it is important to emphasize that in light of the many critiques of this endeavor, a more scientific approach would bring more respectability to the field. The need for such a scientific approach is addressed in this and succeeding chapters.

Crime scene profiling was developed in the United States in the 1970s by the **Behavioral Science Unit (BSU)** of the Federal Bureau of Investigation (FBI) to provide investigative assistance to law enforcement in cases of serial homicide or serial rape (Homant & Kennedy, 1998). In 1984, the **National Center for the Analysis of Violent Crime (NCAVC)** was created (see Focus 2.1) and within it, the **Behavioral Analysis Unit (BAU)** and the **Violent Criminal Apprehension Program (ViCAP).** As noted in Focus 2.1, one division of the NCAVC is devoted to crimes against children, particularly those involving child abductions. In field offices across the United States, the FBI has **Child Abduction Rapid Deployment (CARD)** teams to provide expertise to state and local law enforcement, and these teams sometimes bring in profilers to assess who the perpetrator may be. In addition, many state police agencies have their own CARD-like teams, sometimes referred to as **Child Abduction Response Teams (CARTs).** We will discuss this in more detail in Chapter 5, but for the moment it is important to state that the number of *stranger* abductions in a given year is quite small—just over 100 nation-wide—though even one such abduction is of great concern.

Today, most of the work in the area of crime scene profiling is under the auspices of the BAU, although the BSU remains as a separate unit that sponsors research and seminars and works closely with the various divisions of the NCAVC. According to the FBI website, the tasks that are commonly associated with profiling are performed by Supervisory Special Agents assigned to the NCAVC. Importantly, the website stresses that these agents

> do not get vibes or experience psychic flashes while walking around fresh crime scenes. Rather, it is an exciting world of investigation and research—a world of inductive and deductive reasoning; crime-solving experience; and knowledge of criminal behavior, facts, and statistical probabilities. (http://www.fbijobs.gov/611.asp)

We begin the chapter with a historical overview, starting with the development of crime scene analysis in the BSU. Although we maintain the use of our term *crime scene profiling* for consistency—and although we often use the terms *profiler* and *behavioral profiler*—please remember that many professionals who engage in the practice today prefer to use other titles, such as investigative analysts, crime scene analysts, or behavioral crime analysts. There is no "profiler" job title in the BSU or BAU, although "profiler" is a term that appears frequently in its literature as well as in the research literature.

Early FBI Profiling Origins

The FBI itself began as a bureau of investigation within the Justice Department in 1908; J. Edgar Hoover became its director in 1924, and the agency was renamed the Federal Bureau of Investigation in 1934. Hoover had little use for psychology or behavioral or social sciences in general (J. E. Douglas & Olshaker, 1995)—at least publicly. During his strong control over the Bureau—over nearly 50 years—psychology and the "soft sciences" were something of a "back room" endeavor. Numerous books, scholarly articles, and documentaries have focused on the FBI, with some of the books having been written by former agents. Moreover, in November 2011, a film about Hoover, *J. Edgar*, directed by Clint Eastwood and starring Leonardo DiCaprio, was released.

Although it could be said that Hoover himself used psychology to his advantage, he did not support the creation of a publicly recognized, psychologically oriented unit in the agency specifically geared toward helping in the investigation of crimes. Hoover's controversial reign over the FBI and his control over many political and other public figures are well documented (e.g., Jeffreys-Jones, 2007; Kessler, 2002). Under his direction, agents spied on student protestors, activists, writers, politicians, professors, actors, and numerous other citizens throughout much of Hoover's tenure, and particularly during the tumultuous period of the 1960s. He is also known to have kept extensive files on the private lives of many individuals, and he was able to maintain power and his own high-ranking position as a result of the incriminating information he had obtained.

THE BEHAVIORAL SCIENCE UNIT AND THE NCAVC

Following Hoover's death in early 1972, restrictions on the practice of psychology within the agency became more relaxed. A new FBI Academy was opened that year in Quantico, Virginia, and the Behavioral Science Unit was developed. The BSU's mission was to bring behavioral science into the training curriculum for federal law enforcement officers. Behavioral science was meant to be an umbrella term to encompass specific social science disciplines—criminology, psychology, and sociology—in the hope of understanding human behavior, particularly criminal behavior, along with the social factors that influence it. The BSU also evolved into a resource for various state and local law enforcement agencies interested in obtaining help in solving difficult cases.

As noted above, and illustrated in Focus 2.1, the NCAVC was created in 1984. Today, the NCAVC, BSU, BAU, and ViCAP engage in numerous activities (see www.fbi.gov/), not all of which receive much public attention. For example, they offer courses, such as on terrorism, conflict and crisis management, gangs, death investigation, applied criminology, and biopsychological aspects of criminal behavior. In many cases, participants receive college credit from the University of Virginia. With the help of the popular media, however, crime scene profiling has become one of the best-known contributions of the BAU. On many networks, fictional profilers lend their assistance to fictional detectives, and television shows like *Criminal Minds* focus directly on the work of the "real" professionals, often mentioning the agencies themselves by name.

Focus 2.1

National Center for Analysis of Violent Crimes (NCAVC)

In 1984, President Ronald Reagan announced the establishment of a center designed to provide behavioral-based operational support to federal, state, local, and international law enforcement agencies involved in the investigation of unusual or repetitive

(Continued)

(Continued)

violent crimes, threats, and terrorism. The center, called the National Center for Analysis of Violent Crime (NCAVC), had the primary mission to consolidate research, training, and operational support activities for the express purpose of providing expertise to any law enforcement agency confronted with unusual, bizarre, or particularly vicious or repetitive violent crimes. The NCAVC is under the auspices of the FBI and consists of four units:

(1) Behavioral Analysis Unit 1 (counterterrorism threat assessment);

(2) Behavioral Analysis Unit 2 (crimes against adults);

(3) Behavioral Analysis Unit 3 (crimes against children); and

(4) Violent Criminal Apprehension Program (ViCAP).

Unit 1 focuses on matters involving terrorism, threats, arson, bombings, stalking, cyber-related violations, and anticipated or active crisis situations. Unit 2 focuses on serial, spree, mass, and other murders; sexual assaults, kidnappings, missing persons cases; and other violent crimes targeting adult victims. Unit 3 concentrates on crimes perpetrated against child victims, including abductions, mysterious disappearances of children, homicide, and sexual victimization.

The mission of ViCAP (Unit 4) is to facilitate cooperation and coordination between law enforcement agencies and to provide support to those agencies in any effort to apprehend and prosecute violent serial offenders, especially those who cross jurisdictional boundaries. ViCAP maintains a large investigative repository of major crime cases in the United States, including homicides, sexual assaults, missing persons, and other violent cases involving unidentified human remains.

The NCAVC is a prized assignment, and according to its website, positions there are so competitive that individuals selected usually possess 8 to 10 years of experience as an FBI special agent (with 3 years as the basic requirement). Other important qualifications include overall experience as an investigator specializing in violent crimes. NCAVC staff members are trained to conduct detailed analyses of crimes from behavioral, forensic, and investigative perspectives. The purpose of these analyses is to supply law enforcement agencies with a better understanding of the motivations and behaviors of offenders.

One of the pioneers of profiling at the FBI was Howard Teten, who taught Applied Criminology at the FBI Academy. In an effort to incorporate more practical and useful content in his course, Teten consulted with psychiatrist James A. Brussel, who had become well-known for his profiles of the Mad Bomber and, to a lesser extent, his consultation in the Boston Strangler case (both discussed in Chapter 1). Brussel agreed to teach the fundamentals of his profiling technique to Teten. After consulting with Brussel, Teten—along with Special Agent Patrick J. Mullany, who had a master's degree in counseling psychology—made profiling a more central theme of his Applied Criminology course. Eventually, Teten and Mullany changed the course's title to Applied Criminal Psychology.

Teten's experience with Brussel resulted in a breakthrough in Teten's approach to analyzing crime (J. E. Douglas & Olshaker, 1995). Although Teten did not agree with many of Brussel's Freudian interpretations, he came to the conclusion that one could learn about the motives and personalities of the offender by focusing on the evidence found at the crime scene. In fact, identification of the motivation of offenders in committing crime became the early hallmark of the FBI approach to crime scene profiling. It is a form of **deductive analysis.** The deductive approach to profiling is *case focused* and attempts to infer characteristics of an offender from an analysis of the evidence gathered from a particular crime or series of crimes (Alison et al., 2004). "Deduction involves drawing a conclusion from what we already know" (Carson, 2011, p. 83). In contrast, **inductive analysis** concentrates on statistical averages of the characteristics of the "typical" offender. "Induction involves making an inference from what we already know. With inductive reasoning, we are not certain about our premises and, therefore, we cannot be sure about our conclusions" (Carson, 2011, p. 84). Inductive analysis plays a central role in the profiling methods developed in the United Kingdom, to be covered in Chapter 3. Nevertheless, as we saw in the quote above from the FBI website, both deductive and inductive reasoning are essential components of the profiling endeavor in the United States as well.

Deductive reasoning also is more closely aligned with the clinical approach to profiling, while inductive reasoning is more closely aligned with the actuarial approach. We will review these approaches in more detail shortly. For now, it is important to stress that the FBI's deductive process—which was its main focus during the early years of the BSU—puts heavy emphasis on discovering the reasons a perpetrator committed the crime. The process assumes that the perpetrator's offense-related behavior reflects specific motivations, which in turn will be associated with specific personality characteristics of the offender. For example, if the profiler thinks the crime was motivated by desire for revenge, he or she might look for such traits as hot-headedness or reactive aggression. The FBI's approach also relies heavily on the reasoning, experience, insight, and intuition of the profiler, thus making it very clinical in orientation.

From these early origins, crime scene profiling in the United States developed rapidly. According to Anthony Pinizzotto (1984), in its earlier years, between 1971 and 1981, the BSU provided profiling assistance on 192 investigations. J. E. Douglas (2007) states that when he created a special criminal profiling unit within the BSU in 1981, the Unit received requests for assistance in 54 cases, and the caseload expanded every subsequent year. By the time Douglas retired in 1995, the agency was analyzing more than 1,000 cases a year.

TWO SEMINAL ARTICLES

In 1980, profiling was introduced to the broader law enforcement community in the United States by two articles in the *FBI Law Enforcement Bulletin*, one written by BSU Special Agents Richard Ault and James Reese (1980) and the other by Special Agents Robert (Roy) Hazelwood and John Douglas (1980). These articles set the early stage for profiling as it is conducted in the United States today. The men would have long careers with the FBI, and in some cases they continued their consulting activities beyond that time. For example, Hazelwood is the former agent who was ready to testify on linkage analysis in the *Fortin* case cited at the beginning of this chapter. He and other retired FBI agents have formed consulting groups that offer services to public agencies to this day. Douglas would go on to publish books and articles in this area, including such memoirs of his experiences as *Mind Hunter* (1995), *The Anatomy of Motive* (1999), and *The Cases That Haunt Us* (2000), all written with Mark Olshaker. Douglas would also be instrumental in developing the *Crime Classification Manual* (J. E. Douglas, Burgess, Burgess, & Ressler, 1992, 2006), to be discussed later in the chapter. He also was consultant on the motion picture *The Silence of the Lambs* (Demme, 1991) and the apparent inspiration for Agent Jack Crawford in that film.

The first of the two important articles mentioned above, written by Ault and Reese in 1980, was titled "A Psychological Assessment of Crime Profiling." In it, the authors described a case involving a serial rapist who sexually assaulted at least seven women over a 2-year period in an East Coast city. Investigators had no suspects in the case and asked the BSU for help. After examining the evidence gathered by investigators, the BSU advised that the rapes were probably committed by the same person. They described the offender as a white male, 25 to 35 years of age, divorced or separated, marginally employed, with a high school education. The BSU also gave the opinion that the offender had a poor self-image, lived in the immediate area of the rapes, and probably engaged in voyeurism (was a Peeping Tom). Three days after receiving the profile, police investigators identified 40 suspects in the neighborhood who met the age criteria. Then, using additional information from the profile, they were able to narrow their investigation to one individual, who was arrested within a week.

The purpose of the Ault and Reese article was to familiarize the police community with the concept of profiling and to underscore the importance of considering the psychological aspects of any crime. The authors as well as others within the BSU believed that the personality of the perpetrator or perpetrators is especially important in the investigation of hard-to-solve crimes. According to Ault and Reese (1980), "A crime may reflect the personality characteristics of the perpetrator in much the same fashion as the way we keep and decorate our homes reflects something about our personality" (p. 24). They added that the profile may include the following information about the perpetrator:

- Race
- Sex
- Age range
- Marital status
- General employment
- Probable reactions to questioning by police
- Degree of sexual maturity
- Likelihood that the individual will strike again
- The possibility that he or she committed a similar offense in the past
- Possible police record

Ault and Reese concluded the article by noting that "profiles are not the result of magical incantations and are not always accurate" (p. 24). They added that it was important for profilers to have wide exposure to crime scenes and some exposure to criminals who had committed similar crimes. Officers or investigative teams seeking evaluations from a profiler were advised to send the profiler the following:

- Complete photographs of the crime scene, including photographs of the victim if it is a homicide;

- Complete autopsy, including any results of lab tests done on the victim;

- Complete report of the incident, including date and time of offense, location, weapon used (if known), investigators' reconstruction of the sequence of events, and a detailed interview of any surviving victims or witnesses.

This very practical article in a widely read law enforcement publication likely encouraged police agencies to contact the BSU or seek individuals within their communities who were willing to offer help in this regard. Note, though, that Ault and Reese believed the profiler should have wide exposure to crime scenes, suggesting that law enforcement experience was crucial. To this date, there is debate in the literature as to the relative merits of the practitioner versus the scientist model of profiling (Carson, 2011).

The second seminal article, by Hazelwood and Douglas (1980), was titled "The Lust Murderer." In the article, they described characteristics of individuals who commit heinous sexual offenses, even more heinous than those of other sadistic murderers. The lust murderer could be distinguished because he engaged in mutilation of the breast, rectum, or genitals. However, Hazelwood and Douglas also introduced, in this article, the **organized nonsocial offender** and the **disorganized asocial offender,** along with an accompanying crime scene dichotomy, the **organized** versus **disorganized (O/D)** crime scene. With very few exceptions, lust murderers could be placed into one of the above two categories, and lust murders fell into one of these two crime scenes.

The organized nonsocial offender was methodical and cunning, could be quite amiable, and usually carried out his crimes at a distance from his residence. By contrast, the disorganized asocial offender lacked cunning, had an aversion to society, and experienced difficulty maintaining relationships. He tended to commit his crimes closer to his residence, where he felt secure. The crime scenes left behind in the wake of these offenders' actions—a deliberate, cold, systematic scene, or a chaotic and messy one—reflected their personalities.

Hazelwood and Douglas (1980) indicated that their conclusions were based on case reports of lust murders, interviews with investigative personnel, and a careful review of the literature. However, during the same time period, Douglas also was beginning field research with imprisoned sexual murderers, so it is likely that the information he derived from them had some effect on his conclusions. As Douglas continued his prison research, he and his colleagues also continued to develop the O/D dichotomy. (See Tables 2.1 and 2.2 for the FBI summaries of these concepts.) Because that research provided a backdrop for much of the scientific research on profiling that is conducted today, we give it more attention in the following section.

Table 2.1 Profile Characteristics of Organized vs. Disorganized Offenders as Classified by the FBI in 1985

Organized	Disorganized
Average to above-average intelligence	Below-average intelligence
Socially competent	Socially inadequate
Skilled work preferred	Unskilled work
High birth-order status	Low birth-order status
Father's work stable	Father's work unstable
Sexually competent	Sexually incompetent
Inconsistent childhood discipline	Harsh discipline as a child
Controlled mood during crime	Anxious mood during crime
Use of alcohol with crime	Minimal use of alcohol
Precipitating situational stress	Minimal situational stress
Living with partner	Living alone
Mobility (car in good condition)	Lives/works near crime scene
Follows crime in news media	Minimal interest in news media
May change job or leave town	Significant behavior change

Source: Federal Bureau of Investigation (1985), p. 19.

Table 2.2 Crime Scene Differences Between Organized and Disorganized Offenders as Classified by the FBI

Organized	Disorganized
Planned offense	Spontaneous offense
Victim a targeted stranger	Victim/location known
Personalizes victim	Depersonalizes victim
Controlled conversation	Minimal conversation
Crime scene reflects control	Crime scene random and sloppy
Demands submissive victim	Sudden violence to victim
Restraints used	Minimal use of restraints
Aggressive acts prior to death	Sexual acts after death
Body hidden	Body left in view
Weapon/evidence absent	Weapon/evidence often present
Transports victim or body	Body left at death scene

Source: Federal Bureau of Investigation (1985), p. 19.

It is important to emphasize that, like Ault and Reese, Hazelwood and Douglas (1980) acknowledged that there were limitations to profiling. They referred to the profile as a useful investigative tool, but one that "must not alter, suspend, or replace prescribed investigative procedures" (p. 133). They also wrote, "The process is an art and not a science" (p. 133). As we will see throughout this book, many profilers today would disagree with this appraisal, maintaining that profiling as practiced today is more scientific. However, both critics of profiling and supporters of more intuitive profiling would argue that Hazelwood and Douglas called it right back then, and that even today, profiling as it is often practiced is more art than science.

THE DOUGLAS AND RESSLER INTERVIEWS

Between 1979 and 1983, John Douglas and fellow agent Robert Ressler, while on the road providing training to various law enforcement agencies, conducted a series of informal interviews with convicted murderers, including sexual murderers. In 1977, Douglas had become one of the instructors of the Applied Criminal Psychology course at the FBI Academy that was first designed by Howard Teten, but he was not satisfied with the course content. In his book *Mind Hunter* (Douglas & Olshaker, 1995), Douglas complains that as popular and useful as the course was, it was based primarily on theories from the academic world and not from experiences and talents of the law enforcement world. In addition, much of the course included anecdotes or "war stories" told by instructors, some of whom had never been out on the street. Douglas' prison visits, then, were undertaken to add some depth to the Applied Criminal Psychology course. He would later write, "The prison visits became a regular practice whenever Bob Ressler or I were on a road school and could get the time and cooperation" (Douglas & Olshaker, 1995, p. 111). He goes on to say,

> By the time Bob and I had done ten to twelve prison interviews, it was clear to any reasonably intelligent observer that we were onto something. For the first time, we were able to correlate what was going on in an offender's mind with the evidence he left at a crime scene. (p. 117)

Douglas also began to realize that although he and Ressler were learning about the "criminal mind," the material they gathered at the prisons was not well organized or systematic.

In the early 1970s, Douglas had met Dr. Ann Burgess, a professor of psychiatric nursing at the University of Pennsylvania and a leading authority on rape and its psychological consequences. The two agreed to work together on a more systematic research project with felons convicted of sexual homicides, often more than one. Burgess obtained a grant from the National Institute of Justice to fund the project and developed a 57-page questionnaire for Douglas and Ressler to use while interviewing the inmates. The project was called the Patterns of Homicide Crime Scene Project (A. Burgess, Hartman, Ressler, Douglas, & McCormack, 1986).

The project was concluded after a total of 36 imprisoned sexual killers had been interviewed. They were asked questions regarding their backgrounds, their behavior at the crime scene, and their post-offense behavior. In addition, the agents reviewed their criminal records. It should be mentioned that there were significant gaps in the information in the data set obtained by Douglas and Ressler, as some offenders refused to answer a number of the questions. As will be noted later in the chapter, contemporary researchers have focused on these and other limitations of the research. Regardless, the agents' goal was to establish a core basis for profiling crimes based on a psychological framework.

Burgess, Douglas, Ressler, and other colleagues began by looking for identifiable patterns in the killers' background, personality, and characteristics of their crimes. The pattern they believed they found was essentially the one described in the 1980 article Douglas had written with Roy Hazelwood: Some killers were well organized and self-controlled in their strategies and methods of selecting and killing victims, whereas others were disorganized and impulsive in their approach. Based on this interpretation, Douglas and Ressler were able to divide the killers into a distinct dichotomy, with 24 classified as organized (involving 97 victims) and 12 classified as disorganized (involving 21 victims). This "discovery"—which seemed to document the theory put forth in the 1980 article— became one of the core guiding elements in crime scene investigations.

FURTHER DEVELOPMENT OF THE O/D DICHOTOMY

In 1986, Ressler, Burgess, Douglas, Hartman, and D'Agostino, using the original Douglas-Ressler interview data, further elaborated on the organized/disorganized classification model, proposing that the crime scene itself would reflect these characteristics. Recall that the BSU believed the offenders' behavioral and personality characteristics can be determined from the evidence at a crime scene. "Like a fingerprint, the crime scene can be used to aid in identifying the murderer" (p. 291). That fingerprint could take one of two forms, either organized or disorganized.

One of the primary objectives of the above study was to bring more scientific respectability to the Douglas-Ressler data by subjecting it to statistical analysis. As the authors wrote,

> In meeting the study's first objective, we demonstrated that there are in fact consistencies and patterns in crime scenes that are objectively quantifiable and that distinguish organized from disorganized sexual murderers. The labels "organized" and "disorganized" are not only convenient because of their visual connotations to the crime scene but also have an objectivity to them. (Ressler, Burgess, Douglas, et al., 1986, pp. 293, 297)

Using the same interview data, Ressler, Burgess, Hartman, Douglas, and McCormack (1986) examined to what extent these sexual murderers had been subjected to sexual abuse as children and adolescents. The study was prompted by frequent law enforcement requests for help in solving "motiveless" homicides. Preliminary investigations by the FBI had revealed that most of these motiveless murders clearly had a sexual component. The prevailing theory at the time was that sexual offenders assaulted others because they had been sexually assaulted themselves (e.g., Groth, 1979b). As hypothesized, the researchers discovered that when the sexual killers were questioned about prior sexual abuse, 43% of them said they had been sexually abused as children (age 1–12), and 32% reported being abused in adolescence (age 13–18). The investigators concluded that, for those men who commit sexual murder, their cognitive processes appear to sustain and perpetuate fantasies of sexually violent actions. In other words, murder that appears to be motiveless is largely driven by sexual gratification propelled by fantasies.

The researchers discovered that murderers who had been sexually abused began to fantasize about rape at a significantly earlier age than murderers who had not been sexually abused. Moreover, sexually abused murderers were more likely to mutilate victims than non–sexually abused murderers. Mutilation was defined as the deliberate cutting—usually after death—of the sexual areas of the body, such as breasts and genitals. Ressler, Burgess, Hartman, et al. (1986) found that the sexually abused murderers' life paths were characterized by a high level of aggression toward children, peers, and adults. The authors speculated that "undisclosed and unresolved early sexual abuse may be a contributing factor in the stimulation of bizarre, sexual, sadistic behavior" (p. 282).

Today, the organized/disorganized distinction is one of the most widely cited classification systems of violent, serial offenders (Canter et al., 2004), but as we will note later in the chapter, it is not without its critics. John Douglas and his colleagues (Douglas, Ressler, Burgess, & Hartman, 1986) eventually introduced a third category to the typology, which they called the mixed offender. The **mixed crime scene**—left behind by the mixed offender—has characteristics of both organized and disorganized behavior. For example, a crime may have begun as carefully planned, but deteriorated into a disorganized crime when things did not go as planned. The O/D classification has also been extended to other crimes, including burglary and arson (Douglas, Burgess, Burgess, & Ressler, 1992).

In summary, an organized crime scene indicates planning and premeditation on the part of the offender. The crime scene suggests indicators that the offender maintained control of himself or herself as well as the victim. It is expected that he or she is socially and interpersonally skillful in handling potential victims. The offender probably relies on a verbal approach in obtaining victims. In addition, the organized killer or assaulter usually selects victims according to some personal criteria. The notorious serial killer Ted Bundy, for example, selected young, attractive women who were similar in appearance. He was also successful in the abduction of these women from highly visible areas, such as beaches, college campuses, and ski lodges, indicating considerable planning and premeditation (J. E. Douglas et al., 1986).

In contrast, a disorganized crime scene shows that the offender very probably committed the crime without premeditation or planning. He or she probably lives close to the location in which the crime was committed. The crime scene reveals that the offender acted on impulse or in a rage, or in a state of extreme excitement. The disorganized perpetrator obtains victims by chance, often without specific criteria in mind. For example, Herbert Mullin of Santa Cruz, California, killed 14 people of varying types (e.g., an elderly man, a young girl, and a priest) over a 4-month period (J. E. Douglas et al., 1986). It is also assumed that the disorganized offender is socially inadequate and unable to maintain interpersonal relationships. Most often, the victim's body is found at the scene of the crime.

The Crime Classification Manual

The above studies, along with others conducted during the 1980s on crimes like murder, rape, child abduction, and arson, provided important information on the distinguishing characteristics of these crimes (J. E. Douglas et al., 1992). These characteristics formed the basis for the profiling techniques used by FBI investigators at that time.

Much of the commentary and research on profiling carried out by the FBI during that time was summarized in the *Crime Classification Manual* (*CCM*), first published in 1992 (J. E. Douglas et al.) and reissued in 2006. Its subtitle is *A Standard System for Investigating and Classifying Violent Crimes*. The manual is a compilation of offender profiling applications and crime scene characteristics related to a wide variety of violent crimes. The defining characteristics of each crime are outlined, and each is accompanied by a case study that includes background information about the crime, characteristics of the victim, crime scene indicators, and forensic findings. The second edition of the *CCM* (2006) adds computer crimes, religious-extremist murder, and elder female sexual homicide. The second edition also contains new information on stalking and child abductions. (See Focus 2.2 for a summary of cult murder, according to the *CCM*.)

Focus 2.2

Cult Murder

The following is an illustration of the type of information contained in the *Crime Classification Manual* (*CCM*). The material is adapted from J. E. Douglas et al., 1992, pp. 144–146.

The *CCM* defines a cult as "a body of adherents with excessive devotion or dedication to ideas, objects, or persons, regarded as unorthodox or spurious and whose primary objectives of sex, power, and/or money are unknown to the general membership" (p. 145). In other words, the cult's leader is aware of what he or she is doing, but most of the followers are not. When two or more members of the cult commit murder, it is classified as a cult murder.

Victims: Random victims are occasionally preyed upon, but generally victims are members of the cult or someone on the fringes of membership. Typically, more than one individual is killed.

Crime Scene Indicators Frequently Noted: The *CCM* notes that the crime scene may contain symbolic items (e.g., artifacts or images), and the status of the body is dependent on the purpose of the killing. If the killing is intended as a widespread message, there will be little attempt to conceal the bodies; if intended to intimidate a small circle within the cult, bodies may be concealed through burial.

Staging: Not usually present.

Common Forensic Findings: Wounds from firearms, blunt-force trauma, sharp pointed objects. Mutilation of the body is possible.

Investigative Considerations: The *CCM* notes that the general membership of the cult may be told the crime was committed as part of the group's belief. However, the leader's motivation "will be a controlling factor: a macho way to justify the homicide, tighten his control of the group, and/or eliminate troublemakers or less devoted followers who threaten his authority" (p. 146).

Case Study: To illustrate cult murder, *CCM* authors used the 1990 investigation in Cleveland of the murder of five members of a family, the Averys, who had joined a radical splinter group of a church led by Jeffrey Lundgren. The family did not wholeheartedly endorse Lundgren's philosophy and were subsequently isolated from the group. They were possibly trying to separate from it at the time of their deaths. Lundgren had persuaded his followers that the family should be killed as a cleansing sacrifice. He was ultimately convicted, sentenced to death, and executed in October 2006. His wife and son are serving sentences of 150 years to life and 120 years to life, respectively.

Note that the *CCM* includes victim characteristics. According to the FBI, in answering the question, "Why was this particular person targeted for a violent crime?" investigators will often be led to the motive. Even if the crime *seemed* to be a random one—for example, the victim was just in the wrong place at the wrong time—the motive of the offender could be gleaned. The victim might share characteristics with other victims of similar crimes. In addition, the *CCM* attempts to standardize the language, terminology, and definitions of these crimes for investigators and criminal justice personnel. Concluding chapters on crime scene analysis in the *CCM* define many of the concepts we will discuss below.

Crime Scene Profiling Today

Although we focused above on the work of investigators in the United States, it is important to stress that crime scene profiling or criminal profiling also has grown dramatically in popularity across the world during the past 40 years (Snook, Eastwood, Gendreau, Goggin, & Cullen, 2007). In Chapter 3, we will discuss in greater detail the work done in other countries, particularly the United Kingdom. Although crime scene profiling has many similarities, there are also discernible differences in the methods used by the analysts. For example, the United Kingdom and Canada have taken a more actuarial or statistical approach to profiling, while the United States has taken a more clinical approach. Nevertheless, there is increasing "cross-fertilization" of training across the globe, so both clinical and actuarial approaches are in evidence.

As we described in Chapter 1, crime scene profiling is the process of identifying cognitive tendencies, behavioral patterns, motivation, emotional dispositions, and demographic variables of an unknown offender based on characteristics and evidence gathered at the scene of the crime. Based on crime scene information and the predicted characteristics and habits of the offender derived from the scene, the analyst or profiler tries to describe general characteristics of the offender or offenders and possibly predict where and how the next crime may occur. In serial murder cases, for example, a profiler may find clues indicating that the span of time between offenses is lessening. In some cases, a possible suspect has been identified and police want to know whether this individual has personality characteristics that are consistent with the crime scene.

Crime scene profiling is used most often when investigators have few clues that could help solve the case, and they are making little headway as to who may have committed the crime. In some situations, however, the behavioral consultant is brought in at the very beginning of a case. This is most likely to occur if the case is a particularly heinous one or if law enforcement officers have a working relationship with the behavioral expert. Crime scene profiling also is often used in rape and homicide investigations, particularly when a crime appears to be committed by a serial offender, or in child abduction cases, where the first few hours after a child's disappearance are crucial. Each of these crimes will be discussed in more detail in Chapter 5.

It should be emphasized that crime scene profiling—even in its most sophisticated form—rarely can point directly to *the* person who committed the crime. Instead, the process helps develop a manageable set of hypotheses for identifying who *may* have been responsible for the crime. The development of the profile is a probabilistic process that requires a considerable amount of information about the offense. For example, police reports, detailed crime scene photographs, witness statements, forensic laboratory reports, and—if the case is a homicide—autopsy reports are important (O'Toole, 1999). If at all possible, the profiler should visit the crime scene. Detailed information about the victim's lifestyle, background, and physical characteristics is also paramount.

If done competently, a profile will provide some statistical probabilities of the demographics, geographic patterns, and psychological features of the offender. (Note, though, that geographic profiling is its own category, one to be covered in Chapter 4.) According to Mary Ellen O'Toole (1999)—an FBI special agent for 28 years who is now associated with a private company that trains criminal justice officials—a profile may suggest the offender's lifestyle, race, gender, emotional age as well as chronological age, marital status, level of formal education or training, occupation, and work history. It may also contain information about the offender's ability to relate and communicate with others, the likelihood of prior criminal behavior, the presence of dementia or other mental deterioration, feelings of guilt concerning the crime, the likelihood of committing the crime again, and motivation for the offense. In addition, the profile report should—if possible—include how the crime most likely occurred and the interaction between the offender and the victim. Profiles also may be able to indicate what type of victim is at risk. Finally, a profile should eliminate substantial segments of the population from further investigation.

Basically, crime scene profiling is usually done in three stages. First, police officers and detectives collect crime scene data, such as forensic photographs, autopsy results, and all relevant physical evidence. Second, this information is then turned over to a profiler or team who analyzes the data and offers an "educated hypothesis" about important characteristics of the offender. Recall from the first chapter that Brussel reviewed information provided by police and produced a preliminary profile within a few hours, while detectives awaited his conclusions. Likewise, the "profilers" in the popular, fictionalized accounts (TV shows such as *Criminal Minds, Bones, Numb3rs*) waste little time in providing their input. Responsible, professional analysts in the real world are more guarded and cautious. Third, the profile report, including predictions, is then communicated to the police investigating the case. In some cases, profilers do not have the luxury of thoughtful, deliberative assessment of the evidence. In child abduction cases, for example, time is of the essence—making information both crucial and, unfortunately, more subject to error.

PROFILING TERMINOLOGY

A review of the literature on crime scene profiling will uncover certain terms that occur with some consistency. For example, in crime scene investigations as outlined by John Douglas and his colleagues in the *CCM* (1992), investigators are advised to look for such clues in the crime scene as the modus operandi; personation or a signature; and whether or not there is any staging, souvenir or trophy taking, or psychological undoing.

The **modus operandi,** or MO, refers to the actions and procedures an offender uses to commit a crime successfully. It is a behavioral pattern that the offender learns as he or she gains experience in committing the offense. However, the MO is subject to change. Repeat offenders may change their MO in an attempt to develop a method that is most effective. For example, serial burglars find new tools or different methods of overriding an alarm system, and serial killers often become more daring and risky in their selection of victims or in the clues they leave for police. Consequently, although the MO cannot be ignored, investigators may make a serious error if they place too much significance on this aspect when linking crimes.

Personation refers to any behavior that goes beyond what is necessary to commit the crime. When such behaviors are demonstrated by a *serial* offender, it is called the **signature.** For example, a serial offender may leave at the crime scene evidence of a repetitive, almost ritualistic behavior from crime to crime. The signature may involve certain items that are left behind or removed from the scene, or other symbolic patterns such as writings or drawings on the wall. Some burglars tailor their styles (or their signature) to convey messages to victims and investigators, hoping to induce some strong emotional reactions from the victims, such as fear or anger. The burglar may leave a frightening or threatening note or "violate" some personal item, such as intimate clothing, a photograph, or a diary. Consequently, the emotional reactions of burglarized victims often run the gamut from anger and depression to fear and anxiety (Brown & Harris, 1989). If there are murder victims, personation or a signature may involve body positioning, mutilation, or other symbolic gestures on the body that are primarily significant only to the offender.

The signature is thought to be related to the cognitive processes of the offender and, because it is relatively consistent in its characteristics, it may be more informative to an investigator and more useful in the profiling process than the MO. In many cases, the signature reveals the motivations of the crime, as it is assumed that it points to the underlying psychological and emotional needs of the offender (Turvey, 2008). For example, an adult victim's body may be positioned in a particularly demeaning fashion, a flower may be left on a child's body, or a burglar may write crude messages on walls implying control over his victims.

According to FBI profiling approaches, the signature is often believed to be a sign of psychopathology. Experienced profilers have argued for many years that profiling serial violent offenders is most successful when the offender exhibits some form of psycho- pathology at the scene of the crime, such as sadistic torture, evisceration, postmortem slashings and cuttings, and other mutilations (Pinizzotto, 1984). The reasoning behind this assertion is that mentally disordered persons, ironically, demonstrate greater con- sistency in behavior from situation to situation than persons not so disordered. The assumption here is that anyone who commits these outrageous offenses must be men- tally disordered, an assumption not necessarily borne out in the research. However— even if we concede the mental disorder—it is open to debate whether persons with mental disorders are more consistent in their behavioral patterns than stable individu- als. Systematic empirical research on the topic is lacking.

Staging is another behavioral pattern sometimes found at a crime scene, a sus- pected suicide, or an accidental death. It is the intentional alteration of the scene prior to the arrival of the police. Staging is believed to be done for one of two reasons: either to redirect the investigation away from the most logical suspect or to protect the victim or the victim's family from public embarrassment (J. E. Douglas & Munn, 1992a). Thus, staging may be done by the perpetrator (e.g., staging a crime scene to make a domestic murder look like a home invasion killing) or by someone who discovers the victim or evidence of a crime. In the case of a death, staging is frequently done by someone who has a close association or relationship with the victim. For example, the victim may have become an accidental death victim by practicing autoerotic asphyxia, obtaining sexual excitement from hypoxia (lack of oxygen), usually through near strangulation.

Trophy taking and souvenir taking are other behavioral patterns sometimes encountered in crime scene analysis, particular with reference to violent crimes. A **trophy** is an item taken from the scene or from the victim that symbolize the offend- er's triumph over the victim, and it typically represents the force used against the victim or the victim's subjugation (Turvey, 2008). The infamous serial killer Jeffrey Dahmer took body parts as trophies and preserved them in formaldehyde; other examples are torn garments or photographs or videotapes taken at the scene. A **sou- venir** is a meaningful item taken by the offender to remember the incident, remind- ing the offender of the pleasure gained from the crime (Turvey, 2008), such as jewelry taken from the victim. Although the souvenir may seem more innocuous than a tro- phy, both types of items may also represent an attempt to psychologically control the victim after the crime, if the victim survives, or to taunt loved ones if the victim does not. Some profilers believe, though, that making the distinction between a trophy and a souvenir is important, because each infers something slightly different about the personality or the motives of the offender.

Another concept sometimes encountered in crime scene profiling or analysis is **undoing.** This is a behavioral pattern evident at the scene in which the offender tries to psychologically "undo" the crime. For example, a distraught or emotionally upset offender, who kills the victim, may try to undo his or her actions by placing the body in bed, perhaps even resting the head on a pillow, and covering the body with blankets. The perpetrator also may place the victim upright in a chair, trying desperately to return the victim to a natural-looking state. Very often, such an offender had a close relationship with the victim. In other cases, an offender may try to dehumanize the victim by engaging in actions that obscure the victim's identity, such as excessive facial battery. Other offenders may objectify their victims by placing them face down. Undoing is similar to staging, but it is less directed at steering police away from the facts of the incident and more directed at making the offender feel better about the offense.

CASE LINKAGE

Case linkage is another important profiling concept, but it is also a process that is gaining increasingly more research attention (Tonkin, Woodhams, Bull, Bond, & Palmer, 2011). Sometimes called linkage analysis, it is a method of identifying crimes that are likely to have been committed by the same offender because of behavioral similarity across the crimes (Woodhams, Bull, & Hollin, 2010). Recall the illustration from the *Fortin* case at the beginning of the chapter. In that case, the profiler focused on several similarities between the two sexual assaults, but critics have also pointed out that there were many differences in these two cases as well (Ebisike, 2008). Case linkage is most often used with crimes such as stranger rape and murder, but may also be used for burglary, arson, and robbery. In fact, there is some evidence that different types of crimes (e.g., a violent crime and a property offense) may be linked to the same offender (Tonkin et al., 2011). The correct linking of cases is likely to be a valuable contribution to police investigation and ultimately reduces the number of suspects (Grubin, Kelly, & Brunsdon, 2001); on the other hand, an incorrect linking of cases can result in a wrongful conviction. In the extensive commentary on the *Fortin* case, no one suggested that Fortin, the person convicted of the crime, was not the perpetrator of both offenses; rather, critics were concerned about the scientific status of linkage analysis (Risinger & Loop, 2002).

The profiler may link crimes in one of two ways: He or she may search for similar crimes among a database of crimes, without a preconceived notion of who the offender might be; the discovery of other crimes with similar characteristics of victims, MOs, or offender signatures will *suggest* that the same individual could have committed them. Or, the profiler may search for other crimes that are highly similar to the crime committed by someone who has already been identified. For example, police may have arrested and charged an individual with a crime and may want to know whether he is likely to be responsible for other unsolved offenses. Victim accounts of the crime are important in the process—provided of course that the victim survived the crime.

Once the profiler has collected all the relevant information, he or she composes a list of the behaviors demonstrated by the offender. According to Woodhams et al. (2010), "Some behaviors might be more spontaneous, whereas others may be produced as a reaction to the victim or witnesses" (p. 120). In addition, the profiler may classify the offender behaviors as modus operandi or ritualistic or signature behaviors (Hazelwood & Warren, 2003). Alison, Goodwill, and Alison (2005) posit that MO behaviors are functionally significant and depend on the context of the crime; they are necessary to commit the crime—such as a belt around the victim's neck. The signature, on the other hand, is psychologically significant, or ritualistic, and is not dependent on the context.

Determining these distinctions generally requires a subjective judgment on the part of the profiler. Discovery of a signature, however, is extremely helpful, if not essential, in linkage analysis.

In order for case linkage to work, the offender must demonstrate consistent but distinct behavior in each crime. In other words, the behavior must be distinguishable from other offender behavioral patterns but consistent across crimes for the offender in question. For instance, the signature may be unique for the offender, and he consistently exhibits it across crimes. This task is not as easy as it sounds, as the profile must be distinctive and unique enough to reveal something about motive, intent, or signature of a particular offender (Santtila et al., 2008). Santtila et al. examined 116 Italian homicides committed by 23 offenders. The researchers found that the offender's crime scene behavior was consistent across serial murders as well as different from that of other offenders. This finding lends support to the serial killer model concerning consistency and variability in behavior; that is, serial killers tend to be more consistent than not, although there is also variability as their crimes progress. For example, their crimes may become more or less brutal, and their choices of victims may broaden. In general, however, research indicates that there is consistency in the behavioral patterns of these offenders (Alison, Goodwill, Almond, van den Heuvel, & Winter, 2011; Canter & Youngs, 2009). However, the consistency is not always found in the offender's MO, as this may change according to the situation and the effectiveness of the MO in prior offending. In fact, a majority of research in criminal behavior finds only a moderate level of consistency associated with the MO (Bennell, Snook, MacDonald, House, & Taylor, 2012). In a recent study of serial rapes, however, researchers found sufficient similarity in MO to conclude that the assumption of behavioral consistency underlying case linkage was justified (Woodhams & Labuschagne, 2012). In addition, research also finds consistency in the manner in which the offender treats and relates to the victims, a distinctive pattern we will cover in the next chapter.

ADDITIONAL RESEARCH ON CRIME SCENE PROFILING

Research in the area of crime scene profiling has largely been preoccupied with the development of offender typologies that are assumed to be useful for profiling violent crimes (Kocsis, 2010). In contemporary psychology, the term **typology** refers to a system for classifying personality or other behavioral patterns. At least 16 typologies have been applied to profiling (Bourque et al., 2009). However, a vast majority of them lack a solid theoretical basis and empirical validation. One of the most heavily researched typologies is the organized/disorganized dichotomy proposed by John Douglas and his colleagues, which was discussed earlier in the chapter and is illustrated in Tables 2.1 and 2.2. Although the Douglas group originally saw all crime scenes as either organized or disorganized, they eventually modified their view to some extent. First, they proposed a "mixed crime scene," one which had elements of both organized and disorganized scenes. Then, in the *CCM*, Douglas and his colleagues (1992) introduced a continuum as being more realistic. They wrote,

It should be emphasized that the *crime scene rarely will be completely organized or disorganized.* It is more likely to be somewhere on a continuum between the two extremes of the orderly, neat crime scene and the disarrayed, sloppy one. (p. 9)

The organized/disorganized (O/D) typology has been endorsed by many (e.g., Hickey, 1997; S. T. Holmes & Holmes, 2002), while others have serious concerns about its validity or usefulness. As John Douglas seems to have recognized from the quotation above, crime scenes are rarely as neat as portrayed in a typology or classification system. Nevertheless, the O/D typology has been and continues to be appealing to many investigators.

Although the organized/disorganized typology seems intuitively logical and appealing, recent research indicates it may have very limited usefulness as an investigative tool (Canter et al., 2004; Kocsis, Cooksey, & Irwin, 2002). In fact, a recent review on the issue finds that, at this point, there is no convincing evidence to support the classification (Snook, Cullen, Bennell, Taylor, & Gendreau, 2008).

Recall that, although the O/D dichotomy was discussed in the Hazelwood and Douglas (1980) article on lust murder, that article was conceptual rather than empirical. While the authors mentioned case reports, interviews with investigators, and a review of the literature, they were not describing systematic research. As Devery (2010) has noted, "In terms of its structure and content, the 1980 article by Hazelwood and Douglas on lust murders falls far short of what would be considered an acceptable social scientific exposition of a concept" (p. 397).

Shortly thereafter, in the early 1980s, Douglas and his colleagues began to publish their research collected on the basis of interviews with 36 inmates, most of whom were responsible for more than one sexual homicide. As admitted by Douglas himself (Douglas & Olshaker, 1995), and discussed earlier in this chapter, the interviews in their early phases were often informal and largely subjective.

Furthermore, as observed by Devery (2010),

It is highly unlikely . . . that the sample of serial killers was representative even of serial killers of their time, as the sample was one of convenience—only available killers who agreed to speak with Douglas and Ressler and their collaborators were included in the study. . . . Research based on such small and unrepresentative samples may identity certain behavioral characteristics of the serial killers, but without a control sample of nonserial killers, the identified characteristics can't tell us much about how common such characteristics are in the general community. (p. 395)

It should be noted that Devery refers to the 36 imprisoned offenders as "serial killers," but it is more accurate to refer to them as sexual murderers, and typically repeat sexual murderers. The numbers reported by Douglas and Ressler indicate that some of their interviewees may have been responsible for only one sexual murder (see, e.g., numbers of disorganized offenders [12] compared to number of victims [21]), and some were probably responsible for just two. As we will note in Chapter 5, serial killing has traditionally been defined as requiring more than two offenses committed by the same person separated by a time interval, although a recent FBI-sponsored symposium on the issue recommended that two offenses separated by time could qualify as serial murders (Morton & Hilts, 2005). These distinctions aside, it appears that the 36 men interviewed by Douglas and Ressler were clearly *sexual* murderers, but not necessarily serial or even repeat murderers, although they are often referred to that way in the criminology literature, as we see in this and later chapters. For our purposes, though, we are most concerned about the validity of the O/D dichotomy.

David Canter and his colleagues (2004) also had concerns about how the Douglas-Ressler interviews were conducted, especially pertaining to their reliability, validity, and the manner in which conclusions about the offenders were drawn. Canter et al. point out that the agents did not select a random, or even large, sample of the offenders. They simply selected those who agreed to talk to them. Therefore, "the widespread citation of this typology is based on an informal exploratory study of 36 offenders put forward as exemplars, rather than a specific test of a representative sample of a general population of serial murderers" (p. 296).

It may be more realistic to assume that crime scenes as well as offenders fall along a continuum, with the organized description at one pole and the disorganized description at the other pole, as the *CCM* seems to acknowledge. Even so, Canter et al. (2004) point out that if most crime scenes are actually mixed, the dichotomy is little more than a theoretical proposal of no real utility.

However, the most troubling aspect of the organized/disorganized typology is the temptation to assume that the offender can be characterized as either a disorganized or organized individual, demonstrating the traits and behavioral patterns associated with each classification. An analyst—particularly an amateur profiler—will thus include these likely traits and behaviors in his or her report. Recognizing the enormous popularity of the O/D system among law enforcement agencies in many parts of the world, David Canter, Laurence Alison, and their associates decided to test this well-cited and heavily relied-on model. The research group point out that the organized/disorganized typology proposes that specific characteristics only happen together (co-occur) with certain other characteristics. If the offender was organized, then it may be assumed that most—if not all—of the behavioral characteristics listed under organized offenders (see Tables 2.1 and 2.2) will be evident. A similar assumption is proposed for disorganized offenders.

The selection of the data and the criteria adopted in the Canter et al. (2004) study were matched to those adopted by the FBI model in the *Crime Classification Manual*. The data for the study were gathered from published accounts of serial killers taken from the Christopher Missen archive of serial killer data. According to Canter et al., "This material consisted of secondary sources of nationally and internationally known U.S. newspapers, periodicals, journals, true crime magazines, biographies, trial transcripts, and case history narratives" (pp. 302–303). The researchers were able to gather 39 aspects of serial killings derived from the murders committed by 100 U.S. serial killers (e.g., facial disfigurement, burns on victim, restraints, body covered post mortem, bite marks).

Interestingly, the actions used by the serial killers varied considerably, with certain aspects being displayed in a high percentage of cases (e.g., victim alive during sex) and others displayed in a very small percentage (e.g., dismemberment). "Such variation alone raises questions about the validity and reliability of the classification dichotomy because such variations indicate that there will be many situations in which very few criteria will be present" (Canter et al., 2004, p. 302). In fact, the researchers found very little co-occurrence of variables in either the crime scenes that would be classified as organized or those that would be classified as disorganized. For example, in 70% of organized cases, the body was concealed and there were also multiple crime scenes. This is a statistically respectable co-occurrence, but it was one of only two situations in which co-occurrences were that high (the other one being sexual activity with a live victim and a body posed in 75% of the cases). Disorganized crime scenes found even less co-occurrence.

The Canter et al. (2004) study is far more detailed than we can present here. Essentially, however, *the researchers did not find any support for the FBI's O/D typology*. "The taxonomy proposed by the CCM ... as a naturally occurring distinction between serial sexual murderers or their crime scenes does not garner even the weakest support from the data examined here" (p. 313). In each crime, there is almost always a mixture of perhaps two organized traits and a random array of disorganized traits. In other words, serial killer behavior is much more complex that the O/D typology suggests. In addition, given the frequency of certain core organized variables in the crime scenes examined by Canter et al., "being organized is typical of serial killers as a whole" (p. 312).

In the United Kingdom, Canter, Alison, and their associates have conducted extensive additional research on profiling in recent years, much of which will be discussed in Chapter 3. In contrast, crime scene profiling in the United States has continued to be more an art than a science, particularly as it relates to the approach taken by the FBI. As we saw earlier in the chapter, however, in recent years investigators in the United States have tried to promote a perspective that welcomes both clinical and statistical approaches.

This may be less true of those not recently trained by the FBI or through the **International Criminal Investigative Analysis Fellowship (ICIAF)**, the program that has taken over the training of behavioral analysts (to be discussed shortly). It may also be less true of those former agents who have continued consulting with investigators on an independent basis. Reporting on an interview with John Douglas on National Public Radio, Gladwell (2009) revealed that he thought that Douglas would have a well-thought-out response to the Canter, Alison, et al. research. "But it quickly became apparent that he had no idea who Alison or any of the other academic critics of profiling were" (p. 356, footnote). This would seem like a harsh appraisal, particularly because Douglas was long retired from his FBI work. However, he continues to attract public attention by consulting and providing media interviews, so as such is "fair game" for critical comments.

Typologies and Profiling

As noted above, typology refers to a particular system for classifying personality or other behavioral patterns, and there have been at least 16 different typologies developed for profiling purposes. They include typologies of murderers, rapists, child molesters, burglars, arsonists, and terrorists. When a profiler mentions the sadistic murderer profile or the child abuser profile, and so forth, he or she is referring to characteristics associated with these typologies, some of which will be discussed in Chapter 5. Usually, the typology is used to classify a wide assortment of behaviors into a more manageable set of brief descriptions, which can be useful but should be employed guardedly. So, by classifying crime scenes and placing the possible perpetrators into categories (organized or disorganized), the FBI is taking a typological approach.

When we place people (in this case, people responsible for a crime scene) into behavioral categories, we assume that behavior is consistent across time and place. Crime scene typologies are constructed on the premise that human behavior (e.g., of the offender) is largely the same from situation to situation—but this is not necessarily the case. For example, typologies assume that the way a person acts at home is pretty much the same way he or she acts in the classroom, with friends, at work, or in public. However, the validity of this assumption is very much open to debate. Some researchers (e.g., Mischel, 1968; Mischel & Peake, 1982) cogently argue that human behavior across different situations is inconsistent, and that notions of stable behavioral dispositions or personality traits are largely unsupported. On the other hand, consistency across time, called *temporal consistency*, is acknowledged. As long as situations are highly similar, people will like respond that same way over their life spans. But when the situations change, behavior is likely to change. Walter Mischel and Philip Peake conclude, on the basis of their research findings, that behavior is highly dependent on the nature of the situation or social environment, and that humans discriminate between situations and react accordingly. Essentially, cross-situational consistency is a critical issue in the formation of any classification system or typology. That is, if behavior is not consistent across situations, we must be very guarded in drawing conclusions from clues left at the scene. As mentioned earlier, behavioral consistency is a very current topic in the research literature, particularly as it relates to case linkage.

Robert Keppel and William Birnes (2003) assert that although typologies have descriptive value, "they have consistently failed to provide investigators with the elements necessary for crime scene assessment" (p. 132). They identify the Holmes and Holmes typology of serial murderers (first proposed by Holmes and De Burger and later expanded upon by Holmes and Holmes) as one prime example. Not only is it of limited value in crime scene investigations, they say, but it is also unsupported by empirical study. In addition, Keppel finds in his more than 30 years of experience of homicide investigations that very few police investigators use the typologies found in the *CCM* published by Douglas et al. in 1992.

In fact, the major homicide tracking systems such as the FBI's Violent Criminal Apprehension Program (ViCAP); the Homicide Investigation Tracking System (HITS) in Washington, Oregon, and Idaho; and the Royal Canadian Mounted Police's (RCMP) Violent Crime Linkage Analysis System (ViCLAS), which are centralized databases for homicide information, do not use either typology to classify murderers . . . because the characteristics of killers and crime scenes by the Crime Classification Manual and Holmes and Holmes are not rich in detail. (Keppel & Birnes, 2003, p. 132)

They conclude by stating that, in general, homicide investigators have found that typologies and other crime classification systems have provided little assistance in solving a particular murder.

Clinical Versus Actuarial Profiling

In large measure, the profiling enterprise supported by the FBI is clinical in orientation, although in recent years there is indication of a move toward more actuarial approaches. The clinical approach is based on experience, expert knowledge, and training, often interspersed with intuition and subjectivity. It is the preferred strategy for most profilers. Unfortunately, it is also most often fraught with an extensive range of cognitive biases and inaccuracies (Grove & Meehl, 1996), the most common of which will be discussed shortly.

The **actuarial method of profiling**—to be discussed in more detail in Chapter 3—is based on how groups of individuals with similar characteristics have acted in the past. It refers to the use of data about prior instances in order to estimate the probability of a particular outcome. The fundamental statistic employed in actuarial prediction is the **base rate,** which is defined as the statistical prevalence of a particular behavior in a given group over a set period of time, usually one year. Insurance companies have compiled extensive statistics on who has traffic accidents. These statistics may show, for example, that 20-year-old male college students who have a mediocre academic record and who drive a specific type of car (say, a new sports car) have a very high probability of being involved in a traffic accident within a 1-year period of time. The base rate for this group may be 40%. If the student falls within this group, he will pay a much higher insurance premium than a 20-year-old female with an outstanding academic record and a 10-year-old Camry.

Although the actuarial method has been extensively used by the insurance industry, it also permeates the field of criminal law and its enforcement.

> From the use of the IRS Discriminant Index Function to predict potential tax evasion and identify which tax returns to audit, to the use of drug-courier and racial profiles to identify suspects to search at airports, on the highways and on city streets, to the risk assessment instruments to determine pre-trial detention, length of criminal sentence, prison classification and parole eligibility, prediction instruments increasingly determine individual outcomes in our policing, law enforcement, and punishment practices. (Harcourt, 2007, p. 2)

One profiling approach that seems very similar to that used by the FBI is that of Gary Copson and his colleagues (Copson, Badcock, Boon, & Britton, 1997), who call theirs the clinical method of profiling. (Copson was superintendent and eventually commander of the Metropolitan Police for London's communities.) According to Copson, clinical profilers try to identify a wider and more sophisticated range of subliminal behavioral signals than are used in other profiling approaches, such as the FBI's. We do not agree that this is necessarily the case. Profilers—or behavioral analysts—associated with the

U.S. government have always favored more clinically based than actuarial approaches to combating major crimes. The clinical method simply refers to heavy reliance on experience and training, and it often encourages intuition and subjectivity. For example, as recently as May 2011, the BAU-2 of the NCAVC (see Focus 2.1) initiated another behavioral interview program to understand the minds of violent offenders. The press release states, "The insights from these consensual interviews are used for research and training, and they also have the potential to help investigators in the field" (Federal Bureau of Investigation, 2011a). The interview process involves asking questions about every aspect of the inmate's life—from his earliest childhood experiences to the abduction, sexual assault, and/or murder for which the inmate was convicted.

The difference appears to be that Copson and his colleagues have been more forthcoming in revealing their methods. For example, they have identified three common features in their practice. One of the key features of the clinical model is to ask the following three basic questions: (1) What happened? (incorporating where and when); (2) How did it happen? and (3) To whom did it happen? Another key feature is a crime scene visit, which is indispensible for understanding the crime. Scene photographs, autopsy photographs and report, maps, and witness statements are also important. Similar to the FBI model of profiling, the centerpiece—and the third important feature—of the clinical model is the inference of motive. Determining motive helps identify the starting point for the development of significant characteristics of the offender. While clinical profilers consider the signature, staging, and the O/D pattern, they go beyond these considerations. According to Copson et al. (1997), "When they pore over case material they are searching for signs of cognition and affect—emotions, moods and desires; for themes of anger, power and control—overt and implicit; for obsessionality; and for any other underlying psychological influences" (p. 15). Another important feature of clinical profiling is the exchange of ideas between the profiler and the police investigators before the report is finalized. The formulation of a good profile can only come after such an exchange. "It is the discussion part of this process which many officers value above all" (p. 16). Copson is critical of the actuarial approach taken by Canter and his associates, an approach to be covered in the next chapter. "It seems to have been assumed by some academic observers that Canter's is the only valid systematic approach to profiling in use in Britain, not least because he says so" (p. 13).

Several other principles of clinical profiling include the recommendation that the profile be custom made. That is, the report should not be based on a boilerplate or generic stereotype of violent offenders. The report should also be directed at the level of sophistication of the police investigators for understanding psychological principles. Moreover, the profiler should be comfortable in viewing the profile as an evolving, reflexive process, subject to change as more information becomes available. The report should include a list of inferred characteristics of the unknown offender, and some profilers will provide a range of observations, predictions, and recommendations. Clinical profilers will often offer advice on personality characteristics, demeanor, and predictions of future behavior. In addition, police investigators will sometimes ask for interview strategies, crimes series linking, and witness evaluation (Gudjonsson & Copson, 1997). It should be noted, though, that some investigators are very cautious about profilers providing interview strategies, particularly if they are not themselves law enforcement officers. In one study, detectives indicated that profilers they had worked with actually provided advice that conflicted with the law on interviewing and interrogation (Gekoski & Gray, 2011). Another concern is that psychologists or psychiatrists acting in a profiling capacity will be viewed as arms of law enforcement rather than as independent professionals.

Copson et al. (1997) emphasize that profiling involves a "a leap of logic, and observing or predicting something which goes beyond what is known at that point" (p. 14). At this stage in the evolution of profiling, they argue, profiling must be practiced this way, as it is far from a science in its current development. This aspect of profiling is one reason why it is so popular and more interesting than the pallid, dry actuarial (statistical) approach, which is more research based and less susceptible to cognitive biases and arbitrary decisions.

Training and Characteristics of Profilers

The training of profilers in North America was initially under the responsibility of the FBI Police Fellowship Program. Between 1966 and 1991, the 10-month program trained 32 police officers from around the world to be profilers. However, in 1992, the FBI terminated the program, although the Bureau continues to train its own agents. It does not formally call them "profilers"—there is no such job title—but informal references to profilers abound in its publications. As emphasized in Chapter 1, we use the term throughout the book with the caveat that alternative terms are often preferred (behavioral analyst, criminal investigative analyst, etc.). Furthermore, we must stress that many self-described profilers today are not psychologists, psychiatrists, or researchers, although others are.

The FBI-sponsored training program, particularly as it relates to the profiling of serial offenders, is so widely known that it is often referenced in the entertainment media and in popular novels. For example, in the 2010 novel by Jo Nesbo, *The Snowman*, the main law enforcement character, a Norwegian detective, was the only one in his agency trained in profiling serial killers by the FBI in the United States. He returns to Norway and successfully captures a serial killer and is hot on the trail of a second using the techniques he learned during his training.

Beginning in 1992, the ICIAF began the training and accreditation for the certification of criminal investigative analysis, and—according to its website—it remains the only organization in the world that trains and certifies profilers. Participants in the training must be police officers with at least 3 years of experience in violent crime investigation, among other requirements. The ICIAF comprises two divisions: the criminal profiling division and the geographic profiling division. It consists of 110 members representing the United States, Canada, The Netherlands, the United Kingdom, and Australia (Behavioural Trace Investigations, 2009).

While it is important to have accreditation and certification of properly trained profilers, there is no evidence that the ICIAF members do better at predicting or estimating criminal behavior than an educated, knowledgeable investigator who did not undergo the training provided by the ICIAF. However, and as asserted by Bourque et al. (2009), "the ICIAF selection and training program should be able to keep the practice of profiling safe from charlatans" (p. 44). Of course, some will argue that the exclusiveness of the ICIAF certification serves as a form of protectionism, allowing police agencies to box out competitors. Bourque et al. further conclude,

> We are, however, of the opinion that profiling methods should be formalized, performance criteria should be developed, and empirical research should be undertaken to measure the true effectiveness of criminal profiling in Canada. (p. 44)

As it now stands, though, "profiling" is not yet a regulated profession in the United States and many other countries, so anyone could legally call themselves a profiler. In most instances—unless a certified individual such as one trained by the ICIAF is available—the police either approach a person they know or have had experience with in the past. In contrast, Britain, Canada, and Australia have some regulations for those who engage in profiling (Rainbow, 2011).

As noted by Gudjonsson and Copson (1997),

> Profiling is not associated with the expertise of any one profession and the police have no way of recognizing the validity of profilers' claims of relevant expertise. Typically, any expert status is difficult to challenge or check. (p. 68)

We will see many illustrations of this problem in Chapter 9, when we consider the issue of profilers providing expert testimony in criminal and civil courts.

In sum, although the practice of profiling can vary significantly from one country to another, much of the profiling is conducted by unaccredited experts. Interestingly, Hazelwood, Ressler, Depue, and Douglas (1995) believed that only individuals with considerable police and investigative experience should be allowed to call themselves profilers. John Douglas (2007) states, "When I train profilers I tell them they must walk in the shoes of both the subject and the victim. You have to experience the feelings and emotions of both" (p. 10). Mary Ellen O'Toole, the long-time FBI agent mentioned earlier in the chapter and considered a leading expert on profiling, offers this portrayal:

> An experienced and well-trained profiler is intuitive, has a great deal of common sense, and is able to think and evaluate information in a concise and logical manner. A successful profiler also is able to suppress their personal feelings about the crime by viewing the scene and the offender-victim interaction from an analytical point of view. Most important, a successful profiler is able to view the crime from the offender's perspective rather than his or her own.
> In addition, the successful profiler possesses an in-depth understanding of human behavior, human sexuality, crime scene investigation and forensics, and has extensive training and experience in studying violent crimes and providing interpretations of his or her insights and observations to investigators. (p. 45)

On the other hand, Canter and Alison (2000) assert it is a misconception that there are some special sets of skills and knowledge for profiling available only to those who have worked with criminals or those who have considerable experience in police investigations. Researchers and thoughtful practitioners can also make significant advances and discoveries in criminal profiling. We might add that a successful profiler—regardless of his or her experiential background—should understand basic concepts of research and statistical methods and be up-to-date on the current research in the field. Profilers also should be fully aware of the many cognitive biases and distortions that are inherent in the profiling process.

Accuracy and Usefulness of Crime Scene Profiles

It is undisputed that the practice of profiling is utilized to some extent by police agencies across the world (Snook et al., 2008). Many police investigators and detectives indicate they find criminal profiling useful in their investigations of certain crimes, particularly violent ones and those committed by serial offenders. In one survey reported by Snook et al., 8 out of 10 police officers in the United Kingdom found criminal profiling helpful in their investigations and would seek profiling help again. In an exploratory Internet survey of forensic psychologists and psychiatrists, Torres, Boccaccini, and Miller (2006) found that 40% of these professionals thought that criminal profiling was scientifically reliable and valid.

In a recent article, Gekoski and Gray (2011) distinguish between accuracy and usefulness. They note that even a profile that is reasonably accurate—as indicated by the number of correct predictive factors once a suspect has been identified, tried, and convicted—may not be *useful* (or cost-effective) to law enforcement. In other words, the law enforcement officers may have arrived at the same conclusions on their own, using routine investigative methods. In addition, the profile may have provided much peripheral information that could have cast suspicion on a much wider range of individuals or led investigators to focus on the wrong suspect.

To investigate these and other possibilities, Gekoski and Gray (2011) conducted semi-structured interviews with 11 detectives in the United Kingdom who had an average of 26 years in police service. Together, these officers had experience with 34 profiles that could be discussed with the researchers. Although as a group they expressed some positive support for the help offered by the profilers, they were also generally dissatisfied. A small number were cynics and dismissed profilers' advice, but others admitted to overestimating the worth of the profiles, which they believe in some cases contributed to damaged investigations. Most of the detectives indicated that the information they had gained from the profilers could have easily been (or in some cases, had been) obtained on their own or from other law enforcement officers. In other words, the profilers did not tell them anything they did not already know. Gekoski and Gray acknowledged, however, that with better and more recent training of behavioral investigative analysts (BIAs), as they are called in the UK, some of the above concerns could be alleviated. On the other hand, they also pointed out that police today have access to technological advances in investigative techniques, such as DNA (see Focus 2.3). "With developments such as these, it is possible that there is simply no longer as much need or enthusiasm for profiling as there was in times gone by when detectives were more limited in the investigative tools available to them" (p. 114).

The research on profile *accuracy* is sparse and limited. Profilers are very reluctant to participate in research involving profiler accuracy (Snook et al., 2007). Kocsis, Irwin, Hayes, and Nunn (2000), for example, asked 40 active profilers in several countries to participate in their study, but only 5 agreed. In order to participate in the study, the only criterion was that they had to have been "consulted by a law enforcement agency for the purpose of constructing a psychological profile in the course of a criminal investigation" (p. 316).

Focus 2.3

Will New Advances Make Profiling Obsolete?

Over the past three decades, criminal investigators have had access to numerous innovations for the collection, identification, and processing of evidence found at crime scenes. Among the most widely recognized is deoxyribonucleic acid (DNA) analysis, with some scholars even suggesting that increasingly more sophisticated methods of collecting DNA could make crime scene profiling obsolete (e.g., Gekoski & Gray, 2011). DNA testing now allows much smaller samples of biological material to be analyzed, and the results tend to be more discriminating. DNA testing of forensic crime scene samples can now be compared against a database of known offenders and other unsolved crimes—and the databases themselves are enormous. Forensic laboratories also have developed advanced analytical techniques through the use of computer technology with systems such as the Combined DNA Index System (CODIS), various Automated Fingerprint Identifications Systems (AFIS), and the National Integrated Ballistics Identification Network (NIBIN). It is plausible that in the future, DNA analysis will provide the physical characteristics of the offender, including hair and eye color.

With such increasingly sophisticated techniques made available to investigators, will behavioral profiling continue to be used? Psychology is the science of probabilities, never certainties; DNA and similar analyses, though always subject to some error, are far less tentative. Richard Mark Evonitz was linked to three homicide victims and a fourth who survived an attack when fibers from his former home, his car, and items from the victims' homes were found to match his DNA. The testing of DNA, when possible, is now routine in many criminal investigations, and investigators also are seeking to reopen cold cases in hopes of obtaining such evidence. However, the demand for DNA testing outstrips the capacity of crime laboratories to process these cases (National Institute of Justice, 2011). Moreover, such testing is not without controversy. Legislation that permits DNA testing on a broader range of suspects, arrestees, and offenders has been accompanied by civil liberties issues. On the other hand, many prisoners are also requesting that their cases be reopened because new DNA evidence has been obtained. In addition, numerous convicted offenders have been cleared by DNA testing, when it has been discovered that DNA found at the scene did not match with their own.

In summary, there are numerous issues involved with DNA analysis and other contemporary tools of forensic investigation, including methods that employ the social and behavioral sciences. As noted by the National Institute of Justice (2011, p. 5), DNA backlog requests "are not a onetime event. They are dynamic and subject to the law of supply and demand. They may go down, but they may go up." The same could be said of demands for the services offered by crime scene profilers.

In a classic and informative study, Pinizzotto and Finkel (1990) tried to assess the accuracy of profiling. Participants, 28 in all, included 4 profiling experts who trained police at the FBI Academy, 6 police detectives across the United States who had been trained at the FBI in personality profiling, 6 experienced detectives without training, 6 clinical psychologists naive about criminal investigation and criminal profiling, and 6 untrained undergraduate students. The participants were given a variety of materials from either a homicide case or a sex offense case, including photographs, victimology information, autopsy and toxicology reports, and crime scene reports. Both cases had been closed, with offenders arrested and convicted. The participants were asked to write a profile of who they thought committed the crime, and were then asked to rank order five individuals from most likely to least likely to have committed the crime, based on brief descriptions.

The results, in general, were not strongly supportive of profile accuracy. Trained experts were somewhat more accurate in profiling the sexual offender, but were not much better than the untrained groups in profiling the homicide offender. The researchers also tried to identify any qualitative differences in the way experts and nonexperts processed the information provided. Overall, the results showed that experts did not process the material any differently from the nonexperts. This finding suggests that the cognitive methods and strategies used by expert profilers are not discernibly different from the way nonexperts process the available information about the crime. The artificiality of the experiment and the quality of information given the groups may have been influential factors in this observation, however. What the researchers did find is that some trained profilers were more interested and skillful in certain areas than other profilers. Some, for example, were good at gaining information from the medical reports, whereas others were better at discerning clues from the crime scene photos. This finding indicates that group profiling by a team of trained experts may be more effective than utilizing one single profiler. We should note that behavioral analysts today typically work in teams rather than singly. Pinizzotto and Finkel (1990) conclude from their research that criminal profiling requires a complex number of tasks that involve a "multilevel series of attributions, correlations, and predictions" (p. 230).

One of the most well-cited studies directly related to the accuracy of profiling is a survey done by Gary Copson (1995) of the Metropolitan Police Service of London. Recall that Copson has described in some detail his clinical method of profiling, discussed above. Copson's study involved 48 of 56 police forces in 184 profiling cases. A total of 29 profilers were identified in the study, including 4 forensic psychiatrists, 4 clinical psychologists, 6 forensic psychologists, 5 academic psychologists, and 4 British police officers. Twelve of the 29 were only used on one occasion. The profiling work was dominated by the work of two individuals, an academic psychologist and a clinical psychologist, who between them were involved in 88 of the 184 cases. The crimes for which profiling was requested were homicides (113), rapes (40), extortion (12), other sex crimes (10), arson (4), abductions (3), and threats (2). The services most often requested were profiling (116 cases) and assistance with understanding the motives for the crime (112 cases). Copson found that the profiler's predictions helped solve a crime in only 14.1% of the cases. However, he also discovered that 82.6% of the police detectives thought that profiling helped to some extent in their overall investigations. More specifically, police investigators stated that profiling led to the identification of the offender in only 2.7% of the cases, but did allow for a better understanding of the crime or offender in about 61% of the cases. The investigators also reported that the profile helped structure the interrogation in 5.4% of the cases. Commenting on this research, Bourque et al. (2009) noted that the police detectives felt the profile was *totally* useless only about 17% of the time. Furthermore, few investigators acted *directly* on the advice of profilers. Bourque et al. posit that the main variable affecting investigators' perception of the usefulness of profiling was who the profiler was. Apparently, the reputation of the profiler largely determined the amount of credibility the investigators gave the profile.

Brent Snook et al. (2007) conducted a meta-analysis of empirical research on the accuracy and effectiveness of profilers. It should be noted that Snook and his colleagues have been critical of profiling endeavors, particularly because profilers do not reveal their methods, and therefore they are not subjected to empirical validation (Snook et al., 2008). In their 2007 meta-analysis, the researchers concluded that criminal profilers do not decisively outperform other groups in predicting the cognitive processes, physical attributes, offense behaviors, or social habits and history of offenders. They further concluded that criminal profiling "will persist as a pseudoscientific technique until such time as empirical and reproducible studies are conducted on the abilities of large groups of active profilers to predict, with more precision and greater magnitude, the characteristics of offenders" (p. 448).

It is worth repeating that profiling very rarely provides the specific identity of the offender, nor is it intended to. Criminal profiling basically tries to narrow the field of investigation to a manageable number of potential suspects (J. E. Douglas et al., 1986). Broadly, criminal profiling suggests the kind of person who might have committed the crime under investigation, but it is highly unlikely to pinpoint an individual's exact identity, as we emphasized earlier. Moreover, while it is difficult to ascertain the accuracy of profiling, its real value may be the introduction of new thoughts in difficult-to-solve cases.

The Psychological and Cognitive Pitfalls of Crime Scene Profiling

Almost all profile reports are replete with inferences and descriptions that are simply not verifiable. Gudjonsson and Copson (1997) note that in one study of 50 solved cases, nearly 50% of the inferences made by profilers were not verifiable. Recall from our discussion in Chapter 1, as well, that profiles contain observations that could apply to numerous individuals (e.g., an unmarried male in a low-income occupation who frequents bars, lives alone, and is conservative in his views toward women).

Robert Keppel and William Birnes (2003) write,

> The profilers simply continue to get it wrong, and yet the police and media rely on them as if they are predictions from the oracle at Delphi. . . . There are dates, places, and times that have more factual merit to the investigative process than the behavioral characteristics identified by FBI, psychological, and psychiatric profilers. (p. 140)

Profilers continue to take it on the chin for their inaccuracies. Why do they miss the mark so often, and what might explain this apparently low hit rate?

The profiler does not approach his or her task with an empty mind. Herbert Simon (1957) developed the concept of *bounded* or *limited rationality*. By this he meant that humans have a limited mental capacity to make sense of the enormous complexity of the world. Each of us constructs a simplified mental model of the world and then works with this model (Heuer, 1999). According to Richards J. Heuer Jr., "We behave rationally within the confines of our mental model, but this model is not always well adapted to the requirements of the real world" (p. 3). Similarly, George A. Kelly (1963) summarized that humans construct a simplified mental model of reality and then perceive and react to the enormous complexity and chaos of the world using this model. Without this model, we would have very little to anchor down our senses, perceptions, beliefs, and thoughts. In this respect, we all have our own versions of the world. There are some similarities to other versions, of course, but there are also many unique differences. The total composite, however, results in a version different from any other. In other words, no two people think alike.

Nelson Goodman (1978) explained human thought and judgment in a similar fashion when he referred to "world making." Each person constructs his or her unique version of the world on the basis of experience and distinctive mental structure. As much as many profilers believe that one must put oneself into the mind of the serial killer to identify motivations and personality, it is extremely difficult—if not impossible—to do so. Keppel and Birnes (2003) point out that the profile is often mistakenly built on what the analyst believes is the killer's or violent offender's own projection of reality. No matter how hard profilers try to enter the mind of the offender, they will ultimately be strongly influenced by their own mental model, biases, and version of reality. As noted by Richards Heuer (1999), who worked for the CIA for nearly 45 years as a staff officer, a substantial body of psychological research on perception, memory, attention span, and reasoning capacity documents the limitations of the mental capacity and "world making" of intelligence officers as well as profilers. This limitation of mental capacity leads predictably to biases and faulty judgments and decision making in the evaluation of evidence. We will now cover in more detail some of the memory and cognitive biases that are likely to explain some of the many inaccuracies and problems in profiling.

MEMORY AND COGNITIVE BIASES

"What is commonly called memory is not a single, simple function. It is an extraordinarily complex system of diverse components and processes" (Heuer, 1999, p. 17). As pointed out by Kocsis (2010), a number of authors (e.g., Copson et al., 1997; P. E. Dietz, 1985; Korem, 1997; Rossi, 1982) have developed models for how a profile should be done. Kocsis finds that these models lack an empirical foundation and are based largely on the authors' anecdotal experiences and observations, which are generally referred to in the literature as the FBI or clinical methods of profiling discussed earlier. However, Kocsis notes that the models all have one thing in common: "All models appear to assume that the mental assimilation of case information, presumably via memory, is an integral component of the mental processes involved in the accurate construction of a criminal profile" (p. 58). Kocsis believes the better the memory of the profiler, the more accurate the profile. A profiler's memory consists of his or her experiences, training, knowledge, and values. When profilers construct a profile, they examine the new information of the case and compare it with their own experiences, usually including previous cases. This is referred to as "working memory." The working memory is continually being reconstructed as new information is gained and old information is partially forgotten. The less experience a profiler has, the more reconstruction of working memory he or she will have to do.

More often than not, experienced profilers have devoted many years to developing a craft and mind-set that has served them well, and they see no need to change it (Heuer, 1999). They are convinced the information embedded in their memory from years of experience allows them to perceive patterns in crimes and make inferences that are beyond the reach of other individuals and investigators. In many instances, they believe this mind-set enables them to achieve whatever success they enjoy in making profiling inferences. This phenomenon is known as **belief persistence** or perseverance, and once formed, it is remarkably resistant to change (Marshall & Alison, 2007; R. Ross & Anderson, 1982). Individuals may continue to cling to beliefs even when the evidential basis for these beliefs is discredited or completely refuted (Nestler, 2010). This point can be well demonstrated by the rigidity with which some experts continue to hold to the O/D typology, formulated by Douglas and Ressler 30 years ago. Based on their past experiences, professional training, and cultural and professional norms, the special agents thought they saw a pattern in the material found in their interviews of violent inmates. As Malcom Gladwell (2009) noted, John Douglas appeared to be unaware of the research that put serious doubts on the reliability and validity of the typology. Moreover, based on Douglas's own website at www.johndouglasmindhunter.com, he still holds to the value of the O/D typology for profiling serial offenders.

The clinical models of profiling are especially subject to all the "distortions, biases, and shortcomings associated with the frailties of human decision making" (Alison & Canter, 1999a, p. 29). These shortcomings are associated with the tendency to use simplifying cognitive templates and constructs when making complex judgments (Marshall & Alison, 2007). Heavy reliance on simple cognitive templates can be potentially damaging to criminal investigations.

CONFIRMATION BIAS

Some studies in the last 10 years—including meta-analyses—indicate that a large proportion of the conclusions and predictions contained within profiles are both ambiguous and unverifiable (Alison, Smith, Eastman, & Rainbow, 2003; Alison, Smith, & Morgan, 2003; Snook et al., 2007). Many of the statements are so vague that they are open to a wide range of interpretations. Compounding the problem is the tendency for police investigators to interpret the ambiguous information contained within the profile report to fit their own biases and hunches about the case or the suspect. They select those aspects of the report that they see as fitting their own cognitive sketch of the suspect while ignoring the conclusions and predictions in the report that do not fit. This powerful tendency is known in psychology as **confirmation bias.** It is the tendency to gather evidence that confirms preexisting expectations or beliefs while failing to acknowledge contradictory evidence or information. "When it operates, it places us in a kind of closed cognitive system in which only evidence that confirms our existing views and beliefs gets inside; other information is noticed but is quickly rejected as false" (Baron & Byrne, 2000, p. 8). In essence, confirmation bias is the tendency to notice and remember information that lends support to our views on something, such as our opinions about a suspect. It is a powerful tendency that might be prevalent not only in the subjective interpretations of a profile, but also in its creation. It is entirely likely that experienced profilers who hold firmly to their working memory and a cognitive template based on many years of experience, selectively search, recollect, or assimilate information in a way that lends spurious support to their traditional way of seeing things.

Investigators and profilers are guided in their search for and evaluation of evidence by their preliminary theories or hypotheses regarding how and by whom a crime was committed. In addition, such working hypotheses are not always based on solid facts surrounding a case, but sometimes on the expectations, preconceptions, and ultimately the cognitive biases of the investigators. As noted by Marshall and Alison (2007), Copson's 1995 report "stated that over 50% of offender profiles were considered 'operationally useful' because they *reinforced* the officer's own belief" (p. 288). That is, there is a tendency for police investigators to creatively interpret the ambiguous information contained within profiles to fit their own biases about the case or the suspect. Does this imply—from the officer's perspective—that the profile was accurate? One common observation about police requests for profiling advice is that they normally occur late in the investigation process, which suggests that police investigative processes and media coverage have already run some—if not most—of the course, with a number of the hypotheses and potential biases already in place.

Ask and Granhag (2005) identify three conditions during criminal investigations that are likely to promote confirmation bias. First, law enforcement agents usually work under substantial time pressures to solve the crime. The workload is not only heavy, but there are often deadlines for strategic decisions, such as whether to retain a suspect in custody. Second, the police culture is characterized by norms that encourage decisiveness. According to Ask and Granhag, these norms are often influenced by significant individuals in the organization who expect results in a timely manner. Time is especially critical if there is a serial killer or rapist on the loose. Third, many pivotal decisions, such as an arrest, entail a specific commitment on behalf of the responsible investigator. "Thus, the loss of prestige that would follow from admitting erroneous decisions may motivate investigators to confirm the adequacy and disregard deficiencies of prior judgments" (p. 47). All three conditions also influence the report and accompanying recommendations of the profilers.

SELF-SERVING BIAS

Self-serving bias is the strong tendency to interpret events in a way that assigns credit to oneself for any success but denies any responsibility for any failure. The self-serving bias is regarded as a form of self-deception designed to maintain high self-esteem. It is the tendency for a person to take more credit for a successful task and less credit for an unsuccessful outcome than he or she actually deserves. Recall the discussion about James Brussel in Chapter 1; Brussel's memoirs offer great detail about his assistance to investigators and even indicate that they did not listen to him when the wrong man was arrested and convicted. Brussel also admitted to making just one mistake in one of his profiles, suggesting that a perpetrator was unmarried when he was in fact married and had been for many years. Self-serving bias is similar to self-*centered* bias, which is taking more credit than one deserves for a task that also involved others. Essentially, self-serving bias accompanies high self-esteem and confidence—or at least the image of confidence and self-esteem one wishes to project to the world.

FUNDAMENTAL ATTRIBUTION ERROR

Fundamental attribution error or bias is a common and powerful tendency to explain another person's behavior in terms of dispositional or personality (internal) factors rather than situational or environmental (external) factors. In other words, there is a tendency to believe that people act in a way that reflects the kind of people they are, not the situation or circumstances in which they find themselves. This tendency is especially strong when we do not know the other person well, a common situation in crime scene profiling. The traditional FBI profiling approach is especially susceptible to this bias, because it often assumes a consistent relationship between offending behavior and personality traits. More specifically, it is assumed that personality traits can be inferred from crime scene behavior, and then used to predict other behavior. Although the clinical approach to profiling often emphasizes victim as an important component in the process, there still may be the tendency to neglect the external influences in the long run. Examples of external factors that might be critical in the profiling process include the victim's reaction, the degree of opportunity in the offense, weapons or self-defense strategies of the victim, and the physical layout of the attack site.

It certainly is not wrong for profilers to lean toward the internal side of the attribution process, because behavioral prediction relies heavily on this aspect. However, it is the *overestimation* that can present problems and lead to misleading conclusions. It can be especially problematic when the profiler assumes a consistent and invariant relationship between offending behavior and certain personality traits or behavioral patterns. For example, J. E. Douglas and Olshaker (1995) refer to the "homicidal triad" as being characterized by bed-wetting, cruelty to animals, and firesetting (p. 139). Research evidence does not support the triad, although one of its components—cruelty to animals—has emerged as a correlate of violent behavior toward people (Stouthamer-Loeber, Wei, Loeber, & Masten, 2004). Douglas and Olshaker also write with certitude that lust murderers have "trouble dealing with authority" and are "anxious to exert control over others whenever [they] can" (J. E. Douglas & Olshaker, 2000, p. 29). Although this may be intuitively appealing, it is an assumption—a fundamental attribution error—that has not been documented in the criminology research.

Together, the above principles from social psychology help us understand why some crime scene profilers tend to miss the mark in the assertions they make.

Clinical profiling is particularly susceptible to cognitive biases, but other forms of profiling are susceptible as well. In addition, as we will note in later chapters, other forms of profiling have their own unique shortcomings.

Summary and Conclusions

Crime scene profiling is the act of closely examining a crime scene for clues about the cognitive, behavioral, and demographic characteristics of a possible perpetrator or perpetrators. It is, in many aspects, what law enforcement investigators have always done. In the hands of trained profilers, however, the scene is examined with the hope that psychological insights will fine-tune this process and provide additional assistance to police.

We reviewed the early history of profiling in the United States, focusing on the work of those associated with the Behavioral Science Unit (BSU) of the FBI, under the leadership of Howard Teten, John Douglas, and their associates. Some agents began to publish accounts of their work in law enforcement publications, which introduced investigators nationwide to the idea of profiling. The interviews conducted by Douglas and his colleague, Robert Ressler, laid the groundwork for the formulation of the organized/disorganized dichotomy, which was central to FBI investigations for many years and continues to be prominent to this day. Though Douglas himself amended the dichotomy to indicate that many if not most crime scenes were mixed, critics have argued that whether it is a dichotomy or a continuum, the approach has questionable validity. Likewise, the FBI's *Crime Classification Manual* has been challenged for its lack of relevance to much crime scene investigation. The *CCM* reflects the FBI's clinical as opposed to actuarial approach to profiling, and it is vulnerable to criticism by academics and more research-oriented practitioners.

Many profilers today have been trained by the FBI as special agents or have received certificates from FBI-sponsored programs. Others have received training from the ICIAF, an international group dedicated to improving training and honing skills of profilers. Unfortunately, however, there is no formal system for regulating profiling; police in some communities simply seek assistance from a self-described profiler who may or may not have the knowledge and skills that are available in this rapidly changing enterprise. As we will note in the next chapter, in which a model report is discussed, professional profiling requires extensive knowledge and familiarity with both theory and research in criminology, together with awareness of investigative procedures.

Concepts encountered in the profiling literature were introduced in this chapter, including the modus operandi, the signature, personation, staging, and trophy taking. We also discussed the process of case linkage or linkage analysis, which is gaining more attention in the research literature as well as in profiling practice. Linkage analysis involves finding similarities among various crimes and attempting to link them to one perpetrator; in addition, it may involve mining a database of crimes in an attempt to determine whether a particular offender might be responsible for more crimes than those for which he or she has been identified. An underlying assumption of case linkage is behavioral consistency; that is, it is assumed that humans are consistent in their behavior over time and from situation to situation. Therefore, an offender's modus operandi should be recognizable, thereby allowing investigators to link multiple crimes to the same offender. As noted in the chapter, researchers have arrived at varying conclusions with respect to behavioral consistency. Absent additional supportive data, it is premature to conclude that such consistency either does or does not exist.

We ended the chapter with a discussion of additional concepts from social psychology that help explain why crime scene profilers often miss the mark in their attempts to help identify what type of individual may be responsible for a crime, particularly a series of violent crimes, such as sexual assaults or murders. Like all human beings, profilers are subject to a variety of cognitive biases. These include confirmation bias, where they emphasize clues that may support their preconceived notions; self-serving bias, where they point out clues that may highlight their specific expertise or make them look good; and fundamental attribution bias, whereby they overemphasize the role of personality to the neglect of situational variables. Nonetheless, with these caveats in mind, crime scene profiling—carefully done—can be an extremely useful investigative tool for law enforcement.

KEY CONCEPTS

Actuarial method of profiling

Base rate

Behavioral Analysis Unit (BAU)

Behavioral Science Unit (BSU)

Belief persistence

Case linkage

Child Abduction Rapid Deployment (CARD)

Child Abduction Response Teams (CARTs)

Clinical method of profiling

Confirmation bias

Deductive analysis

Disorganized asocial offender

Disorganized crime scene

Fundamental attribution error or bias

Inductive analysis

International Criminal Investigative Analysis Fellowship (ICIAF)

Linkage analysis

Mixed crime scene

Modus operandi

National Center for the Analysis of Violent Crime (NCAVC)

Organized crime scene

Organized nonsocial offender

Personation

Self-serving bias

Signature

Souvenir

Staging

Trophy

Typology

Undoing

Violent Criminal Apprehension Program (ViCAP)

3

Scientific Approaches to Crime Scene Profiling

With a morbid fascination reminiscent of the attitudes to freak shows, there appears to be an inability to resist the desire to probe into the darker recesses of the more bizarre features of criminal behaviour.

—Alison & Canter (1999b)

W ithout question, the "bizarre" features of crime scenes capture the attention of the media, the public, and even of investigators themselves. As we noted in Chapter 2, it is often the unique aspects of a crime scene, such as a perpetrator's signature, that are highlighted in discussions of profiling. Furthermore, sensational crimes are the ones most focused upon, whereas in reality the various forms of profiling can be employed with a wide range of offenses, not just homicides or stranger abductions. Laurence Alison (2005) writes that

the beliefs surrounding profiling appear to be so ingrained that many of the keenest and, indeed, brightest students have been so embroiled in the media portrayal of this field that they are often the most difficult students to encourage in developing a critical stance on such methods. (p. 9)

This chapter in many ways is more critical of the current state of profiling than the previous chapters. In fact, the reader is apt to receive a rather bleak picture of profiling as it is too often practiced, and its presumed mysterious aspects may be significantly reduced. Crime scene profiling, at its best, is not about entering "the evil mind of the criminal" or deciding whether a perpetrator is a disorganized or organized offender. Rather, it has more to do with discovering how victims are chosen, how they are treated, what forensic evidence is left at the crime scene or on the victim, and how far the offender traveled to reach his or her victims—a topic that will be addressed in detail in Chapter 4. In addition, a profile should reflect the profiler's extensive knowledge about the psychology of crime.

Misconceptions About Profiling

In a timely article, Lee Rainbow and Adam Gregory (2011) identify several popular misconceptions about profiling, which are held by both the public and many professionals (see Table 3.1). The most common misconception is that—as a matter of routine—profilers make predictions or assumptions about an offender's personality. As Rainbow and Gregory point out, not only does such activity have questionable reliability and validity, but statements about an offender's personality very often do not help police investigators identify the offender. For example, predicting that an offender is extraverted, anxious, narcissistic, or obsessive-compulsive rarely is useful for the investigation. Despite the classic FBI approach that "the crime scene is presumed to reflect the murderer's behavior and personality in much the same way as furnishings reveal the homeowner's character" (J. E. Douglas et al., 1992, p. 21), contemporary profilers should try to focus on *behavioral features* of the offender that are not only helpful to police investigators but also requested by them. For example, investigators may want to know whether the offender is likely to engage in outdoor activities, frequent clubs, or work at a desk job—some of these behaviors can be tied to personality features, but personality terminology need not be used in the profile reports. If they are used, it should be done in cautionary fashion.

A second misconception is that the profiler's role is to solve the case. Rainbow and Gregory (2011) note that this misconception often stems from the published memoirs and biographers of self-promoting profilers, who focus on "successful" cases with which they were involved. "Such accounts are characterized by highly subjective and self-serving memoirs focusing on idiosyncratic personal contributions and incredible levels of insight and accuracy" (p. 20). Many of these authors imply that the case was solved primarily because of their own skill and ability. The psychiatrist James Brussel, whom we met earlier in this book, even devoted a chapter in his memoirs to a case in which he argued that the wrong man was imprisoned; police, he said, ignored his profile, which pointed to the true perpetrator, who ultimately left the United States. (As we noted in the previous chapter, the individual convicted of the crime confessed and remains imprisoned.) *The primary goal of any professional profiler is to support the investigative and decision-making process by providing a different perspective based on solid behavioral science.* The profile report is not intended or expected to solve the case.

Related to the above is the fact that those profilers who are not themselves law enforcement officers can get so caught up in a case that they consider themselves an arm of the police agency investigating the crime. In one noteworthy case in England (see *Regina v. Stagg,* 1994), the profiler was so involved in the investigative phase that he encouraged an undercover police officer to continually goad the suspect into confessing to a brutal crime; the suspect never confessed and was eventually cleared of the crime, but not before spending over a year in pretrial detention. We will return to this case shortly.

A third misconception is that profiling as a whole is an *established* scientific endeavor. This misconception is probably held far more by the public than by police

Table 3.1   Misconceptions and Reality With Respect to Profiling

Misconception	Reality
Profilers predict personality.	Personality prediction has questionable validity and reliability. Statements about personality are often not helpful to investigators. Profilers should focus on behavioral indicators.
Profilers solve crimes.	Profilers provide information that may or may not be helpful to investigators. Profilers who are not law enforcement officers should not consider themselves an arm of law enforcement.
Profiling is an established scientific endeavor.	Although the scientific approach is recommended, profiling is in its early stages and is far from being established as a science.

Source: Adapted from Rainbow & Gregory, 2011.

professionals, thanks to motion pictures and popular TV programs. Although profilers are expected to offer advice that is methodologically sound and based on empirical research and psychological principles, profiling, at this point in its early development, does not possess established scientific status (Kocsis, 2009; Snook et al., 2008). The courts across the globe generally recognize this limitation of the technique and its methods, though testimony from behavioral analysts/profilers is often admitted, as we will point out in Chapter 9. Moreover, while many profilers prefer not to claim expertise in this way, one goal of many researchers as well as practitioners is to get the practice of crime scene profiling recognized as a scientific process.

Making the Case for Scientific Profiling

The American philosopher Charles Peirce outlined four general ways through which we acquire beliefs and knowledge about the world (Kerlinger, 1973). First, there is the **method of tenacity,** where people hold firmly to their beliefs about human behavior simply because they have always believed and known them to be true and correct. These beliefs are held to even in the face of contradictory evidence: "I know I'm right regardless of what others say or what the evidence indicates." The method of tenacity also may rely on intuition or "gut feelings." In forensic circles, this phenomenon is known as **belief persistence** (Rainbow, Almond, & Alison, 2011), mentioned briefly in Chapter 2. This characteristic appears to be a common bias among many profilers. Once they form a prediction and description of the offender, they hold onto their for-mulation regardless of contradictory information or evidence. At times, even the lan-guage used reflects rigid, dogmatic, or unprofessional viewpoints. One prominent profiler who makes frequent media appearances maintains a website and a blog in which she periodically refers to both accused and acquitted individuals as "scumbags."

Police investigators are subject to belief persistence as well. "Within an investigative context, belief persistence effects often arise during the course of an investigation due to investigating officers generating story-like narratives in order to make sense of the information they gather" (Rainbow et al., 2011, p. 44). Once developed, belief persistence is very difficult to alter. It often leads to confirmation bias (also discussed in the previous chapter), where investigators seek out and assign more weight to evidence that confirms their initial views, and ignore or give less weight to evidence that does not support their initial hypothesis.

The second way of developing beliefs and knowledge is the **method of authority.** In this context, something is true because individuals and institutions of authority proclaim it to be so. Education is partly based on this method of knowing, with authority originating from teachers and the "great minds" and literature they cite. School-aged children often quote the authority of their teacher as indisputable evidence in support of an argument; college students often assert, "It says so in the book" or "online." Information gathered this way is efficient and time saving, and it certainly may be valid, but the material gathered must frequently be scrutinized or empirically validated in the long run. The method of authority has relevance to profiling when investigators place too much weight on the report prepared by a profiler without considering competing possibilities. It can also come into play in the courtroom when expert witnesses testify, as will be covered in Chapter 9.

The **a priori method** is a third way of obtaining knowledge. When we use this method, we say our knowledge and beliefs are correct because "it stands to reason and logical deduction." Ultimately, the knowledge is based on logic, and sometime on mathematical formulation. The idea seems to be that through free communication and interactions, people can reach the "truth" because their natural inclinations tend toward the truth (Kerlinger, 1973). Philosophy is generally based on this method, as are many aspects of the American judicial system and the formulation of laws.

Common sense is a dominant ingredient in the a priori method, although it is relevant to all four methods of knowing. *Common sense,* in this context, refers to "a homespun awareness resulting from everyday experience, as opposed to knowledge acquired from formal training in a technical philosophy" (Gordon, Kleiman, & Hanie, 1978, p. 894). In the profiling enterprise, many experienced investigators use the a priori method or common sense to help them solve crimes. It may be "common sense," for example, to focus an investigation on individuals with a prior record, who have served prison sentences for the same type of crime, and who happen to be living in the same geographical area. This is not a bad thing to do, but by itself it does not necessarily result in finding the true offender.

The fourth way of obtaining knowledge is through the **method of science,** which is the testing of a statement or set of statements through systematic investigation and study. On the basis of empirical research and systematic investigation, statements about events and phenomena are revised, reconstructed, or discarded. Science is an enterprise under constant scrutiny, change, modification, and expansion rather than one based on an absolute, unalterable system of facts. Science teaches us that there are few certainties in the world—only probabilities—and we should base our decisions, knowledge, and beliefs on the best information available at any point in time. In the profiling context, practitioners, researchers, and academics who want to bring more respectability to profiling (or behavioral analysis) continually challenge the profiling community to specify their methods and document their findings (see, e.g., Snook et al., 2008).

In his classic work, *The Logic of Scientific Discovery*, Karl Popper (1968) contends that a truly scientific statement not only is capable of being verified or shown to be correct for the time being, but also is capable of being falsified or shown to be incorrect. In fact, Popper argues that one criterion of a scientific statement is its vulnerability to being refuted by common or special experience. The scientist will ask, "Is it conceivable to set up conditions where the statements accounting for the observed phenomena could be shown to be incorrect?" If such conceivable conditions cannot be proposed, the statement is not scientific. A truly scientific statement, then, according to Popper, is constantly at risk of being shown faulty in accounting for observations and experience. A statement that is concrete, precise, and testable is a scientific statement.

In an effort to describe the differences between verifiability and falsifiability, Popper uses the scientific statement, "All swans are white," which is a falsifiable statement. No matter how many times we may observe white swans, our observations do not justify the conclusion that *all* swans are white. If, after one million observations (verifications), a black swan is seen, the statement "all swans are white" will be incorrect. One falsification will have forced a revision of our thinking about swans, rendering the original non-universal. Now we must try to develop a better statement, such as "All young swans are white," a statement which itself is falsifiable.

Why is all this important? What if a profiler concludes that "All serial killers are white" or that "Serial killing is extremely rare in all parts of the world except America" or that "Mass murderers are almost always insane and kill for no apparent reason"? These are statements (all of which have been made by profilers in the past) that can clearly be verified or falsified by science—and in each case the statement has indeed been falsified. Not all serial killers are white; evidence of serial murder across the globe is accumulating; and mass murderers are usually neither legally insane nor mentally disordered, in the clinical sense of that term. Unfortunately, although some profilers do relay information cautiously and in terms of probabilities, many profiler reports to police investigators and oral statements to the police and media are ambiguous and cannot be verified or falsified. Consider the following statement on the behavior of arsonists: "Firesetting is a substitute for a sexual thrill, and the devastating and destructive powers of fire reflect the intensity of the pyromaniac's sexual desires, as well as his sadism" (Abrahamsen, 1960, p. 129). This statement is neither verifiable nor falsifiable, nor is it particularly useful to police investigators for identifying a serial arsonist. Similar statements reflecting a psychoanalytic orientation continue to be made to this day. In one very controversial case, a drawing of a knife-wielding hand cutting a diamond shape, which a suspect had made on his homework, was interpreted as the suspect's rehearsal for the genital mutilation found on a murdered woman's body.

It should be emphasized that Popper's ideas are not entirely embraced by those within the scientific community, especially in the social or behavioral sciences. In contrast to the physical or biological sciences, research data in the behavioral sciences are rarely clear enough or convincing enough to warrant either confirmation or falsification of a lawful relationship or a theory. Most often the data are open to multiple interpretations and subject to varying explanations. The point here, however, is that scientific knowledge is an open system that is tentative, fallible, and developing. The *science* of behavioral profiling, to be presented in this and the next chapter, follows the same tentative, fallible, and developing characteristics.

Although Popper's theory may not be directly on point, Peirce's four methods of knowing are clearly relevant to our discussion. They provide a rough framework for determining the source of our knowledge, but also offer a beginning argument for why behavioral profiling *should be* a scientific endeavor. With the possible exception of the method of tenacity, each method has it place in the accumulation of knowledge, as long as we recognize which method we are using to obtain our knowledge. Authoritative sources and reasoning both are valuable contributors to our beliefs and opinions. The method of science, however, provides us with additional information about the "soundness" of our authoritative and logical knowledge, and it promotes a critical and cautious way of thinking about our beliefs. As we shall point out in this chapter, to be successful, profiling must rely on three methods of knowing—the method of tenacity excepted—but its techniques and procedures must strive toward validation through scientific research.

The Beginnings of Scientific Crime Scene Profiling

It is probably fair to say that *scientific* crime scene profiling began in the United Kingdom, while clinically based crime scene profiling began in the United States, with the work of the FBI's Behavioral Science Unit, discussed in Chapter 2. It is also important to stress that both methods have value. As we learned from the work of Copson and his associates, a *carefully defined* clinical perspective has gained much respectability. In addition, in recent years psychologists have become more accepting of structured professional or clinical judgment in the assessment and treatment of individuals, and it has become apparent that a combination of clinical skills and actuarial knowledge is helpful (Borum, Lodewijks, Bartel, & Forth, 2010; Heilbrun, Marczyk, & DeMatteo, 2002). Nonetheless, profilers do not directly assess or offer treatment to suspects or potential suspects—they rarely even meet them. For this reason, those who recommend a scientific approach to crime scene profiling still favor the actuarial method at this time in its development.

ORIGINS OF INVESTIGATIVE PSYCHOLOGY

In the mid-1980s, social psychologist David Canter was called to Scotland Yard to explore the possibilities of incorporating psychological concepts and theory into police investigation techniques. What prompted the call was a series of rapes, and eventually rape-murders, that had police stymied. Canter's background was in applied social and environmental psychology, so he approached the request not from the perspective of a clinician, but as someone who could draw on his experience and research on criminal behavior. Canter (1994) also believes police investigators found their way to him because of his earlier work studying human behavior in fires and other emergencies.

Beginning in 1982, numerous women were attacked at railway stations in and around London. First, a 23-year-old woman was attacked and brutally raped near the Hampstead Heath Station. Over the next 4 years, 18 more women were attacked and raped, again near train stations. Three women were raped on the same night in 1985 in Hendon, a suburb of London. The investigation and search for the offender involved at least four police forces: Metropolitan, Surrey, Hertfordshire, and British Transport Police (Stevens, 1997). The serial rapist had a distinct method of operation. He used a knife, bound the victim's hands with strong twine, and usually stayed close to the railway tracks. The attacker then used trains to escape quickly from the scene. The attacker was quickly labeled by the media "The Railway Rapist," and flyers were circulated requesting information that could lead to his capture. Interestingly, police suspected there were two different offenders, but they did not reveal this to the media. The police were correct (see Photo 3.1).

In late December 1985, the first death occurred: A 19-year-old woman was dragged off a train at Hackney Wick Station by the attacker, repeatedly raped, and then strangled with twine. Her body was found 2 weeks later. At that point, police investigators launched the largest investigation in the United Kingdom since the Yorkshire Ripper attacks in the late sixties and seventies.

After reports of the murder, the media changed the label to "The Railway Killer." In April 1986, a 15-year-old was abducted on her way to buy candy at a local shop. She was raped, strangled, and her body was set on fire. A month later, a 29-year-old woman who worked for a London weekend television station as an administrative assistant was abducted and murdered as she left the train in Brookmans Park, Hertfordshire. Her badly decomposed body was found 2 months later in a field near the railroad tracks.

Photo 3.1: The Railway Rapists, David Mulcahy and John Duffy

At some point in the investigation, Canter, then teaching and conducting research at Surrey University, was called in to aid the police investigation. Canter thought that the Railway Rapist was a married but childless resident of the Kilburn area of London who had a history of domestic violence. He drew up a profile of 17 personality traits and behavioral characteristics, plus several environmental clues. Canter's contribution was one of the earliest offender profiles done in Britain. Although the profile itself did not lead directly to the arrest and conviction of the main perpetrator, John Duffy (another individual, David Mulcahy, was also later identified), the profile did help pinpoint the area in which Duffy lived, and much of the behavioral profile was found to be somewhat accurate after the trial. (See Focus 3.1 for additional details about the case.) As in most cases involving serial offenses, the offender was arrested after intensive investigative work by many law enforcement agents and a combination of propitious factors coming together. Canter himself downplayed his role and did not claim to have solved the case.

Focus 3.1

SEARCHING FOR THE RAILWAY RAPIST

John Duffy, a former British Rail carpenter and a martial arts instructor, was a suspect in the Railway Rapist case from the beginning of police investigation, but he became hidden among numerous other suspects as the investigation progressed. Investigating officers realized the attacker probably knew the railway system well, since he had committed many of his attacks near railroad lines (Stevens, 1997). The offender usually quickly left the crime scene via trains.

Police had a number of clues that—in retrospect—were significant. A footprint near the scene of one of the murders revealed a relatively small shoe size, narrowing the offender down to 1% of the adult male population in Britain. Duffy had previously been arrested for violence and burglary. In addition, his blood group matched semen found in the body of one of the murder victims. One of the rape victims described her attacker as a white man, 5'4" tall, with ginger/fair hair, and a spotty or acne-pitted complexion, a description that closely fit Duffy. At the time of his arrest for burglary in 1981, his mug shot revealed he was wearing a hooded sweatshirt. Several of the rapes had been committed by a hooded attacker wearing a similar sweatshirt. The photograph also revealed another item reported by rape victims: a balaclava—a cloth headgear that covers the whole head, exposing only part of the face—worn by the offender.

Furthermore, Duffy had been interviewed by two Metropolitan Police officers after one of the attacks in 1986, but had an alibi (Stevens, 1997). However, the officers were not happy with the interview and were planning to interview him again. Perhaps most revealing, Duffy had allegedly raped his ex-wife at knifepoint in a North London park, an attack that began to separate him from the other list of suspects. After Duffy was identified as the prime suspect, he became the subject of surveillance by the police and was arrested in 1987. After examining Duffy's clothes, forensic experts were able to match fibers from one of his sweaters to the fibers found on the first murder victim.

John Duffy was convicted in 1988 of two murders and five counts of rape and a related sexual attack. He was sentenced to six life sentences. For years, he claimed to have no memory of the attacks he committed. However, in 1997, his memory began to return, and he described his crimes in detail to psychologist Dr. Jennie Cutler to set the record straight. In his prison cell, he admitted to the crimes he was found guilty of in 1988, and he confessed to more than 20 additional sexual assaults that he could recall (Pritchard, 2001). He said there were probably more, but he could not remember them all. It is possible that his multiple accounts were hyperbole to some extent, but it is unquestioned that he did commit a series of rapes and murders.

Duffy also eventually revealed what the police already knew: that he had not attacked all of the women by himself. During these confessions, he eventually named his childhood friend, David Mulcahy, as his accomplice in many of his rapes and the three murders. As youth, Duffy and Mulcahy used to go out together shooting at people with air rifles. In 1976, the pair were convicted of causing bodily harm when they shot four victims with air rifles. They also tormented and tortured animals, an indication that they probably had a callous disregard for living creatures throughout most of their lifetime.

During Mulcahy's trial in 2000, Duffy was the chief witness against him, and for 14 days in the witness box he detailed the crimes to the jury, while facing repeated outbursts from Mulcahy challenging him. Mulcahy, a married father of four, was convicted on 15 counts after one of the longest murder trials ever to take place in Great Britain.

During their rape and murder escapades, the pair would carry their "rape kit," which included balaclavas, knives, and tape to gag and blindfold their victims, and listen to Michael Jackson tapes (especially *Thriller*) while they hunted for women who were alone at railway stations. One of the disturbing findings during the Mulcahy trial was that the tape used to bind one of the rape victims had not been tested for fingerprints before it was placed in an evidence storeroom. During the Mulcahy trial, it was reexamined and found to contain Mulcahy's fingerprints—a tragic blunder that could have led to the arrest of the pair years earlier.

In 1992, the Metropolitan Police Service (UK) commissioned a research project to study the usefulness, reliability, and validity of offender profiling (Rainbow, 2011). Canter's work had obviously been of help, and other profilers were beginning to contact police to offer their assistance with other crimes. And, of course, in the United States, profiling was gaining considerable attention, particularly with reference to serial killers. The project researchers discovered that there were no governing bodies for the regulation of professional or ethical standards relating to the practice of profiling, and that there were no formally recognized programs for the training of profilers, in either Britain or the United States, with the exception of the FBI endeavors covered in Chapter 2.

At about the same time, a different case was holding the attention of police, the British public, and the profiling community. In 1992, a young woman named Rachel Nickell was stabbed and killed while walking on Wimbledon Common with her 2-year-old child. Police asked psychologist Paul Britton—who had aided them in other investigations during the 1980s—to help identify a likely suspect. Britton's approach to profiling was much like that described in earlier chapters: somewhat experiential, intuitive, and clinically based. After reviewing the facts of the Nickell case, Britton told police the perpetrator was likely a loner who lived near the Common, was interested in pornography, and likely had had some past encounter with police with respect to a minor crime. The police investigation focused on Colin Stagg, a single man in his twenties who lived with his parents not far from the scene of the crime. Stagg had been admonished by police for writing a sexually explicit letter to a woman whose name he found in the lonely hearts column of a local publication.

Britton then took on a very active role in the investigation. He urged police to set up a "honeytrap," in which a female police officer would pose as someone interested in hearing more about his sexual fantasies, and in great detail. Over many weeks, Britton worked closely with the officer, providing her with suggestions as to how she might bait the suspect into making incriminating statements. We will discuss legal aspects of the Stagg case in Chapter 9, but for the moment it suffices to say that Stagg was not responsible for the death, that another man later confessed, and that police apologized to Stagg some years later. The wrongful accusation and undercover investigation of Colin Stagg were undoubtedly factors that led to calls for more cautious use of profilers during police investigations.

In 2001, the Association of Chief Police Officers (ACPO) in the United Kingdom recommended that the term "offender profiler" be replaced with the term **behavioral investigative analyst**, or BIA. We will continue, however, to use the broad and more common term "profiler" in this book, unless "BIA" is used in a specific study or recommendation. The ACPO also recommended that police investigators only use the services of ACPO-approved BIAs. The ACPO not only called for better operational management of profiler advice, but also demanded a more scientific basis for its application.

Although some progress has been made in recent years, police investigators continue to seek the advice of profilers, not only in the UK but across the globe, without recognizing the need for legal or practice standards, ethical standards, and scientific rigor in the advice they seek. Richard Kocsis (2009) notes that profilers sometimes write books about their success "in the true crime genre" (p. 246):

> Although these accounts certainly provide qualitatively rich illustrations of profiling, their merits in the context of scientifically robust evidence for establishing the validity of profiling must be treated with caution. Given that such accounts are often authored by either current or retired profilers, their objectivity requires judicious evaluation. (p. 247)

Kocsis (2009) also notes that surveys of police indicate they are generally satisfied with the help offered by profilers, even though they report that few profiles actually helped identify a perpetrator. In similar fashion, Alison and Canter (1999b, p. 6) state, "Many of the individuals who are considered the 'old masters' of profiling have produced accounts of their successes in the form of autobiographies." However, rarely do these accounts refer to any commonly accepted psychological research or principles.

Craig Bennell (2008) has also noted that the frequency with which profilers are called on to assist in police investigations has increased dramatically over the past 30 or so years. Yet the amount of profiling *research* has increased at a much slower rate over the same time period. As Bennell states, debates are ongoing about what roles profilers should play in criminal investigations, how profiles should be constructed, delivered, and evaluated, whether the contributions made by profilers are valid and, if so, how, and whether there are new, potentially more productive approaches to profiling that could improve upon or even replace the methods that are currently being used. (p. 49)

In the remainder of this chapter, we explore the current scientific research being conducted in offender or crime scene profiling, primarily in the United Kingdom, Canada, and Australia. This research has been largely spearheaded by David Canter and his students, the work to which we will soon turn our attention.

Prior to doing that, it should be mentioned that some profilers claim that their method of profiling *is* scientifically based. In Germany, for example, Harald Dern and his colleagues (Dern, Dern, Horn, & Horn, 2009) note that "[e]mpirically gained data, case information, and methods of deducting relevant information from given case-specific data are considered the cornerstones of this approach," which they refer to as "behavioural case analysis" (p. 1086). Dern et al. also assert that the German profiling community continually evaluates the reliability of its methods. That is, the profilers try to ensure that when two or more professionals are examining the same crime scene data, and are using the same method, they will reach basically the same conclusions. Furthermore, in Germany profiling is never carried out by individuals alone but rather by teams, the purpose being to reduce cognitive biases.

Scientific advancements in profiling are also being developed in Finland (e.g., Häkkänen, Hume, & Liukkonen, 2007; Häkkänen, Lindlöf, & Santtila, 2004; Häkkänen, Puolakka, & Santtila, 2004); in the Netherlands (e.g., Bijleveld & Smit, 2006; Jackson, Van Koppen, & Herbrink, 1993; Ter Beek, van den Eshof, & Mali, 2009); and, to a lesser degree, in Sweden, Italy, New Zealand, and Israel.

Investigative Psychology Today

David Canter's experience working with police investigators on the Railway Rapist case shifted his interest to what the field of psychology could offer in similar cases. He and his colleagues believe that "there is a wealth of psychological literature that can be drawn upon to aid in the contribution to the psychology of investigations" (Alison & Canter, 1999b, p. 9). Although his early views were based on his previous studies and knowledge in applied social psychology, he saw the opportunity to develop a whole new area of applied psychology he called **investigative psychology** (Canter & Youngs, 2003, 2009). Eventually, he developed a graduate program in investigative psychology at the University of Surrey in England, and, 10 years later, moved to the University of Liverpool to direct a graduate program in *investigative psychology* there. As of this writing, he remains at the Centre for Investigative Psychology and is a professor at the University of Liverpool and the University of Huddersfield. The International Research Centre for Investigative Psychology, in conjunction with the University of Huddersfield, offers a master of science and doctoral degrees in investigative psychology under the leadership of Professor Canter and Professor Donna Youngs.

CLINICAL VERSUS ACTUARIAL PROFILING REVISITED

The work done by Canter and his associates in many ways is in sharp contrast to the work on crime scene and offender profiling conducted in the United States. One striking distinction is the actuarial versus clinical approach, which we discussed in the previous chapter. One is a statistical, research-based orientation; the other is a subjective orientation based on prior knowledge, experience, and sometimes a "gut feeling." In fact, the Canter group has not hesitated to criticize the clinical approach taken by the FBI, which has dominated much of the training provided to profilers. As noted in Chapter 2, individuals across the globe had participated in the FBI training programs, and at times this is even alluded to in films and popular litera-ture. It is important to point out, though, that the training of "profilers" has changed considerably, with investigators now being more aware of the need to integrate empirical knowledge about criminal behavior and statistical techniques into the work they do.

During the 1970s and 1980s, the FBI did not see the need for a strong research basis to their profiling activities, as Canter has noted. "They saw the skill as residing in the 'profiler' rather than being the product of systematic social science" (Canter & Youngs, 2009, p. 9). Canter and Youngs further write, "It is not surprising therefore that many researchers found deficiencies in the accounts that these FBI agents produced in their work" (p. 9). Alison and Canter (1999b) emphasize that

> despite evidence to suggest that current profiling methods are little more than subjective opinion (albeit informed by experience), the notion of an expert profiler, who is able to succeed where the police have failed, appears to be a myth that our culture is unable to shake off. (p. 6)

Canter and his associates argue that "[p]rofiles based on the intuitive creation of an individual with little scientific backing are just flotsam on a sea of crime" (Canter, 2000a, p. 286). Again, it is important to stress that in recent years the FBI and some of its retired profilers have endorsed a more scientific approach to behavioral investigations (Alison et al., 2011), but they still have a very long way to go before it approaches scientifically based profiling. In addition, there are very few instances where the profile report, compiled before the case is solved, reveals a high degree of accuracy that led to the arrest and conviction of the offender. Research on the validity, reliability, and accuracy of profiling is being done, but the discipline as a whole has far to go before it achieves what Lee Rainbow calls the "holy grail" of practice.

POLICE PSYCHOLOGY VERSUS PROFILING

As an aside, we should mention that many psychologists consult with law enforce-ment agencies across the globe in a variety of capacities. Profiling, if it occurs, is a small part of these activities. For example, psychologists assess candidates for law enforcement positions and for promotions, conduct fitness-for-duty evaluations, offer counseling and psychotherapy, give workshops on stress management, and give support to families of law enforcement officers, among many other services (Bartol & Bartol, 2012). Further, as Canter (2000a) notes, psychologists were involved in the practice of prediction of criminal behavior for police agencies long before the formation of the FBI's Behavioral Science Unit. For example, Viteles (1929) reported that police departments in Germany were using psychologists in a variety of ways at least as early as 1919. Martin Reiser (1972), probably the first full-time police psychologist in the United States, described his many roles in his work with the Los Angeles Police Department beginning in 1968. He writes, "The psychologist may find himself consulted by detectives of the homicide division in regard to a bizarre murder having obvious psychological underpinnings with a kind of logical meaning beneath the irrational surface appearances" (p. 52). Reiser did not refer to his work as "profiling," but he and other psychologists consulting with police did offer suggestions that might help investigators develop or pursue leads in certain crimes. Reiser also advised psychologists working with police to do their homework and try to understand criminal behavior, including familiarizing themselves with the research literature.

Nevertheless, Canter (2000b) points out that the process of profiling is unique from the more traditional psychological assessments in two ways. First, the material on which the inference and evaluation is based is restricted to what is available during an investigation. In some cases, the material can be rich in information, such as the details and descriptions of a rapist's sexual behavior. The investigative information also usually includes the time and place of the offense and the characteristics of the victim. However, "it does not include the sorts of material that are the stock in trade of psychologists, such as the mental processes and personality characteristics as indicated in personality questionnaires" (p. 27). Basically, material gathered from a crime scene is incomplete, ambiguous, and sometimes unreliable. Therefore, the psychologist is required to make inferences about an unknown person based not only on what he or she knows about the crime, but also on his or her knowledge of the research literature on offenders, including their cognitive processes, emotional states, and behavioral patterns. Much of this knowledge may come from the research literature on humans in general, but the more the knowledge is directly related to specific offenders, the better. Therefore, the profiler (or behavioral analyst, if you prefer) should be well versed in criminology and criminal behavior.

Secondly, profiling is unique from other forms of consulting with police because the evaluation of the suspected offender must connect directly with behaviors and characteristics that police investigators can actually act on. It may be interesting to make inferences about the motivations of the offender, but it is more helpful to estimate where the offender might live, the characteristics of his or her next victim, or where he or she may strike again. These estimates are far more useful for law enforcement investigators. The profiling process is most productive when there is an ongoing exchange of ideas and hypotheses between the police and the profiler. On the other hand, the profiler also must guard against being too strongly influenced by the views of investigators.

RESEARCH QUESTIONS

A central theme in Canter's method of profiling is that the offender's style of criminality is an integral, natural part of the offender's general lifestyle, not some special, atypical aspect of it (Canter, 2000b). He suggests that the following four research questions must be addressed before behavioral profiling can be a solid science that will truly be helpful to crime investigations of unknown offenders—i.e., what we have called crime scene profiling.

1. What are the important behavioral features of the crime that may help identify the offenders?

2. What are the most appropriate ways of indicating the differences between crimes and between offenders?

3. What inferences can be made about characteristics of the offender that can identify him or her?

4. Are there any other crimes that are likely to have been committed by the same person?

As Canter notes, all four questions are already core issues in other areas of psychology; they are relevant to the study of significant differences between one person and another and the degree of consistency a person demonstrates between similar situations. It is not surprising, therefore, that a considerable amount of research in personality, individual differences, social psychology, environmental psychology, and cognitive psychology offer information that have significance for the study of crime and the scientific approach to profiling. We address each of the four research questions in more detail below.

The Behavioral Features

What are the important—or salient—behavioral features suggested by the scene of the crime that may help identify the offender? Answering this question will require the empirical accumulation of base rates and the identification of co-occurrences of behaviors across specific crimes. **Base rate** refers to the unconditional, naturally occurring rate of a phenomenon in a population (VandenBos, 2007). Said differently, base rate refers to the occurrence of something within a given population. Canter and Youngs (2009) use the example of the base rate for violent crime as a function of gender. In almost all societies, base rates reveal that 90% of all violent crime is committed by men. Consequently, it may not add much to a profile to say that the murder was committed by a male, although it certainly would be significant if there was indication that this particular murder was committed by a female.

It is also helpful to understand the patterns of behaviors that are characteristic of any type of crime, including murder, rape, arson, burglary, and robbery. For example, in what percentage of burglaries do perpetrators leave a signature, or unique identifying sign? Knowledge of the base rates of typical behaviors of crime are necessary before we can determine how a particular offender's behavioral patterns differ from the actions of criminals-in-general—and it is the behavior of this particular offender that we are interested in. Put another way, how can we tell if the actions of *this* rapist or this burglar differ from those of rapists or burglars in general?

In a similar vein, American psychologists Hicks and Sales (2006) also propose a scientific model of profiling that must begin with the development of a large set of databases that represent similar crimes. They argue that the slow growth of adequate databases is due to the fact that most studies in criminology and the psychology of crime examine only very small pieces of the total crime scene behaviors. For example, a common practice is to compare socioeconomic class, gender, or personality with frequency of offending. This approach is generally referred to as *bivariate analysis,* meaning one variable is compared with one other. Hicks and Sales assert that,

> Although the process of conducting these individual studies of the relationships between a small number of variables will gradually add to the knowledge base of criminal offending, a scientific model of profiling requires the conceptualization and investigation of a broader picture of profiling-related variables. (p. 208)

They add that this is necessary because, in order to make the kinds of investigative predictions that are necessary for accurate profiling, a comprehensive understanding of the relationships and pathways that link multiple sets of factors typically found in crime scene investigations is needed. They call for the development of multivariate models that take into account the aspects of motive, personality, and behavior of offenders as a beginning step in the formation of scientific profiling.

Distinguishing Between Offenders and Crimes

What are the most appropriate ways of indicating the differences between crimes and between offenders? This question is concerned with how distinctive the offender's behaviors are—this may include the signature, the nature of the items taken, and treatment of the victim. It also involves discovery of how the offender approaches and captures the victims. Investigators are searching for something odd or unique. For example, a burglar who unnecessarily kills the family pet (even a goldfish) along with taking electronic equipment and other valuables is displaying a distinguishing behavioral pattern. The same can be said of a rapist who always ties his victims' ring fingers together before sexually assaulting them. Distinguishing behavioral patterns are critical in the formation of profiles as well as linking cases to the same offender.

Offender actions that have some distinct theme and are relatively rare will provide the basis for differentiating between crimes. Put another way, it is more helpful for creating a profile if the offender's behavioral patterns differ from the broad database of typical actions for that particular offense—so once again, obtaining the initial database is paramount. One reason that even cautious, highly experienced profilers would have had difficulty with the D.C. sniper case is that highway sniper crimes of this sort are rare. Consequently, there was no extensive database from which to elicit clues about a possible offender.

Databases on other types of murder and rapes are becoming more widely available. Canter (2000a) proposes that one way to distinguish serial rapists and murderers might be how they treat the victim. An important clue for developing a profile is the role an offender assigns to his victims and the roles he assigns to other people in his life. Canter believes that a core ingredient in this role assignment is that violent criminals are incapable of creating private dramas and cognitive scripts in which others share center stage. Salfati and Canter (1999) also proposed several victim-related patterns that would aid investigators in narrowing the search for someone responsible for a crime. We will discuss this more in Chapter 5 when we cover profiling in relation to specific offenses.

Inferring Characteristics

What inferences can be made about the characteristics of the offender that may help identify him or her? Research indicates that offenders share many aspects of their criminal styles with a majority of other criminals, but there are other aspects that are unique to them (Canter & Youngs, 2003). As discussed above, it is these unique or differentiating characteristics that will provide a productive basis for distinguishing between the database of similar offenses and the crimes committed by this particular offender.

To repeat, *a central theme in Canter's method of profiling is that the offender's style of criminality is an integral, natural part of the offender's general lifestyle, not some special, atypical aspect of it* (Canter, 2000b). A reasonable inference, therefore, is that the way the offender deals with victims tells us something about the way he deals with other people who are significant to him. The backgrounds of rapists often reveal exploitative relationships with dates and partners, but there is a specific behavioral theme that the offender follows in each of these relationships. For example, John Duffy, the Railway Rapist, came to the attention of police investigators because he had raped his wife at knifepoint after she had left him. Before they were legally separated, he had a habit of tying her up and violently raping her, a method he used with his future victims. Interestingly, some of the officers had assumed "that a person involved in such domestic violence was not the sort of man who would go on to kill a stranger in a deliberate, planned way" (Canter, 2000a, p. 45). Consequently, Duffy was not considered a serious suspect for some time. Furthermore, sex offenders who break into homes to sexually assault their victims often have previous convictions for burglary and violence; they do not necessarily have convictions for sexual assault. However, the method or "MO" an offender uses to break into homes is most likely to be similar in different crimes and unique to him, especially the subtle aspects of the break-in. "I strongly reiterate that the process of making inferences about a person from the way he commits a crime is a natural development that can be seen in scientific psychology, thus it is a teachable, learnable skill" (Canter, 2000a, p. 287). Moreover, "The identification of the behaviours that are significant comes from understanding what the offence is about psychologically" (Canter & Youngs, 2009, p. 145).

Linking Crimes

Are there any other crimes that are likely to have been committed by the same person? As we noted in Chapter 2, linkage analysis is a hot topic in the profiling literature and has been referred to in numerous court cases in which profiling experts or police investigators have testified.

In the past, serial murderers who moved from jurisdiction to jurisdiction were able to evade detection by police investigators because of lack of communication among police agencies, particularly communication about similar crimes. The notorious serial killer Ted Bundy, for example, is believed to have committed in excess of 30 murders in a number of jurisdictions in the United States over a period of 5 years (Collins, Johnson, Choy, Davidson, & Mackay, 1998). He knew full well that keeping mobile between jurisdictions would enable him to avoid detection.

In 1985, in order to avoid similar linkage problems, the U.S. Department of Justice introduced an automated case linkage system known as the Violent Criminal Apprehension Program (ViCAP) in an effort to generate better communication channels across law enforcement jurisdictions. Likewise, in the 1990s, the Royal Canadian Mounted Police (RCMP) launched a similar advanced, automated, computerized case linkage system called the Violent Crime Linkage Analysis System (ViCLAS) designed to share information associated with serious crime and to enable crime linkages nationwide (Collins et al., 1998; Martineau & Corey, 2008) (see Focus 3.2).

The basic goal of the crime linkage system is to enter information about violent crimes into the computer system database and identify those that show distinct patterns of similarity that might reflect linkages. ViCLAS is mandated in certain parts of Canada and is used as an investigative tool in Australia, Austria, Belgium, the Czech Republic, New Zealand, Switzerland, and parts of the United States (Bennell et al., 2012). Linkages can be established in a variety of ways by police agencies. One way is to look at the crime scene behavior of the offender, such as the MO or the signature.

Focus 3.2

The Violent Crime Linkage Analysis System (ViCLAS)

The Violent Crime Linkage Analysis System (ViCLAS) originated as a national database developed by the Royal Canadian Mounted Police for tracking violent offenders and the crimes they commit. More specifically, it is an automated case linkage system designed to capture, collage, and compare crimes of violence through the analysis of forensic and behavioral data. Quite early in its development, it became clear that the system would have to utilize some of the behavioral principles used in profiling to identify and track serial violent crime and criminals. ViCLAS relies not only on the traditional MO data but also on behavioral information from the crime scene, such as the crime scene signature. In Canada, as of April 2007, there were approximately 300,000 cases on the system, and over 3,200 had been linked by that time. Also, there were over 88,000 crime series on ViCLAS, suggesting that there are a large number of serial offenders in Canada. The linkages are expected to increase significantly as the number of cases entered into the system expands.

(Continued)

(Continued)

The cases in the system include five categories of crime or suspected crime: (1) homicide or attempted homicide, solved or unsolved; (2) sexual assault, solved or unsolved; (3) missing person, where the circumstances indicate a strong possibility of foul play and the person remains missing; (4) unidentified body, where the manner of death is known, or suspected, to be a homicide; and (5) non-parental abduction or attempted non-parental abduction, solved or unsolved (Martineau & Corey, 2008; Police Services Act, 2010).

Currently, there is a ViCLAS center in every province in Canada except for Prince Edward Island, which is served by Nova Scotia. There are nine centers in all, seven of which are maintained by the Royal Canadian Mounted Police, and one each by the Ontario Provincial Police and the Sûreté du Québec. In addition to Canada, ViCLAS has now been adopted by England, Austria, Belgium, The Netherlands, Germany, Australia, and some regions of the United States (Australian Bureau of Criminal Intelligence, 1997).

ViCLAS and other crime linkage systems are not without controversy. Bennell, Snook, et al. (2012) identify four assumptions inherent in these systems that may render them misleading and inaccurate. Specifically, users of crime linkage systems assume that (1) data contained in the systems can be coded reliably, (2) data contained in the systems are accurate enough to draw meaningful inferences, (3) serial offenders demonstrate consistent but distinctive patterns of behavior across their crimes that permit the linking process, and (4) police analysts possess the ability to identify such patterns and link crimes accordingly. According to Bennell, Snook, et al. (2012), none of these assumptions has been convincingly supported by empirical research.

Canter (2000b) contends that there should be some consistencies in the manner in which the offender carries out a crime from one occasion to another, regardless of how indistinguishable it appears at first. That is, even though the crime appears to be very different from other crimes, there will be, after careful and thoughtful examination, something that reflects consistency. Most experts believe these consistencies are typically found in the unique modus operandi, criminal signature, or the style (theme) of the offender. Consistency and differentiation should permit the linking of a series of crimes to a single offender, which often helps police investigators significantly. For example, the consistencies should set the offender apart from a larger pool of suspects.

Realistically though, a few offenders may display very little—if any—*obvious* consistency across their crimes, especially if the offender engages in expressive, emotionally driven crimes characterized by extreme impulsivity. In these cases, it will take a very skillful investigator to identify a consistent aspect to the crime, while being certain it is distinguishable from similar crimes committed by other offenders. On the other hand, some serial offenders are proud of their signatures and MOs, including serial burglars who may be inclined to leave their "calling cards," such as drawings on the wall or destruction of family pictures. In general, recent research does support the view that *most* offenders demonstrate regularity in *some* of their actions from offense to offense

(Bennell & Canter, 2002; Grubin et al., 2001; Salfati & Bateman, 2005). Much of this consistency can be found in the offender's signature. Nevertheless, as Bennell et al. (2012) emphasize, this consistency should not be assumed.

PSYCHOLOGICAL SIGNATURES

So far, we have restricted our discussion of signatures to criminal behavioral patterns. As you may recall from Chapter 2, the signature is the offender's script or mark left at the crime scene; it is unique and unusual. According to J. E. Douglas and Munn (1992b), the signature is the unique "calling card" intentionally left by the offender. However, in psychology the term "signature" refers to a much broader range of behaviors and human activity. The most obvious, of course, is the distinctive way we sign our names and our handwriting in general. Forensic handwriting experts, for example, can usually identify the genuineness of signatures on important documents questioned by the courts. Written signatures have an identifiable and stable pattern that distinguishes one from another. Beyond our written signatures, however, we also have distinctive "signatures" in our cognitive, emotional, and behavioral patterns that occur naturally and often beyond our awareness. We all have subtle but distinctive ways of talking, walking, thinking, problem solving, and even processing information. For example, in his book *Blink*, Malcolm Gladwell (2005) tells the story of how, in World War II, British intelligence officers were able to identify the location of various German military units simply by listening to the cadence of the transmissions of Morse code from the various German radio operators. After listening to the thousands of transmitted signals over an extended period of time, the listeners in British intelligence were able to tell which one of the many German operators was transmitting the signal and where they were located, even though the British teams could not decipher what the signals were actually saying. The German operators did not deliberately try to sound distinctive. They simply ended up sounding distinctive "because some part of their personality appeared to express itself automatically and unconsciously in the way they worked the Morse code keys" (p. 29). Morse code is little more than dots and dashes that must be translated into words. There is nothing distinctive about the dots and dashes during transmission, but the *cadence* of the transmission was the operator's distinctive signature. The British intelligence listeners even had their own names for the German operators. Consequently, when someone high up in British intelligence asked, Can you be absolutely certain that the German fighter squadron is near Tobruk and not in Italy? "[T]he British interceptors could listen to just a few bursts and say, with absolute certainty, 'It's Oscar, which means that yes, his unit is now definitely outside of Tobruk'" (p. 209).

During our daily lives, our signatures creep into behavioral patterns without our awareness, while we concentrate on the main issues and problems at hand. Even our walking patterns may tell an informed observer something about us. Footprint patterns left in the snow by a serial offender may provide important information about the offender, especially linking his crime to others. In fact, a vast majority of signature behaviors displayed by an offender during a crime are unknown even to him. As you will recall, the signature as commonly used in the profiling literature refers to a unique behavior *intentionally* left at the crime scenes. Signatures discussed here are outside our awareness, and they tend to be very consistent and stable. More importantly, they can offer invaluable information for profiling and case linkage. In order to distinguish between the intentional crime scene signatures and unintentional signatures, we will call the former **crime scene signatures** and the latter **psychological signatures.**

At this point in the development of scientific profiling, much more work needs to be directed at the psychological signature. A good example of a psychological signature that may be important for case linkage is the speech patterns of sex offenders. This could range from something as obvious as an accent, a stutter, or a lisp, to something as subtle as the perpetrator using the third person rather than speaking directly to the victim—"I won't hurt her if she doesn't scream"—or using a regional term (*sack* rather than *bag*). Some meaningful attempts at classifying the speech patterns of rapists have been conducted by Woodhams and Grant (2006); Dale, Davies, and Wei (1997); and Kendall, McElroy, and Dale (1999). Woodhams and Grant in their research were able to develop a coding system that was reliable and accurate in the linkage of rape cases, but they admitted that far more research needed to be done in the area.

In a study of 450 homicides committed by 90 offenders, Bateman and Salfati (2007) found that serial murderers did not consistently display the same intentional crime scene behaviors throughout their series of homicides. The behaviors examined by these researchers included both MOs and the more narrowly defined crime scene signatures. Bateman and Salfati concluded that future research on signature consistency needs to focus more on behaviors that are related to the intrinsic psychology (such as psychological signatures) of the offender rather than intentional behaviors that are largely influenced by the situation. One of the contributing variables to the reported inconsistencies found in the Bateman-Salfati study was the influence of situational factors on individual behaviors. For example, we know that rape offenders are highly influenced by *situational* factors (Harris, Smallbone, Dennison, & Knight, 2009), thereby suggesting that intentional consistency is not necessarily guaranteed. For instance, a woman's resistance to sexual assault by fighting, screaming, or running if possible tend to enhance her ability to avoid a rape without increasing her physical injury (Ullman, 1997, 2007; Ullman & Knight, 1995). On the other hand, pleas to the rapist not to harm her have little effect and may even goad or anger the rapist further. In the past, women were often advised not to resist, for fear of being hurt more or even killed. Now we know that trying to maintain some control of the situation—again, by screaming, running, or otherwise resisting—is the most effective measure to take. Thus, the situational factor influences the offender.

The Person–Situation Debate

The debate about human consistency across situations has existed for many years. Consistency forms the basic core of prediction—the more consistent the behavior, the higher the likelihood of being able to predict it. Norval Morris and Marc Miller (1985) identified three kinds of predictions. The first, **anamnestic prediction**, is based on how a *particular* person will act in certain situations. The second, **actuarial prediction,** is based on how *groups* of individuals with similar characteristics will act. Actuarial predictions are largely made with knowledge of base rates, which are the frequency that certain phenomena occur in specific populations. When psychologists refer to the "probability" that someone will be dangerous, they are relying on actuarial prediction. The third predictive method, called **clinical or experiential prediction,** relies heavily on the knowledge obtained by the clinician in his or her practice. The first two methods of prediction are based on observational and statistical data, whereas clinical prediction is more intuitive and subjective. Clinical predictions are immune from evidentiary examination and scientific scrutiny, except in relation to the reputation, experience, and past successes or failures of the predictor (Morris & Miller, 1985). They are intuitive rather than verifiable, except in the end result. As we discussed in Chapter 2, clinical prediction currently characterizes the FBI approach to behavioral profiling, although there are attempts to move toward actuarial approaches.

Canter is asking for the rigorous development of the anamnestic and actuarial prediction methods—as applied to offenders—in order to establish a scientific foundation for profiling. Interestingly, Morris and Miller (1985) argue that the best predictions of human behavior might be based on a combination of all three types of prediction. Canter and other researchers agree that clinical prediction has some place in behavioral profiling, although it should spring from a scientific framework.

Perhaps the best approach in establishing a scientific profiling framework is to build a decision tree model that allows the profiler to make a yes or no decision at each step of the decision-making process. Hicks and Sales (2006) propose a similar idea based on complex regression analysis models. The decision tree model is very close to the filter model for prioritizing suspects proposed by both Goodwill and Alison (2006) and Snook, Wright, House, and Alison (2006).

Decision trees are predictive models that use a tree-like graph to organize information about possible options and decisions. The Goodwill-Alison filter model uses a top-down graph to prioritize offense links based on the most salient and robust aspects of crime scene information collected by police investigators. The advantage of this model is its straightforward application for both police agencies and profilers (Alison et al., 2011). "The result is a decision-making framework that is somewhat malleable to investigator experience while also providing objective and transparent investigative decision support in the form of an empirically based model" (Alison et al., 2011, p. 58). The overall major advantage of a decision tree designed for profiling is that it allows all three kinds of prediction knowledge (anamnestic, actuarial, and experiential) to be used on a graphic model developed from well-researched empirical data and information. The pressing goal at this point is to gather the empirical data and information from the research on criminal behavior.

The A → C Equation

Once consistency and differentiation can be established, the central research questions that encourage meaningful psychological advice to police investigations can begin.

Canter (2000b) summarizes these research questions as the $A \rightarrow C$ equation, where "A" represents all those actions that occurred in and are associated with a crime that are known to investigators before the offender is identified. The "C" refers to the relevant and identifying characteristics of the offender. The $\rightarrow$ symbol refers to the scientific and logical processes that lead to inferences made about the offender, which will eventually lead to his or her arrest and conviction.

The $\rightarrow$ part of the process requires a well-written and meaningful report to police investigators. However, as pointed out by Alison et al. (2004), research or clear guidelines on how to do the report are lacking. "There have been no guidelines on how practitioners might prepare such reports, let alone how reports might serve to promote optimal qualitative and quantitative data for use by academics and practitioners" (p. 75). As emphasized throughout this chapter, the profiler should be thoroughly familiar with the current research literature on criminology in general and the psychology of crime in particular. He or she should also be familiar with police investigative procedures and methods. Saying the offender is between 20 and 30 years old without outlining the grounds on which the claim is made, the strength of the claim, and the reasons why those grounds are an appropriate basis for drawing the conclusion is of no use. The report must have a clear explanation for the basis of any of the opinions given. Usually, this basic requirement is neglected in a vast majority of behavioral profile reports. Profilers should always be encouraged to provide an account of the factors that influenced their opinions. (See Focus 3.3 for a sample outline of a profile report.)

Focus 3.3

What's in a Profile Report?

The following is a partial outline of a model report submitted to police by BIAs in England regarding a murder in which a suspect had been identified. Police had asked psychologists to help them understand the suspect as an individual as well as perhaps identify other possible offenses he might have committed. The lengthy report comprised numerous tables and appendices. Not all headings have been included here. It should be clear from the following, however, that the model profile report is detailed, carefully documented, and guarded in its inferences, while offering helpful suggestions to investigators.

Caveat or Disclaimer

Stresses that report is an investigative tool
Not meant to point toward innocence or guilt
Based on research

Competence and Qualifications of the Psychologists

A brief biographical statement, including credentials, is provided for each author of the report.

Peer Review

Police are encouraged to have the report reviewed by other forensic psychologists.

Case Summary and Evaluation

Psychologists summarize details of the case, in this instance the murder of a 13-year-old girl.

Evaluation of the Murder

Psychologists compare the characteristics of the suspect against those of others who have been found to commit similar offenses. In this case, characteristics such as relatively uninhibited, stream of poor marital relations, and sexual promiscuity were highlighted. Section includes detailed table comparing the characteristics of heterosexual aggressors as a group to characteristics of the suspect.

Evaluation of Suspect Based on Information Provided

Provides research evidence from literature on sexual assault, specifying the suspect as a certain type of rapist. Purpose here is to communicate to other law enforcement agencies with unsolved sex crimes, with a view that the suspect might possibly be responsible. This section essentially focuses on linkage analysis, but the psychologists are very careful and guarded about making inferences.

Risk Assessment and Prediction of Reoffending

Again, authors of the profile are very cautious, giving many caveats about predicting violence. Numerous studies are cited in appendices to the report.

Investigative Recommendations

Authors make a number of recommendations, including focusing on killings in fields or wooded areas, investigating whether the suspect may have abused other young girls in his family, examining the relationship between his partner's pregnancy and violence, and focusing on certain periods of transition in his life during which suspect may have committed crimes.

Source: Adapted from Alison, West, & Goodwill (2004).

Behavioral Investigative Analysts in the United Kingdom

In helpful detail, Rainbow and Gregory (2011) describe the procedures that profilers—behavioral investigative analysts, or BIAs, in the UK—are expected to follow when working with police investigators. It is important to point out that some psychologists consulting with law enforcement in the United States might be taking the same or similar approaches; however, they have yet to publish descriptions of their work in scientific journals and thus cannot be cited here. Moreover, in the United States, there is yet to be an academically based program like that in the UK, devoted to investigative psychology.

The BIA in the United Kingdom is consulted by police investigators in particularly challenging cases as part of their decision-making process. The BIA meets with the police investigative team where an exchange of information and ideas leads to an agreement outlining clear goals and expectations of each party. In many cases, this includes granting the BIA privileged access to sensitive information about the crime scene, the victim(s), autopsy or medical reports, and other pertinent forensic analyses, often with the understanding that any disclosure of this information to the media requires permission from police authorities. In some cases, the BIA may also have access to any available databases of similar crime statistics such as ViCLAS, which, for security reasons, may not be available to others outside certain security clearances. The provisions of the agreement may include the delivery of a detailed report from the BIA within a specific time frame. Interestingly, Rainbow and Gregory (2011) recommend that the report provide a starting point for a dialogue between the BIA and the police investigators. "This is critical to ensure the SIO's [Senior Investigating Officer's] understanding of the inferences and recommendations made, and to promote understanding that such conclusions should be continually evaluated against additional forthcoming information" (p. 27).

In addition, an examination of available databases might enable the BIA to hypothesize about possible linkages between the current crime under investigation and other offenses with similar unique characteristics. If possible, the BIA should try to make predictions from available pools of suspects. Rainbow and Gregory (2011)—who consider geographic profiling a distinct discipline with different theoretical, empirical, and research considerations—suggest that, whenever possible, the BIA should consult with a geographic profiler for predictions concerning where the offender may live. Geographic profiling will be the topic of the next chapter. To repeat the theme emphasized in this chapter, the BIA or profiler should be thoroughly familiar with the current research literature and theory on the psychology of crime as a scientific basis for the opinions, predictions, and conclusions written into the report—as illustrated in Focus 3.3.

Contemporary Theories in Criminology

Currently, there are many theories and research findings rapidly emerging on the psychology of crime. Many of them are far more sophisticated than implied by Hicks and Sales (2006), who lament the bivariate focus of most of the extant research conducted on the psychology of crime. Some of the research agendas and theory-development projects use multiple variables and have sophisticated research programs, which are beginning to move the psychology of crime into a realm that is potentially useful to scientific profiling.

In this section, we briefly describe four major trends, but emphasize that other approaches are also of potential use. Herein we focus on (1) Terrie Moffitt's **developmental**

pathway theory; (2) Laurence Steinberg's **socio-emotional theory**; (3) **deficient interpersonal skills** and **peer rejection**; and (4) the extensive research literature on **psychopathy**, initially spearheaded by Robert Hare. In each case, we provide examples of how this approach has relevance to profiling (see also Table 3.2).

Table 3.2   Implications of Crime Theories for Profiling

Theoretical Constructs	Examples of Crime Scene and Background Indicators (What profilers should look for . . .)	Representative Researchers
Developmental	Early onset of antisocial behavior; persistent offending; signs of early cruelty, callousness	Moffitt, 1993a, 2006
Maturation in self-regulation	Risk taking, impulsive behaviors: likelihood of young offender Cannot assume that MO will be consistent over years	Steinberg, 2008, 2010
Peer rejection/ deficient social skills	Evidence of bullying, either as victim or aggressor; evidence of peer rejection Behavioral, social, cognitive deficits	Dodge & Pettit, 2003 Patterson, 1982
Psychopathy	Excessive brutality, sadism Charming, smooth-talking individual Manipulative May not conceal crimes	Hare, 1996, 1998 Porter, Fairweather, et al., 2000; Porter et al., 2003 Häkkänen et al., 2007

DEVELOPMENTAL PATHWAYS IN OFFENDING PATTERNS

In recent years, the psychological study of crime and delinquency has adopted a developmental perspective in the explanations for crime. If we follow individuals from birth to adulthood, we learn a great deal about how antisocial behavior develops (Hartup, 2005). Developmental psychologists and criminologists have learned that people follow different developmental pathways in their offending or non-offending histories. Some youth engage in defiant and antisocial behavior at a very young age, and this pattern sometimes progresses into more severe forms of violence and criminality during adolescence and young adulthood (Dahlberg & Potter, 2001). There is also solid research that serious, persistent antisocial behavior begins in early childhood and in many cases before the preschool years.

Canter's observation that we can learn about the lifestyles of serial offenders by how they treat their victims has considerable relevance here. Some youth display early signs of cruelty to animals, insensitive bullying, substance abuse, and very little empathy toward peers—and they often carry this pattern well into adulthood (Pardini & Loeber, 2008; Stouthamer-Loeber et al., 2004). Recall that the Railway

Rapist, John Duffy, displayed callous behavior, including the torture of animals, as a child and adolescent. On the other hand, many youth exhibit very few signs of antisocial behavior during their childhood, but participate in some vandalism, theft, alcohol drinking, and drug experimentation during adolescence, and then they mature and reduce or completely refrain from these activities during young adulthood.

The major impetus for the developmental perspective has been the theory and research of Terrie Moffitt (1993a, 1993b, 2003, 2006). Originally, Moffitt's developmental theory identified two trajectories or pathways. On one path, we see a child developing a lifelong trajectory of delinquency and crime beginning at a very early age, probably as early as age 3 or even younger. These offenders show a developmental history characterized by an interaction between neuropsychological deficits and deficient familial and neighborhood environments. Moffitt calls these individuals *life course–persistent offenders (LCPs)*. She writes,

> Across the life course, these individuals exhibit changing manifestations of antisocial behavior: biting and hitting at age four, shoplifting and truancy at age ten, selling drugs and stealing cars at age sixteen, robbery and rape at age twenty-two, and fraud and child abuse at age thirty. (1993a, p. 679)

LCPs continue their antisocial ways across a wide range of situations. Since they never learn to control their antisocial proclivities, they act impulsively as children, adolescents, and adults (Piquero, Brame, Fagan, & Moffitt, 2005).

As Canter (2000a) notes in his book *Criminal Shadows*, "The men I have studied all have committed more than one crime, typically numerous crimes before they are caught" (p. 273). Canter goes on to describe several serial killers who followed early life course–persistent antisocial patterns similar to those outlined by Moffitt.

LCPs continue to miss opportunities to acquire and practice prosocial and interpersonal skills throughout their development. This is partly because they are rejected and avoided by their peers, and partly because their parents, teachers, and caretakers become frustrated and give up on them (Moffitt, 1993a). LCPs are plagued by various psychological and antisocial problems throughout their lifetime. Wiesner, Kim, and Capaldi (2005) find that, "Developmental theories posit that antisocial behavior that onsets early in childhood is likely to lead to a cascade of secondary problems, including academic failure, involvement with deviant peers, substance abuse, depressive symptoms, health risk sexual behavior, and work failure" (p. 252). Although this figure may seem high, research indicates that about 5 to 10% of individuals follow this antisocial development trajectory (Fontaine, Carbonneau, Vitaro, Barker, & Tremblay, 2009; van Lier, Vuijk, & Crijen, 2005; van Lier, Wanner, & Vitaro, 2007). Only 1 to 2% of females show a similar persistent, early-onset pattern (Fontaine et al., 2009).

The great majority of juvenile offenders are those who follow a different developmental trajectory. They begin offending during their adolescent years and generally reduce or terminate offending somewhere between ages 18 and 26 (Moffitt, Caspi, Harrington, & Milne, 2002). Moffitt labels these youth *adolescent-limited (AL)* offenders. Their developmental backgrounds do not show the early and persistent antisocial problems that members of the LCP group exhibit.

Application to Profiling

Alison et al. (2011) posit that, "[considering] the fact that most offenders have criminal antecedents of some kind, the future challenge lies in efficient exploitation of the nowadays vast amount of electronically stored information on previously identified offenders" (p. 58). They go on to say, "The sobering fact is that most criminals appear to be in the system already, investigators just need to know at what, especially where, to look" (p. 58). Prior arrest and conviction records obviously are relevant.

Life course–persistent offenders are usually extremely criminally active. In one study that followed LCPs up to age 35, the researchers discovered that they had committed an average of 40 crimes (both violent and nonviolent) and were responsible for 61% of all crimes in the population sampled (Stattin, Kerr, & Bergman, 2010). Serial offenders, therefore, are highly likely to be found in the offenders' database. In addition, there is a good chance they will be found in domestic violence databases (Piquero et al., 2005), an area with which many law enforcement agencies are very familiar. Another study found that LCPs accumulated a higher-than-average number of convictions between ages 41 and 50, but they also demonstrated a very high level of failure in all areas of life, including employment, relationships, drug and alcohol use, and mental health (Piquero, Farrington, Nagin, & Moffitt, 2010).

However, a juvenile record in and of itself may not be helpful. Many youths have contact with the justice system, and most eventually desist, or age out of crime. Even many youths who have *frequent* contact with the system move out of their adolescent years, have a greater stake in society, become less impulsive, and stop their antisocial activity. Investigators are advised, therefore, to focus their attention on the individual who offended as a youth but did not stop offending—i.e., the persistent offender.

DEVELOPMENTAL AND MATURATION CHANGES IN OFFENDERS

The way a person commits a crime is likely to change over time, even though there always remains some element of behavioral consistency. Life situations change, the offender's MO may improve on the basis of experience, or the offender may undergo developmental changes (Canter & Youngs, 2003). As noted by Canter and Youngs, the unfolding developmental changes that come with age result in many changes in cognitive and emotional processes. For example, developmental psychologist Laurence Steinberg (2008, 2010) hypothesizes that reward seeking and impulsivity develop along different timetables and have different brain-development influences during adolescent and early adult development. In addition, the differences in the developmental timetables account for the well-known high levels of risk taking during adolescence and early adulthood. As most parents and caretakers know, adolescent behavior is generally characterized by impulsiveness, sensation seeking, a lack of future orientation, and strong susceptibility to peer pressure and influence. Risk taking during this period includes reckless driving, binge drinking, drug experimentation, cigarette smoking, and spontaneous unprotected sexual activity. Criminal actions are certainly included in the risk taking and sensation seeking, and some of them may be described as violent. Self-report studies have revealed that nearly 90% of adolescent boys admit to committing offenses for which they could be incarcerated (E. S. Scott & Steinberg, 2008).

Impulsivity and rapid mood swings, so characteristic of many teens and young adults, are likely associated with immature self-control mechanisms. There is, in the rapidly expanding research literature, incontrovertible evidence of significant changes in brain structure and function during adolescence (Steinberg, 2009). Recent research indicates that certain areas of the human brain do not fully develop until at least early adulthood (around age 25) (Steinberg, 2008). As the brain matures, risk taking and criminal behavior decrease for a vast majority of young adults, partly because of developmental changes in the regions of the brain that are responsible for self-control and self-regulation. These regions are primarily located in the front areas of the brain. Moreover, individuals follow different developmental trajectories and reach different levels of maturity at different ages (Steinberg, Graham, et al., 2009). Scientific evidence further suggests that intellectual (cognitive) maturity is reached several years before psychosocial maturity (Steinberg, Graham, et al., 2009). Adolescents age 16 or older have basically the same logical reasoning abilities and verbal skills as adults, but as a group they have the psychosocial maturity level of a 16-year-old. Therefore, while adolescents may have many of the same cognitive processes and capacities as adults, their assessment of and attitude toward risk are significantly different. Adolescents, as a rule, are far more willing and prone to take high risk in a wide variety of situations, including antisocial behavior. The adolescent willingness to take on high risks is especially strong in peer groups compared to when they are alone.

Application to Profiling

Knowledge of these developmental factors would help profilers gauge the approximate age of some offenders and facilitate explanations of changes in behavioral patterns of serial offenders, especially sex offenders. Crime scenes that display some impulsivity or immaturity may be the work of juveniles. For example, burglaries carried out by professionals are usually carefully planned and often meticulous, with very little signs of impulsiveness involved; careless and risk-taking burglary suggests a younger (less than age 24) offender. Professionals sometimes refer to the burglars who demonstrate very little planning or sophistication, and who take high risks, as "cowboys" (Rengert & Groff, 2011). Their strategy is often to impulsively "smash and grab" when the opportunity arises. Changes in developmental factors also may help explain significant changes in the MOs of certain serial offenders, such as sexual offenders, burglars, and arsonists.

DEFICIENT INTERPERSONAL SKILLS AND PEER REJECTION

Research has consistently shown that peer rejection is one of the strongest predictors of later involvement in persistent, serious offending, especially violent crime

(Cowan & Cowan, 2004; Dodge, 2003; Trentacosta & Shaw, 2009). This rejection starts early in a child's life. As early as age 5, excessively aggressive, belligerent children are unpopular and are usually excluded from peer groups (Dodge & Pettit, 2003; Patterson, 1982). Moreover, it has been found that peer rejection exacerbates antisocial development only among youth initially disposed toward aggression (Dodge et al., 2003). Although these children may be rejected for a variety of reasons, aggressive behavior clearly appears to be the most prominent factor. Peer-rejected children are not only aggressive, but they also tend to be argumentative, inattentive, and disruptive. Furthermore, boys who are both peer rejected and excessively aggressive have a number of behavioral, social, and cognitive deficits and display low levels of prosocial behavior in general (Coie & Miller-Johnson, 2001) (see Photo 3.2). This cluster of deficits often results in poor school and academic performances (Buhs & Ladd, 2001; Dodge &

Photo 3.2: Is he sad, defiant, or both? Children rejected by their peers often display antisocial behavior as they grow older.

Pettit, 2003). Peer acceptance is crucial during early development, and those who receive it turn out much differently compared to their rejected peers. Children who are liked and accepted by their peer group in the early school years are far less likely to become persistently antisocial in their later years (Laird, Jordan, Dodge, Pettit, & Bates, 2001; K. H. Rubin, Bukowski, & Parker, 2006). It should be mentioned, however, that a vast majority of the research examining the effects of peer rejection on antisocial behavior has focused on boys, although some research suggests that girls may follow a similar trend (van Lier, Vitaro, Wanner, Vuijk, & Crijnen, 2005).

Application to Profiling

The implications of the peer rejection research for behavioral profiling could be enormous. It is doubtful that investigators reach back into elementary and secondary school records in an attempt to identify "bullies" of earlier years. However, this approach—if possible—could provide valuable leads, particular if an offender has remained in the community throughout his life. There are, of course, many barriers to obtaining academic records, and even juvenile court records are sealed in many states once juveniles reach adulthood. Although this is understandable, it remains true that the age of onset of criminal activity is a significant predictor of later offending. Moreover, it appears that among the many background variables that can help narrow the search for serial offenders, their behavior toward peers has emerged as a factor that may be just as crucial.

OFFENDING PATTERNS OF CRIMINAL PSYCHOPATHS

Research on psychopathy has grown at a rapid rate since early theorists (e.g., Cleckley, 1941; Hare, 1980, 1996) began to discuss the construct. Partly because of their behavioral and psychological characteristics, psychopaths hold a special fascination with the public as well as students of criminology. Descriptions of psychopaths and their exploits abound in the literature.

Psychopathy is best viewed as existing on a continuum, with some people displaying more psychopathic tendencies than others. As a group, psychopaths tend to be "dominant, manipulative individuals characterized by an impulsive, risk-taking and antisocial lifestyle, which obtain their greatest thrill from diverse sexual gratification and target diverse victims over time" (Porter, Fairweather, et al., 2000, p. 220). For example, Gretton, McBride, Hare, O'Shaughnessy, and Kumka (2001) find that criminal psychopaths generally

> lack a normal state of ethics and morality, live by their own rules, are prone to use cold-blooded, instrumental intimidation and violence to satisfy their wants and needs, and generally are contemptuous of social norms and the rights of others. (p. 428)

As emphasized in the literature, however, psychopaths also can be very charming, smooth-talking, and persuasive—they may not fit into the public perception of the typical serious offender. Although psychopaths probably comprise a very small percentage of the adult population—less than 5 percent—when they commit criminal acts, the crimes are often among the most violent (Hare, 1996, 1998).

Psychopathic sex offenders are likely to be more violent, brutal, unemotional, and sadistic than other sex offenders (Hare, Clark, Grann, & Thornton, 2000; Porter, Woodworth, Earle, Drugge, & Boer, 2003). Criminal psychopaths also commit more diverse and severe forms of sexual homicides (Firestone, Bradford, Greenberg, & Larose, 1998; Porter et al., 2003). The relationship between psychopathy and sexual offending appears to be complicated, however. For example, the prevalence of psychopaths among child molesters is estimated to be from 10 to 15%, whereas among rapists it is between 40 and 50% (Gretton et al., 2001; Porter, Fairweather, et al., 2000). Research also suggests that rapists who demonstrate psychopathic characteristics are more likely to have "nonsexual" motivations for their attacks, such as anger, vindictiveness, sadism, and opportunism (Hart & Dempster, 1997). Psychopaths tend to target victims of all ages and physical characteristics, without a discernible consistent preference (Woodworth & Porter, 2002), Some research suggests that psychopaths, because of their high levels of impulsivity and egocentricity, do not make an extra effort to conceal their crimes, not even in homicide cases (Häkkänen et al., 2007).

Application to Profiling

Canter's suggestion that profilers should examine very closely how the assailant deals with the victim is an important one again. Brutality and sadistic attacks may strongly indicate that the assailant may have many psychopathic characteristics and is likely to continue the antisocial behavior. Profilers aiding in the investigation of violent, brutal crimes without a discernible motive would be wise to investigate individuals on suspect lists with extensive criminal histories who may also have typical characteristics of psychopaths, including a callous and unemotional mien, evidence of impulsive and sensation-seeking behaviors, and—often—superficial charm.

Research on psychopathy continues at a steady clip, and it is obvious that profilers should be aware of the latest findings. For example, research reveals that there are probably four clusters of traits characteristic of psychopaths (Salekin, Brennan, Zalot, Leistico, & Neumann, 2006; Vitacco, Neumann, & Jackson, 2005). Each of these identifies behavioral features that could offer leads to criminal investigators. The four trait clusters or core factors are (1) interpersonal impression management, characterized by chronic lying, glibness, grandiose sense of self-worth, manipulating others, superficial charm, and promiscuous sexual behavior; (2) impulsive and irresponsible lifestyle, characterized by unreliability, sensation seeking, lack of realistic goals, poor work habits, poor planning, and parasitic lifestyle (living off others, including spouses, intimate partners, friends, and parents); (3) deficient affective and emotional experience, characterized by low remorse, a weak conscience, the absence of anxiety or nervousness, and a failure to accept responsibility for one's actions; and (4) antisocial tendencies, which includes lack of self-regulation, high rates of recidivism, and a persistent, serious, violent, and diverse criminal history. The fourth core factor was recently included specifically to account for criminal psychopaths.

Potential Error Problems in Scientific Profiling

In the previous chapter, we covered some of the cognitive biases that can influence clinically based crime scene profiling. To some extent, these same biases can influence the more scientific approach to profiling. In this section, we revisit some of these biases but also introduce error problems that are specific to the more scientific approach.

HEURISTICS

The greatest influence on the study of human judgment under conditions of uncertainty has been the heuristic and biases research of Kahneman and Tversky (1973; Tversky & Kahneman, 1974) during the early 1970s (Sloman, Over, Slovak, & Stibel, 2003). **Heuristics** are basically mental shortcuts for dealing with information, making complex decisions, and drawing inferences in rapid and efficient manner. Everyone uses them.

Interestingly, Tversky and Kahneman discovered that we rely on a limited number of heuristic principles and strategies to reduce the complex tasks of assessing probabilities and in making predictions. In other words, we tend to use few decision factors, sometimes even to make important decisions: Where should I go to college? Well, how much will it cost? Money matters (heuristic). Will I be far from home but close enough to get there for emotional support and to do my laundry if need be? Family matters (heuristic). Is there a ski slope/surf nearby? How's the club scene? Recreation matters (heuristic). And, of course, does it offer the major I want? Think future (heuristic). Bingo, decision made.

Here is another example: Should I take this job? What's the salary? What type of health insurance does it provide? Can I have my weekends? Do my future coworkers seem compatible? If all is answered to one's satisfaction, one takes the job.

Tversky and Kahneman (1974) also found that, "In general, these heuristics are quite useful, but sometimes they lead to severe and systematic errors" (p. 1124). (The ski slope may close down, the department offering the major may face budget cuts, the workload is impossible to complete in 5 days, the coworker you share an office with is related to Dracula, and so forth.)

Profilers and investigators are people, and they, too, use heuristics, or mental shortcuts. People with past criminal records—especially if they are on parole—are often the first suspected of crimes. This is a shortcut. However, the true perpetrator may not be on parole. In addition, it should be emphasized that the profilers and investigators are expected to make judgments and decisions under high levels of stress and pressure and under conditions that are often ambiguous. Under high levels of stress and time pressures, mental shortcuts are useful and can contribute significantly to the investigative process, but they also offer potential sources of cognitive and judgment errors.

REPRESENTATIVE HEURISTIC ERRORS

One representative error is a generalization about a given offender based on partial information or on how closely the offender matches the typical or average member of that group of offenders. This is a mental shortcut used to classify someone according to how similar that person is to a typical case. Decisions or judgments by profilers made according to this heuristic error tend to ignore base rates—even when the profilers are aware of them. Instead, the profilers rely on their personal experiences with relatively similar cases. The profiler may conclude, "Okay, this is similar to a case I dealt with several years ago." Although this heuristic may save time, the problem occurs, according to Rainbow et al. (2011), when there actually is no commonality between the two things being compared. The two things may be only superficially similar, or the profiler's mental representation or perception may be incorrect. Many profilers prefer to rely on their own experience over base rates because their personal experiences tend to be vivid, salient, and concrete, whereas statistical or empirical base rates tend to be remote, pallid, and abstract (Rainbow et al., 2011).

In 2010, an interesting article was published in the UK's *Guardian* newspaper (Ronson, 2010). The writer had interviewed Paul Britton, the psychologist mentioned earlier in the chapter who participated in the Nickell case. The writer also had spoken with Lee Rainbow about the research he and his colleagues were conducting. The two men, Britton and Rainbow, had little in common with respect to their views on profiling. Britton showed little interest in research or statistics. Rainbow, by comparison, pointed out that 84% of all rapists had been convicted of some crime, but typically not sexual crimes. Referring to Rainbow, Ronson notes,

> His point is that the 84% statistic is not the kind of intriguing deduction that would captivate an old-style profiler. It doesn't tell you much about the labyrinthine mind of the sex criminal. It's an ungainly, dull fact, but it is real. (Ronson, 2010, last paragraph)

Another representative error is the **availability heuristic.** Consider the following question: Which are more common in the English language, words that begin with the letter "k" or words with "k" as the third letter? When most people are asked this question, they immediately answer, words that begin with "k" (Tversky & Kahneman, 1982). It is easier to think of words that begin with the letter "k" than it is to come up with words with "k" as the third letter (know, kite, ketchup, kale, kill, kitten, kiss, kitchen, kangaroo, and so forth, compared with acknowledge, ask, make, like . . .). Actually, there are more than twice as many words with "k" as the third letter as there are words with "k" as the first letter. The availability heuristic principle indicates that the easier it is to bring information to mind, the greater its importance or relevance to our judgments and decision making.

The availability heuristic operates when judgment is determined by "the ease with which instances or associations come to mind" (Tversky & Kahneman, 1973, p. 208). Availability heuristic errors occur when decisions and judgment are influenced by the memory of associated events or objects (Fanetti & Boles, 2004). People are led astray when the ease with which things come to mind is influenced by factors unrelated to their probability (Heuer, 1999). "Probability" in this context refers to base rate frequencies. For instance, profilers are most likely to incorporate into their decisions and judgments the most vivid cases, or important cases, or cases that come to their minds most readily. Research suggests that it not only depends on how easily the information comes to mind, but also how much of it we can remember (Rothman & Hardin, 1997). The availability heuristic may work well in some cases, and it may bring on errors in others, especially if the profiler neglects to consider research-based base rates. Profilers need to be constantly aware of the pitfalls of mental shortcuts.

BASE RATE FALLACY (OR NEGLECT)

Base rate fallacy is a decision-making error in which information about the occurrence of some common characteristic within a given population is ignored or not given much weight in decision making. This tendency has important implications for understanding error judgments made by profilers. For example, the profiler may focus on a specific offender, pushing into the background useful information about the population of offenders with similar characteristics. Base rate neglect is especially likely to happen if the profiler encounters a case that he or she perceives as unique and outside the usual cases within a particular offense category. It also happens when the profiler believes he or she is better equipped for dealing with the case based on prior experience. Thus, the base rate fallacy may co-occur along with the heuristic principles discussed above.

Rainbow et al. (2011) provide an excellent example of how investigators and profilers may become distracted from the usual crime scene investigative methods because they ignore or are unaware of the base rate. The case involved a 90-year-old woman who was found dead in her home. At the crime scene, her heart had been removed from her body and placed on a silver platter. Blood had been drained from her body and poured into a small container, which had the traces of lip marks on the rim. Candles had been arranged to suggest some kind of ceremony had occurred, and fireplace pokers were placed at her feet in the shape of a crucifix. Adding to the drama, the murder had happened on an island off the coast of Wales that was dotted with ancient Druid ruins. It would be tempting to view this as a horrific illustration of a cult-related murder and assume that a small group of individuals was involved. However, investigators in this case were wise enough to consider base rate data—who kills the elderly?

As Rainbow et al. (2011) note,

> In terms of prioritizing suspects, base rate information from research into elderly homicide together with a logical crime scene interpretation strongly indicated that the offender was likely to have some association to the victim and probably lived in close proximity. (p. 44)

Forensic evidence, including a footprint left at the scene, led to the arrest of a 17-year-old from the same village who had delivered newspapers to the victim's door the previous 3 years and was aware that she had money and jewels stashed in her home. Investigators concluded it was neither a ritualistic sacrifice nor an occult ceremony, but a straightforward robbery-murder situation. The 17-year-old killer, in an attempt to divert attention away from himself, set the stage to make it appear to be a mysterious ritualistic murder.

EXPRESSIONS OF UNCERTAINTY

Few if any profilers would be so foolish as to indicate that the perpetrator definitely possessed certain characteristics. Almost invariably, they will make statements framed as probabilities, communicating that there is some uncertainty in their assessment. According to Heuer (1999), however, probabilities of something happening may be expressed in two ways. **Statistical probabilities** are based on empirical evidence concerning relative frequencies, such as base rates. **Subjective probability judgments** are based on a profiler's personal belief, e.g., that the offender will commit the crime again, or that a particular suspect appears to be the prime suspect, or that the offender lives in a specific area. In many instances, subjective probability statements are ambiguous and misunderstood by police investigators. As Heuer reports, "To say that something could happen or is possible may refer to anything from a 1-percent to a 99-percent probability" (pp. 152–153). The profiler should communicate more clearly by placing a personal percentage on the prediction (i.e., 30%) so that investigators can judge how strongly the profiler believes the event will occur. Nevertheless, it should be emphasized that this is a probability, not a definitive prediction.

It is likely that clinically based profilers will resist the notion of attaching a percentage figure to their predictions—this seems to fly in the face of intuition or clinical judgment. Nevertheless, according to Heuer (1999), without such guidance, investigators may be inclined to interpret ambiguous probability statements as highly consistent with their own preconceptions of the case. It is very important that police investigators be open to alternative viewpoints, and it is equally important that profilers help create alternative ideas. In this context, the profiler should be comfortable enough to consult with outside experts and colleagues whenever possible to formulate alternative perspectives. These colleagues may see things or ask questions that the profiler has not seen or asked. It is likely, then, that a team of profilers working together will produce a more accurate profile than a lone individual.

Even the brief outline of the model report presented in Focus 3.3 indicates that these profilers were careful to avoid many of the pitfalls we have discussed above. For example, they encourage investigators to share the report with other experts, they carefully review the criminology literature pertinent to the case at hand and discuss base rates for the offense, and they discuss statistical probabilities rather than present subjective appraisals of the likely perpetrator.

Summary and Conclusions

With this chapter, we move from a discussion of crime scene profiling as a clinically based, experiential, and somewhat subjective endeavor to one that relies more on the scientific method. This is not to say that a clinically based approach does not have its place. However, as evidenced in the many cases in which intuition, vague images, or gut feelings have led profilers astray, a more objective approach is warranted. Therefore, we suggest that knowledge of the literature and broad database of past crimes, statistical expertise, and sound clinical judgment are the best tools for the profiler to have at his or her disposal. It is important to emphasize that profilers rarely meet or interview the suspect in a crime; therefore, inferences about the suspect must be made very carefully.

Perhaps no individual has done more to steer profiling toward science than David Canter, with the establishment of the Centre for Investigative Psychology. Canter and his colleagues have conducted a research program that makes use of large databases of offenses to draw similarities between crimes and to help police pinpoint possible geographic locations, as we will see in the next chapter. Most importantly, however, the reports prepared by these profilers (who prefer to call themselves BIAs) are extensive, cautious, and research based. Nevertheless, we do not suggest that any one country has a lock on scientific profiling; many psychologists in the United States, included those associated with the FBI, have applauded Canter's work and have integrated his methods into their own procedures. Still, as critics have noted (Kocsis, 2009; Snook et al., 2008), there remain across the world—including in England—other profilers who rely primarily on hunches, past experience, or unvalidated typologies of offenders.

Contemporary theories and research in criminology should be taken into account in preparing profile reports. In this chapter, we highlighted a few, including developmental and maturational theories, theories regarding deficient interpersonal skills, and research on psychopathy. Knowledge of these and other theories can help the profiler recognize behavioral characteristics that may be of help to investigators. In addition, profilers must be careful to avoid the pitfalls of profiling. These include heuristic errors that may lead them to draw conclusions based on personal experiences or generalizations, ignoring base rate data, and offering conclusions based on subjective rather than statistical probabilities.

KEY CONCEPTS

A → C equation

A priori method

Actuarial prediction

Anamnestic prediction

Availability heuristic

Base rate

Base rate fallacy

Behavioral investigative analyst (BIA)

Belief persistence

Clinical or experiential prediction

Crime scene signatures

Deficient interpersonal skills

Developmental pathway theory

Heuristics

Investigative psychology

Method of authority

Method of science

Method of tenacity

Peer rejection

Psychological signatures

Psychopathy

Socio-emotional theory

Statistical probabilities

Subjective probability judgments

4

Geographic Profiling and Mapping

I don't want all this psychological jargon about why he's depressed or how paranoid he is. I just want to know where he lives and where he'll strike next.

The above comment is heard in both real and fictional police precincts, when officers are faced with a series of related crimes and very few leads. What they are requesting is help from a **geoprofiler,** a person trained to see spatial patterns in crimes. In contrast to the crime scene profiling discussed in the previous chapters, geographic profiling concentrates on the locations of various crimes to try to determine where the perpetrator might live. The overriding and primary goal of geographic profiling is to identify roughly where the offender lives or at least sleeps at night, based on the locations of his or her crimes (Canter & Youngs, 2008). It pertains to crimes, especially serial crimes, that occur outside the home.

"Spatial patterning of crime has long been observed" (Brantingham & Brantingham, 1991, p. 27). As far back as the early nineteenth century, Gerry (1833, cited in Brantingham & Brantingham) identified conviction rate differences among regions of France. As we will note below, some of the earliest theories in criminology were based on discoveries that crime seemed to occur at specific types of locations but not at others. Understanding the role that geographic location plays in the occurrence of crime incidents can offer pivotal clues about how to detect offenders' patterns and discover their domiciles or places they frequent. The knowledge gained from geographic patterns will also help in the prevention of crime. For example, law enforcement can change the extent or the nature of its patrol strategies, and social service agencies can adapt their supportive services accordingly.

Contemporary research on offending spatial patterns has demonstrated that crime often occurs or clusters within certain geographic areas, such as a specific area of a city. Moreover, these offending patterns do not seem to be simply the result of opportunity or randomization, or even offender personality characteristics. As noted by Canter and

Youngs (2009), some of whose work was discussed in Chapter 3, "whether they are aware of it or not, offenders are making some sort of active choice about the places in which they will commit their crimes" (p. 170). Studies have shown that the distance traveled by offenders and the spatial distribution of their crimes provide valuable clues in identifying the location of the perpetrators' homes or at least their base of operations.

There are two major ways these crime patterns may be analyzed: geographic mapping and geographic profiling. **Geographic mapping** is concerned with analyzing the spatial patterns of crimes committed by numerous offenders over a period of time. **Geographic profiling** refers to the analysis of geographic locations associated with the spatial movements of a *single* serial offender or a small cohort of offenders. As will be demonstrated in this chapter, these two approaches typically complement each other. The crime scene profiling discussed in earlier chapters has traditionally concentrated on violent crime, such as murders and sexual assaults, though profilers are quick to note that it can and should be extended to other crimes as well. Geographic profiling and mapping also are concerned with violent crime, but they frequently examine property crimes such as burglary, robbery, and motor vehicle theft, which are far greater in number.

Geographic Mapping

Sometimes called crime mapping, geographic mapping provides a visual and statistical analysis of the spatial nature of crime (Boba, 2009). In a sense, geographic mapping focuses on identifying the "hot spots" of certain types of crime, like robberies or drug dealing. Hot spots refer to areas with a greater-than-average number of criminal events or higher-than-average risk of victimization (Filbert, 2008) (see Figure 4.1, illustrating hot spots for auto thefts). A neighborhood or cluster of blocks may represent a hot spot.

Figure 4.1   Crime Map of Auto Theft Incidents in an Urban Area

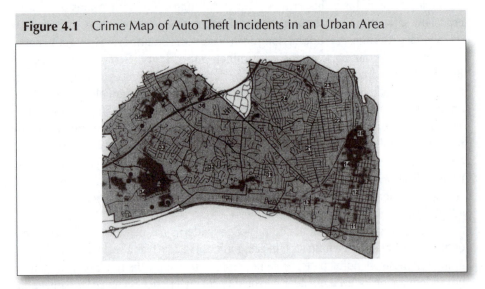

Source: McCue (2011), p. 5.

Smaller locations, such as a particular bar, street segment, bus stop, liquor store, or stretch of road, may represent "hot places." In a survey of more than 2,000 police departments in the United States, 85% reported that crime mapping was a valuable tool for the department (Mamalian & Lavigne, 1999).

HISTORY OF CRIME MAPPING

Crime mapping has been used in Europe since the first half of the 19th century and began to be used in the United States during the early 1900s. Probably the greatest early influence on geographic mapping—and ultimately geographic profiling—was that of the Department of Sociology at the University of Chicago, whose professors became known as "the Chicago group" and whose Chicago School pioneered the ecological study of crime. The two individuals who laid the groundwork for this approach were Ernest W. Burgess and Robert E. Park. In 1915, Park published a theoretical paper on crime patterns in the city of Chicago. The paper probably represents the official beginning of **ecological criminology,** now more commonly called **environmental criminology.** Park and Burgess soon set out to validate the theory by gathering all the information they could about the city. Their students prepared spot maps, conducted interviews, evaluated maps, and in various ways observed and systematically recorded various phenomena in the city. They soon began to discover that extremes in poverty, illness, and crime were found disproportionately in particular sections of Chicago. These observations may seem obvious today, especially in relation to officially recorded crime, but in the early 20th century they were pivotal discoveries. Although ecological studies of crime and delinquency started to be done in Europe several years before, they did not focus on areas and regions *within* a city.

The Chicago researchers also reviewed court records, particularly those of juveniles, and took note of where the juveniles lived. According to their maps, both male and female juvenile delinquents lived and operated in certain locations, and they committed crimes close to their homes. At first, juvenile court officials and youth workers were skeptical about these findings (E. W. Burgess & Bogue, 1967), maintaining that while these strange patterns might be characteristic of Chicago, delinquency in other cities was distributed evenly. Subsequent studies of other cities, however, revealed the same disproportionate patterning (T. P. Morris, 1957). In urban areas, delinquency was concentrated where buildings were deteriorating, poverty was widespread, and the population was in transition. Delinquency was almost nonexistent in the "better" residential neighborhoods. Moreover, delinquency fit neatly into a pattern of circular zones around the centermost areas of the cities.

Burgess began to fine-tune the ecological theory and proposed his "concentric circle theory" (also called the zonal hypothesis). He recognized that, at that time, American cities tended to expand radically outward from their center in five discernible circular patterns. Each circle represented a zone with distinct demographic and physical characteristics. In Chicago, the area of transition (zone 2) was where delinquency, youth gangs, adult crime, poverty, spousal desertion, abandoned infants, and serious health problems were most concentrated. Later, Clifford Shaw and Henry McKay (1969) confirmed the concentric circle theory as it applied to delinquency and crime. Using the home addresses of more than 100,000 juveniles processed by the Juvenile Court of Cook County between 1900 and 1927, Shaw and McKay found that the highest rates of delinquency and adult crime were in areas of transition. They called these areas the "hot beds" of crime.

The term *transition* characterized a literal movement of the population within these areas. That is, individuals and families were continually moving in and moving out. This was a time during which immigrants were arriving and settling in the inner cities, and some families were beginning to move outward to suburban locations. The immigrant population struggled to find work and living accommodations. Furthermore, changes to the architecture of the cities (new buildings to house businesses) and to their infrastructure (roads, railroad lines) disrupted much of the lifestyle of residents. The Chicago School used the phrase "social disorganization" to highlight the connection between the crime patterns they were discovering and the conditions of the residents. It is important to note that these sociologists wanted to shift the study of criminology away from a focus on individual shortcomings of the offender. Juvenile crime did not represent individual deficiencies of the juveniles, but rather the disorganization and disruption within the neighborhoods where they lived.

We could say much more about the work of the Chicago School and its contribution to the field of criminology as a whole. Clifford Shaw, for example, subsequently developed the Chicago Area Project, one of the earliest community-action programs, in which workers went into the streets of Chicago to advocate for and work with youth considered at risk of offending by virtue of the zone in which they lived. Critics of the ecological approach have argued that by placing their focus on poor, inner-city youth, these criminologists ignored the fact that more advantaged youth and adults also committed illegal acts. The contention that criminologists too often ignore the crimes of the wealthy continued through most of the second half of the 20th century and is still expressed today.

INFLUENCES OF ENVIRONMENTAL CRIMINOLOGY

The foundations of more modern crime mapping are found in the environmental criminology developed by Paul and Patricia Brantingham (1991), particularly their **crime pattern theory**, which incorporates **routine activity theory** and **rational choice theory**, both of which will be discussed shortly. To the Brantinghams, the observations and maps developed by the ecological school were interesting, but the explanations were too simplistic. Most earlier theorists focused on correlations between crime and social phenomena—poverty, social disorganization—in their attempts to describe motivations to commit crimes. Between 1970 and 1980, environmental criminology came into prominence with a focus on how the *distribution of opportunities* for criminal acts influences the actual commission of crimes. A consistent finding of environmental criminology was that most offenders commit a large number of their offenses close to home. Brantingham and Brantingham observed that the average crime trip is short. In fact, the farther the distance from home, the less likely the offender will commit a crime, a finding the Brantinghams referred to as "distance decay." They also pointed out that environmental criminologists have found that offenders, both adult and juvenile, are often spatially clustered, residing in the same regions of a city.

According to the Brantinghams (1991), the clustering of criminals was just a special case of human groups in space. "Criminals have also been shown to be disproportionately represented in certain subpopulations which can be identified along sociodemographic dimensions such as wealth, age, sex, and ethnicity" (p. 33). Therefore, criminal residences and associated crimes cluster within certain areas. For those who commit crime, much of any city is really unknown territory, which either does not exist in their minds at all or is saturated with the terrors of the unfamiliar. Consequently, their crimes will be committed in familiar territory, either near their homes or their places of work, entertainment, or shopping.

We will leave the Brantingham theory for the time being but will return to it again in our discussion of geographic profiling.

CONTEMPORARY CRIME MAPPING

A variant of environmental criminology continues today in more sophisticated fashion and is often demonstrated in popular law enforcement shows like *NCIS* or *CSI: Miami*. It is not unusual for urban police departments to train some officers as geographic crime mappers or to hire someone who specializes in that task, either full-time or as a consultant. In fact, crime mapping has become a common analytical tool for many police departments, emergency management agencies, and homeland security agencies (Bourque et al., 2009; R. Wilson, 2008). Since the 1990s, this expansion has been accomplished through the use of desktop *geographic information systems (GIS)*. GIS has enabled police departments to move from tracking criminal activity on maps with dots or pushpins to using advanced spatial statistics to understand and analyze crime (R. Wilson, 2008). The software enables researchers to not only visualize data, but also to evaluate human behavior over geographic space, determine spatial patterns, validate theories, and examine how geography affects crime and public safety. Hot spots or places usually can be identified by using GIS packages with raster (i.e., grid) mapping capabilities, which creates density maps (Filbert, 2008). The technique employed by these packages is often referred to as *street geocoding*. However, as will be emphasized later in the chapter, "The errors in street geocoding can be very substantial and have been well documented in recent years" (Zandbergen, 2008, p. 1449).

One popular software version of crime mapping is CompStat, a system of tracking crime and managing resources that was pioneered in New York and is used in other major cities. Although some departments have credited this system with effecting a decrease in violent crime, it is not without controversy. A segment aired on National Public Radio's *This American Life* in late summer 2010 highlighted abuses of that system by commanders in one precinct who ordered illegal arrests of citizens and downgraded the seriousness of some criminal offenses, making it appear that serious crime had decreased. Another software package frequently used for crime mapping is GeoDa, developed by Luc Anselin and associates at the Spatial Analysis Laboratory at the University of Illinois (Anselin, Syabri, & Kho, 2006).

All software systems designed for crime mapping provide supplemental statistical tools to aid law enforcement agencies and researchers to identify patterns of crime that will help in its detection and prevention. Today, widely available, large datasets and new analytical tools are contributing to what is known as **predictive policing.** The term refers to "any policing strategy or tactic that develops and uses information and advanced analysis to inform forward-thinking crime prevention" (Uchida, 2011, p. 3). Beth Pearsall (2010) offers another definition: "Predictive policing . . . is taking data from disparate sources, analyzing them and then using results to anticipate, prevent and respond more effectively to future crime" (p. 16).

Geographic Profiling

Geographic profiling (GP)—as opposed to mapping—focuses on a *single* offender or small group. It is an investigative technique that attempts to provide information on the likely base of operations of someone thought to be committing serial crimes (Rich & Shively, 2004). Geographic profiling is a technique or process that can help locate the likely area where a serial offender resides, or other place that serves as an anchor point or base of operations (e.g., bar, girlfriend's home, work). It should be emphasized that geographic profiling is not a foolproof method of leading police investigators to the exact house or location of an offender, but it can be a powerful tool that provides police with a better starting place for following up on leads and narrowing their searches. Although there are several ways to create a geographic profile, the field is rapidly moving toward the use of computer programs for estimating offender home locations. These computer programs typically produce a map or series of maps, similar to those used in geographic mapping. For geoprofiling, the maps are usually in the form of a surface with probability gradients similar to elevation lines on a topographical map. The highest peak (often referred to as the top profile area) represents the best estimate of that offender's residence (see Figure 4.2 for an illustration).

The "map" is usually produced through sophisticated software, and it often demands extensive training in the use of the program. These maps and computer programs are becoming increasingly more complex, as the rapid development of computer-based collection of police data around the world encourages the use of computer software for analyzing large-scale patterns of criminal behavior (Canter, 2009). A geographic profile involves more than maps and computer models, however. We will discuss this as well as the computer software shortly. However, before we do, it will be helpful to touch briefly on the history and theoretical background upon which geographic profiling is based.

Figure 4.2   Example of a Computer-Generated Geographic Profile Map

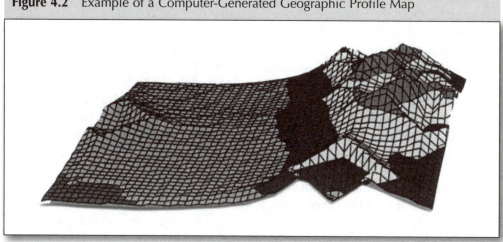

THEORETICAL FOUNDATIONS AND EARLY HISTORY

It is important not to forget the very early work of Park and Burgess, Shaw and McKay, and the Chicago School as reviewed earlier in the section on geographic mapping. These early starts prompted researchers and scholars to continue this approach, although with different emphases.

Two major theories of crime form the foundations of geographic profiling: routine activity theory and rational choice theory. Recall that Paul and Patricia Brantingham incorporated both, but particularly routine activity theory, into their very influential crime pattern theory, which marked the beginning of environmental criminology.

Routine Activity Theory

The theory was first developed by Cohen and Felson (1979) as a theory of victimization, or an explanation for why certain people are victims of predatory crime. The theory's central theme is that criminals learn of possibilities for crime, or seek them out, as part of the daily activities of potential victims, such as going to work, school, visiting friends, shopping, or visiting places of entertainment. In order for such crimes to occur, three factors need to be present at the same time and in the same location: There needs to be a motivated offender, a suitable victim, and the absence of a guardian able to protect the victim. If you remove any one of these three factors, a crime is unlikely to occur.

According to Brantingham and Brantingham (1991), the routine activities of *offenders* as well as those of potential victims should also be considered. That is, the areas where offenders conduct routine activities combine to form what the Brantinghams termed their "action space" or "activity space," which is based on both their illegal and legal activities. The actions of the offenders help form an "awareness space," which includes parts of the city and geography they have some knowledge about. The Brantinghams hypothesized that offenders usually do not go far beyond the area they know (their awareness space) because it is easier to commit crimes in the course of their daily routine than by making a special journey to do so. Furthermore, awareness spaces are primarily based on nodes that are centered at home, work or school, shopping locations, entertainment areas, and the paths connecting these (Figure 4.3). In suburban and rural areas where shopping, entertainment areas, and work locations are spread out, awareness spaces tend to be larger. In urban areas where these activities are more concentrated, awareness spaces tend to be smaller. "For all people, even criminals, much of any city is really unknown territory which either does not exist (cognitively) at all, or is populated with the terrors of the unfamiliar" (p. 37).

During the routine activity of his or her daily travels, the offender develops a target backcloth (Brantingham & Brantingham, 1993). The target backcloth is formed by both geographic and temporal distributions of suitable crime targets or victims (as seen from the offender's perspective) across the physical landscape. "The availability of such targets might vary significantly according to neighbourhood, area or even city, and can also be influenced by time, day of week and season" (Rossmo, 1997, p. 165).

Routine activity theory helped launch geographic profiling, but, as Canter and Youngs (2009) point out, the theory puts the offender in a passive role in relation to the environment, only becoming aware of opportunities for crime by what the environment reveals while the offender is engaging in noncriminal activities. Canter (2005a; Canter & Youngs, 2009) argues that offenders make active choices about their movements through the environment on the basis of their mental maps concerning the

Figure 4.3   Space Awareness Paths

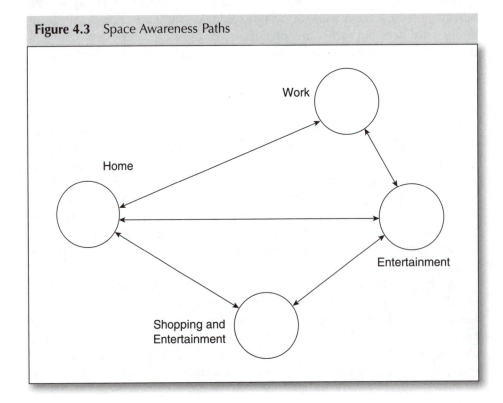

opportunity for crime (Canter & Youngs, 2009). The offender is not just learning about opportunities in the environment, but is also building a mental picture or cognitive map of the area concerning physical structure and activity. In addition, this mental map is continually updated and revised with experiences in the region. We will discuss mental maps in more detail shortly.

Rational Choice Theory

The concept of rationality has a long history in theories of criminology, specifically in what is known as the Classical School. Philosophers in the 18th and 19th century (e.g., Cesare Beccaria [1767] and Jeremy Bentham [1823]) argued that humans had free will and made conscious decisions about whether or not to engage in criminal activity. In other words, criminal behavior—like all other behavior—was the product of choice. Employing a "cost-benefit" analysis, they said that the way to solve the crime problem was to establish punishments that would outweigh the gains offenders received from committing their offenses. However, they emphasized that punishments should not be excessive or inhumane, but rather should be carefully calibrated to fit the crime. For example, Beccaria wrote against capital punishment and denounced physical punishments, such as flogging, that were not uncommon in his era.

Modern rational choice theory, articulated by prominent criminologists (e.g., Cornish & Clark, 1986; Nagin, 2007), has a foundation in these early classical approaches. It views the offender as a rational being, constantly involved in analyzing the costs and benefits of crime. The concept of deterrence plays a large part in this theory: By raising the stakes, the criminal justice system tries to discourage people from committing crime. Therefore, advocates of rational choice theory tend to support policy approaches such as placing more law enforcement officers on the street or attaching stiffer penalties to crimes. In explaining the theory, Cornish and Clark write,

> Its starting point was an assumption that offenders seek to benefit themselves by their criminal behavior; that this involves the making of decisions and of choices, however rudimentary on occasion these processes might be; and that these processes exhibit a measure of rationality, albeit constrained by the limits of time and ability and the availability of relevant information. (p. 1)

Essentially, the theory is based on the assumption that the criminal is a reasoning person who weighs means and ends, and is unlikely to take risks without sufficient benefit.

With specific reference to environmental criminology, the typical criminal is unlikely to commit crimes that take him or her too far away from familiar surroundings. Canter and Youngs (2009) integrate the theory into GP by speculating that the farther an offender travels from home, the greater the risks and costs; thus, if the offender travels far away, it is because an increase in benefits is expected. They use the example of a serial killer's decision regarding where to dispose of a body. The farther he travels from his familiar surroundings to dispose of the body, the higher the risks and costs (apprehension). Some serial killers dispose of bodies in their homes, such as in the basement, freezers, attics, or on the property grounds.

HISTORY OF GEOGRAPHIC PROFILING

According to Canter, Coffey, Huntley, and Missen (2000), Stuart S. Kind (1987) was one of the first forensic scientists to demonstrate the direct application of geographic principles of crime patterns when he conducted a pioneering investigation of the offenses of the Yorkshire Ripper, Peter Sutcliffe. Sutcliffe murdered 13 women and assaulted another 7 in West Yorkshire, England, over the 5-year period from 1975 to 1980. Kind, an ex–Royal Air Force navigator, approached the task of locating the offender as a navigational challenge (Canter & Youngs, 2008). Kind's report was written before Sutcliffe was arrested, and it lay dormant before Canter (2005) rediscovered the report several years later. Apparently, it had not been used to help find the offender, but in retrospect it was quite accurate. Kind's navigational analysis identified the "center of gravity" of the crimes thought to be linked to the case. The center of gravity for Kind was the "only point that simultaneously has the minimum possible distance to each of the offense locations" (Canter et al., 2000, p. 459). In essence, the center of gravity, or "centroid," was most likely where the offender resided or otherwise had his or her base of operations. The analysis proved reasonably accurate in identifying where Sutcliffe lived. The farther a location was from this point, the lower the likelihood the point represented the base of operations of the offender.

GEOGRAPHIC PROFILING SOFTWARE

Like geographic mapping, geographic profiling benefits from increasingly sophisticated software available to its users. As noted above, however, there is ongoing research questioning the accuracy of programs in which street geocoding is employed (Zandbergen, 2008), suggesting that investigators should be very cautious in relying on these approaches.

There are three main geographic profile software programs: Rigel, CrimeStat, and Dragnet. Rigel developed out of the work of D. Kim Rossmo (1995), the first police officer in Canada to obtain a PhD in criminology. Rossmo wrote a doctoral dissertation at Simon Frasier University's School of Criminology (Vancouver, British Columbia) on geographic profiling. Influenced by the work of Paul and Patricia Brantingham, he extended the Brantingham model to answer the question, What does the location of a crime say about where the offender might live? Rossmo, who became the detective inspector in charge of the Vancouver Police Department's Geographic Profiling Section, developed a computer program called Criminal Geographic Targeting (CGT).

Interestingly, Rossmo was dismissed from the Vancouver Police Department in 2000 after working with them for about 5 years, ostensibly because geographic profiling was costly and was not of help to this department. However, his supporters believed some of his superiors in the chain of command were threatened by his academic credentials and resistant to his suggestions, particularly in relation to an ongoing crime problem in the city.

Since 1971, an estimated 40 women had vanished from the streets of Vancouver, including 16 between 1995 and 1998. Rossmo urged police to form an investigative task force and to warn citizens in Vancouver that a serial killer could be on the loose, preying particularly on sex workers. At the time he was let go, Rossmo was apparently offered a 2-year-contract, but he refused it. Instead, he sued for wrongful termination, but his suit was dismissed.

The story has a positive ending, at least for Rossmo, who is now a research professor at Texas State University's Center for Geospatial Intelligence and Investigation. In 2005, Robert Pickton, a 55-year-old Canadian pig farmer, was charged with the murder of 27 women; he was ultimately convicted in 2007 of the murder of 6. Pickton is now serving a life sentence without possibility of parole for 25 years. In 2010, a 400-page report documenting police handling and mishandling of the case was released to the public; shortly thereafter, the mayor of Vancouver issued a written apology to Rossmo, acknowledging that the earlier criticisms of him and his work were unfounded, inaccurate, and misleading.

Following this somewhat rocky start, other departments have been more receptive of Rossmo's approach and those of other geoprofilers and have found their work of value in their day-to-day operations. The computer program CGT is designed to analyze the geographic or spatial characteristics of a specific offender's crimes through the use of algorithms. An algorithm is a step-by-step problem-solving procedure—algorithms are the basis for most computer programming. CGT generates a three-dimensional map that assigns statistical probabilities to various areas that seem to fall into the offender's territory. The three-dimensional map is then placed over a street or topographical map where the crimes have occurred. The program considers known movement patterns, possible comfort zones, and victim searching patterns of the offender. The primary goal of the technique is to pinpoint the location of the offender's residence or base of operations.

The CGT program was later patented and incorporated into the **Rigel and Rigel Analyst** software applications (Rich & Shively, 2004). The Rigel Analyst is primarily designed for serial property crimes rather than serial murders or serial rapes. The Rigel and Rigel Analyst are expensive but can do a lot of things. Rigel even has a report-creating function, has a built-in base map, and can prioritize suspects. According to Patricia Brantingham (2004), information obtained through Rigel is beginning to be regarded as supportive evidence in court cases. However, as we will see in Chapter 9, many courts are suspicious of new technological advances whose scientific validity has not been established.

Another software package for GP is called **CrimeStat**. The program was developed by Ned Levine (2000, 2002) and funded by the National Institute of Justice. The software package is Windows-based and interfaces with most desktop geographic information system programs. A GIS allows us to view, understand, interpret, and visualize data in ways that reveal relationships, patterns, and trends across a geographic landscape or maps. CrimeStat Version 3.0 was released in 2004, and Version 3.3 was released in 2010. CrimeStat software builds on Kim Rossmo's work, but extends its modeling capacity. The program uses a crime travel demand model that analyzes crime travel behavior of serial offenders over a specific area. The travel demand model utilizes available roadways and transit networks in the analyses. Within the model, mathematical equations are employed to represent each traveler's decision-making process of why, when, where, and how to make the trip, and what route to follow. According to Rich and Shively (2004),

> The model, which is an application of travel demand theory that is widely used in transportation planning, including modules for predicting crime origins and crime destinations, predicting trips from each origin to each destination, estimating the travel mode used in committing a crime trip, and guessing the likely travel route taken. (p. 12)

CrimeStat is based on a GP strategy and statistic called spatial distribution (Levine, 2000). That is, the program calculates a central point from a distribution of crime site locations, and it relies on the spatial statistic referred to as the *center of minimum distance* to do this. The importance of the center of minimum distance is that it is a location where *distance to all the crime incidents is the smallest*. Obviously, the model is highly complex and requires considerable data collection and calibration on the part of the user.

Canter (1999, 2004) developed his **Dragnet** software in the mid-1990s based on his work with police investigators in the United Kingdom, discussed in Chapter 3. Dragnet is an interactive system intended for use on a PC with minimal training. It was "developed as a support tool to indicate the likelihood of the offender living at any given location and the implications of linking crime" (Canter & Youngs, 2009, p. 405). Currently, Dragnet is designed to be both an operational tool for police investigations and a research tool for analyzing offender decision-making choices in crime site selections.

The three software applications are very different. Rigel, because it is commercial software), has more extensive input, analysis, and output capabilities than the other two. Rigel is the only program of the three that automatically creates the search area, the primary goal of geographic profiling. As pointed out by Rich and Shively (2004), it is clearly useful to display all three GP software packages on a geographic information system because the system also shows streets, landmarks, political boundaries, and other geographic features of the areas around the crime. At this writing, Dragnet does not incorporate GIS into the package.

In the following subsection, we discuss briefly some of the ways in which software developers promote the use of their materials. Following this, we cover concepts relating to geographic profiling. Later in the chapter, we will discuss emerging research in this area.

Measures of Accuracy

Various measures of effectiveness for GP software have been identified (Harries & LeBeau, 2007). The measures all require the eventual detection of the offender—that is, we do not know how well they perform until an offender is at least arrested and preferably convicted. (Of course, the same can be said of crime scene profiling: We do not know whether a profile was accurate until someone is arrested and convicted.) **Error distance** indicates how far off—in terms of distance—the profiler was in predicting the exact point of the home base of the offender. Harries and LeBeau, however, suggest that it might be unrealistic to use this measure for accuracy. It is more useful for investigators to be able to focus on an area rather than a point, "since it is highly unlikely that the point at the peak of a probability surface will actually coincide with the domicile of an offender" (p. 329). *Search cost/hit score* refers to "the percentage of cells, in an overlaid grid, that need to be searched to locate the cell that contains the offender's base of operations" (Rich & Shively, 2004, p. 17). This measures the extent to which the profiling process reduces the total search area, which is a key goal of software applications, and all three major geographic profile programs produce hit score surface maps. However, this measure is highly dependent on how the search area is originally defined and how capable the profile programs are in producing hit score surface maps.

As mentioned above, error distance is the distance from the offender's residence or anchor point to the nearest point in the highest probability part of the geographic grid. Stated differently, it is the distance from the offender's actual base of operations to the area predicted by the software to be his or her base of operations (see Figure 4.4). **Top profile area** is defined as the "ratio of the total area of the top profile region to the total search area" (Rich & Shively, 2004, p. 17). More simply, the top profile area is the predicted area that most likely contains the base of operations of the offender, such as residence, place of employment, or other frequented location. It is the most important prediction criterion for determining the effectiveness of profiling software, as it represents the search area for police investigators. **Profile accuracy** is a determination of

Figure 4.4   Illustration of Profile Error Distance

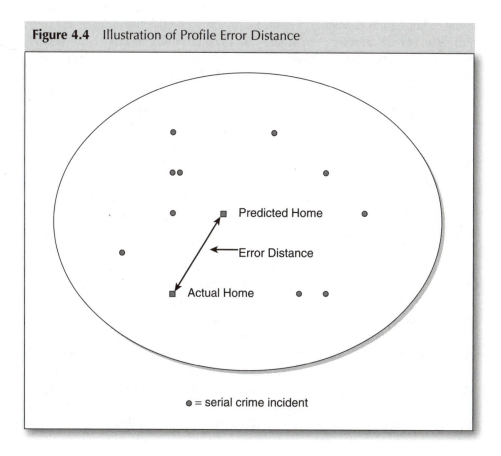

● = serial crime incident

whether the offender's base point is within the predicted top profile area. This measure provides a simple indication of whether or not the profile was correct. Unfortunately, much of the work in geographic profiling computer programs has been driven by the numbers and algorithms and not by theory concerning why certain statistical relationships exist (Canter, 2009). It is therefore important that we turn our attention to the key concepts that highlight some of the theoretical and empirical foundations upon which geographic profiling is based.

KEY CONCEPTS IN GEOGRAPHIC PROFILING

Distance Decay

Rossmo (1995) used the concept of **distance decay** to produce a more sophisticated model of the likely base of the serial offender. Distance-decay function is a term that describes the effect that distance has on cultural interactions or patterns between locales. In fact, it is considered a core concept of geography (J. D. Eldridge & Jones, 1991). The distance decay hypothesis states that the social or cultural interaction between communities declines as the distance between them increases. In geographic profiling, distance-decay function refers to "the relationship between the probability of offending and the distance from home" (Canter et al., 2000, p. 459). More specifically, as the distance from an offender's home increases, the probability of his or her committing an offense decreases (see Figure 4.5). In other words, the probability "decays" the greater the distance from the offender's base. There are many variables that affect distance decay. For example—and as pointed out by Canter et al.—the home of a serial killer might have a very strong influence on his activity and how far he is willing to travel to commit his murders. In this case, the decay function is apt to be very steep and rapid. In other words, he is not willing to travel far from his base. On the other hand, an offender also might have a wider base or anchor, in which case distance decay occurs slowly and more gradually. For example, there might be a "buffer zone" around the offender's place of residence in which there is a reduced likelihood of offending, possibly because the offender is fearful of being recognized by neighbors (Turner, 1969).

The **buffer zone,** a concept developed by the Brantinghams (1984), is a small zone around the offender's residence in which he or she has a strong tendency not to commit crime (see Figure 4.6). (This excludes crimes committed within one's own residence, however.) For most offenders, the buffer zone is less than a quarter of a mile from their residence, but there are exceptions. The Brantinghams believed that a buffer zone most likely exists for some crimes, such as robbery or larceny, but not for others, such as rape and homicide. This is because the distance traveled indicates the amount of planning (Rhodes & Conley, 2008). The farther the distance traveled to commit the crime, the greater the amount of planning required. Rapes and homicides tend to be more impulsive, opportunistic crimes. In general, bank robbers have a 5-mile buffer zone, whereas car thieves have about a 1-mile zone. Overall, the size of the buffer zone appears to depend on the distribution of opportunities perceived by the offender. For example, there are numerous cars within a 1-mile radius and far fewer banks.

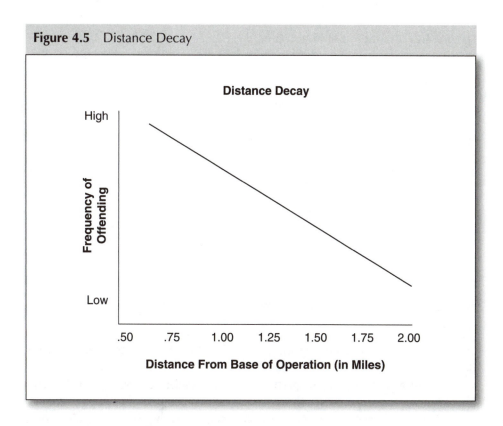

Figure 4.5   Distance Decay

Some researchers (e.g., Snook, Taylor, & Bennell, 2005) have argued, however, that there is little general agreement about how to define or measure a buffer zone. Others point out that crimes are sometimes committed very close to the offender's home, and they conclude that there is no buffer zone for some offenders. The idea of a buffer zone may have some value, but at present it is clearly a concept in more need of research.

Interestingly, serial murderers have a tendency to cover a narrower area in which to leave bodies of their victims as the number of murders they commit increases (M. Godwin & Canter, 1997). As the number of victims gets larger (close to 9 or 10 bodies), the offender has a tendency to leave bodies close to home (less than 2 miles away). In the words of Godwin and Canter,

> It accords with the proposal that their offenses become increasingly integrated with their daily lives, and that some sort of growing confidence, or growing determination to reduce the risk of transporting bodies, leads to the dump sites and the encounter sites being close together. (p. 36)

This "home dump site" is illustrated in the cases of many notorious serial killers, including Jeffrey Dahmer; John Wayne Gacy; Robert Pickton; and—most recently—Anthony Sowell, who was sentenced to death in August of 2011. Sowell murdered 11 women and disposed of their bodies around his property in Cleveland, Ohio.

A considerable amount of research has also demonstrated that serial offenders who commit crimes against property tend to, on average, travel farther to commit their crimes

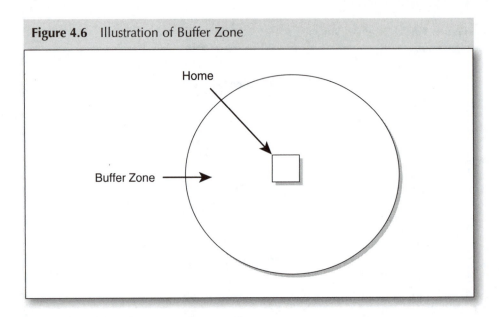

Figure 4.6   Illustration of Buffer Zone

than those who commit crimes against persons (Block, Galary, & Brice, 2007; Canter & Hammond, 2006; Leclerc, Wortley, & Smallbone, 2010). This observation supports rational choice theory, as for many property crimes the offender perceives that the benefits (e.g., financial rewards) outweigh the costs (e.g., risks of being caught and punished).

The literature is by no means unequivocal on this issue, however. According to some research, violent offenders are more likely than property offenders to commit their crimes farther from home. This may be particularly true of sexual offenses, such as rape. J. Warren et al. (1998) examined 565 rape cases that were committed by serial rapists; on average, the rapes occurred 3 miles from the offender's home. Likewise, studies by Canter and Gregory (1994) and Lundrigan and Czarnomski (2006) found that serial sexual offenders committed their crimes at least a mile and a half away from their homes, and sometimes considerably farther.

We must emphasize, however, that as a group, sexual offenders are the least likely to reoffend, so serial sexual offenders are the exception rather than the norm. When they do reoffend, their offenses are typically not sexual in nature (A. J. R. Harris & Hanson, 2004; Langan, Schmitt, & Durose, 2003). Duwe, Donnay, and Tewksbury (2008) studied spatial patterns in a database of 3,166 sex offenders released from correctional facilities in Minnesota between 1990 and 2002. Of these, 374 were rearrested for a new sexual offense and 224 were reincarcerated for a new sexual offense. Focusing on these 224 individuals, the researchers learned that they were most likely to commit their crimes in or near their place of residence, and that the great majority of their victims were someone the offenders knew, such as family members, neighbors, or acquaintances. Stranger sexual assaults were rare and were most likely to occur more than a mile away from the offender's home; fewer than one quarter of these assaults occurred within a mile of the offender's home.

In summary, distance decay is an important concept to consider in geographic profiling, but it has many facets that researchers continue to explore, and thus far the results are anything but clear-cut. There are many mathematical models to describe distance decay functions, and all three major software programs designed for geographic profiling rely on them. For example, CrimeStat incorporates five distance decay functions in its analysis. Distance decay functions measure either the difficulty of traveling though a populated heavy traffic area, or the willingness of a person to travel different distances to access opportunities.

Mental Maps

Another key concept in geographic profiling is that of **mental maps**. Kim Rossmo (1997) posits that geographic profiling has both quantitative (objective) and qualitative (subjective) components to it. The objective component employs a series of scientific geographic techniques and statistical measures to analyze and interpret the spatial and time movements of an offender. "The subjective component of geographic profiling is based primarily on a reconstruction and interpretation of the offender's mental map" (p. 161). This subjective component can best be understood if we make reference to key concepts in psychology, particularly cognitive psychology, which addresses how people make sense of the information they obtain from their environment.

In general, a mental map—also called a cognitive map—is a construct we use to understand and know the environment (Kitchin, 1994). It reflects an individual's perceptions and preferences for certain places. It influences the way in which persons acquire, classify, store, retrieve, and decode information about locations in their physical environment. According to Kitchin, "In effect, a cognitive map is a mental device and store which helps to simplify, code and order the endlessly complex world of human interaction with the environment" (p. 2). In short, it represents geographic survival knowledge. But these maps are not just a set of spatial mental constructs denoting relative position. They also contain values and meanings for the individual who holds them.

The Brantinghams (1991) many years ago talked about mental maps, which they called "cognitive maps" (p. 36). They found that these maps vary by age and socioeconomic class. Individuals with less ability to move around the city have less elaborate cognitive maps than those who travel the city extensively. In addition, "The old, those with young children, women, and those who were unemployed had more limited action space and spent more time at home" (p. 36). Of course, these observations would have to be modified to reflect modern times.

Nevertheless, research indicates that mental maps vary widely by nationality, religion, ethnicity, gender, education, and socioeconomic class (VandenBos, 2007). Mental maps are basically those internal representations that help us find our way around. Without them, we would become lost and have difficulty finding our way home. People with various forms of dementia, such as Alzheimer's disease, become disoriented and can easily get lost, even in familiar surroundings, as their disease progresses. Care facilities for these individuals keep some doors locked or have fenced-in grounds so that those with advanced dementia do not wander away. Essentially, they have lost their mental maps.

As mentioned previously, many researchers have discovered that repeat offenders commit their crimes in a limited area, and that area tends to be close to where they live (Canter & Hodge, 2008). This is largely because their mental maps are well developed for places around where they reside or spend most of their time. Because of their extensive experience with their home base, they feel most comfortable with and knowledgeable about the area. On the other hand, this is less likely to be the case with violent crime (Duwe et al., 2008), with violence within the home excepted. In addition, recall as well that offenders sometime have buffer zones, or areas around their homes where they are unlikely to commit crimes.

Canter and Hodge (2008) believe that asking repeat offenders to draw maps that indicate where they have committed crimes would offer considerable potential for understanding their ways of thinking about their crimes (p. 251). Ultimately, this approach should offer many helpful clues for developing a more refined approach to geographic profiling. In their detailed book on investigative psychology, Canter and Youngs (2009) include an example of a map drawn by an offender that revealed his pattern of burglaries, including the centrality of his home—referred to by the authors as "domocentricity" (p. 180). Canter and Youngs observe that offenders often produce maps with great detail, even marking—with pride—buildings with particular forms of security devices or other limits on accessibility. The maps represent mental constraints as well as opportunities perceived by the offender.

A similar approach was used in the early 1980s by T. Bennett and Wright (1984). The researchers undertook a 3-year project on convicted burglars confined in various prisons throughout southern England. Their primary interest was to learn the decision-making processes and perceptions of the residential burglars at the time of the crime. The principal method of data collection in the study was semi-structured interviews with the burglars themselves. Although most of the burglars had committed a variety of property crimes, almost all of them considered burglary their main criminal activity. Therefore, most of them probably qualified as professional burglars rather than amateurs.

T. Bennett and Wright (1984) discovered that a vast majority of the burglaries reported by these offenders were planned. Very few were the result of spur-of-the-moment decisions. Rather, most of their burglaries appeared to be the result of well-learned cognitive scripts accompanied by detailed mental maps of areas in which they were most comfortable. **Cognitive scripts** refer to mental images and plans for how one will act and react in certain situations. The mental maps in these cases were developed on the basis of familiarity with the neighborhood and routes for escaping successfully from the scene. The mental maps were likely formed during their daily rounds to select promising targets.

Canter and Youngs (2008) caution that the mental map is not simply the knowledge of a route to get to a place of crime; rather, the offender makes "choices on the basis of his/her mental map of the opportunities for crime" (p. 14). The offenders may not have a clear notion of what specific route they need to take to get to their crime location, but they do know the general direction. A good illustration of using mental maps can be found in both classic and contemporary "heist" movies (e.g., *Heat*, with Robert DeNiro and Al Pacino; *The Town*, with Ben Affleck). The robberies are meticulously planned, with the masterminds being familiar with their targets and aware of the comings and goings of individuals associated with them, be they various banks or sports stadiums. Scenes from heist films often depict the perpetrators drawing maps (translated from their own mental maps) to show their partners which strategy will be undertaken.

The Circle or Centrality Theory

Another fundamental concept in geographic profiling is the issue of centrality, or "center of gravity." As noted previously, a basic assumption of geographic profiling is that places people are familiar with exert considerable influence over where they are likely to go (Canter & Youngs, 2008). The same is assumed to be true of most offenders. The **centrality theory** hypothesizes that the crime spatial patterns of *many* serial offenders will approximate a circle around their homes or anchor points—referred to above as domocentricity (see Figure 4.7). The word "many" is italicized because this pattern is not always the case. Some serial offenders' crime scenes do not surround their homes but demonstrate clustering patterns that do not include the anchor point near the center. This observation led to the very important distinction between two offender types: the *marauder* and the *commuter.* The first is associated with the concept of centrality; the second is not.

The **marauder** is the offender who travels from his or her base to commit crime and then returns, going out in different directions and on different occasions (Canter

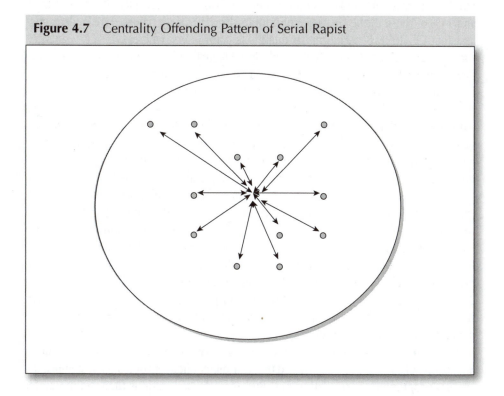

Figure 4.7 Centrality Offending Pattern of Serial Rapist

& Gregory, 1994). The simplest way to define the area circumscribed by the marauder crimes is to identify the two crimes farthest from each other and use the line joining them as the diameter of a circle (Canter & Youngs, 2008). The center of the circle will approximate the anchor point or the home of the marauder type of offender. For example, Canter and Larkin (1993) found that 87% of the serial rapists in the UK committed their crimes in a manner that confirmed the centrality assumption. That is, their residence or anchor base was determined to be near the center of their surrounding crime scenes. A similar pattern was reported by Kocsis and Irwin (1997) who found that 82% of the offense patterns of serial arsonists in Australia verified centrality. Research has also indicated that a majority of serial murderers are marauders who reside within a circle defined by their area of criminal activity (Bennell, Snook, Taylor, Corey, & Keyton, 2007; Canter, 2003; Lundrigan & Canter, 2001; Snook, Cullen, Mokros, & Harbort, 2005).

For the **commuter,** on the other hand, there is little overlap between his or her criminal and home ranges. In other words, the crime sites do not radiate out (like the spokes of a wheel) from the home or anchor point. While marauders commit their crimes with their home base as a nexus of criminal activity, commuters travel from their home into a separate area to offend and do not surround their home base with their crime incidents in the same manner (see Figure 4.8). For the commuter, the preferred area of crimes may be chosen for its abundance of suitable targets or potential victims.

Numerous studies on offender travel indicate the distance traveled depends to some extent on the type of crime as well as the country in which the crimes were committed. Lundrigan and Canter (2001) found that only 11% of the U.S. *serial killers* they studied and 14% of those in the UK were commuters. However, data reported by Paulsen suggest that 51% of U.S. serial *rapists* qualify as commuters, whereas 43% of Canadian serial sexual assaulters qualified. Similarly, 63% of Finnish commercial robbers and 52% of Australian burglars met the criteria for the commuter model. These data indicate that geographic profiling based on the assumption of centrality may fail in approximately 50% of certain crimes. Put another way, if we consider just the above studies, we see that the centrality assumption can be made with some confidence with serial killers—they are typically marauders rather than commuters—but we must be far more cautious with other serial or repeat offenders. Unfortunately, the research into predicting commuter/marauder distinctions is currently very limited.

In one recent, relevant study on marauders and commuters, Derek Paulsen (2007) examined 106 crime series from 25 jurisdictions across the United States. The data were obtained from official case files of solved crimes, which contained a complete listing of all crime locations and all known anchor points of the offender, including home, work, and all other relevant locations. The crimes included arson, murder, robbery (commercial and street), burglary, and sexual assault. It should be mentioned that 24% of the 106 crime series had *multiple* anchor points that were known to the police. In other words, in about a quarter of the cases, the offenders had more than one residence or other base of operation.

The data revealed that 64 were identified as marauders and 42 were commuters. Surprisingly, Paulsen (2007) discovered that commuter offenders operated in significantly smaller geographic ranges with more clustered offense locations than did marauder

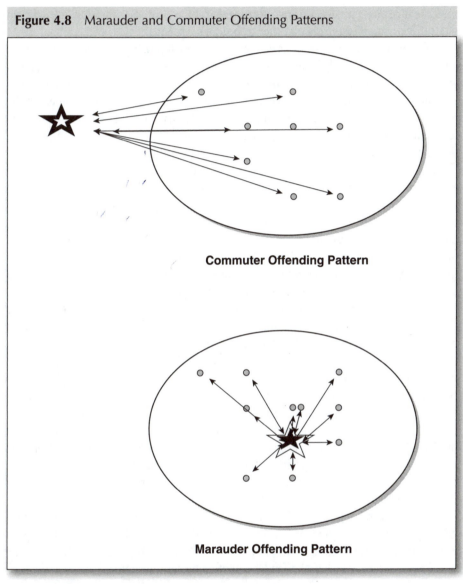

Figure 4.8   Marauder and Commuter Offending Patterns

Commuter Offending Pattern

Marauder Offending Pattern

Note: Stars represent home base. Dots represent serial crime incidents.

offenders. This finding may appear in opposition to the hypothesis that marauder offenders would be most likely to operate in smaller geographic areas closer to their anchor point. However, Paulsen also found that the marauders continued to offend in a circular fashion around their anchor point, even though the distance range was, on average, greater than the commuter offender's travel range. In other words, the marauder anchor point or place of residence still approximated the center point of the circle. On the other hand, the commuter committed his crimes in roughly the same area, closer to his anchor point, but the anchor point did not fall near the center of the crime sites (see Figure 4.8). Rather, the anchor was most often on the edge or just outside the circle. Paulsen recommends the following: "Improving the ability to predict whether an offender is a marauder or commuter before a profile is conducted could reduce time wasted on inaccurate geographic profiles and allow agencies to focus investigative resources on other techniques" (p. 350).

Think of your travel patterns as you leave home each day. If you plotted your travels on a map to work, school, friends, shopping, entertainment places, Internet cafes, pubs, and other frequented places over the past 2 or 3 weeks, what would you find? Would your home or residence be somewhere in the middle of a circle if you connected the dots to home base, or would the assumption of centrality not hold? Are your travel patterns more like those of the marauder or the commuter? This is a relevant exercise because the theory of centrality sometimes holds, but often it does not.

Some researchers have found another variable that must be taken into account: the emotional state of the offender. Specifically, if the offender is emotionally or sexually aroused—thereby committing what is referred to as an *expressive* crime—the distance to the crime scene is likely to be shorter (Laukkanen, Santtila, Jern, & Sandnabba, 2008). Consequently, the logic follows that emotion-laden, expressive crime is most likely to be committed by marauders and basically support the centrality theory. Crime that is committed to gain something (e.g., money, goods), referred to as *instrumental* crime, is more apt to be characterized by commuter-type offending.

Katarina Fritzon (2001) examined a total of 156 cases involving a single crime scene that was set on fire by either a sole arsonist or a small group. The data came from solved police cases. Fritzon discovered that arsonists whose behavior contained a strong emotional factor tended to travel much shorter distances than arsonists who sought a direct instrumental benefit from the fire. Vindictive, angry arsonists traveled less distance to set the fire than those arsonists hoping for instrumental gains, such as covering up another crime. Fritzon also found that arsonists traveled farther to target people than to set fire to objects. These findings underscore the importance of adapting geographic profiling to the type of crime and offender under consideration. In addition, the research evidence to this point indicates that when an offender conforms to the centrality theory, as described by Canter and Larkin (1993), predictions of place of residence or anchor point tend to be more accurate.

Recall from the beginning of the chapter that the overriding and primary goal of geographic profiling is to identify roughly where the offender lives or at least sleeps at night, based on the locations of his or her crimes (Canter & Youngs, 2008). However, the behavioral patterns of a serial offender can often be complicated.

> For instance in a murder case there may be a point of first contact with a victim; a location to which the victim was taken and assaulted; another location where the victim was murdered, and yet another location where the body was disposed of. (Canter & Youngs, 2008, p. 7)

All of these locations may be of interest to law enforcement investigators, including the relationships among them. But these multiple locations may also cause some havoc in the geographic analyses to locate a home base or anchor point of the offender. The anchor point can be the offender's place of residence, place of work, or some other location important to the offender. Furthermore, the offender may not operate from a typical home base. He or she may operate out of a bar, pub, or nightclub, or the

offender may be homeless. Offenders may also operate out of the home of a significant other or friend.

Canter (Canter & Youngs, 2009) also admits that the circle or centrality hypothesis
may be an oversimplification for all marauder offenders. A major challenge to the
hypothesis is that it ignores the actual geography of an area by assuming that offenders
will travel equally in all directions. For one thing, it may not be possible to travel into
certain areas because of physical barriers such as lakes, rivers, dead-end streets, industrial parks, arterials, or interstate highways. In addition, offenders may have a preference or predisposition to go off in certain directions. The "windshield wiper effect"
might illustrate a common pattern (see Figure 4.9). This is a pattern reported by
Lundrigan and Canter (2001), who looked at the average angle between crime for 79
U.S. serial killers and found it to be about 60 degrees. Put another way, the home is at
the bottom of a fan, and the crimes fan out from that point rather than circling the
home for 360 degrees.

Figure 4.9   Windshield Wiper Effect

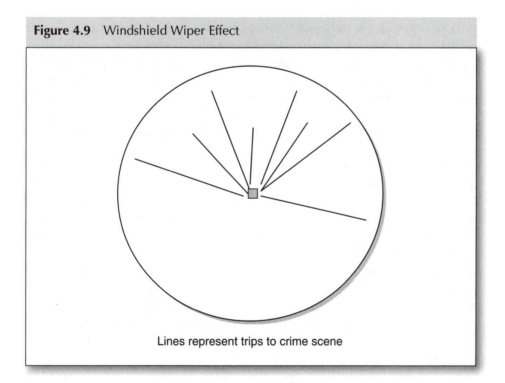

Lines represent trips to crime scene

Geographic Hunting Patterns

In an approach not unlike the marauder-commuter distinction outlined above, Kim
Rossmo (1997) developed a typology that highlights the complexity of spatial and
time-related movements and geographic patterns of *different* serial offenders.
Rossmo argues that predatory criminals use various hunting styles in their efforts to

seek out and attack victims. Some serial offenders tend to commit their crimes within a certain region and are therefore geographically stable. Others are more transient, moving from place to place. He further maintains that the preferred hunting style will affect the spatial distribution of the offender's crime locations, indicating that any attempt to predict the base of operations of predatory-type offenders must consider their hunting style.

Rossmo (1997) classifies the "hunting patterns" or search methods of offenders into four groups: (1) hunter, (2) poacher, (3) troller, and (4) trapper. "Hunters are those criminals who specifically set out from their residence to look for victims, searching through the areas in their awareness spaces that they believe contain suitable targets" (p. 167). The crimes of the **hunter** tend to be geographically stable and often occur near the offender's place of residence or neighborhood. **Poachers** tend to be more transient, usually traveling some distance from their residence or neighborhood in search of victims. Rossmo observes that the terms "hunter" and "poacher" are similar to the marauder and commuter classification proposed by Canter and Larkin (1993).

The third group, the **trollers,** are not specifically searching for victims but rather randomly encounter them during the course of routine activity. The fourth group, the **trappers,** create situations to draw victims to themselves. "Trapping" may be accomplished through entertaining a date or someone one just met, placing want ads, taking in boarders, or assuming positions or occupations where potential victims come to them. "Black widows, 'angels of death' and custodial killers are all forms of trappers, and most female serial murderers fall into this category" (Rossmo, 1997, p. 169).

Rossmo (1997) also describes three primary victim attack methods used by these four types of offenders. The *raptor* refers to an offender who attacks a victim upon encounter. The *stalker* is an offender who first follows a victim upon encounter, then attacks. The third method, the *ambusher*, is defined as an offender who attacks a victim once he or she has been enticed to a location, such as a residence or workplace, which is controlled by the offender. The victims' bodies are most often hidden somewhere on the offender's property.

Target patterns are influenced by offender activity space, hunting method, and victim backcloth. According to Rossmo (1997), poachers and stalkers do not usually produce target patterns that are amenable to geographic profiling. Moreover, hunter/raptors and trapper/ambushers are much more common than hunter/stalkers or trapper/raptors.

Rossmo recommends that geographic profiling be combined with crime scene profiling for maximum effectiveness in developing probabilities for offender identification. According to Rossmo (2000), geographic profiling is a combination of good police work, local knowledge of the physical landscape, knowledge of suspects and the relevant database, crime scene investigation, and the many other factors that go into skillful investigative activities. In addition, he admonishes that geographic profiling is essentially an investigative tool that does not necessarily solve crimes but should help in the surveillance or monitoring of specific locations. It is good that he has offered this caveat; the hunting pattern typologies he recommends have not been extensively documented in the literature to this point, and critics argue that this approach is of minimal use to investigators. Though "interesting," they are not necessarily scientifically valid.

The Basic Assumptions of Geographic Profiling

Geographic profiling is a fascinating area of study and may well be a crucial enterprise for the investigation of crime, particularly serial offenses by either one or a small group of offenders. However, six basic assumptions must be met if GP is to estimate effectively the base of operations or anchor point of the offender. If these assumptions are not met, then inferences drawn may be in error.

1. A series of cases are linked to one offender.

2. At least three or four crimes are needed; otherwise they cannot be effectively linked to a single offender.

3. Offenses should be widely dispersed, with a central location.

4. The offender should have a stable base of operations.

5. There should be a short time interval between offenses.

6. The crime series must occur continuously over time.

CASE LINKAGE

In order for GP to be effective, a series of crimes must be linked to a common offender. We discussed case linkage briefly in earlier chapters and will discuss it again in Chapter 9, because it has been the subject of important court cases. Some agencies prefer to call case linking "tactical crime analysis," and they sometimes hire tactical crime analysts for this purpose. Case linking may be accomplished by forensic evidence, such as a DNA profile, fibers, tool marks, notes, or latent fingerprints. As we learned in Chapter 2, the crime scene signature or distinguishing modus operandi is another useful means of case linking. However, as we have emphasized previously, many offenders often change their MO over time as a function of situational and learning factors. Bennell and Jones (2005) write, "As a result, the use of MO as a tool to link serial crimes is presently applied sparingly and with extreme caution" (p. 24).

Nevertheless, despite questions about the consistency of the MO, there is a growing body of empirical evidence that offenders are to some degree consistent and distinctive (Tonkin et al., 2011; Woodhams & Toye, 2007).

These studies have investigated the consistency and distinctiveness of a variety of offender behaviors, including (but not limited to) the methods of entry, the type of property stolen, and the type of property targeted (in studies of auto theft, burglary, and robbery) and the degree of planning, control, sexual behavior, and violence (in studies of robbery, rape or sexual assault, and homicide). (Tonkin et al., 2011, p. 1070)

Furthermore, the research is beginning to demonstrate that two behaviors in particular display significant consistency and distinctiveness that frequently exceeds other types of offending behavior: spatial and temporal behavior. More specifically, the accuracy of the distance between offense locations (the spatial or inter-crime distance) and the number of days between offenses (temporal proximity) exceeds all other identifiable offending behaviors (Tonkin et al., 2011).

Canter and Youngs (2008) believe that perhaps, in the absence of forensic evidence, one useful way to link crimes to a single offender is to identify crime scenes or sites that occur close together. For example, if the offender commits crimes close to home, then the offender must be committing crimes in geographic areas that are close to each other. In addition, when crime scenes are close to each other, it may well indicate that they were committed by the same person. Empirical support for this observation was provided by Grubin et al. (2001) in their study of serial rapists. They found that by far the simplest way of linking crimes to a single offender was to look at crime sites that occur close together in location.

Moreover, despite their belief that traditional ways of looking at MO have questionable value in linking serial crimes, Bennell and Jones (2005) did find some aspects of commercial and residential burglary that allow linking. More specifically, it is possible to identify certain behavioral characteristics of burglars that are relatively stable and distinct across a crime series, one of these being inter-crime distance. Both commercial and residential burglars appear to choose relatively distinct geographic areas in which to commit their crimes that were close together. "Shorter distances between crimes signalled an increased likelihood that burglaries were linked" (p. 23).

LINKAGE AS A FUNCTION OF MULTIPLE OFFENSES

Another important assumption for improving the efficiency of geographic profiling is that there should be at least three to five crimes linked to a single offender, and preferably even more. The more crimes in the equation, the more accurate the estimate, especially if a computer GP program is used. Small sample sizes have the potential for a very large error. Nevertheless, some scholars are questioning how strongly we should hold to that assumption.

Knabe-Nicol and Alison (2011), for instance, make the case that geoprofilers can be helpful to police investigators even in single crimes. For example, a case where the offender encounters the victim in one location, takes the victim somewhere else to rape or murder, and releases the victim or dumps the body in another location offers many crucial clues. Perhaps the offender also deposits the property taken or objects used in the attack in another location, behavior that will further provide clues about the offender's familiarity with various locations and his or her decision-making processes. Investigators and geoprofilers may gain knowledge about other locations from such things as sightings, CCTV, or cell phone data. The movements of the offender through space and time give investigators considerable information about where his or her base of operations may be located. Even if the crime appears at first glance to be a single case, it might lead to linking it with another case. Research has shown a high level of consistency in geographic MO of serial offenders, as most repeatedly use the same location set (Rossmo, 1997). That is, although they may not return to the same place, they will return to the same *type* of place, such as a warehouse, or a private home, or a public park.

Knabe-Nichol and Alison (2011) also argue that geoprofilers can assist investigators on even a single crime that took place in *one* location, although the information provided is apt to be far less accurate than for a single crime that involved multiple locations. A single offense with one location is one in which the encounter, attack, victim release or body disposal, and property disposal sites are all at the same place. More specifically, the offender encounters a victim, engages in an attack or crime in the same location, and then leaves without moving the victim or the victim's body. A single offense involving multiple locations may reveal that the offender encountered the victim in one location, took him or her to another to carry out the rape or murder, took the victim or body to still another for disposal or release, and deposited property taken or objects used in the attack somewhere else on the way back to his base of operations. Therefore, in the case involving the single offense with several crime locations, there is more opportunity for drawing conclusions about the home base of the offender.

Knabe-Nichol and Alison (2011) conducted a study asking professional geoprofilers to make predictions about the home base of the offenders committing 13 single-offense cases. Some involved a single-location crime scene, while others involved multiple crime scene locations. As expected, the profilers performed significantly better in the cases involving multiple locations, but they were reasonably accurate in the single-location crimes, too. The profilers were 75% accurate in identifying bases of operation of the offender in multiple-site crimes and 52% accurate in single-location crimes. In both study conditions, many of the investigative suggestions were regarded as helpful. However, the number of professional geoprofilers participating in this study was extremely small (N = 4), as was the number of cases (N = 13), so the results must be viewed as merely suggestive. The researchers agree that much more research needs to be done in this area, but perhaps eventually the definition of geographic profiling will not require the inclusion of the term "serial."

RELATIVELY EVEN DISTRIBUTION OR WIDE DISPERSION OF OFFENSES

A third basic assumption is that the crime scenes must be fairly evenly distributed around the offender's home or anchor point. Crimes that are closely clustered around one location, such as those found in the Paulsen study regarding commuter and marauder offenders discussed above, would probably hamper the identification of a base of operations of an offender. For example, if all the offenses occurred in one specific location compared to a wide-dispersion pattern, determining the location of the offender's base of operations would be extremely challenging.

Although most crimes are committed close to home, the distance traveled from home to the scene of the crime is related to a number of considerations, including the characteristics of the offender, the target, and the offense. Geographic detection will be facilitated if the offender follows the characteristics of a marauder rather than a commuter. Crimes that cluster around a single location imply a base of operations somewhere in the center regions of the incidents.

As touched upon earlier, Laukkanen and Santtila (2006) hypothesize that crimes that are more expressive or emotionally driven, such as rape, vindictive or revenge arson, and sexual assault, tend to have a shorter journey-to-crime distance than those of a more instrumental nature, such as robbery or burglary. It has been found, for example, that *some* professional robbers who carefully plan their crimes are willing to travel significant distances from their homes, especially if the rewards are high (van Koppen & Jansen, 1998). In fact, their research indicated that commuter-type spatial behavior was the majority (63%) of commercial robbery. This is especially true if the robber is armed with a firearm (Capone & Nichols, 1975).

SINGLE, STABLE BASE OF OPERATIONS

One principal assumption of geographic profiling is that the offender has a single, stable anchor point or base of operations over the time period of the crimes. Geographic profiling is unlikely to work in locating an offender who lives and sleeps in multiple locations. For example, in the Washington, D.C., sniper case, the offenders John Allen Muhammad and Lee Boyd Malvo lived in a Chevrolet Caprice car and possibly in motels and homes of acquaintances, and they moved around the area. As noted by Harries and LeBeau (2007), an initial cluster of sniping in Maryland hinted at a Maryland residence, but later events occurred in Virginia. Serial killers who traveled across the country also would be difficult to detect if one were relying on the concepts promoted by geographic profiling. For example, the long-haul truck driver Keith Hunter Jesperson, known as the Happy Face Killer because of the smiley face he drew on his letters to the media, claimed to have killed for over a year before bodies were even found (Quinet, 2007). He killed at least eight women over a 4-year period, including his long-term girlfriend, and is now serving sentences of life-without-parole. Even when found, bodies might not be linked through geoprofiling, but rather more likely through the crime scene evaluation techniques discussed in earlier chapters.

RELATIVELY SHORT TIME INTERVAL BETWEEN OFFENSES

For geographic profiling to be the most effective, the crime incidents should cluster in time as well as space (Harries & LeBeau, 2007), meaning they were committed within a reasonable amount of time (weeks or months rather than years). Long intervals between offenses mean it is less likely the crimes will be linked by investigators, at least initially. The same situation would hold if the offenses were committed in different law enforcement jurisdictions. Harries and LeBeau comment,

> The worst-case scenario that could be envisioned in this context would be a set of serial crimes, each of which is committed in a different adjacent jurisdiction, with none of the affected agencies recognizing interrelatedness or [being willing to] share information. (p. 324)

The Beltway Sniper case in 2002 might have resembled this worst-case scenario had the 10 murders not received so much media coverage and the perpetrators not been so sensational in their MO.

CRIME SERIES MUST OCCUR CONTINUOUSLY OVER TIME

A series of crimes committed simultaneously (on the same day) is unlikely to prove useful for identifying the offender's base of operations. It is assumed to be most helpful for GP if the offender returns to his or her base of operations several times during the commission of the crimes. In fact, time factors have the potential to add significantly to the ease of estimating the base of operations of the offender. By adding time or temporal factors to spatial analysis, geography theoretically and statistically becomes four-dimensional rather than three-dimensional. The spatial analysis covers three dimensions (longitude, latitude, and elevation of location), and time analysis adds the fourth. What is more, the four-dimensional approach to GP more accurately corresponds to how the offender not only moves through space, but across time as well. Knabe-Nicol and Alison (2011) point out that a park, street, or footpath may be used by a very different demographic of people during the night, especially weekend nights, than during the day. Each crime location should be visited during the time the crime was committed (including the day of the week) in order to estimate who is usually there at that particular time.

> For instance, the location of an offence that occurred late at night but that offers no late-night entertainment, shops or other reasons why someone would be there, indicates that the offender may reside around that area. (p. 137)

On the other hand, a crime committed during rush hour might suggest that it occurred when the offender was en route to or returning from work, a phenomenon some geographic profilers refer to as "displacement."

Another point that Knabe-Nichol and Alison (2011) make concerning temporal factors is the observation that some offenders return to the location of their crime, often at the same time of day they committed the crime, to relive the event. Therefore, geographic profilers might be wise to encourage law enforcement to maintain surveillance at the crime location and at the same time it occurred. This behavior of returning to the scene of the crime appears to be especially characteristic of serial rapists.

Focus 4.1

ATF Criminal and Geographic Profiling Program

Since 1986, the Bureau of Alcohol, Tobacco, Firearms and Explosives (ATF) has assigned special agent criminal profilers to the FBI National Center for the Analysis of Violent Crime (NCAVC) in Quantico, Virginia. Currently, one ATF behavioral profiler and one geographic profiler are assigned to the NCAVC. The behavioral profiler's mission is to support arson and bombing investigations in the identification, arrest, and prosecution of the offender by analyzing the behavior of the offender. The geographic profiler's mission is to analyze the location of connected crimes in an attempt to pinpoint the most probable area where the offender lives. Currently, the ATF is the only U.S. federal agency to have a geographic profiler (Bureau of Alcohol, Tobacco, Firearms and Explosives, n.d.).

ATF profilers undergo an intensive 2-year training program in behavioral science principles, crime scene analysis and interpretation, forensic science, and pathology. Upon completion of their training, the profilers are certified by the International Criminal Investigative Analysis Fellowship (ICIAF), discussed in Chapter 2. The certified profilers are able to offer their services to various law enforcement and fire service agencies in the United States and worldwide.

Among the services provided are statement analysis, which is analyzing a suspect's language, both oral and written, in order to identify possible areas of deception, find hidden meanings and motivations, and develop interview themes. The services also include threat assessment, which is assessing the potential of a known individual to act violently in a particular situation, or developing a psycho/sociolinguistic profile of an unknown subject to assess the risk of the subject carrying out threats. Other services include crime link analysis, profile development, and interviewing techniques. The ATF profilers provide training to law enforcement and fire personnel on behavioral and geographic profiling techniques, and they conduct research on bombing and arson profiling.

Recent Research on Geographic Profiling

Although there have been a number of reported successes with geographic profiling, there have also been several instances where the technique has been wrong in predicting the approximate location of the offender's residence or base of operations. Some software packages, for instance, are so complicated that they are highly dependent on the quality and accuracy of the informational input. Incomplete or inaccurate information can seriously distort the outcome. In addition, the practice of geoprofiling consists of two stages: (1) linking a series of crimes to the same offender, and (2) developing a geoprofile that estimates the approximate area of an offender's residence or place of operations. The first stage is often the more challenging and subject to error. Thus far, none of the geographic profiling software packages have been subjected to rigorous, independent, or comparative assessments to evaluate their accuracy, reliability, validity, or appropriateness for various situations. The following section will examine some of these problems.

SIMPLE HEURISTICS MAY BE
BETTER THAN COMPUTER PROGRAMS

In addition to the use of sophisticated GP computer programs to estimate the base of operations of serial offenders, researchers have examined alternatives to GP approaches. Much of this research has focused on the use of simple rules for predicting the locations of offenders' home base (Bennell et al., 2007). One research approach concentrates on how simple cognitive heuristics can help some individuals make accurate decisions and predictions. Bennell et al. define *heuristics,* for their purposes, as "cognitive mechanisms that allow decisions to be arrived at quickly and with little mental effort" (p. 120). Recall that we discussed heuristics in Chapter 3 and noted that they, too, can produce inaccurate results. However, Bennell et al. cite research indicating that heuristic-based decisions can be as accurate as more computationally expensive methods, such as the GP programs discussed previously. Moreover, individuals can be trained to use simple heuristics to predict with accuracy the base of operations of serial offenders. In Chapter 3, we did not discuss training in the use of heuristics, so this is an important point to make.

Snook, Canter, and Bennell (2002) found that simple heuristics can be quickly understood and utilized by individuals without any special knowledge about criminal behavior or experience in criminal investigations.

> They can understand well enough to improve their accuracy in predicting the likely home location of serial murderers and can utilize them so effectively that, at least for the sample of serial killers used here, their judgments are, on average, as accurate as a geographic profiling system. (p. 116)

In the Snook et al. (2002) study, two groups of students were provided with 10 maps, each indicating the location of five crimes committed by a different serial killer. They were asked to designate where they thought each serial murderer lived by placing an X on each map. Before the task, one group (the experimental group) was educated about the circle heuristic, which corresponds very closely to the centrality theory discussed above. Group members were told that a majority of offenders' homes can be located within a circle with its diameter defined by the distance between the offenders' two furthermost crimes. They were also educated about the distance decay heuristic. They were told that the majority of offenders commit offenses close to home. The second group (the control group) was asked to do the same task but was not provided with the simple heuristic training given to the experimental group. The researchers also had the computer program Dragnet produce a series of probabilities for each location on the map.

Overall results demonstrated that simple training had a significant impact on accuracy, with the experimental group improving to the point where their predictions were as accurate as Dragnet. The findings raise questions about the specific benefits of using geographic profilers and computer-based GP programs. The results also have implications for police agencies. They suggest that police agencies may be able to correct any use of inappropriate heuristics by providing investigators with those that are more research-based. In addition, the conclusions indicate that police organizations may not need to purchase expensive GP systems. Training officers on research-based heuristics provides a quick, cost-effective, and accurate way to predict serial offenders' base of operations. The analogy could be made to driving to a new location with the help of a road atlas or map or a GPS device in one's car; once one knows how to read a map, finding the location is not difficult, and maps are the less expensive alternative. Moreover, if you've ever had the experience of being led astray by the disembodied voice on your global positioning system, it is possible that you place more trust in the map.

The avid fan of *NCIS* or similar TV crime shows would argue that the computer programs are faster, which is clearly a good point. Furthermore, together with the indispensable "apps," they guide us to restaurants, landmarks, hospitals, and various places of interest. Nevertheless, they are not necessarily accurate. As we see below, there is some evidence that—for crime-solving purposes—people with some training in heuristics can exceed the performance of the computer programs.

In a later study, Snook, Taylor, and Bennell (2004) modified the procedure used in their earlier study. Two hundred and fifteen prospective undergraduate students ("prospective" because they had not yet started classes) received booklets containing 10 maps displaying the first three crime sites for solved serial murders. The booklets had separate pages, which, in order, contained (1) a blank cover sheet, (2) instructions to indicate (by marking an X) on each of the 10 maps a place where they thought the offender's home was most likely to be located, (3) the 10 maps, (4) instructions to record the strategies they used to reach their decisions, (5) instructions to place the completed maps out of their reach, (6) heuristic training material, (7) the same 10 maps, and (8) instructions to record the strategies they used to reach their decisions.

The heuristic information section of the booklet differed, depending on which group participants were assigned to. Students assigned to the control group did not receive information about heuristics. The decay group received information about the distance decay heuristic, whereas the circle group received written information regarding the circle heuristic. These two experimental groups first made predictions without reading the supplementary material, then again made predictions after reading about distance decay or the circle hypothesis. Results revealed that, on average, information about decay and the circle heuristic improved the predictions of the experimental groups to a level of accuracy that equaled—and in some cases exceeded—the computer program CrimeStat's predictions. In conclusion, the researchers write, "the present findings suggest that technological advances in the field of geographic profiling over the last 10 years may have overcomplicated what may, in reality, be a relatively simple task" (Snook et al., 2004, p. 119).

The Snook et al. studies used college students as participants, which the researchers admit was a limitation. The typical student, of course, does not have any investigative experience. Bennell et al. (2007) used police officers from a large police department in the UK in a study that followed the basic design of the Snook et al. investigations. However, the Bennell et al. study added two factors that may influence accuracy in predictions: the number of crimes and the level of topographical detail. These two factors were added because some professional geographic profilers have maintained that both factors should be taken into account when making GP predictions. Also, the previous studies have used scenarios involving serial killers, whereas the Bennell et al. project used serial burglars. As noted previously, serial killers tend to be marauders, whereas property offenders are more likely to be commuters.

The 91 police officers from a large police force in the United Kingdom were randomly assigned to a control, circle, or decay group. All participants also completed a demographic questionnaire. There were no significant differences among the police participants in age, gender, or years of police experience. A majority of the officers had very little experience or knowledge of geographic profiling methods.

There were two phases in the study: a pretraining phase and an after-training phase. In the pretraining phase, the officers were asked to predict the likely home location of 36 serial burglars. This procedure established the baseline. The officers were then briefly trained—depending on their group assignment—in either the circle hypothesis or the distance decay hypothesis of home location. The control group, of course, did not receive training. The three groups were then asked to predict home location again, a procedure called the retest (see Figure 4.10). The participants were told to work individually and at their own pace.

The accuracy of police officers' predictions was compared across the three groups as well as with the home-location predictions of the computer program CrimeStat. The measure of accuracy was the distance error (Figure 4.4).The overall results showed that police officers are able to accurately predict an offender's home location. "Even without any training, many police officers made predictions that were as accurate as those provided by a computerized geographic profiling system" (Bennell et al., 2007, p.128). In the pretraining phase of the study, police officers in the control and circle groups (but not the decay group) made predictions that did not differ in accuracy from

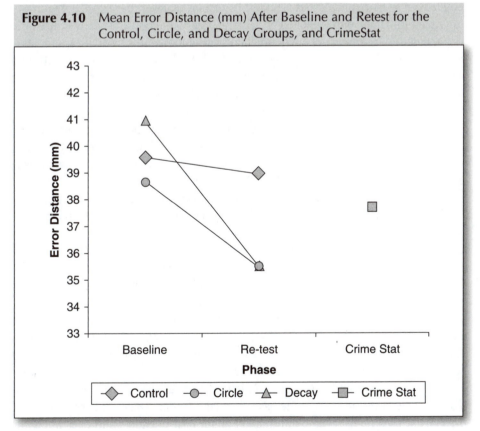

Figure 4.10 Mean Error Distance (mm) After Baseline and Retest for the Control, Circle, and Decay Groups, and CrimeStat

Source: Bennell, C., Snook, B., Taylor, P. J., Corey, S., & Keyton, J. (2007).

the predictions of CrimeStat, suggesting that officers may have available implicit knowledge, experience, and heuristics that they apply in estimating crime locations. The data did indicate, however, that there were significant individual differences in the use of heuristics before training. Some of the officers were either unaware of heuristics that allow others to make accurate predictions, or they favored a different, inappropriate heuristic. However, brief training concerning the circle or decay heuristic (as done in the Snook et al. studies) was sufficient to increase the officers' predictive accuracy. Both groups trained with circle and decay heuristics did better on average with their predictions than the computerized system CrimeStat did. The effect of additional information involving the number of offenses or more topographical features to the maps did not support the argument that geographic profiling needs more information to increase accuracy. Police officers apparently did not need the number of crimes or topographical details to improve their predictions of the base of operations of serial burglars.

COMPUTER MODELS TRY TO
GET BETTER THROUGH BAYESIAN METHODS

The above-described research seriously questions the theoretical and practical applications of computer-driven estimations of home locations of offenders. As pointed out by Block and Bernasco (2009), "The tools that were developed, for journey-to-crime estimation, only exploited the distance decay function and barely utilized the rich theoretical framework of environmental criminology, routine activities, and rational choice on which it was allegedly based" (p. 188). Levine (2009) agrees with this assessment. The computer software models are mathematical, not geographic. As a consequence, the tools downplayed environmental characteristics and opportunities in the community, and as Snook, Bennell, and their colleagues demonstrated, the computer models came up short. Overall, the accuracy of the computer programs was disappointing. "They were often less accurate than simpler techniques, such as the centre of minimum distance, and did not outperform students and police officers who visually applied one or two heuristic rules" (Block & Bernasco, 2009, p. 188).

Levine (2000) reported similar shortcomings of geographic computer models in his study of 50 serial offenders in Baltimore County, Maryland. He found that relying exclusively on the distance decay function while ignoring the many other factors resulted in a high degree of error (Levine, 2009). Likewise, Paulsen (2006) conducted an analysis of 247 serial offenders from Baltimore County by using a number of different measures, including four different software packages. He found that the simpler measures, such as the circle heuristic, were more accurate than the more complex computer packages.

In order to correct the shortcomings of the computer models, researchers have begun to incorporate the empirical Bayes method (also called the Bayesian method) into their procedures and algorithms. The method not only uses the distance of the journey to crime, but also incorporates previous knowledge of offenders (where previous offenders lived) and destinations (where they offended) and the links between them to predict the home or home base of serial offenders (Block & Bernasco, 2009). In short, it uses more specific information about past offenders and does not allow distance to completely dictate the outcome of the prediction.

For example, CrimeStat 3.1's new empirical Bayes journey-to-crime estimation method calculates three risk surfaces on the map display. The first risk surface is generated by the regular journey-to-crime and distance decay method. The second risk surface corresponds to zones where previous offenders lived, independent of where they committed their crimes. The third risk surface is based on the "origin-destination zone matrix" (Block & Bernasco, 2009, p. 190). The method selects the zones where the current crime series (the crimes being investigated) occurred and then calculates for each zone the probability that an offender lives within that zone The procedure not only automatically accounts for the distances between two zones, but also considers travel time, specific attractions, and barriers that may impede or facilitate criminal travel between the two zones. For example, the costs involved in travel may be a consideration. Some areas are controlled by gangs and may be avoided by an offender. An offender who owns a vehicle has much more flexibility than one who is constrained by travel on foot or by public transportation (Levine, 2009). On the other hand, parking limitations may restrict use of vehicles, and in certain locations travel by bicycle may be a preferred mode of transportation for some offenders.

Block and Bernasco (2009) were able to demonstrate that, based on their study of 62 burglars, the homes of serial burglars were more accurately estimated with the new Bayesian method compared to the traditional distance decay method. As might be expected, the estimates were more successful for marauders than for commuters.

Michael Leitner and Josh Kent (2009) expand the new Bayesian journey-to-crime computer model to include multiple types of crime committed by a single offender. The research literature continually finds that serial offenders usually commit multiple types of crime. For example, the database from Baltimore County, Maryland, consists of 41,979 solved crimes, including 3,484 crime series with three or more incidents apiece. Approximately 73% of the crime series involve multiple types of crime, such as two burglaries, three motor vehicle thefts, and one arson. The other 27% of the crime series include offenses of the same crime type, such as six robberies or eight burglaries. A vast majority of the research on geographic profiling has focused on one type of crime in the series, such as serial murder or rape. The Leitner and Kent study used 850 multiple crime–type series from the Baltimore County database. The results showed that most geographic profiles were significantly more accurate and precise when the offenses from different crime types are integrated in the same series, as compared with crime series with only one type. The results challenge the traditional way of creating geographic profiles. One of the main reasons for the increase in accuracy and precision is that a higher number of marauder-type serial offenders were found among the multiple crime–type series. The researchers recommend that law enforcement agencies reevaluate their standard practice of constructing geographic profiles with only the same-type crime series, provided, of course, all the cases were linked to a single offender.

Summary and Conclusions

Geographic profiling—which has everything to do with identifying spatial patterns in crime—has its U.S. origins in the ecological school of criminology, which emerged at the beginning of the 20th century in opposition to the more psychological approaches that centered crime on deficiencies within the individual. The ecological school hoped to draw attention to the fact that some geographic areas were more susceptible to criminal activity than others. Pinpointing these areas on elaborately detailed maps captured the interest of many criminologists during that time period. In addition, some of them partnered with social service agencies to offer services to the residents of crime-prone communities.

These early approaches to preventing crime led to the more sophisticated crime mapping and geographic profiling of today. Although these terms are often used interchangeably, we have adopted a subtle difference in this chapter. Contemporary crime mapping is helped by the availability of elaborate computerized systems that pinpoint crime occurrences in specific geographic areas. Law enforcement agencies can identify hot spots or hot places of crime and can allocate their resources accordingly. Geographic profiling tries to identify specific offenders based on their patterns of routine activities as well as the active choices they make in committing their crimes. Together, routine activities and rational choice theories emphasize that offenders make deliberate decisions regarding criminal activity, decisions that are often influenced by their awareness of the environment around them and the activities of their potential victims.

Geographic profiling is used particularly when series of crimes are occurring—burglaries, car thefts, arsons, rapes, or murders, for example—but some of its advocates consider it valuable even when investigators seek to solve a single crime. Although it was originally designed to help investigations of murder, rape, and arson, it is now being used for serial bombings, bank robbery, and child abductions (Guerette, 2002). Geoprofilers draw together their knowledge of crime patterns and their awareness about the research in this area (e.g., research on distance decay, centrality, or buffer zones).

Geographic profiling still has a way to go before it establishes its predictive validity across a variety of serial offenses, however. As we reviewed in this chapter, its accuracy depends upon certain assumptions being met, including, for example, that a series of crimes are linked to one offender and that there is a span of time between incidents. Equally important, research on many of the widely available and expensive computerized systems indicates that they may be no more accurate than the predictions of law enforcement officers and even students trained in using simple heuristics to hone in on the area of operations of given offenders. Programs based on Bayesian models appear to have some promise, however.

KEY CONCEPTS

Buffer zone

Centrality

Cognitive scripts

Commuter

Crime pattern theory

CrimeStat

Distance decay

Dragnet

Environmental (ecological) criminology

Error distance

Geographic mapping

Geographic profiling

Geoprofiler

Hunter

Marauder

Mental maps

Poacher

Predictive policing

Profile accuracy

Rational choice theory

Rigel and Rigel Analyst

Routine activity theory

Top profile area

Trapper

Troller

5

Profiling Applied to Specific Crimes

The crime scene and geographic profiling discussed in Chapters 3 and 4 typically occur when heinous or serious crimes, especially a series of such crimes, pose a challenge to the law enforcement community. Serial rapists, bombers, and killers often stymie police, as we saw in earlier chapters. It took at least 20 years to capture the Green River Killer in the Seattle area; nearly 20 years to capture Theodore Kaczynski, alias the Unabomber; and 6 years to capture the Railway Rapist. Serial rapes, a string of arsons or burglaries, or a child abduction can terrify a community and tax the resources of police. These crimes tend to draw the most profiling requests. When profilers or behavioral analysts are brought in to assist in the investigations, their work is more valuable if it is based on scientific data obtained from the study of various crimes—this point was made in earlier chapters, but it is central to the material in the present chapter. Here we will focus on specific offenses and discuss what criminologists have learned about the individuals who commit them as well as—in some cases—the victims themselves.

For each crime covered in the chapter, we will include brief background information defining the crime and its prevalence; research evidence on victimization, when available; and characteristics of offenders, again if available. For some offenses, we will cover various typologies that have been offered by researchers and clinicians. In summarizing this information, we emphasize that we are not offering definitive profiles of victims or offenders. Rather, the demographic and behavioral characteristics covered in the chapter—as well as the typologies—are intended to suggest leads, not to establish criteria. You will learn, for example, that nonfamily child abductors *tend to* be males under 40. While it is understandable that investigators, armed with this information, would focus on these demographics, it would be unwise to overlook a 45-year-old woman involved in a previous abduction attempt as a possible suspect.

Profiling in Child Abduction Cases

Etan Patz, Adam Walsh, JonBenet Ramsey, Madeleine McCann, Caylee Anthony, Jaycee Dugard, Elizabeth Smart, Amber Hagerman, Leiby Kletzky—if there is a public repository of the names of children who were allegedly abducted, the above are surely included. Some survived their abductions and are now adults; others were never found; and still others were found dead, but the perpetrators were never discovered and punished. In some cases, it is not certain that an abduction actually occurred. According to the National Center for Missing and Exploited Children (NCMEC), more than 200,000 children are abducted by family members every year (cited in A.-J. Douglas, 2011). An additional 58,000 are abducted by nonrelatives, primarily for sexual motives. It should be mentioned that registered child sexual offenders are rarely the problem, accounting for less than 1% of the child abduction cases in 2010 (A.-J. Douglas, 2011).

Nevertheless, we must be cautious about the above figures. It is difficult to obtain accurate information on child abduction for a number of reasons (Boudreaux, Lord, & Etter, 2000). Highly publicized stranger abductions often result in a social climate of heightened concerns and tend to yield an overestimation of the incidence rates. In addition, national statistics often combine many different types of abductions due to a wide range of definitions (e.g., family and nonfamily abductions, preteen and teenager abductions, kidnappings versus abductions). David Finkelhor and his associates (Finkelhor, Hotaling, & Sedlack, 1992) suggest there are two important definitions at work when people think of child abductions: the legal definition and the popular-media definition of abduction, which they call the **stereotypical definition.** According to the **legal definition,** a person is guilty of child abduction (or kidnapping) if he or she unlawfully leads, takes, entices, or detains a child under a specified age with intent to keep or conceal the child from its parent, guardian, or other person having lawful custody (Finkelhor et al., 1992). Variants of this definition are used in federal statutes and the laws of most states. Note that this definition can cover a very broad range of situations, including a child taken by a non-custodial parent or a 14-year-old girl persuaded to accompany her 20-year-old boyfriend to Texas.

On the other hand, the popular stereotype draws its imagery from nationally notorious and tragic cases of abduction (Finkelhor et al., 1992) or presumed abduction. These are cases in which the victim is kept for long periods of time or is killed soon after the abduction. Two-year-old Caylee Anthony was presumed to be abducted; her body was ultimately found, her mother was acquitted in her death, and we may never know whether the child was indeed abducted and how she died. Jaycee Dugard was abducted at the age of 11, was held for 18 years by her captors until their arrest, and has recently written a book about her experiences. Leiby Kletzky was walking home from a neighborhood day camp when he was abducted and killed, allegedly by Levi Aron, whose lawyers stated in October 2011 that they intend to present an insanity defense. These cases terrify us, but it is important to remember that they are extremely rare.

The popular stereotype of abduction refers to severe kinds of cases where strangers are the offenders and

(a) the child was gone overnight, or (b) the child was transported a distance of 50 miles or more from the point of abduction, or (c) the child was killed, or (d) the child was ransomed, or (e) the perpetrator evidenced an intent to keep the child permanently. (Finkelhor et al., 1992, p. 228)

Regardless of whether the case meets the legal or stereotypical definition, it is not unusual for law enforcement investigators to begin questioning parents or caretakers of the child as suspects (Canning, Hilts, & Muirhead, 2011). After all, the United States has the fourth-highest rate of child murder by a parent among 21 developed countries (Briggs & Cutright, 1994). Furthermore, "because most of the cases occur in and around the home or in other private locations, there are generally no identifiable witnesses, outside of family members" (Canning et al., 2011, p. 794).

For the remainder of this section, we will concentrate on cases that follow the definition of stereotypical abductions, as these are the incidents in which investigators most often seek the advice of profilers. We will also restrict this section to completed abductions rather than attempts.

THE NUMBERS

In an attempt to get some handle on the incidence of child abductions in the United States, Finkelhor et al. (1992), using multiple prevalence measures, found that 200 to 300 cases met the criteria for the stereotypical abduction (SA) of children in 1988. In a second study conducted in 1999, Finkelhor, Hammer, and Sedlak (2002) estimated that 115 children were the victims of SAs that year. The researchers speculated that the difference in numbers was primarily due to differing methodologies and measures used in the two studies. It could also be a reflection of 10 years' difference—the public being more attuned to child abduction, and early warning systems like the popular **AMBER Alert** being in place, despite the fact that researchers have questioned its effectiveness (e.g., Griffin & Miller, 2008; Sicafuse & Miller, 2010), as we will discuss below.

The number 115 is consistent with the FBI estimates, however, and seems to be more reflective of reality. Because of the seriousness and duration of child abductions, federal law enforcement is typically involved, putting into action its **Child Abduction Rapid Deployment (CARD) teams** (see Focus 5.1). Although 115 is a relatively small number (slightly over two per state), the nature of the crimes has traumatizing effects on communities (Finkelhor et al., 1992). In addition, these abductions received considerable extended publicity and have been highly influential in molding public opinion about the risk and frequency of stranger abduction homicides.

Focus 5.1

CARD Teams

Child Abduction Rapid Deployment Teams (CARDs)—also referred to as Child Abduction Response Teams (CARTs)—are becoming commonplace in the law enforcement community. Team members and prospective members can be a variety of professionals within a community that may be involved in the immediate response to a missing, abducted, or endangered child incident. This would include police officers, social service workers, teachers, day care providers, or recreation officials, to name but a few. They are typically trained in programs sponsored by the U.S. Department of Justice and offered by police academies or on college campuses.

The training curriculum includes general information—e.g., the prevalence and forms of child abduction—and strategies tailored to the specific needs of team members. It includes information about investigative strategies, legal issues that may arise, and pointers on dealing with the media in the unfortunate event that an abduction occurs. The trainees receive information on where to obtain resources, and they often hear from families of murdered and/or abducted children to gain a victim's perspective. The training also often includes practice with a mock incident.

It should be emphasized that stereotypical child abductions by strangers are rare, and the great majority of trainees never have to apply what they have learned to an actual situation. The FBI first deployed its CARD teams in March 2006, and by December 2007, there were 26 deployments of those CARD teams in 18 states (Office of the Inspector General, 2009). In 11 deployments of the teams (42%), the missing children were recovered alive. In the 13 other deployments (50%), the missing children were recovered dead, and in the remaining 2 deployments (8%), the children remained missing. The ages of the missing children ranged from infants (as young as 4 days old) to 17 years.

The FBI's CARD teams consist of special agents with experience in conducting investigations of child abductions in multi-jurisdictional settings. Once deployed, CARD team members travel to the crime scene and serve as technical consultants to the law enforcement agency leading the search for the missing child. The intention of the CARD teams is not to take over the investigation but to provide assistance to the law enforcement agencies involved in the investigation.

The FBI divides its investigation of child abductions into three classifications: child abduction without ransom (nonparental abduction), international parental kidnapping, and domestic parental kidnapping. Child abduction cases with ransom demands are handled by the National Violent Crimes Unit. The following table illustrates the number of cases opened by the FBI from FY 2000 through 2007. It is clear that in a majority of these cases, the FBI's CARD teams were not deployed.

FBI Cases Opened on Child Abductions and Kidnapping

Investigative Type	FY 2000	FY 2001	FY 2002	FY 2003	FY 2004	FY 2005	FY 2006	FY 2007	Total
Child Abduction—No Ransom	106	94	102	90	79	87	87	77	722

Investigative Type	FY 2000	FY 2001	FY 2002	FY 2003	FY 2004	FY 2005	FY 2006	FY 2007	Total
Domestic Parental Kidnapping	139	118	100	81	66	57	44	48	653
International Parental Kidnapping	126	84	73	83	87	65	72	58	648
Total	371	296	275	254	232	209	203	183	2,023

Table Source: Office of the Inspector General (2009).

It is noteworthy that only 10% of the stereotypical abductions lasted 24 hours or more. However, in 40% of all stereotypical abductions, the victims were killed, and in another 4%, the victims were still missing (Finkelhor et al., 2002). These data suggest that there is approximately 1 child abduction murder for every 10,000 reports of a missing child (Hanfland, Keppel, & Weis, 1997). When the child is killed, it is usually within the first 24 hours after abduction (Lord, Boudreaux, & Lanning, 2001), and some statistics indicate that the first 3 hours are the most critical (Hanfland et al., 1997). The 24-hour time limit is repeated incessantly in popular TV programs. However, it is usually interpreted to mean that, when a child is abducted, death *will* occur within 24 hours if he or she is not found; the correct interpretation is that, *if* the child is killed, the killing will likely occur within 24 hours.

Another 32% of stereotypically abducted victims received injuries that required medical attention. If there is any comfort to parents, this suggests that two thirds of serious child abductions by strangers result in a return of the child without serious physical injury.

As stated above, some research suggests that the first 3 hours after the abduction are crucial, as the majority of abducted children (74%) *who are murdered* are dead within that time period (Hanfland et al., 1997). More shockingly, in 44% of the cases, the victims are dead within the first hour after abduction (Hanfland et al., 1997). Unfortunately, nearly half are killed before they are reported missing. In a 2011 child abduction case in Brooklyn, New York, part of an 8-year-old child's body was found in the alleged abductor's apartment 2 days after the child disappeared.

AMBER ALERT

Family members and the media often complain about the slowness of the response of law enforcement when the abduction of a child occurs. In an effort to speed up that response, AMBER Alert was created. The AMBER Alert system was inspired by the brutal abduction-murder of 9-year-old Amber Hagerman in Arlington, Texas, in 1996.

The killer has never been found. Because there were witnesses to the abduction, some believed that Amber could have been rescued had the information about her abduction been quickly publicized (Griffin & Miller, 2008). AMBER Alert is premised on the belief that more rapid official response is necessary to save an abducted child's life. But, as noted by Griffin and Miller (2008), "Slow response does not necessarily lead to death; rather, in the worst cases, the perpetrator's inclination to kill generally ensures that any response will be too slow" (p. 165). They further write, "Victims die quickly in such cases because the offenders execute their crimes with cruel rapidity, preventing stereo-typical child abduction-murders from being amenable to any simple solution" (p. 165). Still, AMBER Alert provides some comfort (and some hope) for family members that the missing child is being publicized, and someone may come forward to provide help-ful information. According to the U.S. Department of Justice (2008), AMBER Alert has helped rescue hundreds of children from abductors, and the system continues to have the near-unanimous support of the public, policy makers, and law enforcement (Sicafuse & Miller, 2010). The Department of Justice further asserted that the AMBER Alert system has become part of America's public safety landscape. All 50 states now have statewide AMBER Alert systems.

The AMBER Alert system was inspired by and designed for stranger abductions in which a child is taken for the purposes of serious harm and/or sexual exploitation. An AMBER Alert can be activated when an investigating law enforcement agency has rea-sonable cause to believe that (1) an abduction of a child (someone under the age of 18) has occurred, and (2) the child is believed to be in danger of serious bodily harm or death. However, some writers believe that the system has been commonly used for reporting "abductions" by non-custodial parents or other family members that gener-ally do not meet the criteria for AMBER Alerts (Griffin & Miller, 2008; Griffin, Miller, Hoppe, Rebideaux, & Hammack, 2007).

The precise number of children abducted by strangers (stereotypical abductors) each year is difficult to determine, and, to date, there is very little research on the topic. Available data suggest that roughly one quarter are abducted by nonfamily members, but the data often include boyfriends, ex-boyfriends, and close acquaintances. In a study of 275 AMBER Alerts, Griffin et al. (2007) reported that about 20% involved abductions by strangers or acquaintances. Recent data by the National Center for Missing & Exploited Children (2010) indicate that about 29% of the total AMBER Alert cases involved nonfamily members, including boyfriends and ex-boyfriends.

During 2009, nine children involved in AMBER Alert cases were recovered deceased (National Center for Missing & Exploited Children, 2010). Four of the cases involved family abductors, and the identity of the abductors in the remaining cases could not be determined. The children could have been abducted by family members, by a stranger, or they might have wandered off on their own. One child whose disappearance was publicized via AMBER Alert, for instance, was discovered drowned in a lake near the child's home. It was unclear whether this was an abduction or a case of a young child wandering off from supervision. These data do indicate, however, that in some cases, even family abductions may pose a serious danger to the child. For example, in one AMBER case, a 3-year-old girl was thrown over a bridge by her uncle. On the other hand, non-custodial parents are very rarely motivated by a desire to harm the child

(Griffin et al., 2007). But there are exceptions even in these cases. In 2003, local police in Concord, New Hampshire, notified the FBI of a case of child abduction by a father who kidnapped his two children from his estranged wife during a visitation (Office of the Inspector General, 2009). He later murdered them.

In summary, although the AMBER Alert system is not a perfect one, it has garnered support from the public and the law enforcement community and will likely be continued. Criminology and public policy researchers have studied it from various angles and have recommended possible improvements. For example, Gier, Kreiner, and Hudnell (2012) have suggested that the alerts may be more effective, resulting in fewer false sightings, if more than one photograph of a missing child is displayed to the public. Typically, the AMBER Alert photos depict smiling images, often from school photographs. The children we see on milk cartons, flyers, the Internet, and television broadcasts are usually smiling, well-groomed, and happy. A child who has been abducted, particularly by a stranger, will not have this appearance.

In a study involving three complex experiments, Gier and her colleagues (2012) showed participants a mock AMBER Alert created by a university television station, resembling the Alerts often seen on television. Then, participants viewed a notebook of photos that included these "missing" children along with other children.

Both "clean" (i.e., smiling and happy) and "dirty" (that is, disheveled, bruised, and sad) depictions were employed. Participants were significantly better at recognizing the children when they were depicted in a similar fashion as in the original mock alert. The Gier et al. research was complex, and the researchers themselves noted that many questions remain about facial recognition, accuracy of recall, and characteristics of a witness in a child abduction case. However, it appears that at the least, law enforcement agencies and organizations dedicated to finding missing children should encourage parents and caretakers to have on hand photographs that depict their children in both well-groomed and disheveled states.

THE VICTIMS

Most of the child victims of stranger abductions are victims of opportunity, and in most cases the abductor was not actively looking for a particular child at the time of the abduction. Hanfland et al. (1997) describe these abductors as "'killers-in-waiting'—given the right opportunity coupled with an available child, they are more likely to spring into action, changing from a chronic hunter to an occasional predator to an episodic killer" (p. 42). Furthermore, usually the victim is not selected because of some physical characteristic such as hair color, body type, or race/ethnicity. The gender and age of the child, however, are very important.

Children aged 6 to 14 are most likely to be abducted by strangers for sexual gratification (Lord et al., 2001). Preschoolers are rarely targeted. School-age females are at least 3 times more likely to be abducted and murdered than school-age males. The average age of the female child abducted is slightly over 11 years of age (Hanfland et al., 1997). Abductors find them physically mature enough to be sexually desirable and vulnerable enough to be easily controlled and exploited.

Most abductions of elementary school children occur in or around the victim's home, with the vast majority of victims abducted within a quarter mile of their residence. Middle school children tend to be abducted from more distant locations, such as playgrounds, shopping malls, and other areas of recreation. Children are rarely abducted from school grounds (Hanfland et al. 1997; Lord et al., 2001).

According to Lord et al. (2001), the bodies of elementary school children generally are found within a mile of the abduction site. The bodies of older children (middle school) are usually found within 5 miles of the abduction site. The disposal site is usually very close to the murder site, so a thorough search in the area is critical for identifying forensic evidence. Offenders are usually very familiar with their disposal sites, suggesting that the sites are near their residence or place of work. Generally, they do try to hide the bodies at the disposal site, although they are rarely buried (Hanfland et al., 1997). In most cases, the offender disposes of the body as quickly as possible, for fear of detection. However, 15% keep the body longer than necessary to dispose of it, but they keep it in convenient and accessible places where it can be concealed or moved quickly. In most of these cases, the killer keeps the body in his residence. In these child murder cases, 69% kept the body in their possession for less than 24 hours. Those killers who kept the body longer often treated the body as a trophy or to stimulate sexual fantasies.

The investigative implications of these spatial relationships are that if the place of initial contact is not identified, it is likely to be more difficult to find the body of the child. In addition, about 25% of the abductor killers return, at some point, to the disposal site, and another 20% leave town. Many return to the disposal site within 3 days after the murder for a variety of reasons (e.g., to be sure incriminating evidence was not left behind, to see if there is any indication of discovery), unless they know the body has been found (Hanfland et al., 1997).

THE OFFENDERS

Almost all children kidnapped by strangers are taken by men (98%), and about two thirds of stranger abductions involve female children. The average age of killers of abducted children is 27 years old, and the vast majority are under 30 (Hanfland et al., 1997). Only 10% are older than 40. They are predominantly unmarried (85%), and half of them (51%) either live alone or with their parents (Hanfland et al., 1997). They usually display poor social skills, have marginal work habits, and have very few friends (Lord et al., 2001). Most have less than a high school education (Beyer & Beasley, 2003). Half are unemployed, and those that are employed work in unskilled or semi-skilled labor occupations. "They are not integrated, personally or socially, into the kinds of relationships or activities that produce or sustain effective self or social controls" (Hanfland et al., 1997, p. 25). They move frequently and do not stay anywhere very long. Consequently, they rarely have ties to the local community (Beyer & Beasley, 2003). Their inability to interact effectively with others may persuade them to obtain victims by abduction, usually forcibly. They are often described by others as "strange," and alcohol and drug problems are frequent. These individuals often reside (at least temporarily), work in, or frequent the area where they commit their crimes. About two thirds of stereotypical abductors have prior arrests for violent crimes, most of them for violent sexual crimes (rape or sexual assault) against children. A large number of them are likely to be found in the active files of law enforcement or the correctional system.

Sixty-seven percent of the child abduction killers follow the same MOs in each of their crimes (Hanfland et al., 1997).

> These findings regarding the similarity of M.O.s across the great majority of crimes committed by child abduction killers show that there is more consistency in the M.O.s of these types of killers than expected and as compared to other types of murderers. (p. 38)

Recall that in our brief discussion of serial murder in Chapter 2, we noted that the MO frequently changes, perhaps deliberately to confound investigators or because the offender is seeking more challenge. Murderers of abducted children tend to be more consistent in their behavior.

Law enforcement usually is under heavy pressure to solve horrific abductions, and many states have special teams to react quickly to a serious missing child report. As mentioned above, and highlighted in Focus 5.1, the FBI has Child Abduction Rapid Deployment teams in their regional field offices across the nation. Many states have similar teams. CARD teams of 4 to 6 experienced personnel are deployed to provide on-the-ground investigative, technical, and resource assistance to state and local law enforcement. The disappearance in 2009 of 10-year-old Lindsey Baum as she walked home from a friend's house in the small town of McCleary, Washington, prompted calls for assistance from the FBI's CARD team. The team brought in profilers to analyze who the perpetrator might be, and they also studied Lindsey's behavior and personality for clues (Thomas, Jones, & Gerstein, 2010). Unfortunately, to date, Lindsey has not been found. In 2009, FBI CARD teams were deployed in 7 AMBER Alert cases, compared to 55 times in 2006 (National Center for Missing & Exploited Children, 2010). At this writing, it is unknown to what extent the CARD teams have been helpful in solving the more serious cases of abducted children.

Profiling in Serial Murder Cases

THE NUMBERS

The U.S. Department of Justice estimated that there were about 35 to 40 serial murderers active at any time in the United States during the 1970s and the 1980s (cited in P. Jenkins, 1988). Hickey (2010) offers a similar and more recent estimate of the number of active and unapprehended serial murderers. Realistically, though, there are no accurate data on the prevalence and number of serial murderers active at any one time in the United States or internationally (Brantley & Kosky, 2005), only estimates.

It is equally difficult to gauge the annual number of serial murder *victims*. Many serial offenders are adept at hiding their victims. Gary Ridgway, the Green River Killer, confessed to killing 45 women, and he skillfully hid their bodies over many

Photo 5.1: Green River Killer Gary Ridgway, right, talks with his attorney, Mark Prothero, during Ridgway's February 2011 arraignment on charges of murder in the 1982 death of one of his victims, Rebecca Marrero.

years. (See Photo 5.1 of Ridgway consulting with his attorney.) The long-haul truck driver Keith Hunter Jesperson, the Happy Face Killer described in the previous chapter, was convicted of killing eight women, but he claimed to have killed 160 persons in multiple states. He later recanted this seemingly preposterous assertion, but it is not unlikely that he had additional victims. In one case of a serial murder described by Wolf and Lavezzi (2007), the offender hid the bodies of eight women in the house inhabited by his parents and sisters. Some of the bodies were found in the crawl space for the basement, and others were found comingled in the attic. We will provide examples of other serial killers with multiple victims in the chapter.

THE VICTIMS

Many serial killers select victims who apparently are not missed by others or, if missed, they are given up as runaways or adults who have left on their own volition. An examination of the victim selection of known serial murderers will reveal that killers prefer the group of people offering easy access, transience, and the likelihood of disappearing without seeming to cause much alarm or concern. Victims are often prostitutes (especially streetwalkers), street runaways, young male drifters, and itinerant farm workers. However, even a killer who focuses on sex workers will not necessarily choose victims from only that group. Family members of victims of the serial killer Arthur Shawcross, who killed in and around Rochester, New York, in the late 1980s, were devastated to learn that police, the media, and the public assumed that their sisters, daughters, or nieces were prostitutes. Some of these victims were; others were not.

Young women on or near a university or college campus or the elderly and solitary poor appear to be the victims next preferred. Young victims are more likely to be reported missing, however. The strongest determining factor in victim selection for each of these groups—the factor that victims seem to have in common—is their vulnerability or easy availability. Serial murderers rarely break in and kill strangers in their homes, for example, despite media and entertainment portrayals. It should be pointed out, however, that although serial killers begin their murderous careers by selecting highly vulnerable victims, they may, as their killings continue, gain significantly more confidence in their ability to abduct and kill more challenging victims—thus, the previously made observation that changes in MO are not unusual.

Unlike the victims of *single* murderers—who are most often family, friends, and acquaintances—the victims of *serial* murderers are most often strangers, and there is no apparent consensual relationship between the offender and the victim (Kraemer, Lord, & Heilbrun, 2004), although even here there are exceptions. Many of the victims of Robert Pickton were sex workers who willingly accompanied him to his farm; once there, they were killed and their bodies disposed of on or near his property. Nonetheless, although their initial relationship may have been consensual, they were still strangers. Godwin (2000) states that 90% of the victims in his study of serial killers were strangers to the killer. The lack of a preexisting relationship in serial murders makes identifying suspects especially difficult.

The preferred method of killing is often different for single-victim murderers and serial killers. Serial killers often prefer more hands-on killing through strangulation or beating with hands or feet, while single-victim offenders prefer firearms (Kraemer et al., 2004). However, the serial killer known as the Grim Sleeper used a gun, with ballistic evidence eventually linked to at least 10 homicides of women whose bodies were found on the streets of South Los Angeles over two decades. The alleged perpetrator, Lonnie Franklin Jr., was arrested in July 2010 and charged with the 10 murders. Over a year later, he was linked to six additional murders in the same geographical area (J. Rubin, 2011). The Grim Sleeper was so called because there appeared to be a 14-year hiatus between the two time periods when similar killings occurred (1985–1988 and 2002–2007). Nevertheless, investigators have expressed suspicion that his alleged killings continued during the 1990s (J. Rubin, 2011).

Single-victim offenders often kill out of anger or lack of control stemming from interpersonal conflict, whereas serial killers often murder in accordance with a carefully thought-out plan, which is frequently sexually predatory in nature. The murder is not typically precipitated by an interpersonal disagreement. Serial homicide offenders also exhibit more planning by moving the victim from one location to another, by using restraints, and by

Photo 5.2: Forensic scientists and an investigator examining a murder scene.

disposing of the body at a site with which the offender is very familiar. Single-victim murderers are much less skillful in disposing of the victim's body (Kraemer et al., 2004). (See Photo 5.2 depicting a single-murder crime scene.) All of the above crime scene factors are of use to law enforcement officers investigating homicides.

P. Jenkins (1993) contends that the current popular image of the serial murderer— a white male who kills for sexual motives—is an inaccurate one. He argues that lack of a *victimological perspective* encourages confusion and distorted information about serial murder. He suggests that our current knowledge about serial murderers is strongly influenced by two factors: availability of the victims and the attitudes of law enforcement agencies toward those victims. Rather than strictly focusing on individual and personality attributes of the offender, he believes we should also examine the *social opportunity* to kill. In other words, what we know about serial murder may be strongly influenced by the nature and type of the potential victims.

To illustrate, Jenkins (1993) cites the case of Calvin Jackson, who was arrested in 1974 for murder committed in a New York apartment building. Actually, Jackson was a serial murderer, but none of his victims led the police to suspect a serial killer. Jackson's killings took place in a single-occupancy hotel where the guests were poor, socially isolated, largely forgotten, and mostly elderly. Time after time, the police were called to the hotel to deal with cases of death or injury due to alcohol, drugs, or old age. When foul play was suspected, the police never considered it the work of a serial murderer, because the victims did not fit the stereotypic profile. Since there was no evidence of grotesque sexual abuse of the victim (the victim stereotype), there was little reason for the police to entertain the possibility of a serial murderer. Other serial murderers may set up situations where murders resemble drug-related homicides. Therefore, our current knowledge of serial murderers may be restricted to a certain category of offender.

THE OFFENDERS

Serial killers may come from all ethnic and racial groups, but accurate and comprehensive data are difficult to establish. However, the widespread belief that only whites are serial killers and blacks and other minorities never commit this type of crime is basically a myth (A. Walsh, 2005). Walsh found that approximately 22% of the serial killers in the United States have been black, and was able to document 90 black serial killers during the post–World War II era. Research on Latino and other minority serial killers is virtually nonexistent.

The number of victims that black killers admit to or are suspected of killing does not differ significantly from the number associated with white serial killers either. Jake Bird, for instance, was verified to have killed 44 victims, just 4 victims short of white killer Gary Ridgway (the Green River Killer), with a record-setting 48. Moreover, some of these killers' stories are equally chilling. Anthony Walsh (2005) describes the methods of black serial killer Maury Travis when he writes,

> Travis had a secret torture chamber in his basement, where police found bondage equipment, videotapes of his rape and torture sessions, and clippings relating to police investigations of his murder victims (mostly prostitutes and crack addicts). Travis hanged himself in jail after confessing to 17 murders. (p. 274)

We may have assumed that serial killings are perpetrated almost exclusively by whites because of how serial murder is identified and investigated. For example, law enforcement agencies may be less prone to investigate African American victims as casualties of serial murderers if they are found in a rundown apartment complex located in a poverty-stricken, crime-infested neighborhood. Under these circumstances, law enforcement officials are more likely to conclude that the victim is simply another fatality in the long stream of never-ending violence found in parts of inner cities. This point was made by Jenkins (1993) in the previous section.

Also, as Anthony Walsh (2005) has observed, the media tend to cover the sensational serial killings by whites but fail to cover in any detail those offenses committed by blacks and other minorities.

> The extensive media coverage of Bundy, Gacy, and Berkowitz cases have made these killers almost household names, but African Americans such as Watts, Johnson, Francois, and Wallace are practically unknown, despite having operated within the same general time framework (1980s and 1990s). (p. 274)

Similar disparity in media coverage of other crimes has occurred, often with reference to the race of the victim. In many communities, it is not unusual to see extensive coverage of the disappearance or murder of a white child and very little attention given to a similar tragedy involving a black victim.

Despite Walsh's assertions, it is important to remind readers of the difficult case of Wayne Williams, which represents a different problem—specifically, possibly attributing more blame because of one's race. Williams is a black man who was convicted in 1982 of murdering two men in their twenties. He is presently serving life terms in the Georgia prison system. More significantly, though, he was suspected in the deaths of over two dozen young black men and children between 1979 and 1982, collectively referred to as the Atlanta Child Murders. The case received very widespread media attention at the time and has stayed alive for many of Williams's supporters, including some of the families of his alleged victims who doubt that he was the killer.

After Williams was convicted of killing the two young men, investigators stopped looking for other killers and essentially closed the books on the Atlanta murders. Many supporters of Williams have maintained that he did not get a fair trial for the murders for which he was convicted, that DNA evidence was inconclusive, or that other exculpatory evidence was withheld from the defense, and that he has been unjustly accused of being a serial killer. There are suggestions, although thus far no evidence, that the Ku Klux Klan was involved in killing many of the black children. Supporters have also asserted that the killings did not stop with Williams's arrest. Williams has filed appeals on a number of grounds, all of which have either been denied or have not resulted in any change in the status of the case—Williams remains imprisoned. Nevertheless, the Atlanta child killings represent an unsettling chapter in crime history, one that has yet to see a satisfactory ending.

Criminal Background

Serial murderers are products of their genetic makeup, their upbringing, their social environment, and ultimately the developmental path that myriad circumstances influence. There is no *single* identifiable causal factor in the development of a serial killer. (See Focus 5.2 for conclusions from a recent FBI-sponsored symposium on this topic.) The motives of many serial killers appear to be based on some combination of psychological rewards such as control, domination, media attention, and personal or sexual excitement rather than financial gain. However, a very large number of serial murderers (75 to 80%) have a persistent history of criminal convictions, often involving a violent crime (Canter, Missen, & Hodge, 1996; Harbort & Mokros, 2001). Additional research (e.g., DeLisi & Scherer, 2006) indicates that serial killers have a persistent and extensive criminal history, with many of their crimes being predatory in nature, such as rape and residential burglary. Obviously, then, it is wise for investigators to mine the data banks of previous offenders.

Focus 5.2

The FBI Serial Murder Symposium

In an effort to develop a better understanding of serial murder, the FBI Behavioral Analysis Unit 2 (BAU-2) organized a multidisciplinary symposium in San Antonio, Texas, for 5 days in late summer 2005. One hundred and thirty-five experts on serial murder from 10 different countries offered their views on the topic (see Morton & Hilts, 2005). This important symposium represents contemporary views of the law enforcement community on serial murder and is likely to influence significantly the manner in which profiles are prepared.

For a number of years, some criminologists have struggled with definitions of serial murder, mass murder, and spree murder, particularly the last. In an apparent attempt to settle this, the final report of the symposium defined **serial murder** as the unlawful killing of two or more victims by the same offender(s) in separate events, at different times. It is distinguished by a cooling-off period, a time period between the killings. **Mass murder** is the murder of three or more persons at a single location with no cooling-off period.

Interestingly, the symposium participants had difficulty with the definition of **spree murder**, which has been considered the killing of three or more individuals without any cooling-off period at two or more locations. Most observers would find this definition confusing, particularly if the locations are close to one another, such as might occur when a murderer kills people in more than one building on a college campus. Was this a mass murder or a spree murder? Consequently, the majority of participants at the symposium advocated dropping the designation of spree murder altogether. More importantly, they concluded that the designation does not actually provide any real benefit for use by law enforcement. One of the major reasons is that the characteristics involved in spree murder are largely indistinctive from mass murder, and most cases are indistinguishable.

With respect to serial killing, the experts further concluded the following:

- Predisposition to serial killing, much like other violent offenses, is biological, social, and psychological in nature, and it is not limited to any specific characteristic or trait.

- The development of a serial killer involves a combination of these factors, which exist together in a rare confluence in certain individuals. They have the appropriate biological predisposition, molded by their psychological makeup, which is present at a critical time in their social development.

- Although the majority of professionals thought there are no specific combinations of traits or characteristics shown to differentiate serial killers from other violent offenders, some experts did identify certain traits common to *some* serial killers. They include sensation seeking, a lack of remorse or guilt, impulsivity, the need for control, and predatory behavior. These characteristics are common features of psychopaths. Psychopaths who commit serial murder (and most do not) do not value human life and are extremely callous in their interactions with their victims. Furthermore, participants believed it was very important for law enforcement professionals to understand psychopathy and its relationship to serial murder. The crime scene behavior of psychopaths is likely to be distinct from other offenders.

- There is no generic template for a serial killer. Each serial offender is different from any other.

- Serial killers are driven by their own unique motives or reasons. Identifying motivations in the investigation of a crime is a standard procedure for most law enforcement agencies, and it is believed to narrow the potential suspect pool. Most homicides are committed by someone known to the victim. Serial murder, by contrast, involves strangers with no apparent relationship between the offender and victim, and motives can be difficult to identify. The killer may have multiple motives, and these may evolve throughout the murder series. The classification of motivations should be limited to observable behavior at the crime scene.

- An offender selects a victim based upon availability, vulnerability, and desirability. *Availability* refers to the lifestyle of the victim or circumstances in which the victim is involved. *Vulnerability* refers to the degree to which the victim is susceptible to attack by the offender. *Desirability* refers to the appeal of the victim to the offender; it may involve such victim characteristics as race, gender, ethnic background, age, occupation, or other specific features preferred by the offender.

- Serial killers themselves are *not* limited to any specific demographic group, such as gender, age, race, or religion.

- The majority of serial killers who are sexually motivated eroticized violence during development. For them, violence and sexual gratification are inexplicably intertwined in their psyche.

More research is needed to identify specific pathways of development that produce serial killers.

Many serial killers are especially drawn to committing murders that attract media interest, or send spine-chilling fear into a community. Sometimes, they commit atrocities that are incomprehensible to the public. At other times, they seem to "toy" with the media. Jesperson apparently became so irritated that his killings were not highly publicized that he began writing letters to the media, signing his letters with a smiley face. Serial killer Dennis Rader (discussed below) also sent letters to the police and newspapers in which he recommended a number of names for himself. The one that eventually stuck was BTK, an acronym for "bind, torture, and kill."

Most of the research and clinical data indicate that serial murderers rarely kill on the basis of some compulsion or irresistible urge. Rather, as discussed in earlier chapters, the murder appears to be more a result of opportunity and the random availability of a suitable victim, most probably during the offender's routine activities. In addition, it should not be assumed that serial killers are social misfits who have trouble fitting into the local community, such as is the case for child abductors. Serial killers often have families; are gainfully employed; and appear to be regular, even religious members of their communities. Many blend into the community well and are often overlooked by law enforcement investigators as potential suspects. Rader killed 10 victims in and around Wichita, Kansas. He was married for 33 years, had two children, and was a Boy Scout leader. He was a long-time and dedicated church member who had held elected office in his church council. He was employed as a local government official and served on several community boards. Robert Lee Yates Jr., who murdered 13 women, worked as a corrections officer in the state prison in Walla Walla, Washington, and was a highly decorated helicopter pilot during his 19 years of military service. Although the cognitive processing and values of serial murderers may be considered extremely aberrant when it comes to empathy, concern, and sensitivity for their victims, a vast majority of them fail to qualify as seriously mentally disordered in the traditional diagnostic categories. They probably would not be described as unusually "strange," although eccentricities are not uncommon.

As we learned in Chapter 4, most serial offenders commit their crimes within their geographic comfort zones, and there is sometimes a "buffer zone" in which they do not operate. However, the comfort zone can extend a few miles beyond their domicile. Serial killers do tend to find their victims, do their killing, and dispose of the bodies of their victims near their residence, place of work, or places of entertainment and recreation. However, as they become skillful and confident, they may abduct victims and kill outside their immediate comfort zones, although most do not. And rarely do they move from state to state for their activities. Those few who do continue their serial killings across state lines usually travel extensively, typically in their line of work. Examples would include itinerant workers, truck drivers, traveling salesmen, and military personnel (Morton & Hilts, 2005). Some experts believe that their extensive travel provides extended comfort zones for their killing activities.

Serial Killer Typologies

David Canter and Donna Youngs (2009) note that, when profiling serial murder cases, most experts and profilers rely on the motivational and psychopathological aspects they infer from information gathered at the crime scene. For example, James Fox and Jack Levin (1998, 2005) distinguish five types of motivation for serial murder: power, revenge, loyalty, profit, and terror. Likewise, R. M. Holmes and DeBurger (1988) propose a motivation-centered typology that has received some research attention. Because of its heavily psychological approach, we discuss it in some detail here.

As noted in Chapter 2, the term *typology* refers to a particular system for classifying personality or behavioral patterns. Usually, the typology is used to classify a wide assortment of behaviors into a more manageable set of brief descriptions. There are many problems with typologies, however, such as considerable overlap between categories. Rarely is one classification independent and separate from the others. Consequently, it is often difficult to place an offender "cleanly" into one category. In addition, some individuals can qualify for two or more classifications at once. For example, if the typology is based primarily on motive, the offender may demonstrate a combination of motives for the crime. Moreover, placing individuals into various categories is based on the questionable assumption that behavior is consistent across both time and place. Still, typologies are useful in highlighting the complexity of human behavior and the variety of motives and scripts.

Several typologies of serial killers have been proposed in recent years, but for illustrative purposes we will concentrate only on the R. M. Holmes and DeBurger (1985, 1988) and R. M. Holmes and Holmes (1998) classification, based on motive.

The Holmes-DeBurger Serial Killer Typology

R. M. Holmes and DeBurger divide serial killers into four main categories, some of which are further subdivided into additional groups. The main categories are the **visionary**, the **mission-oriented**, the **hedonistic**, and the **power/control** killers.

The *visionary* type is driven by forces or visions that demand that a particular group of people be destroyed, such as prostitutes, college students, gay men and women, or derelicts. The visionary killer often operates on what he believes to be directives from God or some other perceived higher authority. This type of killer is driven by delusions or hallucinations that compel him to kill, and he is usually very *disorganized* in his methods of killing. According to R. M. Holmes and DeBurger (1988), this serial killer is psychotic—which is atypical because serial killers are not usually mentally disordered—and suffers from a severe break with reality. He or she is probably the most difficult to understand for investigators and the public alike. The crime scene is chaotic and has an abundance of physical evidence, often including fingerprints and even the murder weapon (R. M. Holmes & Holmes, 1998). The visionary group may be further divided into subgroups, depending on who or what is advocating the killing. Two of the most common subgroups are the *demon mandated* and the *God mandated*.

The visionary offender will usually commit his crimes well within his comfort zone (near his residence, place of recreation, or workplace). Therefore, geographic profiling would seem to be a very useful tool in the detection of this offender. Unlike most serial killers, however, the visionary murderer has no ideal victim type (IVT). That is, there are rarely any common physical (hair color, sex, age, or race), occupational, or personality traits that connect the victims. In addition, the murder is usually spontaneous and characterized by very little planning, and the victim is simply in the wrong place at the wrong time—and of course belongs to the group the killer has vowed to destroy.

Compared with the visionary offender, the *mission-oriented* type determines *on his or her own* that there is a particular group of people who are undesirable and must be destroyed or eliminated. No voices or forces command the offender to do so. The victims of the mission-oriented type may be similar to the victims of the visionary, and they may also be members of a particular religious, racial, or minority group. This killer does not demonstrate any discernible, serious mental disorder. He or she generally functions on a daily basis without exhibiting observable psychologically aberrant behavior. "However, he acts on a self-imposed duty to rid the world of an unworthy class of people: prostitutes, Catholics, Jews, young Black males, or any other specific identifiable group" (R. M. Holmes & Holmes, 2009, p. 120). This type is *less disorganized* in his or her methods of killing compared to the visionary type, and has characteristics of both organized and disorganized behavior. In other words, he falls within the mixed classification, but more toward the disorganized pole.

The *hedonistic* type strives for pleasure and thrills, and perceives people as mere objects to use for one's own enjoyment. The hedonistic killer gains considerable pleasure from the act of murder itself. He is primarily motivated to induce pain or a terrified reaction from the victim. The pain and terror created, in combination with the murder itself, are highly stimulating and exciting for the killer. His method of killing is often more *organized* than that of the mission-oriented murderer, but still has a mixture of both organized and disorganized features.

According to R. M. Holmes and Holmes (1998), hedonistic killers may be divided into three subtypes based on the primary motive for the murder: lust, thrill, and comfort. The *lust* serial killer's primary motive is exclusively sex, even if the victim is already dead (an activity called necrophilia). "He kills for sex; it is a propelling element in the motivation to kill and in the enjoyment he receives from his activities" (R. M. Holmes & Holmes, 1998, p. 93). Furthermore, "The killer kills in ways that reflect both the fantasy and the manner in which the fantasy is to be satisfied" (p. 93). The lust killer is always seeking the IVT that is sexually appealing to him. Ted Bundy, for example, reported that the way a woman walked and talked was an important factor in his victim selection.

The *thrill* killer is primarily motivated to induce pain or a terrified reaction from the victim. Usually, the killer has no relationship with his victim, although he may have followed her for some time. Similar to the lust killer, the thrill murderer selects victims based on certain physical characteristics that feed into his fantasies.

The motive for the *creature-comfort* killer is to acquire activities (business interests) or objects (money) that provide a comfortable and luxurious lifestyle. The killer's victims presumably stand in the way of achieving this. "The comfort killer's main objective is to enjoy life and to be sufficiently in control of immediate circumstances so that 'the good life' can be attained" (R. M. Holmes & Holmes, 1998, p. 119). Moreover, "overt, blatant displays of fatal aggression are not characteristics of this type; most comfort-oriented murderers tend to kill quietly if the situation permits" (p. 119). For the comfort killer, the act of murder is incidental to the pursuit of material gain and a comfortable lifestyle. Presumably, comfort killers dispose of their victims when they have identified a potential new "mark." In many ways, comfort killers resemble the behavioral characteristics of a criminal psychopath. Some writers (S. T. Holmes, Hickey, & Holmes, 1991) have pointed out that female serial killers often fall into this category (e.g., women who kill a series of husbands or boyfriends, or those who appropriate the funds of elderly patients in their care, kill them, and move on to other victims).

The *power/control* type of killer endeavors to obtain satisfaction by having complete life-or-death control over the victim. Sexual components may or may not be present, but the primary motive is the total power and control over the helpless and often restrained victim. These killers tend to seek specific victims who appear especially vulnerable and easy to victimize, such as children. This type of serial killer will demonstrate *organized methods* throughout the murder.

R. M. Holmes and Holmes (1998, 2002, 2009) further developed the serial killer typology and provided a series of case examples to illustrate the types of killers. In their book *Profiling Violent Crimes: An Investigative Tool* (2009), they assert that the O/D dichotomy discussed in Chapter 2 "can be useful when the crimes involve sex as a primary motive. The offenders who commit such crimes as rape, sexual assault, mutilation, necrophilia, and picquerism are particularly amenable to categorization as organized nonsocial or disorganized asocial offenders" (p. 80). *Picquerism* refers to the very rare phenomenon—some even contend there is no such perversion—of obtaining sexual pleasure through repeated stabbing, cutting, or slicing the body of another person with a sharp object (Keppel, Weis, Brown, & Welch, 2005). Jack the Ripper is believed to have demonstrated this behavior as the primary motive in his murders. In one noteworthy court case that will be discussed in Chapter 9, a judge severely reprimanded a profiler who speculated that an offender displayed "picquerism" because the victim's body had numerous bite marks. The judge called the profiler a charlatan whose claims relied on a nonexistent phenomenon.

Typologies are fascinating, and they seem to help us make sense of something that is otherwise incomprehensible. However, as noted above, they are often overlapping and not mutually exclusive, and latching onto a typology can lead a profiler astray from helping investigators find the true perpetrator. Furthermore, a typology of motivations without empirical foundations usually provides little assistance in the process of profiling. Canter and Youngs (2009) contend that the motivation-based approach is fraught with problems, which often result in marginally useful or unsuccessful profiles of the offender. As Canter continually argues, one of the best approaches for the development of helpful profiles is to examine the offending style or dominant theme that can be found in the way the offender interacts with the victim and the role the offender assigns to that victim. In order to understand the killing, it is necessary to try to understand the chain of events that led up to the offender–victim interaction. For example, is there evidence that the victim was specifically targeted, or was the victim simply one of opportunity? If the victim was likely targeted, the profiler should try to discover the offender's selection criteria. Turvey (2002) points out the primary criterion could be one of location (indoor, outdoor, wooded paths, parking lots); occupation (prostitute, homeless and unemployed, college student, exotic dancer); vulnerability (young and naïve, intoxicated, distracted); physical characteristics (hair color or style, clothing, weight, height); or activity (jogging, hiking, shopping, driving). Turvey suggests that a reconstruction of the victim's lifestyle, habits, and routines may provide some insight into the offender's own lifestyle, habits, and routines. Perhaps even more important than selection criteria, however, is the manner in which the offender treated the victim before and after the victim's death.

ROLE OF THE VICTIM

As mentioned previously, profilers today are attentive to the role played by the victim in heinous crimes, and most particularly in how perpetrators treat their victims. We are not suggesting here that the victim plays an active role; rather, it is the role *assigned by the offender*. According to Canter and Youngs (2009), the serial killer may treat the victim in one of three ways: as an object, a vehicle, or a person. The researchers consider these to be general themes of a serial murder. Thus, we can refer to the **object theme,** the **vehicle theme,** or the **person theme.**

If a victim was considered an object, it will be apparent from examinations of the victim's body post mortem. In extreme forms of this theme, the body was destroyed through dismemberment and decapitation. The offender also may have severely dehumanized the victim, both while alive and after death. Dehumanization is a cognitive process where the offender reduces human beings to the level of nonhuman creatures or inanimate objects, especially by denying them individuality and a sense of dignity. The injuries to the victim are sometimes multiple and severe, involving various parts of the body. The offender sees the victim as an object without human qualities, to be explored and played with. In all aspects of the crime, there appears to be a complete lack of empathy.

The role of the victim as vehicle is most apparent in actions that are emotional attacks on or exploitations of the live victim—the victim is considered merely a vehicle for the expression of the offender's desires and anger. However, the victim also is seen as more than a body. Victims frequently carry special meanings to the offender by what they represent and signify in the offender's life history. Despite the association with previous experiences in the offender's life, he still may engage in cruel, direct exploitation through torture, the use of blindfolds, props, and specialized offending kits containing items he or she typically uses to carry out the crimes (Canter & Youngs, 2009). This attack is usually opportunistic or spontaneous in nature. Extreme forms of this theme result in obliterating attacks on the victim and his or her belongings, but these will fall just short of dehumanization of the victim that is found in murders that display the object theme.

Many violent offenders see the victim as a human. The role of the victim as a person is seen in offender actions that indicate attempts at some distorted form of intimacy and recognition that the victim is a person with an identity. Bite marks on the victim's body—as forms of attempting intimacy—are consistent with this interpretation, and they occur in 5% of murder cases (Canter & Wentink, 2004). By contrast, burn marks or punctures made with a weapon are consistent with the object theme (and possibly also the vehicle theme). Offenders who interact with their victims as persons often use reassuring language and display knowledge about the victims, such as where they live (Fritzon & Ridgway, 2001). Extreme variants of this theme are characterized by such things as facial disfigurement or other physical distortions, because the offender is making an effort to obscure the identity of the victim whom he recognizes as a human being.

The Canter three-theme model, as growing amounts of research continue, is soon apt to have subtypes, as all models of human behavior eventually do during their evolution. The model is important, because it is likely that one serial killer will adopt the same approach to all his victims. In other words, he will consider them all objects, or vehicles, or persons.

Profiling in Serial Rape Cases

THE NUMBERS

There were an estimated 84,767 forcible rapes reported to law enforcement in the United States in 2010 (Federal Bureau of Investigation, 2011b). In addition, the total arrests for rape that year were 15,586; arrestees were below the age of 18 in 2,198 of those cases. Unfortunately, neither the reported rape nor the arrest figures reflect the true incidence of rape or the number of rape offenders in the nation. Furthermore, through 2011, FBI rape data counted only cases in which the victims were female. In 2012, Attorney General Eric Holder announced that male victims would be included in rape statistics. This change is still in the implementation stage, however, and it is unclear whether these expanded statistics will be available before 2013.

It is estimated that between 64% and 96% of all rapes are not reported to criminal justice authorities (Fisher, Cullen, & Turner, 2000; Lisak, Gardinier, Nicksa, & Cote, 2010; Lisak & Miller, 2002). Furthermore, a majority of rape cases reported are never prosecuted for the rape (Lisak & Miller, 2002; M. P. Ross, 2000). This is especially the case for acquaintance rape.

These figures also fail to estimate the number of serial rapists who go undetected. In one of the very few studies designed to obtain a reasonable estimation of undetected, serial rapists in the general population, David Lisak and Paul Miller (2002) collected survey data from 1,882 college men attending an urban university. The participants, who were paid a nominal sum for their participation, were asked to complete a packet of questionnaires that included the Abuse-Perpetration Inventory (API; Lisak et al., 2000). Although sexually explicit language is used to describe particular acts in the API, the words "rape," "assault," "abuse," or "battery" are never mentioned.

Of the 1,882 men in the total sample, 120 (6.4%) met the criteria for having committed rape or attempted rape. Of these, 76 (63.3%) admitted to repeat rapes, either against multiple victims at different times or more than once against the same victim. The 76 serial rapists admitted to a total of 439 rapes, averaging 5.8 rapes each. Not only did they report committing a large number of rapes, but they also said they committed a large number of other interpersonal violent attacks, including battery, physical abuse, and/or sexual abuse of children. Overall, non-rapists committed a mean of 1.41 acts of violence, compared to a mean of 3.98 for single-act rapists and a mean of 13.75 for serial rapists. The serial rapists represented only 4% of the sample, but they were responsible for 28% of the violence.

Based on these limited data—which admittedly represent only one urban university—it could be estimated that the prevalence of undetected serial rapists in the male college population in the United States is approximately 4%. Obviously, much more research is needed, but the Lisak-Miller study is a good beginning. Its primary importance is its attempt to gauge the prevalence of undetected serial rapists, and it suggests that a majority of rapes in fact are part of a series of such offenses that are committed by one individual.

The Lisak-Miller study was recently replicated by McWhorter and colleagues (McWhorter, Stander, Merrill, Thomsen, & Milner, 2009). Their participants were 1,146 newly enlisted male Navy personnel. The researchers identified 144 (13%) men who had committed a sexual assault. Of this total, 103 (71%) reported committing more than one rape, with an average of 6.4 each—a result similar to that reported by Lisak and Miller (2002). Again, the results suggest that a vast majority of the rapes are committed by undetected serial rapists. In addition, the McWhorter et al. study demonstrates that a sizeable group of undetected serial rapists exists in other populations besides college males. Moreover, the study also discovered that there was a tendency for most serial rapists to use the same specialized method and select similar targets over the course of their offending. For example, some offenders consistently made certain the victim was intoxicated or drugged before the assault.

THE VICTIMS

It would be misleading to make statements about the victims of rapists, or serial rapists, because generalizations are unwarranted. Rape victims (many prefer to call them survivors) can be found in any social class, occupation, race, age range, geographical location, and so forth. Serial rapists, like serial murderers, sometimes have cues for finding victims, but these cues are vastly different and can range from age to mode of travel (recall the Railway Rapist discussed in Chapter 3). Nonetheless, as we will see below, some rapist "types" do look for vulnerable victims, or victims that they associate with socially or otherwise interact with on a frequent basis. Also important, and again as we will see below, is the behavioral interaction between the victim and the offender, as reported by the victim. In other words, how does the offender treat the victim during the crime? Although rape is always a violent crime, some offenders display MOs that are distinctive from those of others.

Victim Selection

Victim selection refers to the process by which an offender chooses or targets a victim. Research has demonstrated that each offender has his or her personal selection criteria that enter into the somewhat rational decision-making process in committing a crime. Serial rapists make decisions and choose how to proceed with a victim not only based on the perceived characteristics of the potential victim, but also based on situational characteristics at the time. As indicated by Deslauriers-Varin and Beauregard (2010), "previous studies have shown that the target selection processes of sex offenders depend heavily on the social, physical, and geographic environment as well as the victim's behaviors and location prior to the crime" (p. 320).

It is important to discuss the selection of a rape victim in detail because, similar to victim selection with regard to serial murder, it is likely that an offender will use the same approach to selecting individuals who are the targets of his assaults. Therefore, profilers should always be alert to cues that indicate an offender's method of selection.

As we note below, some researchers are beginning to identify distinctions within these methods.

Deslauriers-Varin and Beauregard (2010) identified three target selection scripts based on the victim's activities prior to the crime: the home, outdoors, and social scripts. The home script includes the (a) intrusion track and (b) invited track. The outdoors script includes the (a) noncoercive track and the (b) coercive track. Finally, the social script consists of the two target tracks of (a) onsite and (b) off-site.

In the home intrusion track, the rapist often breaks into the victim's home and sexually assaults an adult female victim while she is alone. Often, he uses a weapon to control the victim. This category of victim selection is considered to be "rational" in the sense that the benefits will usually outweigh the risk associated with the rape. In these cases, the offender will look for cues that the woman is alone and will enter the home through an entry point that is undetected. In the home-invited track, the rapist most likely will become acquainted with the victim until she invites him into her home or apartment. In this case, he is easily identifiable by the victim, and he relies on the fact that the victim is unlikely to report the crime.

In the outdoors script, the victims are usually outside when approached. In these cases, the serial rapists will spend a considerable amount of time preparing for the crimes and selecting victims. In the noncoercive track, they will approach the victim without using violence. For example, the targeted victim may be jogging or reading; the rapist will gradually gain the victim's trust (perhaps on several different occasions) and will invite the victim to his home or other location; she consents, where he then commits the crime. This is similar to the home-invited track, except that here the victim does not invite him to her home. The outdoors coercive track represents a situation where the serial rapist waits outside for an opportunity and then attacks the victim. Often, the serial rapist will kidnap the victim. This track tends to involve higher risk for the offender because the attack occurs outside and the victim's resistance may draw attention.

A good illustration of the outdoors coercive track is the so-called Teardrop Rapist, whose attacks began in Los Angeles in 1996, continued until 2005, and apparently resumed again with the rape of a 15-year-old girl on her way to school in the fall of 2011. Police observed a clear pattern in his offending: Victims were walking alone, generally in the early morning, and were attacked by a man holding a gun or a knife, who pulled them into a wooded area. Most victims have described him as a Latino with a tattoo resembling a teardrop under his eye. He has yet to be found. Thus far, 28 attacks have been attributed to the Teardrop Rapist.

The social script is used with targets who are engaged in social or recreational activities prior to the assault, such as at a bar, swimming pool, concert, shopping mall, theater, or ski area. Serial rapists who employ this script will usually travel to specific recreational locations to identify suitable victims, most often without planning the crime or selecting victims ahead of time. In these encounters, the rapist will frequently use coercion to control the victim. These serial rapists will often act directly, without any initial interaction, having waited for the best available opportunity to attack. The social onsite rape is characterized by the rape occurring indoors, such as in a shopping mall restroom or swimming pool changing room. The off-site target selection track is distinguished by the encounter and attack occurring outdoors when the victim is alone, similar to the outdoors coercive track. Often, the offender will move the victim to a different location for the commission of the crime.

In recent years, researchers also have suggested that some serial rapists tend to show a "crime switching" or "crossover tendency." **Crossover sexual offenses** are those in which the victims are from multiple age, gender, and relationship categories (Heil, Ahlmeyer, & Simons, 2003). Many serial offenders do not select only one type of victim. This appears particularly true of opportunity rapists, or those who have not necessarily planned their crimes and targeted their victims but, rather, take the opportunity to assault when it is presented. Depending on the opportunity, they may select male children or young or older women. Furthermore, Heil et al. concluded that their findings "suggest an opportunistic, malleable nature in sex offending that contradicts traditional sex offender typologies" (p. 233). This is especially the case of typologies based solely on victim characteristics. If one were to speculate and attempt to draw together the target selection scripts discussed above and the crossover findings of Heil et al., one would say that the coercive, onsite, and off-site tracks are the most likely to be associated with the crossover offenders.

False Allegations

As we learned in the previous section, a vast majority of serial rapists remain undetected. Over half of all rapes, and perhaps as high as 90%, are never reported to police, and these are conservative estimates (Belknap, 2010). It is also a fact, however, that some reported rapes are false allegations. Lisak et al. (2010) found evidence that false allegations represented 6% of the 10-year data they examined. Rape awareness programs often use the 2% statistic, a figure drawn from the FBI's Uniform Crime Reports (Lonsway, 2010). Most studies have found that false allegations range between 2% and 10% of total reported rapes (Lisak et al., 2010; Lonsway, 2010).

Canter and Youngs (2009) point out that determining the truthfulness of a victim's allegations in rape cases is an important task for police; therefore, psychologists— including behavioral analysts—consulting with police should inform investigators of the available research in this area. For example, Lonsway (2010) identifies three possible explanations for false allegations. The alleged victim may be suffering from a mental or cognitive disorder or have suffered some emotional and interpersonal disruption. Or—closely related to this—the person may desire attention and sympathy from others for being attacked. Canter and Youngs report that 18% of the false allegation cases fall into this category. In still other cases, the alleged victim seeks revenge and retaliation against a rejecting male. For example, she is angry at the male for leaving her and wants to get him into trouble. According to Canter and Youngs, 27% of the false allegations fall into this category.

However, the majority of false allegations, according to Canter and Youngs, are associated with a fourth explanation, offered by Kanin (1994): The alleged rape provides an "alibi" of sorts. The complainant searches for a plausible explanation "for some suddenly foreseen, unfortunate consequence of a consensual encounter, usually sexual, with a male acquaintance" (Canter & Youngs, 2009, p. 304). Kanin believes that many false allegations represent impulsive and desperate attempts to cope with personal and socially stressful situations. An example of this would be the young woman who consents to sex with an acquaintance, then realizes that her boyfriend would likely find out (the suddenly foreseen unfortunate circumstance); therefore, she alleges that the encounter was not consensual.

Although false allegations of rape can be devastating to the person accused, it should be emphasized that they are small in number compared to the total number of reported rapes, and reported rape figures themselves represent an extremely small percentage of what is believed to be the true prevalence of this crime. When alleged victims recant their accusations, the recantations are often covered extensively in the media. This coverage is fortunate for the accused perpetrator, but it also may perpetuate the notion that false allegations are more common than they are, and it obscures the reality that the great majority of rapes go unreported.

THE OFFENDERS

Serial rapists tend to target strangers (Petherick, 2006). Consequently, we will focus on stranger sexual assault in this subsection. Available data (from the United States and the UK) suggest that serial rapists, on average, commit about five or six rapes, and the average age is about 26 (Canter & Larkin, 1993; Warren et al., 1998). Younger rapists (ages 20 to 23) offend close to home (approximately within a 2-mile radius), whereas older rapists tend to travel farther (approximately within a 5-mile radius; Petherick, 2006). In this sense, younger rapists tend to be marauders, and older rapists tend to be commuters. Research clearly suggests that, as a general rule, rapists tend to be marauders, committing their crimes close to their residence or place of employment (Canter & Larkin, 1993; Kocsis, 1997). The single rapist usually rapes impulsively, but the serial rapist often prepares in detail the manner in which he will commit his sexual assaults.

Many rape typologies have been proposed, including that used by the FBI (Hazelwood & Burgess, 1995), the Nagayama-Hall typology (Nagayama-Hall, 1992), and the heavily cited Nicholas Groth typology (Groth, 1979a). By far, the most research-based typology is the Massachusetts Treatment Center's (MTC), which has drawn considerable attention and is now in its third revision (MTC-R3). Because of its importance, we will briefly cover the MTC model below. It should be emphasized that the limitation of this typology (at least for behavioral profiling) is that it focuses largely on the psychological characteristics of the offender. We believe it is more helpful to the profiler if crime scene information concerning how the rapist treats the victim is also included, as it highlights how the offender interacts with others in his life. As identified by the research of David Canter and his colleagues (Canter, Bennell, Alison, & Reddy, 2003), stranger rapes can be distinguished according to the interaction between the offender and his victim. Consequently, this subsection will also concentrate on behaviors that are reported directly by the victim, which leads to behavioral classification systems that complement the motivational systems such as that from the MTC program (Canter et al., 2003).

Before we proceed, however, it is important to remind readers that behavioral and motivational classification systems are permeated with problems and drawbacks. One obvious problem is that individuals do not usually fit neatly into a discrete category. We discussed this above, and we emphasize that it is no less true with respect to serial rapists.

THE MASSACHUSETTS TREATMENT CENTER CLASSIFICATION SYSTEM

The Massachusetts Treatment Center (MTC) offers a rough framework for conceptualizing and simplifying the behaviors and motives involved in sexual assault. After a series of analyses and further development, the MTC classifies rape offenders into four major types and nine subtypes. The classification system is illustrated in Figure 5.1.

Figure 5.1 Massachusetts Treatment Center Classification System

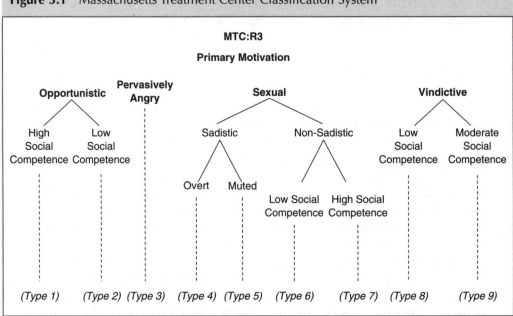

Source: Knight, R. A., Warren, J. I., Reboussin, R., & Soley, B. J. (1998). Reprinted with permission from Sage, on behalf of the International Association for Correctional and Forensic Psychology.

Opportunistic Rapists (Types 1 and 2)

The **impulsive or opportunistic rapist** engages in sexual assault simply because the opportunity to rape presents itself. This offender is driven more by situational factors and opportunity than by any internally driven sexual fantasy (Prentky & Knight, 1991). The rape may occur within the context of some other crime, such as a robbery or burglary. One of the most prominent characteristics of these offenders is their impulsivity and lack of self-control and forethought. This lack of self-regulation leads to a pervasive and enduring lifestyle of impulsive and irresponsible behavior, frequently resulting in an extensive criminal career. Moreover, they view their victims only as sexual objects and are not concerned about the victims' fear or discomfort. In order to be classified as an opportunistic rapist, the offender must exhibit the following features:

- Callous indifference to the welfare and comfort of the victim;

- Presence of no more force than is necessary to obtain the compliance of the victim. Any excessive force or violent behavior rules out this type;

- Evidence of adult impulsive behavior, such as frequent fighting, vandalism, and other impulse-driven antisocial behaviors.

Opportunistic offenders may be subdivided (Types 1 and 2) on the basis of their social competence and the developmental state at which their lack of self-regulation is first noticed. The offender who is high in social competence and highly impulsive in adulthood is labeled a Type 1 rapist. The Type 2 rapist, on the other hand, is low in social competence and shows high levels of impulsiveness during adolescence.

Pervasively Angry Rapists (Type 3)

The **pervasively angry rapist** is an offender who displays high levels of anger that pervades all areas of his life. The anger is directed at a wide range of people. His actions are capricious and randomly violent, and are directed at whoever gets in his way at the wrong time and wrong place (Prentky & Knight, 1991). When these men attack women, their violent and aggressive behaviors do not show sexual arousal, and the attacks often inflict considerable injury to the victim.

The occupational history of this offender is usually relatively stable and often reveals some level of success. He perceives himself as strong, athletic, and masculine. More often than not, his occupation is "masculine" in nature, such as truck driver, carpenter, mechanic, electrician, or plumber. He is often described by others who know him as having a quick, violent temper.

The pervasively angry rapist must show the follow characteristics to qualify for this classification (Knight & Prentky, 1987):

- Presence of a high degree of nonsexualized aggression or rage expressed through verbal or physical assault that clearly exceeds what is necessary to gain compliance of the victim;

- Evidence of adolescent and adult violent and anger-driven antisocial behavior;

- Carries out attacks that are usually unplanned and unpremeditated.

So far, no particular subtypes have been identified for the pervasively angry rapist. Therefore, this type of rapist is referred to simply as Type 3.

Sexually Motivated, Sadistic Rapists (Types 4 and 5)

The motivation for the next four types is sexual in that their attacks are characterized by the presence of sexual or sadistic fantasies and cognitions that strongly influence the assaults. A discernible pattern of sexual preoccupations and fantasy are the aspects that all four have in common. The **sexually motivated rapist** is subdivided into sadistic or non-sadistic (see Figure 5.1). Sadistic sexual offenders are classified as either overt (Type 4) or muted (Type 5), depending on whether their sexually aggressive behaviors are directly expressed in violent acts (overt) or are only fantasized (muted). The muted sadistic rapist exhibits similar characteristics to the overt sadistic rapist, except that the physical assaults of the former inflict less victim damage (Knight & Prentky, 1990). The muted offender's motive is the victim's fear or some violent fantasy that aids his sexual arousal. More specifically, the victim's fear excites him, or he relies on some rehearsed sexual fantasy to excite him. The overt sadistic attacker exhibits both sexual and aggressive features in his assault. In addition, the victim's actual pain and discomfort are prerequisites for his sexual excitement. He believes his victims basically "enjoy" being abused, forcefully raped, aggressively dominated, and controlled. At first, the assault may begin as attempts at seduction, but with increasing resistance from the victim, aggressive behaviors become increasingly prominent.

The overt rapist is usually married, but displays little commitment to the marriage. He usually has an extensive antisocial background from adolescence to adulthood, ranging from truancy to rape-murder. On occasion, the overt rapist engages in sexual sadism that is so extreme that the victim may be murdered.

To qualify as a sexually motivated, sadistic rapist, he must exhibit the following:

- A level of aggression or violence that clearly exceeds what is necessary to force compliance of the victim;

- Explicit, unambiguous evidence that aggression is sexually exciting and arousing to the offender. This can be illustrated either by indications that the offender derives sexual pleasure from injurious acts to the victim, or by the fact that injurious acts are focused on parts of the body that have sexual significance;

- Aggression or enough force to gain compliance;

- Evidence that sexual fantasies of violence or the victim's fear excite him.

Sexually Motivated, Nonsadistic Rapists (Types 6 and 7)

The nonsadistic rapist engages in a sexual assault because of an intense sexual arousal promoted by specific stimuli he perceives in the targeted victim. Aggression or violence is not a significant feature of the attack, although rape by definition is a violent act. The fundamental motivation is the desire to prove his sexual prowess and adequacy to the victim. These offenders live in a world of fantasy oriented around themes of how victims will yield eagerly under an attack, and be impressed by the offender's skill and performance. These attackers fantasize that they will be able to prove their masculinity and sexual competence to themselves and their victims. In their sexual attacks, these rapists are described as being highly sexually aroused and displaying obvious disturbances involving lack of control and distortions of reality.

Although the victim is usually a stranger, the offender has probably watched and followed the intended victim for some time. During the sexual attack, he will display very low levels of aggressive behavior. Sometimes, if he is successful, he may contact the victim at a later time and ask about her well-being or even request a date. Generally, this type of offender confines his criminal behavior to sexual assault and is usually not involved in other forms of antisocial behavior.

Assignment to the non-sadistic categories requires the following behavioral indicators:

- Presence of verbalizations aimed at self-reassurance and self-affirmation;
- Behaviors that reflect, albeit in a strange fashion, an attempt at establishing an amorous relationship with the victim;
- Expressions of concern for the victim's welfare, comfort, and enjoyment during the sexual experience.

Research (e.g., Knight & Prentky, 1987; Knight et al., 1998) has shown that there may be at least two subtypes of non-sadistic, sexually motivated rapists, similar to the two subdivisions of the opportunistic offender. Type 6 is described as quiet, socially inadequate, and submissive. Although they are dependable workers, their poor interpersonal skills and low self-esteem prevent them from succeeding at career advancement. Type 7, on the other hand, is depicted as more interpersonally competent and achieves more career advancement and professional success. This rapist is classified as highly socially competent (see Figure 5.1).

Vindictive Rapists (Types 8 and 9)

The vindictive rapist is driven by his anger toward women. He uses the act of rape to harm, humiliate, and denigrate women. A violent sexual assault is, in this offender's view, the most humiliating and dominating act possible. The victims are brutally assaulted and subjected to sadistic acts such as severe biting, cutting, or tearing of parts of the body. In most cases, the victims are strangers. In addition to physical abuse, the offender will use a great deal of profanity and emotional abuse through threats.

Although most of these offenders are married, their relationships with women are distinguished by periodic abuse and domestic violence. They generally see women as demanding, hostile, and unfaithful individuals who need to be dominated and controlled. In many cases, they select their victims based on some characteristic they perceive as indicating assertiveness, independence, or professional status. The attack usually follows some precipitating event with another woman (wife, girlfriend, mother, supervisor) that he interprets as demeaning to him personally.

Similar to the opportunistic and non-sadistic rapists, the vindictive offenders can be subdivided by their degree of social competence, although in this situation they are divided into low and moderate rather than low and high.

In order to qualify as a vindictive rapist, the follow behaviors must be displayed:

- Clear evidence, in verbalization or behavior, of the intent to demean, degrade, or humiliate the victim;
- No evidence that the violent behavior is eroticized or that sexual pleasure is derived from the injurious acts;
- The injurious acts are not focused on parts of the body that have sexual significance.

CANTER'S LEVELS OF VIOLATION AND THEMES OF RAPE

While David Canter and his colleagues (Canter & Heritage, 1990; Canter et al., 2003) recognized the value of the MTC-R3 in the investigation of stranger rapes, they believe that it does not go quite far enough. They proposed that stranger rape can be investigated from three levels of violation, as well as four underlying themes of the offense. The three levels are personal, physical, and sexual, and as listed, represent increasing *levels of violation*. That is, the personal represents the lowest level of violation, and the sexual the highest.

At the personal level, the offender may apologize to the victim, force the victim to "participate" verbally, or imply that he knows the victim. The physically violating actions include verbal violence; anal penetration; demeaning the victim; signs of multiple types of violence; tearing the victim's clothing; and binding, gagging, and/or blindfolding the victim. The sexually violating actions include fellatio, expectation of victim participating in the act, cunnilingus, and kisses. He may also expect the victim to make complimentary comments about his performance. It is important for the profiler to take levels of violation into consideration, because a serial rapist is apt to display the same level in his various rapes.

In addition to the different levels of violation, Canter and his colleagues (2003) describe "themes" that correspond to the three roles of victims discussed in the serial murder cases earlier in the chapter: the victim as a person, as a vehicle, and as an object. However, the terminology is slightly changed when applied to rape cases, although the descriptions remain similar. More specifically, Canter et al. introduce the term "control" when the rapist uses the victim as an object, "hostility" when the rapist uses the victim as a vehicle, and "involvement" when the rapist uses the victim as a person. These terms are treated as "themes"—and the researchers add a fourth, the "theft" theme—each of which is explained below.

In the **control theme**, the offender regards the victim as an inanimate object that must be trussed and coerced, but the attacker will not try to demean the victim. The term *control* is used because the overall theme is to demobilize the victim. The methods of control may include binding, blindfolding, or gagging the victim. A weapon is often used. The offender has no empathy for the victim and experiences no remorse for his crime. Behaviors typical of the **hostility theme** include verbal violence, insulting or demeaning language, tearing the victim's clothing, and a general tone of violence toward the victim. The **involvement theme** is characterized by the offender's desire for social contact and intimacy. In this situation, the victim is treated as a reactive, living person, rather than as merely a sexual object. The offender may kiss the victim and expect the victim to make sexual comments. He may also compliment her appearance. In the **theft theme**, the rape occurs during the commission of other crime, such as burglary, carjacking, or robbery. "The offender is using the opportunities presented by the crime for some future instrumental goal, not just for the immediate gratification of the rape" (Canter et al., 2003, p. 162).

Canter et al. (2003) propose that the three levels of violation plus the four modes of interaction will provide a composite model of stranger rape that will help in the investigation and profiling of the offender. In a study of 112 stranger rapes, Canter et al. concluded that 73% of the rapes could be assigned a clear, dominant theme. Specifically 26% of them could be classified as hostility, 10% as control, 5% as theft, and the remaining 32% as involvement. These results suggest that stranger rapes may be explained more in terms of hostility and involvement (pseudo-intimacy) than by power and control factors. In addition, control offenses tend to be predominantly physically violating, the theft rapes are predominantly personally violating, involvement offenses are predominantly sexually violating, and hostile offenses tend to be a combination of all three levels of violation.

Canter et al. (2003) concluded that the sexual and physical aspects of the rape do not usually offer the best clues for distinguishing the rapist from other rape offenders. The distinguishing features are more likely to be found in the styles of the interpersonal interactions that are typical of the assault. That is, "Rapes can be distinguished in terms of the mode of interaction between an offender and his victim" (p. 171). Furthermore, the identification of behavioral themes in rape attacks opens up the possibility that it might not be the specific behaviors an offender demonstrates during his crime that are important, but rather the function these behaviors serve. "In other words, discrete crime scene behaviors may be less significant than the underlying themes of the offence" (p. 171). In essence, it is far more important to identify the dominant theme, not only in burglary, but in other serial crimes as well, rather than focusing on detailed consideration of specific actions (Yokota & Canter, 2004). As discussed in Chapter 3, the crime scene themes provide valuable clues about how the offender lives his daily life, particularly in relation to how he treats other people, including his family.

Although much more research needs to be done, the Canter method combined with the MTC model offers the best research approach and beginning data for profiling stranger rapes to date.

Profiling in Serial Arson Cases

THE NUMBERS

Arson is defined as "any willful or malicious burning or attempt to burn, with or without intent to defraud, a dwelling house, public building, motor vehicle or aircraft, personal property of another, etc." (Federal Bureau of Investigation, 2005, p. 53). In 2010, there were nearly 60,000 arsons in the United States (Federal Bureau of Investigation, 2011b). In addition, there were an estimated 8,806 arrests for arson that same year. Forty percent of those arrested were under age 18, and 23% were under age 15. It is further estimated that many arsons are set by serial arsonists, defined as individuals who intentionally set three or more separate fires. It is extremely difficult to estimate the number of serial arsonists who are active at any one time, but if recidivism rates of convicted arsonists are any indication, the number is large. In addition, many arsons by serial offenders go unsolved. According to the U.S. Fire Administration (2011), many communities in the United States are currently experiencing a significant increase in serial arson–related fires.

THE VICTIMS

Hundreds of lives are lost each year in arson-related fires, and thousands more suffer burns and serious injuries as a result of these crimes. In addition, deliberate firesetting is financially costly to the victims and to the community as a whole. What is more, no particular socioeconomic, religious, or demographic group, business, or institution is immune from being victimized by a serial arsonist.

THE OFFENDERS

Currently, there is very little reliable information available to guide investigators or profilers in their search for serial arsonists (Ducat & Ogloff, 2011). Some research indicates that those who persistently and repeatedly set fires are often involved in a variety of other antisocial and criminal behaviors (Del Bove & Mackay, 2011; Lambie & Randell, 2011; Vaughn et al., 2010). In addition, research has further suggested that many arsonists also have a variety of mental disorders (Brett, 2004; Dickens et al., 2009).

Firefighter Arson

Interestingly, among serial arsonists is a small percentage of firefighters who intentionally set the fires they are dispatched to put out. The precise incidence of this behavior remains unknown (Stambaugh & Styron, 2003). According to investigators, a "tell-tale" sign that a firefighter may be setting fires is a sudden increase in nuisance fires within a company's "first due" area, or the area the company has primary responsibility to cover. Firefighter arsonists tend to be relatively new to the department, usually serving fewer than 3 years. The primary motive appears to be excitement for a young firesetter wanting to appear as a hero to fellow firefighters and the community served. Firefighter arsonists usually begin by setting nuisance fires—setting fire to grass, brush, Dumpsters, or trash piles—then move on to abandoned vehicles and unoccupied structures. The arsonist also may be the first firefighter to arrive at the scene and may appear very eager. (See Focus 5.3 for illustration of one of the most notorious firefighter arsonists on record.) Firefighter arsonists are, of course, the exception rather than the rule for serial arsonists; it is far more likely that they are juveniles, young adults, or emotionally disturbed individuals, as we will discuss below.

Focus 5.3

Fire Investigator-Turned-Arsonist

John L. Orr was fire captain, an apparently dedicated career firefighter, and chief arson investigator for the Glendale Fire Department in Southern California. Unfortunately, he was also an arsonist.

Throughout the 1980s and into the early 1990s, cities in Southern and Central California experienced a rash of suspicious major fires that caused millions of dollars in damages and claimed four lives. The MO for many of the fires was highly similar: an incendiary time-delay device consisting of a lit cigarette and three matches wrapped in sheets of lined yellow notebook paper, held together by a rubber band. In 1984, one of the fires broke out in a hardware store in Pasadena, killing four people including a 2-year-old boy. At the time, fire investigators concluded the fire was caused by an electrical malfunction, but Orr insisted it was caused by arson.

Subsequently, several suspicious fires were set in Fresno and Bakersfield, ironically during a convention for arson investigators. All fires were set in stores at shopping malls near expressways. Digging through the debris at one of these fires, investigators found a fingerprint on a piece of yellow notebook paper from the partially burned incendiary device. Bakersfield Fire Department investigators began to suspect that an arson investigator from the Los Angeles area may have been responsible for the fires, since at least 10 from that area had attended the conference.

After an extended search of almost 1.2 million fingerprints, a match was made to John Orr. Officials, including federal authorities, began conducting a thorough investigation of Orr, which included using various forms of surveillance. In 1991, a federal grand jury indicted him on charges that he set or tried to set blazes in eight stores during a 3-year period (Stambaugh & Styron, 2003). Though he was also suspected in at least 15 other fires, including those that took lives, there was insufficient evidence to charge him. However, Orr was convicted and sentenced to three consecutive terms of 10 years in prison for the eight fires.

Interestingly, Orr himself provided clues to his misdeeds, and they may have contributed to additional, more serious charges. Investigators found in his possession an unpublished novel he had been working on, which he titled *Points of Origin*. The book detailed the escapades of a firefighter who became a serial arsonist. At one point in the book, the arsonist torched a hardware store in Pasadena, killing a woman and her young son. Police accumulated more evidence against Orr, and in 1998 he was convicted of four counts of first-degree murder as a result of the hardware store fire. He was sentenced to life plus 20 years in prison without the possibility of parole.

Juvenile Firesetters

In a comprehensive investigation of more than 1,000 juveniles and adults convicted of arson, Icove and Estepp (1987) found that vandalism was the most frequently identified motive, accounting for nearly half of the firesetting. Research has consistently shown that most fires set by juveniles appear to be motivated by the wish to get back at authority, the desire to gain status among their peer group, or the urge for excitement. The Icove-Estepp study revealed that the vast majority (96%) of the vandalism fires were set by juveniles, who often set the fire within a 1-mile radius of their homes. It is not unusual for these children to have been maltreated, and their primary motive is anger directed at those who maltreated them. In addition, they are usually accompanied by friends and peers. About half of juvenile firesetters remain at the scene, watching the firefighting activity. "Studies indicate that fire-setting is strongly correlated with family dysfunction, a history of abuse, school difficulties, antisocial traits including impulsivity and hostility, and co-occurring delinquent behaviors" (Vaughn et al., 2010, p. 217). Firesetters (ages 18 to 35) tend to engage in multiple forms of antisocial behavior, including cruelty to animals, robbery, forcible rape, assault, aggravated assault, and weapons use (Vaughn et al., 2010). The prevalence of lifetime firesetting (ever having set an arson fire in one's lifetime) in the U.S. population was found to be 1%.

Serial Arsonists

Broadly speaking, persistent firesetters are considered highly dangerous if they have a history of setting multi-point fires and of using fuel and other accelerants (Dickens et al., 2009). Serial adult firesetters (over age 18) tend to be young and single and to have started their criminal careers early (Dickens et al., 2009). They also typically have spent more time in prison and have an extensive history of other property crime.

Canter and Fritzon (1998) developed a classification scheme of arsonists based on information gathered from arson investigations. It is based on behavioral as well as motivational indicators rather than exclusively on firesetting motives, on which so many previous arson typologies have been based. A valid and reliable typological mode of crime scene behavioral indicators would be far more valuable to law enforcement agencies as an investigative tool than a classification system based largely on motives (Häkkänen, Puolakka, et al., 2004). More often than not, motives are determined after the arrest of the firesetters, and police investigators are more likely to be able to narrow their search with a thematic approach. The view that Canter and Fritzon hold is consistent with the general conclusions of many writers that firesetting has a number of very different psychological origins. "Some arsons may be a consequence of a deviant lifestyle, being used as a criminal tool, for people who have little other intellectual or physical resource" (p. 90). For others, arson may be the product of an ineffectual way of dealing with interpersonal conflict. For still others, it may reflect self-destructive tendencies. That is, they are troubled individuals who are seeking attention.

The Canter-Fritzon classification scheme. Canter and Fritzon (1998) developed a four-theme model that classifies arson according to its target and the motivations underlying the firesetting behavior. The model is based on the analysis of 175 solved arson cases from across England and revealed four distinct themes to firesetting.

The researchers learned that arson could be distinguished according to two basic motivational and behavioral features, (1) expressive and (2) instrumental. In the **expressive motivating theme**, the offender is driven to express anger or other emotions. In the **instrumental motivating theme**, the offender is driven to achieve certain goals, such as financial gain or to hide another crime.

The behavioral component is identified by the characteristics of the target of the firesetting, and it, too, can be instrumental or expressive. The target may be an object with which the firesetter does not have any personal identification, or a person who is part of the offender's personal or social identity. The combination of the two motivating sources and the nature of arson targets provides four hypothesized forms of firesetting. Those motivation sources that are of an instrumental nature have the direct objective of achieving goals.

In sum, in the Canter and Fritzon (1998) study, targets could be differentiated according to whether they were objects (e.g., schools, vehicles, institutions, businesses, or residences) or specific people who were significant to the arsonist. Motivation distinctions could be classified according to whether an obvious instrumental outcome was desired (e.g., revenge or crime concealment) or whether the act was expressive in that the firesetting drew attention to some underlying emotional problem (see Table 5.1). An expressive

Table 5.1 Four Themes of Arson	
Expressive-Person Arson	Expressive-Object Arson
Instrumental-Person Arson	Instrumental-Object Arson

Source: Adapted from Canter & Fritzon (1998).

arson directed at a person usually is associated with emotional distress, such as depression or feelings of helplessness. An arson that is expressive and directed at an object is characteristic of someone who is acting out and selects a target that has some symbolic, emotional significance to the firesetter, such as school or church (Santtila, Häkkänen, Alison, & Whyte, 2003). Fortunately, most of these firesetters select uninhabited buildings or residences (Häkkänen, Puolakka, et al., 2004). The selection of objects suggests that they are not attempting to injure anyone, but they do enjoy watching the fire, the firefighting activity, and the accompanying excitement of other watchers. An example of arson that is instrumentally motivated and directed at an object is one in which a burglar sets fire to a residence to hide evidence of his or her theft. The theme can also be found in insurance fraud, such as when the owner of an abandoned apartment building sets fire to the building to collect insurance. An instrumental arson directed at a person is usually due to anger or frustration caused by another person whom the firesetter wishes to hurt or remove. In some cases, the firesetting may be directed at someone in authority, such as a teacher or church personnel. The instrumental aspect of this action is that firesetting presumably changes the emotional state of the firesetter. That is, he or she feels better after administering some form of revenge to the targeted victim(s).

The Canter and Fritzon study also produced information pertaining to arsonists' personal characteristics. For example, the analyses demonstrated that instrumental-object behavior was highly characteristic of juvenile and young offenders; the expressive-person theme was associated with persons with a psychiatric history of emotional problems and who used firesetting to draw attention to their problems; the expressive-object behavior was characteristic of serial arsonists as well as those with a psychiatric history; and instrumental-person firesetters set fires in reaction to failed relationships, and firesetting represents their dominant way of expressing anger and frustration.

Action system model. Based on action system theory (Shye, 1985), Fritzon, Canter, and Wilton (2001) have proposed a model highly similar to the Canter and Fritzon (1998) classification scheme. However, the more recent model goes beyond describing only arson behavior. It is intended to include other types of criminal behavior, such as hostage taking. The terminology of the four themes is slightly different, but it still corresponds very closely to the original Canter-Fritzon findings. The four themes of the slightly revised model are listed and described below:

Expressive Theme: These individuals tend to be serial arsonists or other offenders who regard their illegal behavior as the best way to deal with others. They choose targets with some symbolic, emotional significance.

Integrative Theme: These offenders often have a history of mental disorders and suicide attempts. They might engage in attention-seeking behavior that could endanger both their own lives and the lives of others.

Conservative Theme: These offenders use fire, property destruction, or even hostage taking as a way of affecting a person significant to them. For example, the firesetting may be prompted by a failed relationship, or desire for personal revenge for a real or imagined wrongdoing.

Adaptive Theme: Similar to the integrative theme, these offenders use their crimes as a means of getting attention. However, they typically do not display mental disorders—such as severe depression—in the usual psychiatric sense. In most cases, they have a delinquency or criminal record and exhibit behavioral problems in school or at home. An arsonist who sets fire to cover up evidence of his theft could also be seen as an adaptive firesetter.

In terms of profiling implications, object-oriented firesetting is associated with repetition. That, combined with the fact that these offenders tend not to travel far from home, suggests the importance of establishing surveillance in areas recently subjected to arson (Fritzon et al., 2001). It is also likely that offenders who set fires to public properties (e.g., hospitals and schools) will be known to the police for previous firesetting activities. In addition, when there is evidence of planning the fire and the use of accelerants, it is most probable that firesetting is a targeted attack and that the victim will have known the offender.

The model also provides some direction on interviewing suspects. For instance, in relation to expressive arson, the questioning should center on the emotional problems of the suspect. In expressive arson, it is not unusual for the offender to have burns, sometimes severe ones, as a result of setting the fire. "If these problems have proved overwhelming enough to prompt the individual to set fire to themselves, then it would be expected that they would show willingness to talk to police officers on the subject" (Fritzon et al., 2001, p. 677). In reference to integrative arson where there is a desire to draw attention to the arsonist, the offender may be drawn out by deflecting the attention away from him or her. The adaptive theme is more challenging, as the offender may not wish to draw attention to the other crime. In the conservative arson, the offender may be drawn out by emphasizing that what he or she did was understandable, considering the argument or failed relationship problem.

Other arson models. G. T. Harris and Rice (1996) also found four categories of arsonists, labeled as psychotics, underassertives, multi-firesetters, and criminals. The subtypes differed on many clinical characteristics and in their likelihood of firesetting. Subjects were 243 male firesetters in a maximum-security psychiatric facility. The *psychotics* were men whose motives for firesetting were primarily delusional. They had set few fires in their lives and had little in the way of criminal histories. The *underassertives* were men who set fires out of anger or revenge. These firesetters had little criminal activity in their backgrounds and good employment histories. *Multi-firesetters* demonstrated high amounts of aggression and had set many fires as children and adults. They were usually unmarried. The *criminals* had extensive criminal histories, and had a history of aggression as adults.

They were least likely to know the victim(s) of the fire, were most likely to have set the fire at night, were least likely to confess to the fire, and were most likely to commit new fireset-ting offenses and other violent crimes upon release. They were also the most likely to be described as assertive. According to Fritzon et al. (2001), the underassertives are similar to the conservative theme of functioning. The multi-firesetters represent an extreme form of the expressive mode in that emotional relief is obtained from setting fires. The criminals are similar to the adaptive in that their firesetting is employed as a way of cov-ering up other crimes they committed. Psychotic may be seen as integrative, since they are plagued by emotional disturbances.

PYROMANIA

Pyromania is defined as "the presence of multiple episodes of deliberate and purpose-ful firesetting" (American Psychiatric Association, 2000, p. 614). It is often described as an intense fascination with fire, characterized by an irresistible urge to light fires. The firesetting is not done for any apparent motive, such as financial gain, anger or revenge, or to gain recognition. It is, however, characterized by high levels of emotional arousal before the act, followed by relief or reduction of arousal when firesetting. In the psycho-logical and psychiatric literature, it is often referred to as an impulse control disorder. Although pyromania is a concept that has existed for approximately 100 years in the clinical literature, it has received very little empirical research to support its existence. If it does exist as a meaningful diagnostic category, it is very rare (Brett, 2004; Doley, 2003). Moreover, it is difficult to determine how useful the concept of irresistible urges to set fires is in the profiling process. It is clear, however, that the vast majority of serial arsonists do not meet the criterion of being driven by irresistible impulses to set fires.

Profiling Serial Burglars

THE NUMBERS

Burglary—defined as the unlawful entry into a structure for the purposes of com-mitting a crime—often falls under the radar of psychological researchers. As a non-violent offense, it tends not to capture the interest that more sensational crimes do, and its motivation may seem clear-cut—the individual wants goods, drugs, or money. However, as noted earlier in the chapter, some burglaries turn into rapes or murders. Recall Canter's observation that—in the search for serial rapists—investigators should not neglect those with burglary convictions.

Burglary is a common offense, comprising approximately 23% of all nonviolent crimes in the United States reported to police and 9% of both violent and nonviolent crimes com-bined. About 1 in 4 burglaries result in the arrest of someone under the age of 18 (Pollock, Joo, & Lawton, 2010). Burglars have a wide range of reasons for committing their offenses. While most, particularly professional burglars, are in search of goods that they can use or can turn into cash, others are in search of fetishes, want to vandalize the property to put fear into their victims, or case a property for the purpose of committing a future crime.

Moreover, as indicated above, many rapists have prior records, not for sexual offenses, but for burglary. Burglary is largely a male enterprise. Consistently, over the last 10 years, approximately 85% of all offenders arrested for burglary in the United States have been male. Gathering information about burglars and burglaries and being aware of the research literature on the topic are crucial for anyone engaged in profiling.

THE OFFENDERS

We focus in this section on residential burglaries as opposed to commercial burglaries, because the former are more likely to attract the attention of the crime scene profiler. Residential burglary accounted for 73% of all reported burglaries in the United States during 2010 (Federal Bureau of Investigation, 2011b). More than 30 years ago, Dermot Walsh (1980) proposed that all residence burglary exhibited an interpersonal dimension. He observed that residential burglary represents a very different psychological aspect compared with commercial or industrial burglary. "(T)he situation of a residential burglary is very different from a theft in a public place or at a place of work, since any burglary is far more personally disturbing because of its enforced intimacy" (p. 17). In some cases, the burglar's actions in residential burglary are intended to elicit some psychological response from the victim or victims. On the other hand, it is likely that most burglaries are *not* so intended.

More recently, Simon Merry and Louise Harsent (2000) proposed a four-theme (or dimension) burglary classification scheme based on crime scene evidence that extends Dermot Walsh's proposal. The unique feature about this typology is that it considers how the burglary affects the victim. Similar to Walsh, Merry and Harsent emphasize that residential burglary has a unique invasive quality to it. This aspect not only feeds the psychological needs of the burglar, but it also is emotionally upsetting to the victim, even if the offender did not intend this. Merry and Harsent refer to this as the **interpersonal script dimension** of home burglary. They argue that the interpersonal factor exists on a continuum, ranging from implicit to explicit interpersonal behavior. **Implicit interpersonal behaviors** are defined by entry into the home while the residents are away and the theft of material items that have less emotional gain. In these situations, the offender does not desire to upset the victims of the burglary. **Explicit interpersonal behavior,** on the other hand, is characterized by behavior designed to cause fear or psychological reactions in the victims. These behaviors include entry into the home while the occupants are present, causing damage, or stealing items that clearly have significant sentimental value to the occupants—such as framed photographs.

The second dimension of burglary is the **degree of craftsmanship** involved. It also is seen as existing on a continuum, ranging from **low craft** to **high craft**. "Low craft is exhibited in the form of comparative lack of planning, knowledge and skills together with a tendency of reactiveness rather than proactiveness" (Merry & Harsent, 2000, p. 48). The crime scene shows risky behaviors, stealing items that are easily carried, very little search behavior for more valuable items, and being careless about leaving forensic evidence. High craft, on the other hand, reflects high cognitive ability, careful planning, and prudent forethought. The high-craft burglar, sometimes referred to as the professional burglar, spends more time in the home looking for more valuable items, quickly recognizes what items are valuable (antiques, coins, clocks, jewelry), and frequently knows the occupants' favorite hiding places for their valuables. A combination of the interpersonal script and the craftsman dimension results in a typology based on four themes (see Table 5.2). In keeping with research on serial offenders discussed so far, we view the burglar's behavior in terms of themes and discuss examples from each.

Table 5.2   The Four Themes of Burglary

	Low Craft	High Craft
Implicit Interpersonal	Pilferers	Raiders
Explicit Interpersonal	Intruders	Invaders

Pilferers

These burglars generally have the least impact on their victims. Once this burglar enters the residence, he or she creates little disturbance and tends to steal portable and impersonal items, such as cash. This burglar exhibits low levels of dominance and hostility toward the victims and their property. The burglar seems to be more driven by the challenge, excitement, and curiosity of entering another person's home. Overall, there is usually very little material gain from the burglary. Usually, the home has minimal security and is an easy target for entry. For example, the doors are unlocked and non-occupancy clues are apparent. These burglars are likely to be juveniles.

Raiders

These burglars are interested in significant material gain. Items stolen may be laptop computers or other electronic equipment, jewelry, cameras, and antiques. In addition, these offenders tend to show some respect for the victim and demonstrate very little hostility, doing little damage to the home. They are skillful at gaining entry and try very hard to avoid contact with occupants. These offenders are most likely professional and experienced serial burglars.

Intruders

These burglars "are triggered to act through a desire to intrude and violate another's home in a cruder manner than the other themes" (Merry & Harsent, 2000, p. 49). They do malicious damage, are willing to climb and take unnecessary risks, and are prepared to encounter victims. Their style adds an invasive and disturbing quality beyond the theft itself. They demonstrate a lack of planning and are largely driven by a short-lived fulfillment of desire. The theme is expressive, and their impact on victims is significant. According to the most recent data on household burglary in the United States (Catalano, 2010), 28% of the 3.7 million burglaries over a 5-year period were conducted while a household member was present during the burglary. In addition, in 7% of all these burglaries, a household member experienced some form of violent victimization. Furthermore, those household members who were violently victimized knew the offender in 65% of the cases.

Invaders

These offenders show behaviors that have both an instrumental and expressive component. They usually make a mess of the home, strewing things about, and also steal items that have sentimental value for the victims, such as marginally valuable family jewelry. They may destroy family photos, write messages, and leave signature items. They leave "explicit evidence of power, hostility, revenge, and excitement" (Merry & Harsent, 2000, p. 51).

Merry and Harsent (2000) maintain that the four themes of burglary will be consistent from crime scene to crime scene, and should help in the profiling of the offense. Although some aspects of the burglary will be situationally specific and may result in some variation from crime to crime, "the making of mess and damage, items stolen and particularly items left behind are more likely to remain consistent over longer periods" (p. 52). It is further hypothesized by the researchers that juvenile offenders will tend to be pilferers, while older, more experienced offenders will show raider or invader behavioral patterns.

The four-theme classification proposal of Merry and Harsent is a very positive development in the much-neglected area of burglary profiling. However, it demands much more research before we can assess its validity. Attempting to link burglaries to a single offender on the basis of modus operandi or themes has some limitations. For example, in some cases, a burglar's entry behavior may be determined to some extent by the security measures and the physical layout of the residence. Also, as noted by Bennell and Jones (2005), the property stolen may depend on what is available in the residence. Still, and as pointed out by David Canter (2004), there is always some consistency in certain behaviors associated with the themes, regardless of the situations the burglar encounters. Moreover, once again, how the victims are treated by the offender is a very important feature that deserves careful research attention.

Some recent investigations of residential burglary reveal that one of the best predictors of case linkage is the distance between burglary locations, indicating that this is one of the most consistent aspects of offender behavior (Bennell & Jones, 2005; Goodwill & Alison, 2006; Markson, Woodhams, & Bond, 2010). In fact, a combination of the distance between burglary locations and burglaries that occur closer together in time appears to be the most effective way of identifying case linkage in residential burglary. Interestingly, research has consistently found that many houses are targets of repeat burglaries by the same burglar within a relatively short period of time (Bernasco, 2008). "A property with minimal natural surveillance and good escape routes, little security, or flaunting wealth in a high crime area, is likely to be victimized time and again" (Sagovsky & Johnson, 2007, p. 3). In addition, houses next to houses that have been burglarized are at substantially greater risk than those farther away, particularly within 1 week of an initial burglary (Bowers & Johnson, 2005), a phenomenon known to investigators as a "near-repeat" (Bernasco, 2008; F. Morgan, 2001). Research further indicates that near-repeats are done by the same offenders that burglarize the nearby house. Also, a disproportionate number of repeat or near-repeat burglaries occur around the same time of day as the initial crime, usually within a few weeks (S. D. Johnson, Bowers, & Hirschfield, 1997; Sagovsky & Johnson, 2007). The risk of victimization drops as the weeks pass by. Near-repeats may be undertaken when the residents of the initially burglarized property do not take adequate prevention measures (Bernasco, 2008). It should be mentioned that the near-repeat phenomenon also has been found in other crimes besides burglary, including shootings, robbery, and car theft (Youstin, Nobles, Ward, & Cook, 2011).

Why would a burglar return to the same location? First, a vast majority of these offenders appear to be skilled professionals who wish to minimize risk and use their knowledge of the layout of the house and neighboring houses. Once an offender burglarizes a home, the home moves from being a presumed suitable target to a known suitable target (S. D. Johnson, 2008; Youstin et al., 2011). In these cases, one event increases the probability of another event (Youstin et al., 2011). Burglars also learn the habits of the residents, including their work, shopping, and school comings and goings. In addition, the same burglar may return to remove things of value seen the first time but which had to be left behind, probably because the burglar did not have a buyer at that time or because it was too heavy, or he already had his arms full (Sagovsky & Johnson, 2007). Another possible reason is that the burglar returns to steal new items replaced by the victim.

As we learned in earlier chapters, a growing body of research indicates that offenders do not travel far to commit their crimes. The research on residential burglary continues to strongly support this observation.

Summary and Conclusions

Knowledge of the research literature about specific crimes and offenders is crucial for profiling to gain respectability as a scientific endeavor. The profiler (or analyst) called in during the investigative phase of a case must be aware of what criminological research has already uncovered, but in many if not most situations, this will have to be stated in terms of probabilities—for example, stranger abductions are extremely rare, residential fires tend to be set by juveniles, and most burglars are men. Single variables such as this are of little help, however. As emphasized in Chapter 3, to establish profiling as a science, we need very large databases and information on a large number of variables.

This chapter attempted to pull together information on specific offenses, specifically those that are most likely to come to the attention of profilers. With the exception of child abduction, we have discussed crimes that occur in a series; profilers are more likely to be called in when several offenses have been reported and are believed to be the work of one offender than when one single crime has been reported. Thus, the concepts of crime scene signature, crime linkage, and modus operandi discussed in previous chapters are relevant, as are principles of behavioral consistency, including consistency across situations. As we have noted, there will always be some consistency, but behavior is not invariably consistent.

Unfortunately, much of what is available about these offenses comes in the form of typologies—or categories of offenders based on their presumed personality characteristics as evidenced from behavioral indicators at the crime scene. The typologies mentioned in this chapter have varying degrees of validity; the Massachusetts

Treatment Center's profile of rapists, for example, is based on extensive research and has gained considerable respectability. In recent years, researchers have begun to refer to themes rather than typologies. That is, they look for aspects of the crime that have common features, often related to how the perpetrator treats the victim of the offense. In general, the role served by the victim is gaining increasing attention in the research literature; more specifically, crimes often can be categorized according to whether the victim was treated as an object, a vehicle, or a person.

The thematic approach has been discussed predominantly with reference to crimes of serial burglars and arsonists. The crimes of arsonists may be viewed as expressive or instrumental in nature, depending upon whether the arsonist is motivated to express anger or other emotions or is attempting to achieve certain goals. In an updated version of this thematic approach, expressive, integrative, conservative, and adaptive themes are proposed. Likewise, burglars often display behaviors and motivations that allow them to be placed in typologies representing thematic groups. Common groupings are pilferers, raiders, intruders, and invaders.

Although much research is still needed in these areas, the work discussed in this chapter is a promising beginning for those involved in the profiling enterprise; it represents a place to start in the search for serial offenders. For example, confronted with a series of burglaries or arsons, investigators can look at the behaviors that are apparent from the crime scene and attempt to fathom comparable lifestyles and motivations of the offenders, which may in turn help eliminate segments of the population from suspicion—or better yet, provide important clues about the true perpetrator.

KEY CONCEPTS

AMBER Alert

Child Abduction Rapid Deployment (CARD) teams

Control theme (of rape)

Crossover sexual offenses

Degree of craftsmanship (low and high)

Explicit interpersonal behavior

Expressive motivating theme (of firesetting)

Hedonistic killers

Hostility theme (of rape)

Implicit interpersonal behaviors

Impulsive or opportunistic rapist

Instrumental motivating theme (of firesetting)

Interpersonal script dimension

Involvement theme (of rape)

Legal definition (of child abduction)

Mass murder

Mission-oriented killers

Object theme (for victims of serial murder)

Person theme (for victims of serial murder)

Pervasively angry rapist

Power-Control killers

Serial murder

Sexually motivated rapist (sadistic and non-sadistic)

Spree murder

Stereotypical definition (of child abduction)

Theft theme (of rape)

Themes (of arson)

Themes (of burglary)

Vehicle theme (for victims of serial murder)

Victim selection

Vindictive rapist

Visionary killers

6

Psychological Profiling

A Focus on Threat and Risk Assessment

[He] has not exposed himself to a really intimate relationship either with man or woman. He has cut himself off from the world in which love plays any part for fear of being hurt and what love he can experience is fixated on the abstract entity—Germany, which, as we have seen, is a symbol of his ideal mother.

—From a psychological profile of Adolf Hitler (Langer, 1943)

As we noted in earlier chapters, terms associated with profiling are often used interchangeably, and there is also considerable overlap between different categories. It should come as no surprise, then, that psychological profiling is often called criminal profiling, crime scene profiling, offender profiling, or suspect-based profiling. As we use the term here, however, psychological profiling refers to gathering data on a *known* individual or individuals, such as by background investigations, observations, psychological tests, personality inventories, risk assessment instruments, and interviews with that person or with those who know him or her. In that sense, psychological profiles should be prepared only by psychologists or other mental health professionals who have been trained to administer these measures and conduct these observations. By contrast, geographic profiling and crime scene profiling need not be conducted by mental health professionals; as we saw in earlier chapters, law enforcement personnel sometimes receive specialized training for certification as behavioral analysts or behavioral investigative analysts (BIAs) (e.g., from the International Criminal Investigative Analysis Fellowship).

It is important to note that psychological profiling can have a positive spin, and social and behavioral scientists often engage in these more positive enterprises. For example, police psychologists sometimes help administrators in the selection of candidates who might "fit the profile" of a successful officer or who might be a good candidate for promotion (Bartol & Bartol, 2012). Political psychologists conduct research on personalities of individuals who are good candidates for political office, even for the presidency of the United States (Simonton, 1993). Discussing these aspects of profiling would take us far afield from our intended mission, however. This chapter focuses on psychological profiling that is done to prevent harm from occurring; it is profiling intended to help law enforcement or other authorities in identifying and understanding persons who might cause harm to themselves or others in some way.

As in crime scene profiling, when the psychologist "profiles" a specific individual, a report is prepared that focuses less on who the person is (because that is usually known) than on judgments and predictions of how dangerous the person may be and how his or her behavior might be managed. David Canter—whom we credited with coining the term "investigative psychology"—and his colleague Laurence Alison (2000) point out that psychological profiling is basically an offshoot of traditional psychological testing and assessment procedures. As you will see throughout the chapter, psychological assessment of various types is an integral part of psychological profiling.

A Brief History of Psychological Profiling

Psychological profiling was used by the U.S. Office of Strategic Services (OSS) during World War II in an effort to identify the tendencies and thought processes of Adolf Hitler (Ault & Reese, 1980). The psychological profile resulted in a secret wartime 281-page report on Hitler, authored by Walter C. Langer (1943), a psychologist with a heavy psychoanalytical leaning. Langer, working with colleagues including Harvard psychologist Henry A. Murray, hoped that the profile would be helpful in gaining a deeper insight into Hitler, including the motivations underlying his actions.

In keeping with Langer's psychoanalytic orientation, the report was filled with allusions to Hitler's Oedipal conflict, his mother's excessive tidiness and its effect on her son's toilet training, witnessing his parents' sexual activities, his food-related pleasures and revulsions, and—as suggested by the quote opening this chapter—his failure to find a meaningful love relationship.

Murray (1943) also prepared a 240-page psychological profile for the OSS on Hitler's personality and its development. The analysis was used to predict what Hitler would do after an Allied victory and how he should be dealt with if he was captured. The profile was also intended to provide the OSS with suggestions for how to influence Hitler's mental condition and behavior. Interestingly, Murray predicted that Hitler would commit suicide when he realized the end of the war was near, and history indicates that he did. It is very likely, though, that the technique of psychological profiling leaders and politicians predated the OSS by several hundred years in earlier efforts to understand the thinking of kings and military leaders.

Psychological profiling like the above has often been used by military and intelligence organizations, sometimes with embarrassing results when the information is leaked. In 1993, for example, CIA representatives mistakenly told Congress that Haiti's exiled president, Jean-Bertrand Aristide, was prone to manic depression; the report—which was uncorroborated and denounced—nevertheless prompted one U.S. senator to refer to Aristide as a "psychopath" on the Senate floor (Omestad, 1994). Almost assuredly, psychological profiles of the now-deceased Osama Bin Laden, his influential followers, and both living and dead political figures are buried somewhere in government files. Again, it is not our mission to broach these uses; instead, we focus on the type of psychological profiling that is the most acknowledged and researched—psychological profiling that is used to identify and predict the behavior, not of individuals with a large number of followers, but rather of single individuals in non-leadership positions who are possibly dangerous to others. Two highly similar procedures for accomplishing this task are threat assessment and risk assessment.

Both threat and risk assessments involve predicting the likelihood that a specific individual will be dangerous or violent to others *at some point in time*. These assessments examine psychological risk factors that reveal a propensity for violence in threatening or potentially dangerous individuals. The assessment also tries to determine what specific situations or circumstances might have or will set the person off. Although there are many similarities between the two enterprises, they are also distinct and will be treated separately in this chapter whenever possible.

Threat assessment is a process to determine the credibility and seriousness of a threat—the probability of it being carried out. In other words, it is concerned with predicting future violence or other undesirable actions directed at specified individuals or institutions *after an expressed threat has been communicated*. **Risk assessment** is often used in evaluating "individuals who have violated social norms or displayed bizarre behavior, particularly when they appear menacing or unpredictable" (Hanson, 2009, p. 172). Violence risk assessment tries to evaluate an individual's likelihood of engaging in future violence directed at unspecified individuals, in unspecified situations, across an unspecified time frame, usually in the absence of an expressed threat. Threat and risk assessment predictions are probabilistic tasks that require clinicians and other professionals to make judgments about the likelihood of violence (Hatch-Maillette & Scalora, 2002). Both threat and risk assessments should have a firm empirical foundation, especially if legal consequences may be involved.

Regardless of whether it is a threat or a risk assessment, the agency or parties requesting the assessment will want more than a statistical statement about the chances of a damaging or violent act occurring. They usually desire an estimate of the potential consequences and what can be done to reduce or mitigate them (Hanson, 2009).

We will begin by providing an overview of threat assessment, and to illustrate the process we will use the examples of school violence and shootings and workplace violence, because they often involve direct threats, sometimes long before an actual act of violence occurs. We will return to violence risk assessment later in the chapter, using the troubling issue of stalking to illustrate.

Threat Assessment

Threat assessments concentrate on the probability of a threat being carried out. Consider Mitchell, a 14-year-old with a history of marginal performance in his academic work.

Mitchell is having particular difficulty with his ninth-grade English teacher, a 32-year veteran of classroom wars who is just biding his time until retirement. Mitchell has on several occasions mentioned to fellow students that he would like to "off" the teacher, and a disturbing drawing of the teacher with daggers throughout his body was discovered by a school janitor in Mitchell's desk. Mitchell's in-class comments to the teacher have resulted in visits to the principal's office and the school guidance counselor, and on one occasion he was suspended for 3 days. A recent altercation, in which Mitchell shook his fist at the teacher and told him he knew where he lived, led to a referral to a community psychologist who consults with the school. The psychologist was asked by the principal, are we right to be worried about Mitchell?

The threat assessments that have been most heavily researched are those that occur relative to school settings, such as in the above scenario. Although schools have always been faced with similar situations, they became particularly worrisome in the aftermath of school shootings during the late 1990s, and, to a lesser extent, in the apparent recent rise in bullying behavior. School districts began to set up or consult with threat assessment teams for evaluating the seriousness of various student threats toward other students, school personnel, or the school as a whole. These teams may consist of psychologists, school counselors, police officers, the school principal, and other school personnel. On college campuses, these teams may consist of faculty, campus police, mental health professionals, and other representatives.

Outside of school settings, another form of threat assessment is the assessment by mental health professionals of an individual who threatens to commit a serious crime. Research has found that those persons who commit mass murder, for example, often had threatened violence sometime prior to their killings (L. J. Warren, Mullen, & Ogloff, 2011). However, not all persons who make such threats carry out their stated intentions. Therefore, mental health professionals may be called upon to "profile" persons to assess the credibility of their threats, or a threat assessment team may be called in to evaluate the seriousness of the threat.

Threat assessments are also conducted when threats are made toward political or well-known persons. For example, the U.S. Secret Service is continually involved in threat assessments. The agency is responsible for protecting the president and vice president, their families, and certain national and international leaders. In 1998, the Secret Service completed a 5-year study (called the Exceptional Case Study Project [ECSP]) on the behavior of individuals who assassinated, attacked, or approached to attack a prominent person of public status (Fein & Vossekuil, 1998). The study employed an incident-focused, behaviorally based approach in examining investigative reports, criminal justice records, medical records, and other source documents. The project identified and analyzed 83 persons known to have engaged in 73 incidents of assassination, attack, and near-attack behaviors from 1949 to 1995. This information and the ongoing accumulation of relevant threat data provide training materials for conducting threat assessments for law enforcement agencies and other personnel involved in psychological profiling.

Threat assessment usually involves three major goals (Fein, Vossekuil, & Holden, 1995). The first goal is *the identification of the potential perpetrator*, in the event that he or she is unknown. The second goal is to *evaluate the risks the potential perpetrator may pose* to particular targets. This goal requires the gathering of multiple sources of information on the potential perpetrator, including his or her behavioral patterns, interests, and state of mind at various points in time. These sources include interviews with the person or persons; material created or collected by the suspect, including notes, journals, letters, books, magazines, and relevant electronic media; contacts with persons who know or have known the suspect; and record or archival information, including police, court, probation, mental health, and correctional records. This goal also requires gathering as much information as possible concerning the suspect's knowledge of and skills with weapons, and the nature of the weapons the suspect has in his or her possession.

Note, though, that even when an individual is identified, he or she cannot necessarily be legally charged with a crime. The 15-year-old who writes a note threatening to kill the principal may be suspended or expelled from school, but—in most jurisdictions—he has not committed a crime, nor has the student who creates a Facebook page devoted to demanding that a teacher be fired. However, a threat assessment expert may be asked to predict whether these individuals are likely to escalate their behavior to more serious outcomes. Moreover, if the threatening activity continues, it may constitute a breach of stalking laws, thereby enabling police to charge the individual with a criminal violation.

The third goal is to *manage both the suspect and the risks that he or she presents to a given target*. This step requires the clear identification of potential targets gathered from the nature of the threats. It also necessitates the development of a strategy that discourages the suspect from violence or moves him or her away from the intended target. For example, the evaluators may request the help of a prosecutor to use enforceable anti-stalking laws against the suspect.

Threat Assessment and School Violence

School shootings took a significant turn for the worse with the Columbine High School (Littleton, Colorado) massacre on April 20, 1999, which resulted in 15 dead and 23 wounded. (See Photo 6.1, depicting a scene from the library after the incident.) Although there had been a number of school shootings prior to Columbine (at least 10 between 1996 and 1999), the Columbine shooting prompted a great deal of alarm and concern nationwide. The Columbine rampage was the second-most covered news story in the decade of the 1990s and represented the deadliest school shooting in history at that time (Larkin, 2009; Muschert, 2002).

Photo 6.1: Evidence tags mark papers, books, and a calculator strewn across a library table at Columbine High School. Ten of the 12 students who died in the shooting were killed in the library.

Accumulating evidence indicates that the Columbine shooters, two teenage boys, sought fame through the shootings, and, perhaps more alarming, they provided a vivid and powerful model that later school killers have emulated (Kiilakoski & Oksanen, 2011; Larkin, 2009). The Columbine killers "left behind videos, photos, diaries, proto-blog Internet pages and created a brand for school shootings to come" (Kiilakoski & Oksanen, 2011, p. 247). Prior to Columbine, there was no documented evidence of student conspiracies to bomb or shoot up one's school for some perceived "greater good" or political agenda. Pre-Columbine rampage shootings focused on perceived personal injustices such as intimate friend rejections, misogyny, and revenge for bully-ing and public humiliation (Moore, Petrie, Braga, & McLaughlin, 2003). Columbine and many subsequent school rampages have been driven by attempts at recognition and some ill-conceived endeavor to change life for other student social outcasts.

Columbine also produced a record of carnage that some shooters sought to exceed. As Larkin observes, the shooters attained a mythical status in the eyes of outcast stu-dent subcultures. In his research of subsequent school shootings, he found that, "In all cases, perpetrators either admitted links with Columbine or police found evidence of Columbine influences" (p. 1314).

In essence, then, Columbine has become a "cultural script" for aspiring school shooters to follow. For example, of the 12 documented school shootings in the United States between Columbine and 2007, two thirds emulated the Columbine script to a significant degree. Kiilakoksi and Oksanen (2011) assert that school shootings have become an international phenomenon since 1999, with most following the Columbine script. For instance, in 2007, Pekka-Eric Auvinen killed 8 students and staff and wounded 12 at Jokela High School in Tuusula, Finland, before committing suicide. Auvinen closely mimicked the Columbine script, right down to the music. The Columbine shooters were avid fans of the German/American rock band KMFDM, and planned their attack for the day the band released their *Adios* album. As Kiilakoski and Oksanen note, many other school shooters cite KMFDM in their diaries and videos, including Auvinen. "Auvinen used almost the same songs by KMFDM . . . that were cited by the Columbine killers" (p. 257). Larkin (2009) reports in his research that of the 11 school shootings outside the United States, 6 made direct references to Columbine before and during the incident. The latest publicized incident occurred in Salt Lake City, Utah, in January 2012. An 18-year-old and a 16-year-old were arrested after offi-cials learned of their plot to bomb their school during an assembly. The younger of the two bragged to police that he was smarter than the Columbine killers. It was later learned that he had traveled to Colorado in the fall of 2011 to interview Columbine's principal about the massacre. These observations suggest some modeling of the script in school shootings since Columbine. In the next subsection, we discuss whether these script similarities allow the development of an accurate profile of the school shooter.

PROFILING SCHOOL SHOOTERS

After the attack at Columbine, some professionals were intent on identifying and developing a psychological profile of the typical school shooter (Borum, Cornell,

Modzeleski, & Jimerson, 2010; McGee & DeBernardo, 1999). However, considering our present knowledge about the dynamics and precursors of student school shooters, we are still a long way from developing such a profile. As stated by Sewell and Mendelsohn (2000), "We do not know how to identify which youngsters will indeed perpetrate extreme violence—at least not beyond meager probability statements regarding previously violent adolescents" (p. 166). To begin with, school shootings are very rare events, despite media accounts that may suggest otherwise. Rare events do not allow a sufficient database for developing meaningful profiles—at least in the traditional sense of "profiling," where a predictive description of the typical shooter is formulated.

In addition, there is a risk—even with relatively accurate predictors—that many students identified as likely to commit serious violence in the school will not, and consequently will be labeled unjustly. As asserted by Heilbrun, Dvoskin, and Heilbrun (2009), "'Profiling' potential school or college shooters is a futile exercise that will inevitably identify far more individuals than would ever go on to commit such violence" (p. 95). Some professionals have developed checklists that represent early warning signs of individuals likely to commit violent acts in the school. Even the developers of these early-warning checklists admonish against using the indicators as decision tools, but they are often misused, especially in the hands of untrained evaluators (Sewell & Mendelsohn, 2000). Another difficulty with early-warning signs of violence listed on checklists is that they have extremely high base rates—meaning many students display them (see Table 6.1)—whereas the violent acts themselves have very low base rates. In addition, many of these checklist instruments do not provide specific cut-off scores that indicate a risk significant enough to warrant particular action. More importantly, there often has been no empirical research on the checklist to establish either reliability or validity with regard to predicting violence.

Table 6.1   Early Warning Signs of Violence

Loss of temper on a daily basis
Feelings of rejection and loneliness
Victim of bullying
Threatens others frequently
Frequent name calling, cursing, or abusive language
Prefers music expressing violent themes
Lack of impulse control, especially dealing with anger
History of discipline problems
Poor school performance
Has threatened or attempted suicide
Carries a weapon
History of violent or aggressive behavior
Fascination with guns and explosives
Does not respect authority
Uses drugs and alcohol

The above discussion leads us to an important question: What is a school district expected to do when threats from students to other students, teachers, or school administrators are made? One good beginning is to establish a threat assessment team in the school or in the community, comprising individuals who are trained to provide careful consideration to the nature of the threat, the level of risk posed by the individual, and the necessary actions to prevent the threat from being carried out. We will discuss these threat assessment teams shortly.

THE SAFE SCHOOL INITIATIVE (SSI)

The U.S. Department of Education (ED) (Dwyer, Osher, & Warger, 1998), the FBI (O'Toole, 2000), and the Secret Service and ED (Vossekuil, Fein, Reddy, Borum, & Modzeleski, 2002) have all examined and published reports on the dynamics and causes of school shootings. The most influential of these studies was the one produced by the U.S. Secret Service in conjunction with the Department of Education. The two agencies initiated a comprehensive study exploring the thinking, planning, and other pre-attack behaviors displayed by school shooters. The study, called the **Safe School Initiative (SSI),** drew from the Secret Service's experience in studying and preventing targeted attacks. "The objective of the Safe School Initiative was to attempt to identify information that could be obtainable, or 'knowable,' prior to an attack" (Vossekuil et al., 2002, p. 3). The SSI examined incidents in the United States from 1974 through May 2000, analyzing a total of 37 incidents involving 41 student attackers.

The SSI concluded that the following 10 findings were thought to be the most important background knowledge when evaluating the level of threats:

1. Incidents of targeted violence at school rarely were sudden, impulsive acts.

   Some attackers planned the attack as few as 1 or 2 days prior to the incident; other attackers planned the attack for as long as a year prior to carrying it out.

2. Prior to most incidents, other people knew about the attack's idea or the plan to attack.

   In over three quarters of the attacks, at least one person had information about the planned attack, and in many cases (two thirds) at least two persons knew about the plan or intentions. In nearly all these cases (93%), the person(s) who knew beforehand was a peer, a friend, a schoolmate, or a sibling. Rarely did an adult know of the planned attack.

In virtually all school shootings, other investigators discovered that the violent intentions of the assailants were repeatedly made clear to others, particularly peers, often including the time and place. They often verbalized their impending attack in the form of threats, boasts, and assertions of intent. It is estimated that at least 50% of school shooters make their intentions known to others, a phenomenon known by investigators as *leakage*. Documents show that the Columbine school shooters repeatedly dropped hints at school about their murderous intentions (Meadows, 2006).

However, peers rarely reported these threats to the authorities. The reasons for this behavior are not well understood, but fear seems to play a major role. A survey by the Safe School Coalition of Washington State (1999, cited in Verlinden, Hersen, & Thomas, 2000) revealed that fear of not being believed, fear of retribution, and fear of what might happen to the youth threatening the school violence were the most frequently reported concerns of peers. Verlinden et al. (2000) concluded that the risk for school violence is high when there are multiple warning signs and risk factors. "The more signs there are and the greater the opportunity, motivation, and access to weapons, the greater the possibility that the child may commit a violent act" (p. 47).

3. Most attackers did not threaten their targets directly prior to the attack.

   In most cases (83%), attackers did not tell the targets they intended to harm them, whether in direct, indirect, or conditional language, prior to the attack.

4. Most attackers engaged in some behavior prior to the incident that caused others concern or indicated a need for help.

   Almost all of the attackers (93%) exhibited some behavior prior to the attack that caused school officials, parents, teachers, police, or peers to be concerned. The behaviors included efforts to get a gun, or the writing of notes, poems, or essays for class assignments that indicated such intentions.

5. Most attackers had difficulty coping with significant losses or personal failures. Furthermore, many had considered or attempted suicide. Most attackers had a history of extreme depression or desperation.

6. Many attackers felt bullied, persecuted, or injured by others prior to the attack.

   The SSI study found that about three quarters of the attackers felt persecuted, threatened, attacked, or injured by others prior to the incident. Some had experienced severe bullying and harassment over a long period of time.

Investigations of school shooters have consistently found that the three characteristics that emerge are peer rejection, social rejection, and victimization of persistent bullying. One key conclusion made by Leary, Kowalski, Smith, and Phillips (2003) is that "The typical shooter is a male student who has been ostracized by the majority group at his school for some time, and has been chronically taunted, teased, harassed, and often publicly humiliated" (p. 213). Being the victim of vicious and public bullying by peers consistently emerges in the school experiences of shooters. One of the Columbine High School shooters, Dylan Klebold, wrote in his diary how lonely he was without friends and that he was especially tortured by his failures with girls (Meadows, 2006). The other shooter, Eric Harris, wrote in his diary that everyone continually made fun of him. A vast majority of shooters had poor social and coping skills and felt picked on or persecuted (Verlinden et al., 2000). They expressed anger about being teased or ridiculed and vowed revenge against particular individuals or groups. Moreover, as a group, "they lacked social support and prosocial relationships that might have served as protective factors" (Verlinden et al., 2000, p. 44).

7. Most attackers had access to and had used weapons prior to the attack.

    About two thirds had a known history of using weapons, including knives, guns, and bombs or explosives.

8. In many cases, other students were involved in some capacity.

    Although a majority of attackers carried out their attacks on their own, many attackers (44%) were influenced or encouraged by others to engage in the attacks.

9. Despite prompt law enforcements responses, most shooting incidents were stopped by means other than law enforcement intervention.

    Most of the attacks (75%) were stopped by school administrators, teachers, and/or students; alternatively, the shooter stopped attacking on his own. About half of the incidents lasted about 15 minutes or less prior to intervention.

10. Currently, there is no accurate or useful profile of students who engaged in targeted school violence.

Although all the attackers have been boys, there are no sets of traits that describe all or even most of the attackers. In addition, they varied considerably in demographic background and other characteristics, and came from a variety of family situations. The students who carried out the attacks were different from one another in many significant ways. Their targets also varied. It may have been a specific individual, such as a classmate, an administrator, or teacher; it may have been the school in general; or the attack may have been directed at a group or category of students, such as "jocks" or "geeks." This is essentially the same conclusion the Secret Service advanced on adult assassins, published a few years earlier in the ECSP (Fein & Vossekuil, 1998).

Both the school shooter study and the ECSP concluded that the use of profiles is not an effective approach to identifying students who may pose a risk for targeted school violence, or for assessing the risk that a particular student may pose for a school shooting once a particular student is identified.

In addition, the authors of the SSI study asserted that reliance on profiles carries two potential risks: (1) the great majority of students who fit the profile of a "school shooter" will not actually pose a risk of targeted violence, and (2) using profiles based on current research knowledge of shooters will fail to identify some students who actually do pose a risk of violence but share few if any characteristics with prior school shooters. And, as pointed out by Nader and Mello (2002) and as mentioned above, falsely identifying an adolescent as potentially violent may negatively affect his adjustment and social-emotional development. For example, a label of potentially dangerous or violent placed on an adolescent leaves him (or her) vulnerable to emotional and social debilitation when the label impugns the person's social position among peers.

Vossekuil et al. (2002) propose that, rather than creating a traditional profile for a potential school shooter, the inquiry should focus on a student's behavior and communications to determine if that student appears to be planning or preparing for an attack. However, it is unclear what specific type of profiling Vossekuil et al. are referring to in the above statement. It appears that they are referring to the traditional FBI or clinical approach to profiling, rather than the more scientific, multidimensional predictions of psychological profiling. In the next section of the report, they emphasize the need to rely on the "fact-based threat assessment approach" that can facilitate efforts to gather and analyze information regarding student behavior and communications (p. 41). They further write,

> Threat assessment, as developed by the Secret Service and applied in the context of targeted school violence, is a fact-based investigative and analytical approach that focuses on what a particular student is doing and saying, and not on whether the student "looks like" those who have attacked schools in the past. (p. 41)

SCHOOL THREAT ASSESSMENT TEAMS

After the Columbine shooting, the media and some experts were quick to make gross generalizations about the school violence problem. In addition, these horrific incidents have placed greater demands on clinical and school psychologists and other educational practitioners to be competent in conducting various assessments for determining violence risk. However, some practitioners in recent years have questioned the use of violence risk assessments, stressing their potential for stigmatizing effects on students as well as the danger of making far too many false positive predictions of future behavior (McGowan, Horn, & Mellott, 2011). A *false positive* prediction is predicting that someone will be violent when they turn out to not be; a *false negative* is predicting that someone will not be violent, and they turn out to be (see Table 6.2).

Following the Safe School Initiative, school districts in the United States have been encouraged to put together threat assessment teams designed to distinguish serious student threats from low-risk threats (Daniels et al., 2010). Put another way, some threats are more credible than others. This has prompted researchers to conduct studies in an effort to understand these distinctions. In one such study, Cornell and his associates (Cornell et al., 2004) examined 188 student threats that occurred in 25 schools over a 1-year period in Virginia. The researchers make a distinction between two types of threats: transient and substantive. **Transient threats** are statements that do not communicate a lasting intent to harm someone and that can be resolved with an apology or explanation. These were threats school authorities said they encounter frequently and that can be addressed as a routine disciplinary matter. Transient threats reflect emotional states that dissipate rapidly once the student realizes what he or she has said. "The most important feature of a transient threat is that the student does not have a sustained intention to harm someone" (Cornell et al., 2004, p. 533).

Table 6.2 Prediction Table

		Did	Did Not
Prediction	*Will*	*True positive*	*False positive*
	Will Not	*False negative*	*True negative*

Substantive threats are serious in that they represent a sustained intent to harm someone beyond the immediate occasion when the threat was made. Substantive threats can be identified by five indicators, as suggested by O'Toole (2000):

1. *Specific, plausible details have been described in the plan.*

   This indicator may include the identity of the intended victims; the reason(s) for making the threat; the means, weapon, and method by which it will be carried out; and the date, time, and place where the incident will occur. In the 2012 alleged plan to bomb a high school in Salt Lake City, one of the youths had asked a girl he liked whether she would agree to stay home from school on a certain day if he were to ask her. Interestingly, the emotional content of messages may not signal anything significant beyond the emotional state of the student at the time. Emotional content may be conveyed by melodramatic words and unusual punctuation, such as, "You have ruined my life!!!!!!!" Although these types of messages frighten the recipient, the association between emotional content in the threat and the risk that it will be carried out has not been validated.

2. *The threat has been repeated over time or passed on to a number of peers.*

3. *There is evidence that planning to carry out the threat has taken place.*

4. *The student has recruited accomplices or has invited an audience to observe the incident.*

5. *There is evidence that the student actually has acquired firearms, bomb materials, and considerable ammunition.*

Some combination of the above indicators would strengthen the level of the threat. However, threat assessments must take into consideration the context of the threat and try to make reasoned judgments based on as much information as possible.

Students at all grade levels, including kindergarten students, make threats. According to the Cornell et al. (2004) research, most of the intended victims of the threats are other students, usually at the same grade level. There were 146 threats made by boys and 42 by girls in that study. The most common threat (41%) was to hit or beat up a targeted victim. In addition, there were 27 threats to kill, 24 threats to shoot, and 18 threats to cut or stab. There were 32 cases in which the threat was vague or nonspecific ("I'm going to get you"), and 10 other miscellaneous threats, such as threats to set fires or set off bombs. Of the 188 threats studied by Cornell et al., only 3 were considered serious enough to expel the student from school. In one case, a sixth-grade boy picked up a pair of scissors and threatened to stab a classmate. A second case involved an eighth-grade girl who threatened a male classmate, telling him she intended to shoot him. In the third incident, a ninth-grade girl was expelled for threatening to stab another student, and school authorities discovered a knife in her locker following the threat. About 50% of the students who threatened someone were suspended from school, with durations ranging from 1 to 10 days.

As mentioned in the Safe School Initiative, school threat assessment teams are cautioned that an adolescent who is struggling with social and peer rejection and feelings of social incompetence who is then labeled a potential threat may complicate the situation even more. Moreover, as mentioned above, promoters of using early-warning signs to identify potential school shooters often caution against using the indicators as a simple checklist, but unfortunately these cautions are often ignored (Sewell & Mendelsohn, 2000).

In an effort to help school threat assessment teams, Dewey Cornell (Cornell & Allen, 2011; Cornell, Gregory, & Fan, 2011; Cornell & Sheras, 2006) has spearheaded a project designed to develop student threat assessment guidelines, called the Virginia Student Threat Assessment Guidelines. These were developed for K–12 schools in response to the FBI and Secret Service recommendations that schools utilize a threat assessment approach to reduce school violence. The guidelines are described in a 145-page manual that leads team members step-by-step through the threat assessment process (see Figure 6.1).

In summary, school shootings are understandably frightening and are of deep concern, but statistically they are rare. At this writing, since 2000, there have been 46 school shootings (in high, middle, and elementary schools) in the United States, resulting in 48 deaths. Some of these deaths were teachers or other school personnel. At the college level, there were 21 shootings, resulting in 64 deaths. As in the school shootings, some of the deaths of the college shootings were professors or other college personnel. The worst of the college incidents occurred in April 2007, when 32 persons were shot and killed at Virginia Tech. The Safe School Initiative report emphasized that, although school shootings are rare, the psychological impact on the students, school personnel, and the community is immense and long-lasting.

However, even prior to these violent incidents, anecdotal and media accounts of children being victimized at school by other children prompted researchers to study the issue to document the magnitude of the problem. Violence in schools is more than school shootings. It includes rape, aggravated and simple assaults, and robbery. Although in this section we are largely concerned with profiling and prediction of school shootings, it should be noted that hostage takings, bombings, arson, sexual assault, and bullying are all forms of school violence. Therefore, school violence *in general* remains a serious problem, and the Safe School Initiative and the Department of Education advocate for the development of threat assessment teams in a number of school districts to evaluate the possibility of various kinds of violence.

ADULT SCHOOL SHOOTERS

So far, we have talked about school-aged shooters killing or otherwise harming classmates and teachers. Adults unaffiliated with the school have also been involved in school violence incidents. Attempts to predict these attacks are often considered futile, similar to attacks by mass killers. Schools can, however, take protective measures such as installing video cameras on school premises and ensuring that points of entry to the school are clearly visible. Many schools today also have "intruder drills," during which students and teachers practice barricading their classroom doors and hiding behind barriers, such as desks and tables.

Figure 6.1 Decision Tree for Student Threat Assessment

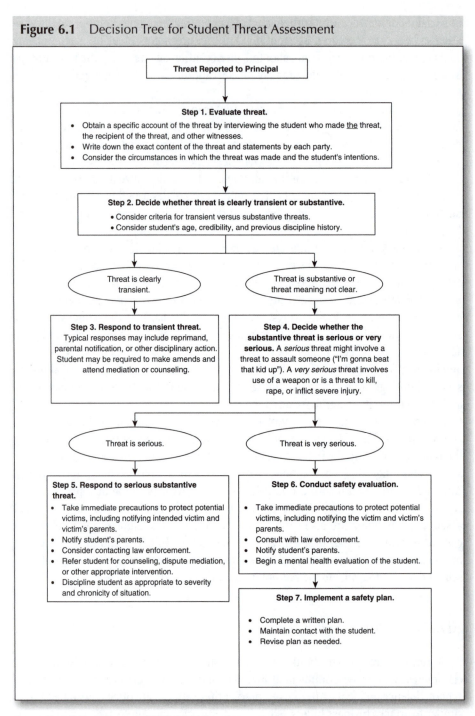

Source: Cornell, D., & Sheras, P. (2006). "Guidelines for responding to student threats of violence." Longmont, CO: Sopris West.

In recent years, a number of adult males have barged into school buildings, killing students and staff. Though horrific, instances such as this are rare, but unlike student shooters, the adults do not typically make threats. In West Nickel, Pennsylvania, on October 2, 2006, 32-year-old Charles Carl Roberts carried three guns into West Nickel Mines School, an Amish one-room schoolhouse. The gunman took hostages, all girls, and sent the boys and adults outside. He barricaded the doors and then opened fire on a dozen girls, killing five and seriously wounding five others before committing suicide. His motivation was unclear, but he indicated that his actions were not directly related to school or the Amish community, but were driven by events in his childhood. More likely, "he may have viewed himself as powerless or his own life circumstances as hopeless and acted out in a school environment that was simple, peaceful—and completely at his mercy" (Gerler, 2007, p. 2).

A week earlier, 53-year-old Duane Roger Morrison, armed with an assault rifle and carrying a backpack full of explosives, walked into Platte Canyon High School in Bailey, Colorado. He took six female students hostage and sexually assaulted five of them. He then released four of them. When a SWAT team broke into the classroom, Morrison shot and killed one 16-year-old student before turning the gun on himself. The other remaining hostage managed to escape. The motive of this adult attacker remains unclear. These two incidents occurred so close together in time that a copycat effect is suspected.

Two infamous adult shooters who massacred college students were Marc Lépine and Kimveer Gill. Lépine was responsible for the "Montreal Massacre" in which he killed 14 women attending class at the École Polytechnique in December 1989. His attack appears to have been primarily motivated by hatred toward feminists, whom he blamed for ruining his life. Gill shot 20 persons, killing 1, at Dawson College, Westmont, Quebec, in September 2006. Police investigators learned that Gill planned on committing similar attacks at other institutions throughout Montreal. Both Lépine and Gill were about 25 years old at the time, and both committed their attacks at colleges they never attended (Langman, 2009). According to Langman, Gill modeled his attacks after Columbine and apparently admired Eric Harris. From all indications, Gill completely withdrew from life and most social contact about a year before his rampage. Lépine's shooting appears to follow the characteristics of a mass murder prompted by hatred of a subgroup. The Gill attack, on the other hand, shows some of the characteristics of a school shooting and seems to follow the cultural script of Columbine to some extent.

PSYCHOLOGICAL CHARACTERISTICS OF STUDENT SCHOOL SHOOTERS

Subsequent to the Safe School Initiative report, other researchers have examined more closely the psychological characteristics of school shooters. We must caution, though, that discovery of a few common characteristics does not mean that a profile of a school shooter is warranted, as we repeatedly have stated throughout this section. Leary et al. (2003) scrutinized the psychological patterns and backgrounds of offenders involved in 15 school shootings between 1995 and 2001. They discovered that peer rejection was involved in most cases of school shootings. Most of the rejected shooters experienced an ongoing pattern of teasing, bullying, or ostracism, and a few had experienced a recent romantic rejection. In many cases, some of the victims of the violence were those who had rejected or humiliated the shooter.

Peer rejection alone did not seem to be enough to inspire them to kill classmates and school personnel, however. In addition to the social rejection, perpetrators showed at least one of the following three risk factors: *psychological problems*, an *interest in guns or explosives*, or a *morbid fascination with death*.

The psychological problems centered around low impulse control, lack of empathy for other people, serious depression, aggressiveness, and antisocial behavior. Many of the shooters had been in trouble for aggressive behavior toward peers, and some had abused animals. Depression appears to be especially important in identifying potential school shooters. In one comprehensive study, three fourths of school shooters had expressed thoughts of suicide or had attempted suicide before the attack (Vossekuil et al., 2002).

Fascination with firearms, bombs, and explosives is also a common theme. School shooters seemed to be comfortable with instruments of destruction. Wike and Fraser (2009) note that police in Plymouth Meeting outside of Philadelphia arrested a 14-year-old school dropout who, with his parents' assistance, had collected swords, guns, grenades, bomb instruction manuals, black powder used in bomb making, and videos of the Columbine massacre. According to police—who acted on a tip from students—this alienated student had plans to attack his former school.

The third observation is that shooters tend to be highly fascinated with death and dark lifestyles and themes. They are not as horrified by sadistic and brutal carnage as most of their peers. In March of 2005, Jeffrey Weise, a 16-year-old at Red Lake High School in Minnesota, killed his grandfather and his grandfather's girlfriend, and then drove to the high school and fatally shot a security guard, a teacher, and five students. He wounded six others before shooting himself. Weise left many messages with dark themes on websites, posted photos of himself dressed all in black, and wrote stories about school shootings and zombies (Weisbrot, 2008). However, these dark themes also may be characteristic of depression or thoughts of suicide. Weise had been hospitalized for suicidal behavior. Eric Harris and Dylan Klebold, the Columbine High School shooters, are often referred to as devout believers in the macabre, but the evidence does not hold up that this was clearly the case. Rather, it appears that they were both simply angry and possibly severely depressed young men.

In a vast majority of school shootings, the perpetrators apparently had very little attachment or bonding to their schools, teachers, or peers (Wike & Fraser, 2009). School attachment and bonding appear to be crucial in any strategy designed to reduce school violence. Some investigators have found that school attachment plays an important role in producing high levels of academic achievement and in reducing substance use, violence, and high-risk sexual behavior (Catalano, Haggerty, Oesterle, Fleming, & Hawkins, 2004; Wike & Fraser, 2009).

Workplace Violence

Very broadly, workplace violence is any act of physical violence, harassment, intimidation, or other threatening behavior that occurs in the workplace (U.S. Department of Labor, 2011). In the public mind, workplace violence often refers to a worker or ex-worker killing his or her coworkers, as in the expression "going postal," minted in the late 20th century after a rash of violent incidents involving postal workers. "Mass murders in the workplace by unstable employees have become media-intensive events" (Critical Incident Response Group, 2001, p. 11). However, multiple homicides represent a very small portion of workplace violence incidents. For example, it is estimated that only 4 to 7% of workplace homicides occur between coworkers (LeBlanc & Kelloway, 2002). Workplace violence also applies to violence directed at employees by customers, visitors, robbers, spouses, unhappy clients, patients, or any person who comes into contact with employees.

STATISTICS ON SERIOUS WORKPLACE VIOLENCE

Data collected by the Bureau of Labor Statistics (2010) indicate that, on average, 564 people are murdered at work each year, making it the second leading cause of occupational death in the United States. In 2008, there were 30 multiple-fatality workplace homicide incidents, accounting for 67 homicides and 7 suicides. On average, about two persons died in each of these incidents. Shootings accounted for 80% of all homicides in the workplace. Robbers were the assailants in about 40% of the cases. Coworkers and former coworkers were the assailants in 12% of all workplace shootings, and women are most often the recipients of the violence (Hayes, Outten, & Steer, 2000). There are three apparent reasons for this. First, women tend to be the front people, such as the receptionists, and if someone is going to harm somebody in the workplace, they often begin with the front person. According to Hayes et al., the second reason is that women are often in the personnel and human resources fields. The perpetrator is often angry because of a poor review or for being fired, reprimanded, or laid off, which he or she attributes to the personnel department, at least in part. The third reason is that domestic violence frequently spills over into the workplace. Ex- or current husbands or angry boyfriends may come into the work environment and try to harm the woman, as well as any employees who try to stop the violence.

Although the impression derived from media reports over the past two decades is that workplace violence is expanding, it must be emphasized that a large majority of workplace homicides do *not* involve murder between coworkers or between workers and supervisors *within* an organization, but occur in robberies and related crimes by people *outside* the organization (Neuman & Baron, 1998). Convenience store clerks or fast-food restaurant workers are often the victims of robbery and other forms of violence while working, especially those employees who work at night and alone.

CATEGORIES OF WORKPLACE VIOLENCE

In an effort to organize the research about and accounts of workplace violence, the California Division of Occupational Safety and Health (1955) divided the incidents into four major categories based on the perpetrator's relationship to the workplace.

In Type I, the assailant has no legitimate relationship with the targeted workplace and enters the organization or business to commit a crime, such as a robbery. Convenience store, liquor store, or fast-food restaurant employees are often the victims. In Type II, the perpetrator is the recipient of some service provided by the workplace, such as health care, social services, counseling, education, or psychotherapy. Nurses, social workers, teachers, and therapists are often the recipients of this type of violence. In Type III, the offender is an employee or former employee of the workplace. The perpetrator in these cases is often a disgruntled employee who has been fired, laid off, demoted, embarrassed, or has lost benefits. In Type IV violence, the offender does not have a legitimate relationship with the workplace but has a personal or intimate relationship with an employee. Often, Type IV is a form of domestic violence spilling over into the workplace.

Our focus here will be on Type III violence, where a current or former coworker engages in violence at his or her workplace or former workplace (see Photo 6.2). We will especially concentrate on the extent to which this violence can be predicted in a psychological profile. To date, there is limited research that examines the predictors of workplace violence. Those studies that have investigated Type III violence have concentrated on either (a) describing the person who engages in coworker violence, or (b) identifying the job characteristics that increase the probability of violence from a current or former coworker (LeBlanc & Kelloway, 2002). There have been very few investigations to validate what factors best predict who will become violent in the workplace, but researchers have identified some warning signs.

Photo 6.2: Two men engage in a violent altercation in their workplace, while a fellow employee makes an effort to intercede. Although no weapons are in evidence, such eruptions contribute to a hostile work environment and may escalate into more serious violence.

THE WARNING SIGNS

When the violence comes from an employee, there is a much greater chance that some warning signs have been observed by other employees or supervisors. In many cases, there are several warnings of verbal threats to kill or do harm to oneself or others. In other cases, the perpetrator has demonstrated a pattern of escalating threats that appear well planned, or made frequent references to other incidents of workplace violence. Often, the threatening behavior or commentary builds over time, with the employee making progressively hostile comments or threats over a relatively short period of time. Usually, they are directed at a specific target or the organization in general.

Table 6.3 lists some problematic behavior or warning signs that may lead to more serious violence. Like the list of warning signs for school violence, these indicators should not automatically be assumed to be precursors of violence in the workplace. In addition, no one behavior necessarily denotes a red flag; there must be several behaviors that cause concern.

Table 6.3 Employee Warning Signs of Potential Workplace Violence

- Increasing belligerence
- Ominous, specific threats
- Hypersensitivity to criticism
- Recent acquisition/fascination with weapons
- Apparent obsession with a supervisor or coworker or employee grievance
- Preoccupation with violent themes
- Holds serious grudges, especially against supervisors
- Interest in recently publicized violent events
- Outbursts of anger
- Extreme disorganization
- Noticeable changes in behavior
- Homicidal/suicidal comments or threats
- Drug or alcohol use on the job

Source: Critical Incident Response Group (2001), pp. 21–22.

As emphasized by the Critical Incident Response Group (2001), workplace violence is often preceded by a threat. Sometimes, however, the threat is difficult to detect because it is subtle and subjective. "The threat may have been explicit or veiled, spoken or unspoken, specific or vague, but it occurred" (p. 23). Fortunately, many threats turn out to be harmless blowing off of steam, but all should be considered serious when first made. Perhaps even more serious is any pattern of aggressive behavior, including constant harassment, stalking, and unwanted physical contact; a pattern of these behaviors is a red flag that an employee may pose a danger to coworkers.

BEHAVIORS AND CHARACTERISTICS
THAT MAY PREDICT WORKPLACE VIOLENCE

Barling (1996) makes the case, largely based on the research literature on family violence, that there are four personal factors that tend to be predictive of Type III violence: alcohol use, past history of aggression and violence, lack of self-esteem, and the use of psychological aggression in the workplace. As noted by Barling, "Profiles of potentially violent employees emphasize their excessive alcohol consumption" (p. 33). Alcohol consumption and a history of aggression and violence are related to aggression and violence toward coworkers and subordinates (Greenberg & Barling, 1999; LeBlanc & Barling, 2005). In fact, alcohol abuse appears to be very common among those employees who kill at the workplace (LeBlanc & Barling, 2005), as is substance abuse (Hayes et al., 2000). Excessive alcohol consumption or substance abuse increases workplace violence because it amplifies the probability of a situation being misread and decreases intellectual and verbal functioning (Cox & Leather, 1994).

In reference to the second factor, history of aggression and violence, an employee who has such a history is likely to resort to resolving conflict and disagreement via the same strategies in the future. One way to reduce the possibility of an employee being violent is to conduct background checks for aggression and a history of violence of prospective employees before hire. The best predictor of future behavior is past behavior in similar situations. If the employee has been aggressive, violent, and threatening to other employees or supervisors in previous workplaces, he or she is likely to show a similar pattern in future work environments.

The third factor, lack of self-esteem, is highly characteristic of aggressive and potentially violent individuals. Any event or series of events that diminishes self-esteem in certain employees has the potential of pushing them over the edge. Closely related to low self-esteem is the fourth factor, that of psychological aggression directed at the worker from coworkers or supervisors. This may be in the form of hostile teasing, harassment, and humiliation. For example, in 1999, Ottawa, Ontario, transit worker Pierre Lebrun shot and killed four of his coworkers and seriously wounded two others before shooting himself (LeBlanc & Barling, 2005). Reports indicated that Lebrun was continually taunted at work because of his stutter.

Another form of psychological aggression, at least from the victim's perspective, is interpersonal injustice. Recent research indicates that perceptions of interpersonal injustice in the workplace may lead to workplace violence (Dupré, Barling, Turner, & Stride, 2010).

> Interpersonal injustice is an individual's perception of the extent to which he or she is treated with a lack of respect, courtesy, and dignity by someone who is in a position to execute practices and procedures that relate to him or her. (Dupré et al., 2010, p. 360)

Interpersonal fairness is of great concern to employees, particularly as it relates to job evaluations that can lead to promotions and salary increases. Evaluations that are perceived as unfair or unjustified can generate strong emotional and hostile reactions. In addition, perceptions of interpersonal injustice may spill over to other situations and across relationships. When a person experiences or perceives something that generates anger, it is possible that that person may take it out on others, not only in the workplace but in the home as well. It is important that professionals conducting threat assessments in the workplace take this point into careful consideration in understanding the dynamics of a risky situation.

Type III workplace violence is very complex, and predicting whether a disgruntled or angry employee will attack is extremely challenging. Perpetrators can be either employees or supervisors, and the attack can be directed at one or several targets, including current or former supervisors, coworkers, subordinates, or any agent representative of a targeted organization or company. Perpetrators also often have a wide range of reasons for their attacks. A vast majority of Type III victims, however, are killed (often randomly) by disgruntled employees who were fired or who felt mistreated by the company or agency. It seems that a particularly autocratic work environment, such as that found in large, impersonal bureaucratic organizations, can be a problem. However, as the examples provided by the Critical Incident Response Group (2001) indicate, no workplace seems immune. As we discussed previously, when an employee feels frustrated and angry, he or she may be prone to engage in violent actions. Nevertheless, in benevolent work environments, violence has a low probability of occurring.

Hayes et al. (2000) in their research on workplace violence suggest that another serious dangerous characteristic is the possession of extremist opinions or attitudes. Anyone who frequently expresses strong attitudes of hatred toward people of color or toward people's sexual orientation or religious beliefs, or who has rigid and extreme attitudes about women in the workplace, is himself a warning sign for potential work environment violence, especially if the expression of these attitudes increases in intensity.

In sum, effective threat assessment in the workplace must include a thorough analysis of the following: (1) the nature and context of the threat; (2) the identified target; (3) the apparent motivation of the person who threatens; (4) the ability of the person to carry out the threat; and (5) the person's background, especially past violent behavior and previous work history and job behavior.

Organizations must develop clear policies and guidelines for what to do when an employee is evaluated as dangerous but has yet to commit any serious crime. Termination of the employee in the heat of the moment without time for preparation may be exactly the wrong thing to do if an employee is considered dangerous. The organization would also be wise to have designated personnel trained to oversee the organization's antiviolence policy, including when to seek threat assessment experts and crisis management professionals.

In light of the above-reported research findings, threat assessment teams might want to consider a number of factors in deciding whether or not a particular individual presents a credible threat of harm. In school settings, such aspects as peer acceptance/ rejection; involvement in activities; access to and fascination with weapons; fascination and preoccupation with death or morbid topics; and communication to others of intent to harm, particularly over a period of time, are all relevant. Psychological problems, such as highly aggressive behavior, depression, or even attempts at suicide represent other red flags. In addition, the overall climate of the school itself is crucial. In a national study of school violence, Gottfredson, Gottfredson, Payne, and Gottfredson (2005) reported that schools in which students find the rules fair and in which discipline is managed consistently experience less violence and disorder. High teacher morale and strong leadership were also important factors.

With regard to the workplace, we have less research information, but here, too, the culture of the organization appears to be an important factor, at least in protecting employees from Type III violence. However, some threats are issued in the context of stalking behaviors, which will be addressed further on. Therefore, we now turn our attention to violence risk assessment, which is similar to threat assessment but involves a much broader spectrum of potentially violent situations and targets.

Violence Risk Assessment

Violence risk assessments are used in the evaluation of a wide range of potentially violent situations, including domestic violence, juvenile violence, prison and jail violence, workplace violence, and violence to oneself. In risk assessments, forensic psychologists and other professionals are often asked to predict the likelihood that a known individual will be "dangerous" to himself or herself or to society in general.

The area of violence risk assessment has come a long way since John Monahan (1981) published a seminal monograph on the topic. In that paper, Monahan provided a comprehensive review and discussion of the relevant scientific and technical literature pertaining to the prediction of individual violent behavior at that time. Monahan has continued working in that area in the years since, publishing numerous scholarly works, many in association with the MacArthur Research Network (e.g., Monahan, 1996; Monahan et al., 2001; Skeem & Monahan, 2011).

Today, risk assessments are one of the most common functions performed by psychologists, particularly those in forensic or correctional practice. Risk assessments are relevant when courts or the criminal justice system decides whether to grant bail, whether to confine people to secure institutions, and whether to grant parole—or conditional release—to prisoners. The development of a number of short-form, rapid risk assessment tools has made it possible for non-psychologists to screen such individuals for risk of violence. The risk assessment need not be accompanied by a full psychological profile, however. A mental health practitioner may be asked just one thing: Is this individual likely to commit violence in the future? On the other hand, a complete psychological profile on a given individual should include an assessment of risk, that is, of whether the individual is suspected to be a danger to self or society.

Many instruments are used to assess the risk of violence. Among the most empirically valid are the Violence Risk Appraisal Guide (VRAG), Historical Clinical Risk-20 (HCR-20), the Level of Service Inventory–Revised (LSI-R), the STATIC-99, and the Sex

Offender Risk Appraisal Guide (SORAG). Risk assessment methods for domestic violence have become increasingly valuable in recent years. Two of the more popular and well-researched instruments for this purpose are the Ontario Domestic Assault Risk Assessment (ODARA) and the Domestic Violence Risk Appraisal Guide (DVRAG) (see Hilton, Harris, & Rice, 2010).

As is true of all forms of profiling, risk (and threat) assessments involve judgments about uncertainty. While they provide some statistical probability of occurrence, they are never certain. In addition, research has consistently demonstrated that common sense is not a reliable guide to what matters in these assessments (Hanson, 2009). For over 50 years, statistical models that rely on measurable, valid risk factors have been, in a majority of cases, superior to clinical judgment or professional opinion (K. S. Douglas & Ogloff, 2003; Grove & Meehl, 1996; Hanson, 2005, 2009; Meehl, 1954). Nevertheless, many clinicians today argue very persuasively that these instruments must be balanced with sound, clinical judgment developed through years of experience and training.

The debate regarding statistical or actuarial prediction versus clinical prediction has led to a third approach for assessing violence risk or threat (McGowan et al., 2011). This third method—called the structured professional judgment (SPJ) model—views violence as a contextual, dynamic construct that exists on a continuum. The method relies on *both* structured clinical and actuarial judgments. More specifically, the SPJ model uses empirically validated risk factors (the actuarial part) as a "means for informing clinical judgments concerning an individual's risk for violence" (McGowan et al., 2011, p. 479). These empirically validated risk factors are used as a starting point, and then clinical judgments are employed, allowing the assessment to be case specific. That is, the judgment considers the specific context and the specific individual factors that statistical data cannot account for. "Taken together, this decision-making model represents a hybrid that draws on empirical knowledge and clinical judgment to guide the assessment of an individual's predisposition toward violence as well as the ecological influences that elicit it" (McGowan et al., 2011, p. 479). So far, the research has been supportive of this method (McEwan, Pathé, & Ogloff, 2011; Melton, Petrila, Poythress, & Slobogin, 2007; Webster & Hucker, 2007). We will integrate this new approach as it pertains to violence risk assessment, especially concerning stalking risk assessment, which will come later in the chapter.

At this point, it is important that we again turn our attention to some additional psychological concepts that are important to understanding violence risk assessment. The ultimate goal of profiling is prediction. Psychologists have long been involved in the enterprise of behavioral prediction, with the assumption that if we can predict with reasonable accuracy, we can prevent and treat those behaviors that are most dangerous to society and to the individual. If we can predict that an individual will be violent, for example, we can take steps to prevent the violence, including offering treatment addressing the violent tendencies. Psychological profiling, then, very often involves the assessment of one's risk of violent behavior.

Unfortunately, as we saw in the earlier chapters, predicting behavior is not easy or simple—and many psychologists today prefer to forego that enterprise entirely. Crime scene profiles, psychological autopsies, suspect-based profiling, geographic profiling, and psychological profiling all assume to a large extent that psychologists can predict (or *postdict* [after the fact]) human behavior. However, in past years, forensic evaluators were wrong twice as often as they were right in predicting crime and violence (Hanson, 2009). It may be that crime scene and geographic profilers are even less accurate, but there is no way to know for sure, since currently the field lacks testable theory and empirical support (Lilienfeld & Lanfield, 2008; Snook et al., 2008).

The two concepts that are among the most important in understanding predictions of potentially violent persons are dynamic and static risk factors, to which we now turn our attention.

DYNAMIC AND STATIC RISK FACTORS IN PREDICTION

An important issue in psychological profiling is the distinction between dynamic risk factors and static risk factors (Andrews & Bonta, 1998; Andrews, Bonta, & Hoge, 1990). They are referred to as "risk factors" because they are associated with or predictive of antisocial behavior. **Dynamic risk factors** are those that can change over time and situation. For example, one's employment status and substance abuse have potential for change, and are thus dynamic. In contrast, **static risk factors** like parental criminality or one's own early onset of antisocial behavior are historical and cannot be changed.

Dynamic factors can be subdivided into stable and acute (Hanson & Harris, 2000). **Stable dynamic factors,** although they are changeable, usually change slowly and may take months or even years to do so, if they change at all. Consider, for example, one's attitudes about violent pornography or one's long-time association with deviant peers. **Acute dynamic factors,** on the other hand, change rapidly (over days, hours, or even minutes), sometimes dependent upon mood swings, emotional arousal, and alcohol or other drug-induced effects. In some research (e.g., Hanson & Harris, 2000), acute dynamic factors were better predictors of reoffending—in this case, with regard to sex offenders—than were stable dynamic factors.

During the 1980s and 1990s, violence risk assessment was directed at improving prediction and largely concentrated on using static, unchangeable risk factors in predicting the behavior of individuals at high risk of violence (McEwan et al., 2011). The methods of violence risk prediction utilized past behavior and static personal factors in the assessment process. Since that time, violence risk assessment procedures have increasingly focused on dynamic, changeable factors as meaningful and powerful components in assessment equations. Perhaps more importantly, the utilization of dynamic, changeable factors in violence risk assessment is more closely aligned with most clinicians' existing practice and helps greatly in the management of dangerous individuals. "The most effective interventions to reduce violence risk will be those that target the dynamic risk factors causally related to violence for that individual" (McEwan et al., 2011, p. 182). In the next section, we cover the topic of stalking as a prime example of the value of violence risk assessment.

Stalking

Stalking, also called obsessional harassment, is "characterized by persistent unwanted contact and/or communication with a victim, resulting in the victim's fear or distress" (Sheridan & Roberts, 2011, p. 255). The term refers to

> repeated and often escalating unwanted intrusions and communications, including loitering nearby; following or surveying a person's home, making multiple telephone calls or other forms of unwanted direct and indirect communications, spreading gossip, destroying personal property, harassing acquaintances or family members, sending threatening or sexually suggestive "gifts" or letters, and aggressive and violent acts. (Abrams & Robinson, 2002, p. 468)

Stalking is an extremely frightening, emotionally distressful, and depressing crime of intimidation, and it is gender related. Eighty percent of the victims are women, and the vast majority of stalking is done by men (Meloy & Felthouse, 2011). In addition, persistent stalking behavior is associated with violent behavior (Sheridan & Roberts, 2011). Spitzberg (2007), for example, found that long-term stalking behavior has an overall violence rate of 32% and a sexual violence rate of 12%. Violent behaviors in the study included assault, injury, suicide, rape and attempted rape, murder and attempted murder, the use of a weapon, and vandalism. Serious violent episodes occur in less than 10% of those stalking incidents reported (Rosenfeld, 2004; Sheridan & Roberts, 2011).

Although stalking is associated with violence, it is distinctive from violence in several important ways (Kropp, Hart, Lyon, & Storey, 2011). First, the perpetrator usually knows or is familiar with the victim, whereas violence is often directed at strangers. Second, stalking may only be indirectly or implicitly threatening to the victim, although it often remains very frightening and stressful to the victim. Third, stalking can persist for many months or years, in contrast to many other forms of violence that occur one time. Not surprisingly, clinicians have discovered that the longer the duration of the stalking—regardless of whether the behaviors are intrusive, violent, or some combination of both—the greater the potential danger to the victim (McEwan, Mullen, & Purcell, 2007).

Stalking took on national concern in the United States when actress Rebecca Schaeffer was killed by an obsessed fan in 1989 (Rosenfeld, Fava, & Galietta, 2009). Probably due to a copycat effect, four other California women were murdered within 2 months after the Schaeffer killing by individuals who were stalking them. These stalking-based murders prompted the California legislature to enact the first anti-stalking law. Anti-stalking laws now exist in all 50 states, the District of Columbia, and Canada. During the years before stalking legislation was enacted, little was known about stalkers and the relationships with their victims (Schwartz-Watts, 2006). Although most states define stalking in their statutes as the willful, malicious, and repeated following and harassing of another person, some include such activities as lying-in-wait, surveillance, nonconsensual communication, telephone harassment, and vandalism (Tjaden & Thoennes, 1998b). Some states require that at least two stalking incidents occur before the conduct is considered criminal.

PREVALENCE

It is estimated that stalking affects 5 to 16% of adults at some point during their lifetime (Eke, Hilton, Meloy, Mohandie, & Williams, 2011). Stalking behavior is often unreported, with only one third to one half of stalking victims reporting the crime (Schwartz-Watts, 2006). Consequently, self-report surveys of stalking victims provide the most comprehensive picture of the amount of stalking, because these reports include incidents in which the victims did not contact police. The now-classic study on stalking was conducted by the Center for Policy Research and published in a monograph titled *Stalking in America: Findings From the National Violence Against Women Survey* (Tjaden & Thoennes, 1998b). It was a nationally representative phone survey of 8,000 women and 8,000 men, 18 years or older, conducted between November 1995 and May 1996. The survey found that 8% of women and 2% of men reported that they had been stalked at some point in their lives (Tjaden, 1997). In most instances, the stalking lasted less than 1 year, but some individuals were stalked for more than 5 years. According to the research reported by Mullen, Pathé, and Purcell (2001), however, repeated unwanted communications and imposed contacts that go on for more than 2 weeks are highly likely to last for months or even years.

In other international studies, 15% of women in Australia reported being stalked, and in England and Wales 16% of women and 7% of men reported being stalked (Sheridan & Roberts, 2011). In Canada, 9% of persons aged 15 or older reported that they had been stalked during the past 5 years in a way that caused them to fear for their safety (Canadian Centre for Justice Statistics, 2005; Kropp et al., 2011). These data indicate that stalking is a serious problem internationally. Researchers believe that the motive of most stalkers is to control, intimidate, or frighten their victims.

RISK ASSESSMENT OF STALKING VIOLENCE

As emphasized by Kropp et al. (2011), risk assessments of stalking must involve a full explanation of the risks involved, including the nature, imminence, severity, and frequency of the stalking the perpetrator might commit, and the conditions under which the victim is likely to live. Research shows that nearly all stalking cases will ultimately involve face-to-face contact between victim and stalker (Mullen, Pathé, & Purcell, 2000; Sheridan & Roberts, 2011). Consequently, in most cases, the victim is quite familiar with the stalker and probably is the best source of information on the nature of the stalking.

Many—perhaps most—stalking victims want to know the likelihood that they will become the victim of a violent act (Rosenfeld & Harmon, 2002).

Determining which stalkers represent a significant risk of violence, and differentiating those individuals from the remaining offenders who may pose less risk of physical harm, has clear and significant implications for victims, clinicians, and the legal system. (p. 685)

In an effort to identify features that may differentiate violent stalkers from nonviolent stalkers, Rosenfeld and Harmon analyzed 204 stalking and harassment cases referred for court-ordered mental health evaluations in New York City. Results supported the findings of previous researchers (e.g., Palerea, Zona, Lane, & Langhinrichsen-Rohling, 1999) who found that former spouses or intimates of stalkers were most at risk. Specifically, intimate stalkers threatened persons and property (including physical violence toward the victim), were more likely to "make good" on their threats by following them with some form of violent behavior, and used more physical approach behaviors in contacting their victims than non-intimate stalkers. This observation is known as the *intimacy effect* (Calhoun & Weston, 2003); research has established that the more intimate the relationship between a stalker and a victim, the more likely a threat will be carried out (Mullen, Pathé, & Purcell, 2009; Warren et al., 2011). These results underscore the importance of accounting for the presence of an intimate relationship when assessing for violence risk in stalking cases (Palerea et al., 1999).

Additional studies by Barry Rosenfeld and his colleagues (Rosenfeld, 2004; Rosenfeld et al., 2009) report that another strong predictor of violence is a history of prior threats of harm. As emphasized by Rosenfeld et al. (2009), "the overall association between threats and subsequent violence is substantial and should raise concerns whenever a credible threat of violence is expressed, and such verbalizations must be thoroughly evaluated" (p. 103). The Rosenfeld group also confirmed their findings from a previous study that the existence of a prior intimate relationship between the victim and the offender is also a strong predictor of violence. That is, persons who stalked prior intimates were more likely to be violent than those who stalked strangers, family members, or acquaintances. Moreover, availability of weapons or a history of using weapons increases significantly the risk of life-threatening violence. Finally, when the stalking behaviors increase in frequency or severity, this represents an important cue to a heightened risk of violence. Interestingly, in most cases severe mental disorders are not strong predictors of violent stalking.

However, it should be noted that some mental health professionals who deal regularly with persons having mental or emotional difficulties have become the victims of stalking by their clients (Gentile, Asamen, Harmell, & Weathers, 2002). The stalkers of mental health professionals may be either single or divorced at the time of the stalking (Gentile et al., 2002). The majority of these clients (62%) were diagnosed as having a mood disorder. In another survey, about 2 out of 3 university counselors had experienced some type of harassing or stalking behavior from a current or former client (Romans, Hays, & White, 1996).

Sheridan and Roberts (2011) discovered that an additional robust predictor of serious stalking violence is when the stalker visits the victim's home, a finding also reported by James and Farnham (2003). More specifically, the Sheridan-Roberts research revealed that those stalkers who visited the victim's home, workplace, or other places frequented by the victim more than three times a week are those most likely to be violent. Those stalkers who camp out on the victim's property may be especially dangerous.

As noted by McEwan et al. (2011), "In the absence of a unifying explanatory theory for stalking, researchers and clinicians have developed numerous taxonomies to group the heterogeneous stalking population into more manageable subtypes" (p. 187). They go on to say that such classification systems provide a broad guide for clinicians and law enforcement personnel for understanding the range of stalking behavior, but these systems are in desperate need of supportive empirical research and unifying theory. The following are some examples of classification systems, or typologies.

STALKING TYPOLOGIES

There have been at least 12 published attempts to categorize the different patterns of stalking behavior (Mohandie, Meloy, McGowan, & Williams, 2006). Many of these have used both mental health problems and motivations as the foundation for the typology. Others have relied almost exclusively on the motivations of the perpetrators. The vast majority of these typologies have been used only marginally for law enforcement investigations or risk/threat assessment. As emphasized by Mohandie et al.,

> A typology should be parsimonious, stable (interrater and temporal reliability), behaviorally based, and useful (concurrent and predictive validity) for a variety of applied settings and professionals, including law enforcement, prosecutors, defense attorneys, judges, juries, forensic mental health experts, and victims' rights activists. (p. 147)

The RECON Typology

One of the most extensively studied and cited stalking typologies is known as RECON, initially developed by Mohandie (2004). The acronym stands for relationship (RE) and context (CON). As described in the prior sections, research has shown that the degree of prior relationship intimacy is a very important variable, especially as it pertains to risk for violence. Research has also demonstrated that there is a difference between those persons who stalk public versus private persons, a pattern that refers to the context. The RECON typology, which is based on more than 1,000 stalkers, divides the pursuit patterns of stalkers into two main categories and four subcategories. The two main categories are Type I, where the perpetrator has had a previous relationship with the victim, and Type II, where the perpetrator has had no or very limited contact with the victim (Mohandie et al., 2006). Type I is further subdivided into perpetrators whose prior relationship has been intimate, such as a married, cohabiting, or dating partner; and perpetrators who have more of an acquaintance, coworker, or friendship relationship. Type II is subdivided into those persons who are pursuing a victim considered to be a public figure, and those persons who pursue a victim identified as a private figure. Thus, the four classifications are labeled (1) **intimate**, (2) **acquaintance**, (3) **public figure**, and (4) **private stranger** stalkers (see Table 6.4).

Table 6.4 RECON Typology

Type I: Previous Relationship	Type II: No Prior Relationship
Intimate	Public Figure
Acquaintance	Private Stranger

Source: Adapted from Mohandie et al. (2006).

Mohandie et al. (2006) discovered that nearly one third of their large sample had assaulted the victim, and nearly one half had exhibited some form of violence toward the person or property. Fortunately, homicide was very rare, occurring in only 0.5% of the cases. However, intervention by law enforcement did not deter the majority of the stalkers, and frequently they made contact with the victim within 1 day after law enforcement had intervened.

The researchers found the intimate stalkers to be the most violent, which is a consistent finding in the research literature. "They insult, interfere, threaten, and are violent" (Mohandie et al., 2006, p. 153). In addition, they found that virtually all of the intimate stalkers reoffended relatively quickly compared to other groups of stalkers. The acquaintance stalkers were less violent, but still one third of the sample assaulted the victim or caused damage to property. "If they threaten, they do so repeatedly, and their pursuit patterns are likely to be indirect, sporadic, but relentless, enduring on average for almost 2 years" (p. 153).

Public figure stalkers are distinguished by a greater proportion being female perpetrators (27%), and their pursued victims tend to be males. In addition, public figure stalkers tend to be older, are less likely to have criminal records, and are more likely to be mentally disordered than the three other stalker types. There are, of course, exceptions. Comedian and television personality David Letterman was stalked for nearly 10 years by a disturbed, possibly schizophrenic woman who pretended she was his wife, entered his home, sent him flowers, and ultimately committed suicide by placing herself in the path of a speeding train. Public figure stalkers are also less likely to threaten the targeted person, and a vast majority are considered nuisances rather than dangerous to the pursued victim. In Mohandie et al.'s (2006) research, only 2% were violent, compared to 74% of the intimate stalkers. However, when violence was committed, it was usually quite serious. Perhaps a partial explanation for the low violence frequency may be the extent of security measures that often surround celebrities, politicians, and other high-level authorities or leaders.

Private stranger stalkers, who represent the less common group, tend to be mentally disordered men who may be suicidal. About one half of this group threatened their victims, and nearly one third were violent toward the person or property. Recidivism rates for this group are low (25%).

Eke and her associates (2011) write that "Professionals assessing a stalking case can use the RECON typology to categorize the relationship and context and then use the offender characteristics, offense factors, and recidivism rates typical of that category to inform their assessment" (p. 273). She followed up on the stalkers from the Mohandie sample 9 years later, and found that 3 out of 4 had committed another crime, and 56% had committed crimes related to stalking. The average time before reoffending was less than 1 year, but over half reoffended in less than 3 months. The stalking offenses included criminal harassment, uttering threats, and making harassing phone calls to the victim. Today, various types of cyber messaging would likely be the norm for harassing. As might be expected, most of the reported violence of prior intimate stalkers was directed at a current or previous intimate partner. In addition, intimate stalkers were most likely to recidivate in general, fail on conditional release, and commit new stalking offenses. They are clearly the most risky of the RECON typology categories.

The Mullen et al. Typology

Another useful typology, one attracting research attention, was proposed by Mullen and his associates (Mullen et al., 2000; Mullen, Pathé, Purcell, & Stuart, 1999). They developed a five-category typology of stalkers. The Mullen types are not mutually exclusive groupings, and the placement of an individual is a matter of clinical judgment rather than strict empirical divisions. The five are (1) intimacy-seeking, (2) rejected, (3) incompetent, (4) resentful, and (5) predatory stalkers. **Intimacy-seeking stalkers** are socially isolated, lonely, socially inept, and filled with an inflated sense of entitlement. Although they recognize that the object of their attention does not reciprocate their affection, they nevertheless hope that their behavior will eventually lead to intimacy and everlasting "true" love. These stalkers tend to be intellectually limited, and their knowledge of courting behavior is rudimentary. **Rejected stalkers** make up the largest group and are largely ex-partners. They often acknowledge mixed and confusing feelings of desire for both reconciliation with their victim and revenge. Clinically, they are most often diagnosed with some type of personality disorder. These stalkers are most likely to assault their victims as a form of revenge.

Incompetent stalkers often stalked others previously, and they regard their victims as attractive potential partners but are not infatuated with them. The motives of **resentful stalkers** are to frighten and distress the victim. "Such a stalker persistently pursued a young woman because she appeared, when glimpsed in the street, to be attractive, wealthy, and happy when the stalker had just experienced a humiliating professional rejection" (Mullen et al., 1999, p. 1249). These stalkers tend to be very paranoid and delusional in their approach to victims and the social world in general. However, while they are threatening and prone to damage their victim's property, they rarely physically assault their victim. **Predatory stalkers**

form a small group but are potentially sexually violent. These individuals take plea-sure in the sense of power produced by stalking as well as the power inherent in sexual assault.

WHEN DOES STALKING USUALLY STOP?

Most victims, in addition to knowing the violence risk involved, want to know how to stop the stalking. So what does terminate stalking? Some stalkers stop pursuing their current victim when they find a new "love" interest. About 18% of the victims in the Violence Against Women Survey (Tjaden & Thoennes, 1998b) indicated that the stalking stopped when stalkers entered into a relationship with a new person. Law enforcement interventions short of arrest also seem to help. Fifteen percent said the stalking ceased when their stalkers received a warning from the police. Interestingly, more formal interventions such as arrest, conviction, or restraining orders do not appear to be very effective—perhaps serving to antagonize the stalker. When it comes to persistent, frightening stalking that creates risks to personal safety, such as carried out by the intimate stalker, the survey suggests that the most effective method may be for the victim to relocate as far away from the offender as possible, providing no information of one's whereabouts to the stalker or to individuals who might commu-nicate that information.

CURRENT RESEARCH IN THE DEVELOPMENT OF RISK ASSESSMENT OF STALKERS

Kropp et al. (2011) find that risk assessment of stalking is usually conducted by relying primarily on clinical judgments, due in large part to the lack of alternatives. Actuarial approaches are typically not used, because no instrument or statistical procedure has been developed specifically to assess the nature of stalking. In addi-tion, there is no research that examines the usefulness and validity of existing psy-chological tests or actuarial risk assessment tools for determining the risks in stalking behavior. In Kropp et al.'s view, the best approach to assessing stalking risk is to develop structured professional judgment guidelines, as mentioned earlier in the chapter. They believe that actuarial approaches are not feasible at this time because the scientific literature does not provide enough solid data for developing such a method, but the literature does provide sufficient information for developing SPJ guidelines.

Currently, there are two sets of SPJ guidelines focusing on stalking risk assess-ment and management. One is the Guidelines for Stalking Assessment and Management (SAM; Kropp, Hart, & Lyon, 2008) developed in Canada. The second set of SPJ guidelines—developed in Australia—is called the Stalking Risk Profile (SRP; MacKenzie et al., 2009) and is rooted in the motivational typology developed by Mullen et al. (2006). Both approaches allow clinicians to make final risk ratings of low, moderate, or high and take into consideration risk factors that have support within the scientific and professional literature (McEwan, Pathé, & Ogloff, 2011). According to McEwan et al., this approach has two important benefits for stalking risk assessment. "At a practical level it is flexible and allows for the complexity of many stalking situations, while at a conceptual level it allows the developing stalking risk literature to take advantage of advances in contemporary thinking on violence risk assessment" (p. 181).

The SRP incorporates the nature of the relationship between the stalker and the victim, the stalker's motivations, the general psychological characteristics and social status of the stalker, and the victim's psychological and social vulnerabilities. It is recommended that the risk assessment examine the stalker's history of violence, prior antisocial conduct, substance abuse, psychiatric history, personality disorders, and social and relational instability (Mullen et al., 2006). The stalker's history of the use and knowledge of weapons is also a concern. The SRP also encourages the use of professional risk assessment tools, such as the HCR-20 and the Spousal Assault Risk Assessment.

The SAM is designed to be used by criminal justice, security, mental health, and forensic professionals working in a variety of contexts where concerns of stalking arise. The SAM takes into consideration factors from three domains: the patterns of the stalking behavior, the psychological adjustment and background of the perpetrator, and victim vulnerability factors. Both the SAM and the SRP hold considerable promise for the violence assessment of stalking behavior and may lead the way for crime scene profiling in the future, in those cases where a specific individual is suspected or is in custody.

According to Kropp et al. (2011),

> The SAM helps users to exercise their best judgment; it is not a replacement for professional discretion. Its purpose is to introduce a systematic, standardized, and practical framework for gathering and considering information when making decisions about stalking risk. (p. 305)

Summary and Conclusions

Psychological profiling differs from other forms of profiling thus far covered in this text in one important way: It focuses on one individual and attempts to assess his or her potential. Although the resulting psychological profile can address positive characteristics—such as one's potential for leadership or for performance in a particular position—it is most relevant, for our purposes, as it assesses potential for violence. Thus, in this chapter we have illustrated psychological profiling by discussing threat and risk assessments.

Psychological profiling has a long history, having been employed by government agencies as well as private industry. Perhaps the most well-known profile in history was the lengthy report on Adolf Hitler, prepared by psychoanalytically oriented mental health professionals at the time of the Second World War. Psychological profiling today is more apt to involve standardized psychological measures as well as structured clinical or professional judgment—in other words, it is a mixture of reviewing an individual's risk factors as well as considering circumstances that relate to his or her own particular situations at the time of assessment. A major use of psychological profiling today is for purposes of threat and risk assessment.

Although these terms are often used interchangeably, we noted that threat assessment is conducted when an individual has made an explicit threat of violence or has displayed behaviors that imply that violence may be imminent. To illustrate this, we discussed the potential for school and workplace violence. Risk assessment is a broader term, used to assess risk—even though no threat may have been made—in a wide range of contexts. Risk assessments may be performed when inmates are released from prison, before someone is granted bail, before someone is released from a mental hospital, or when courts are deciding whether to sentence offenders to prison or community programs, among other examples. In the chapter, we discussed risk assessments conducted for the purpose of deciding whether a stalker presented a risk for potential violence. Note that there is some overlap between the terms *threat* and *risk assessment*; in many cases—as in the case of some stalkers—threats may have been made.

Perceived increases in school violence and bullying behaviors have produced requests for psychological profiling of potential school shooters. Many schools now have access to "threat assessment teams" made up of psychology, law enforcement, and education professionals whose role it is to assess the credibility of a threat or series of threats made by a student. The Columbine incident of 1998 spearheaded nationwide efforts to identify potentially dangerous students as well as behaviors that would lead to violence. We now know that there is no one "school shooter profile," although educators should be aware of a number of warning signs and characteristics. Lists of these signs include such factors as being a loner, having an excessive interest in weaponry, communicating intent to be violent to others, and being specific in describing one's planned method of attack. Nevertheless, these characteristics themselves do not necessarily predict a school shooter, so threat assessment teams must be cautious of making false-positive predictions. In addition, some past school shooters fell under the radar, meeting few if any of the identified characteristics.

Similar concerns are raised in the case of workplace violence, which remains a leading cause of death of employees in the workplace. Most workplace violence occurs from the outside, however. Threat assessment enters in when an employee or past employee is regarded as a potential threat to others in the workplace. Researchers have identified a range of problem behaviors that may be precursors of workplace violence, including hypersensitivity to criticism, angry outbursts, increasing belligerence, and noticeable changes in behavior.

Stalking—which we discussed under the topic of risk assessment—is a behavior that has received increasing research attention but defies efforts at profiling. Although at least a dozen different stalking typologies have been proposed, only a few have been extensively researched. We discussed the typologies proposed by Mohandie and his colleagues—RECON—and Mullen and his colleagues. Both take into consideration the relationship between the stalker and his or her victim and the motivation of the stalker. As a group, stalkers are more likely to harm their victims psychologically than physically. Intimate stalkers, however, those who pursue a former intimate partner, are most likely to do physical harm. In recent years, researchers have offered guidelines, such as the SAM and the SRP, that are based on structured professional judgment to help psychological profilers assess the likelihood that stalking will develop into violence.

KEY CONCEPTS

Acquaintance stalkers
Acute dynamic factors
Dynamic risk factors
Incompetent stalkers
Intimacy-seeking stalkers
Intimate stalkers

Predatory stalkers
Private stranger stalkers
Public figure stalkers
Rejected stalkers
Resentful stalkers
Risk assessment

Safe School Initiative (SSI)
Stable dynamic factors
Static risk factors
Substantive threats
Threat assessment
Transient threats

7

Suspect-Based Profiling

"After 9/11, everything changed." This statement is so often made that it is close to becoming a cliché; at best, it states the obvious. Although terrorist incidents occurred in the United States before that time, and although other countries have long been targeted by terrorist attacks, it became clear in 2001 that the United States was not invulnerable to such massive destruction within its own borders, perpetrated by someone outside its borders. The "war on terrorism" thus began. Since that time, more than 300 individuals have been tried and convicted of terrorist activities in U.S. civilian courts; Osama bin Laden, the mastermind of the attacks, has been killed; and the United States and allied nations have struggled with the extent to which they should be involved in the affairs of nations that are suspected of harboring terrorists. In addition, representatives of U.S. government have searched for a balance between protecting civil liberties of citizens and protecting them from further violence. Suspect-based profiling—the topic of this chapter—deals with these critical issues.

It is important to emphasize that many individuals—including some elected officials—prefer to avoid "war" phraseology, and indeed there is good reason to do so. When nations are "at war," officially or otherwise, this invites actions that might otherwise not be tolerated. For example, in the decades *preceding* 2001, the U.S. government had declared its "war on drugs." This declaration was accompanied by law enforcement zeal to intercept the trafficking in illegal drugs and to punish drug offenders severely, sometimes with prison sentences that many considered draconian. Only recently have legislatures and courts made efforts to reduce these sentence lengths and to recognize much drug-related offending as a health problem more than a criminal justice problem.

Specifically related to profiling, the war on drugs—like the war on terrorism—was accompanied by efforts to identify individuals who might be involved in an illegal enterprise, in this case the transportation of drugs for the purposes of sale. Government agencies produced various drug courier profiles, some of which had elements that actually contradicted one another. For example, drug couriers were said to drive old cars (or new cars), to drive at excessive speeds (or carefully observe the speed limit), to wear gold jewelry (or be conservatively dressed), or to purchase one-way airline tickets (or two-way tickets). Of most concern, however—as in the case with possible terrorists—drug couriers were believed to be black, Middle Eastern, or Hispanic.

We could have covered the profiling of terrorists and drug traffickers in previous chapters, particularly Chapter 5, where specific crimes were discussed. However, we discuss them separately because they involve a very different approach from what we have seen thus far in the book, an approach we term "suspect-based profiling." In most instances, the suspect-based profile summarizes the *psychological* features of persons who might commit a specific crime, such as drug trafficking, detonating a bomb, committing a terrorist attack, or hijacking an aircraft. However, suspect-based profiling also has involved *demographic* features of individuals, including race, ethnicity, and national origin—thus making it a controversial topic. In profiling serial murderers, rapists, burglars, or arsonists, profilers do not focus on these features. The "profiling" of terrorists and drug traffickers (as opposed to users) often does.

Recall the following quote from Chapter 1: "[S]omeone driving at a certain speed, at a certain time of day, in a certain type of car, and of a certain general appearance may fit the profile of a drug courier and be stopped for a search" (Homant & Kennedy, 1998, p. 325). "General appearance," as used in the above quote, may refer to suspicious behavior, demeanor, age, or manner of dress, but unfortunately it may also be based on some features related to race or ethnicity.

Some in the law enforcement community contend that, although unfortunate, the utilization of ethnic and racial characteristics in profiling is necessary in some instances, because some crimes are disproportionately committed by people from certain socioeconomic and demographic sectors of any given population. In recent years, this argument has been raised not only with regard to drug couriers and terrorists, but also with suspected "illegal aliens," or individuals whose immigration status has been questioned. Thus, a growing number of states (e.g., Arizona, South Carolina, Alabama, Georgia, Indiana, Missouri, Oklahoma, Utah) have passed legislation or have legislation in process that critics say unfairly targets ethnic minorities and preempts the federal government's authority over immigration issues. In South Carolina, for example, police are required to ask about the immigration status of individuals who are stopped for other reasons if the officers suspect them to be undocumented. The belief that undocumented immigrants are responsible for a disproportionate amount of crime—a belief not supported by the empirical data—has led to this heightened scrutiny. Nevertheless, recent polls show that a majority of respondents favor these laws.

In a highly anticipated decision, the U.S. Supreme Court recently upheld one provision of Arizona's immigration law and struck down three (*U.S. v. Arizona, 2012*). The Court allowed that state to require law enforcement officers to check the immigration status of anyone they stopped or arrested, even for minor violations, if they suspected them to be in the U.S. illegally. However, the Court struck down provisions that would make it a state crime for immigrants to fail to register their status and for undocumented immigrants to seek or obtain employment in the state. A fourth provision, allowing police to arrest someone without a warrant for a deportable offense, was also struck down. Critics of the most controversial provision —the one upheld —maintain that racial profiling is inevitable because races and ethnicities will be singled out for police suspicion. The Court left the door open for future challenges if such profiling is documented.

Suspect-based profiling often focuses on race or ethnicity, but it need not do so, as we will learn in this chapter. When it does, it introduces both legal and moral issues that rarely get resolved satisfactorily. Recall from earlier chapters that profiling in general should be approached in a cautionary fashion, because aspects of a profile may apply to a wide range of individuals. It is particularly problematic when those individuals are singled out on the basis of their race, ethnicity, or religious beliefs. In an effort to interdict drug trafficking, law enforcement agencies in the 1990s disproportionately stopped numerous black individuals compared with whites. In an effort to prevent another terrorist attack after 9/11, agents questioned and detained numerous individuals of Middle Eastern descent, primarily because of the color of their skin or their Muslim faith. As this book is going to press, New York City police are being criticized for wide-ranging surveillance of U.S. citizens with Shiite Muslim backgrounds, and the U.S. Department of Justice has accused police in East Haven, Connecticut, of violating the civil rights of citizens and terrorizing Hispanic neighborhoods. Clearly, what we define as suspect-based profiling remains a problem. We begin with overviews of one of its more objectionable and illegal forms.

Racial Profiling

Some aspects of suspect-based profiling—behavioral observations, for example—are acceptable, if not necessarily effective. Racial or ethnic profiling, however, is not. Racial profiling refers to

> police-initiated action that relies on the race, ethnicity, or national origin rather than the behavior of an individual or information that leads the police to a particular individual who has been identified as being, or having been, engaged in criminal activity. (Ramirez, McDevitt, & Farrell, 2000, p. 53)

The definition also may be expanded to include government officials who are not necessarily "police," such as agents of the Transportation Security Administration (TSA), an agency of the U.S. Department of Homeland Security.

Toward the end of the 20th century, racial profiling became recognized as a serious and troubling issue. Apparent incidents of racial profiling were experienced so commonly by people of color that they began to label the phenomenon "driving while black" or "driving while brown" (commonly abbreviated DWB), as a play on the legally accepted term DWI (driving while intoxicated or impaired). Similar phrases like "flying while Brown" and "walking while Muslim" were coined shortly after the 9/11 attacks (Newman & Brown, 2009).

Since 9/11, racial profiling has been directed toward people of Middle Eastern descent who are feared to be members of terrorist groups or sympathetic to their cause. In the context of drivers, this unwarranted assumption has led to a disproportionate number of "pretext" stops of people of color. These pretext stops were commonly made during the 1980s and 1990s in the search for drugs, and they became more common after a U.S. Supreme Court decision allowed them (*Whren v. United States*, 1996). A pretext stop is one in which a driver is pulled over for a mild traffic infraction, such as crossing the center line, failing to signal properly before switching lanes, or driving a vehicle with a defective taillight. The stop allows the officer to conduct a visual search of the vehicle and, under some conditions, order drivers and even passengers out of the car. We must emphasize that a pretext stop is not itself an illegal action on the part of the law enforcement official; however, when these stops are used disproportionately against people of color, they raise serious moral questions.

Public awareness of racial profiling with respect to the "drug war" was heightened in the late 20th century, when the problem came to the attention of the courts. One of the first such cases was a class action lawsuit against the Maryland State Police (MSP) (*Wilkins v. Maryland State Police*; cited in D. A. Harris, 1999). The case included evidence based on a survey of traffic violations on Interstate 95. The study, conducted by Dr. John Lamberth, a psychology professor at Temple University, revealed that 74.7% of the 5,354 speeders *stopped* by the MSP were white, and 17.5% were African American, which does not appear to be a highly disproportionate figure. However, of the motorists who were *searched*, 72.9% were black and 80.3% were black, Hispanic, or other racial minorities. In other words, just 20% of the whites who were stopped were also searched.

Based on his analysis of these data, Lamberth concluded the following:

> The evidence examined in this study reveals dramatic and highly statistically significant disparities between the percentage of black Interstate 95 motorists legitimately subject to stop by Maryland State Police and the percentage of black motorists detained and searched by MSP troopers on this roadway. While no one can know the motivations of each individual trooper in conducting a traffic stop, the statistics presented herein, representing a broad and detailed sample of highly appropriate data, show without question a racially discriminatory impact on blacks and other minority motorists from state police behavior along I-95. (quoted in D. A. Harris, 1999, p. 24)

THE DRUG COURIER PROFILE

Maryland was by no means the only state that gained attention because of racial profiling. The extensive report cited above (D. A. Harris, 1999) includes numerous anecdotes of people of color across the nation who were stopped by police, questioned, or had their cars searched. One man in Portland, Maine, for example, reported being pulled over and asked where he was going and who he knew in the city. When he responded that he knew the police chief, he was told to move on. "Drug courier profiles" were circulating among various state and federal agencies. In 1985, when the war on drugs was intensifying, the Florida Department of Highway Safety and Motor Vehicles issued guidelines for law enforcement on how to identify drug couriers. The guidelines encouraged officers to be suspicious of rental cars, drivers who are scrupulously obeying traffic laws, drivers wearing lots of gold, drivers whose status did not "fit" the vehicle, and drivers who represented "ethnic groups associated with the drug trade." In 1986, a racially biased drug courier profile was introduced by the Drug Enforcement Administration (DEA) to various law enforcement agencies across the nation. The profile was used extensively in their training methods for officers in "Operation Pipeline" (D. A. Harris, 1999). Operation Pipeline was a highway drug interdiction program that trained law enforcement officers nationwide how to use pretext stops to find drugs in vehicles.

Studies in San Diego, New Jersey, and New York reported that black and Latino drivers were far more likely to be stopped and searched than were other drivers (Dvorak, 2000; Ramirez et al., 2000). Lawsuits alleging racial profiling by law enforcement were brought on behalf of minority motorists in several states, including Pennsylvania, Florida, Illinois, and of course Maryland as mentioned above. It should be noted, though, that the U.S. Supreme Court has allowed the use of the drug courier profile in the investigative process, such as to make traffic stops or briefly detain airline passengers (*United States v. Sokolow*, 1989). Furthermore, as noted above, in *Whren v. U.S.* (1996) the Court allowed pretext stops.

Over a dozen states subsequently passed laws against racial profiling, many of them requiring antibias training for law enforcement agents and the gathering of statistics on every driver who is stopped (Lewin, 2001). These laws have reduced the use of racial profiling to some extent, but it would be naïve to believe it has disappeared. In addition, international data indicate that racial profiling is not restricted to the United States. A 1998 study by the British Government's Home Office investigated the racial and ethnic demographics of the stop-and-search patterns of police agencies in England and Wales. The study found that blacks were 7.5 times more likely to be stopped and searched, and 4 times more likely to be arrested than whites (Ramirez et al., 2000). According to 1999 census data, the population of Britain is 93 percent white and 7 percent ethnic minority. In Canada, one study found that blacks were nearly 4 times more likely to be pulled over than whites or Asians (CBC News, 2007). In addition, as suggested above, the catastrophic events of September 11, 2001, have led to new forms of racial profiling, as well as ethnic and religious profiling, in an effort to prevent terrorist activities.

Terrorism

Following 9/11, terrorist profiling became a common procedure across the United States, especially in security-sensitive locations (Newman & Brown, 2009). Airports and border crossings suddenly began receiving avid attention. Unfortunately, and similar to the "war on drugs," race or ethnicity were critical components in the development of terrorist profiles. Federal law enforcement agents frequently detained Arabs, South Asians, North Africans, and others with Arab-sounding names (Newman & Brown, 2009). Many of the detained individuals were American citizens. Others were tourists, including residents of other nations visiting relatives and friends in the United States.

Some experts and scholars admonished that the rush to create terrorist profiles in the aftermath of 9/11 resulted in many false positives and disproportionately singled out particular cultural groups (Ramirez, Hoopes, & Quinlan, 2003). The terrorist profile was considered more detailed and biased than the typical criminal or crime scene profile (Newman & Brown, 2009). For example, the profile led to the detention and investigation of young Middle Eastern Muslim men with temporary visa status. "Accusations immediately surfaced that the concept of terrorist profiling was going beyond acceptable criminal profiling and easing into the arena of racial profiling and biased practices" (Newman & Brown, 2009, p. 364). We should note that—as a result of the attention given to racial profiling during the "drug war" at the end of the 20th century—the public did not condone the unjust targeting of blacks and Hispanics, those who had been targets during the drug war era. However, in the wake of 9/11, the targeting of Muslims and those appearing to be of Middle Eastern descent was regarded in a different manner.

WHO ARE THE TERRORISTS?

Terrorists are often described as emotionally disturbed individuals. The cruel attacks on innocent civilians defy the view that terrorists are rational, emotionally stable persons. Those terrorists who engage in suicide missions are frequently perceived as mentally deranged individuals by mental health professionals (Aggarwal, 2009). However, there is little cogent evidence to conclude that members of terrorist organizations are emotionally disturbed, irrational, or psychopathic (Maikovich, 2005; Sarangi & Alison, 2005). In fact, some research suggests that terrorists are often psychologically much healthier and more stable than common violent criminals, although they are often deluded by an ideological or religious way of viewing the world (Silke, 2008). Effective, well-organized terrorist groups have discovered that members who demonstrate irrational or unstable behavioral patterns do not make adequate terrorist participants. According to Silke, emotionally disturbed persons "lack the discipline, rationality, self-control and mental stamina needed if terrorists are to survive for any length of time" (p. 104). Skillful terrorist groups expel individuals from their ranks who are emotionally unstable, primarily because they pose a security threat (Post & Gold, 2002). Hudson (1999) found that, although members of a terrorist organization are expected to be emotionally stable, some high-positioned leaders of these groups may show indicators of psychopathy or delusions of messianic proportions, especially if they are religiously motivated. However, this pattern is considered unusual.

The case is different for lone wolves, however. **Lone wolves** are those extremists who operate on their own, independent of any organized terrorist group or terrorist command structure. Spaaij (2010) found in his investigation of lone wolf terrorists that—in contrast to organized terrorist groups—a majority of lone wolves displayed emotional or mental disorders. We will discuss lone wolf terrorists in more detail shortly.

Before proceeding, it should be emphasized that labels and words carry meaning and perspective that ultimately influence judgment (Ginges, Atran, Sachdeva, & Medin, 2011). "[A] terrorist is despicable, whereas a freedom fighter may be a hero" (p. 507). Furthermore, a suicidal act may be interpreted as an act of desperation, whereas religious martyrdom involves an act of meaning and may be considered noble. For example, "Instead of condemning their deaths as suicides, the families of Palestinian suicide bombers have celebrated their martyrdoms as symbolic weddings to God with media publicity, eroding any social disapproval in attacking the enemy" (Aggarwal, 2009, p. 96). How words and labels are interpreted goes a long way toward determining how terrorists are understood and identifying reasons for their actions.

According to federal law, terrorism is defined as "the unlawful use of force or violence against persons or property to intimidate or coerce a government, the civilian population, or any segment thereof, in furtherance of political or social objectives" (Definitions, C.F.R. 18 U.S. C§ 2331). Moreover, terrorism may be either domestic or international, depending on the origin, base of operations, and objectives of the terrorist organization (U.S. Department of Justice, 2000). In the United States, domestic terrorism refers to an organization or an individual based and operating entirely in the United States, without foreign direction.

International terrorism, on the other hand, refers to violent acts instigated under the direction of a foreign power, government, organization, or individual. Although there are many examples across the globe, the most vivid example of international terrorism in the United States includes the events that occurred on September 11, 2001. An example of international terrorism aimed at American citizens is when Pan American Flight 103 was destroyed by a bomb (stored in the baggage compartment) over Lockerbie, Scotland, in 1988, killing all 243 passengers and 16 crew members. Eleven people on the ground were also killed as large sections of the Boeing 747 fell onto several homes. In addition to the aircraft being American owned, 189 of the passengers killed were American citizens, many of them college students. Intelligence investigations pointed to Muammar al-Gaddafi, leader of Libya, as personally ordering the bombing. A Libyan intelligence officer and head of security for Libyan Arab Airlines, Abdel Basset Ali al-Megrahi, was eventually convicted as the mastermind behind the bombing. The apparent motive for the Lockerbie bombing was retaliation toward the United States for its aggressive stance against human rights violations supported by the Libyan government. Gaddafi himself was captured and killed by rebels during the Libyan civil war, on October 20, 2011.

PROFILING TERRORISTS

The diversity of terrorist groups, representing widely different cultural backgrounds and goals, makes developing profiles of members of each group an extremely difficult enterprise. Stereotypes of the typical terrorist, such as being of Middle Eastern descent, should be discarded. In addition, any search for a "terrorist personality" is destined to fail. "There seems to be general agreement among psychologists that there is no particular psychological attribute that can be used to describe the terrorist or any 'personality' that is distinctive of terrorists" (Hudson, 1999, p. 43). There does not seem to be any detectable personality traits that would enable authorities to identify a terrorist.

Some scholars believe that terrorists should not be assumed to be similar to the typical criminal or violent offender. Even those who are supportive of profiling draw the line at profiling terrorists. "In the domain of criminal behavior there is much value in psychological profiling, with a focus on dispositional characteristics at the individual level, but I view this approach less useful and less effective in the domain of terrorism" (Moghaddam, 2004, p. 103). According to Moghaddam, one key difference between criminal behavior and terrorism is that terrorists, unlike the typical criminal offender, strongly believe that justice and fairness are on their side.

Another factor that renders profiling terrorists extremely difficult is that terrorist *groups* change their modus operandi from place to place, from time to time, and use different perpetrators who often die in the attack. For example, targeting aircraft is one way to generate fear in a society, but seaports, trains, and subways are also vulnerable. Furthermore, smuggling a nuclear, biological, or radiological explosive device into the country in a cargo container is another approach a terrorist group is likely to try (Nickerson, 2011). Other attractive targets are likely to be computer networks, including government, corporation, and military networks. Therefore, terrorist organizations and groups challenge the usual approach of profiling that focuses on serial offending by one offender. Predicting international terrorist group actions is more the bailiwick of intelligence agencies working across international borders than local or regional police agencies. In the United States, the intelligence establishment consists of more than a dozen agencies employing over 100,000 individuals whose job it is to evaluate, integrate, and interpret information (Fingar, 2011; Loftus, 2011).

The British Security Service, known as MI5 (military intelligence, section 5), concluded in a classified report that there is no easy way to identify those persons who become involved in terrorism in Britain (cited in Travis, 2008). The research, conducted by MI5's behavioral science unit, was based on several hundred individuals known to be involved in extremist violent activity. According to the report, the "mad and bad" theory to explain why individuals turn to terrorism is unfounded. There is no evidence that mental disorders are higher among British terrorists than is found in the general population. The report concluded that those who become terrorists represent a diverse collection of individuals, fitting no single demographic profile and following no specific path to violent extremism.

Several terrorist classifications have been developed in recent years, but most are only marginally helpful for profiling purposes. However, some do underscore the complexity of terrorism and the many motivations that unite terrorist groups. One basic terrorist typology was developed by the U.S. Army Command and General Staff College (Terrorism Research Center, 1997). The typology integrates research on terrorism conducted at RAND Corporation (Hoffman, 1993). The typology divides terrorists into three basic groups: (1) the rationally motivated terrorist, (2) the psychologically motivated terrorist, and (3) the culturally motivated terrorist.

The **rationally motivated terrorist** is driven by well-defined and theoretically achievable goals that may involve political, social, or economic objectives (Ditzler, 2004). The target selection and type of violence are often strongly influenced by the terrorist's relationship with his or her constituents. In most cases, the rationally motivated terrorist tries to avoid loss of life in target selection, but does try to cause extensive damage to infrastructure and buildings. The **psychologically motivated terrorist** usually commits violence out of a "profound sense of failure or inadequacy for which [he or she] may seek redress through revenge" (Ditzler, 2004, p. 202). In most cases, these terrorists are unwilling to negotiate with authorities, and they focus on physical harm and injury to persons. The lone wolf terrorist, to be discussed below, best fits this category. The **culturally motivated terrorist** is motivated by an overriding fear of losing cultural identity or cultural extermination. "Not surprisingly, the most important and volatile aspect of cultural identity is often religion, especially in national or cultural groups who are largely governed or socially defined by a particular system of faith" (Ditzler, 2004, p. 203). These terrorists undertake their terrorist actions with a profound sense of absolute moral certainty, and they are believed to be unwilling to negotiate unless their wishes are met entirely.

Terrorists tend to be young, usually in their twenties or even younger. There are relatively few older terrorists, in part because terrorism is a physically demanding activity (Hudson, 1999). As Hudson notes, "Training alone requires considerable physical fitness" (p. 61). In addition, many young terrorists are naïve and highly susceptible to convincing ideologies. Terrorist leaders tend to be older, in their thirties to sixties. Both genders are involved in terrorism, although leaders are predominantly male. Leaders also are usually well-educated and capable of "sophisticated, albeit highly biased, political analysis" (Hudson, 1999, p. 62). Individual, lone wolf perpetrators, however, present a slightly different story, as we shall see in the next subsection.

LONE WOLF TERRORISTS

Although many Americans associate terrorism with the attacks of 9/11, a majority of terrorism in this country has been carried out by "lone wolves"—often domestic lone wolves. As you will recall, lone wolves operate on their own, independent of any organized group or directive from others, and they do not rely on group organizational affiliations to validate their mission. Although they may sympathize with terrorist organizations or extremist groups, lone wolves design their own plans, select their own targets, choose their own MO, and make their own decisions (Bartol & Bartol, 2012). Lone wolves "often come up with their own ideologies that combine personal vendettas with religious or political grievances" (Stern, 2003, p. 172). They wish to bring their own perceived injustices to public attention, whatever they may be. Sometimes, they adopt the points of view of an extremist, religious, or outside group, even if the group does not engage in terrorist activities or condone the violence perpetrated by the lone wolf.

Although many countries are susceptible to this type of terrorism, the United States appears to be especially targeted. Available statistics indicate that between the years 1968 and 2007, 42% of all the lone wolf attacks throughout the world occurred in the United States (COT, 2007). In addition, lone wolf terrorism has increased markedly in the United States during the past three decades (Spaaij, 2010).

As mentioned previously, lone wolf terrorists are generally psychologically different from those who are members of organized terrorist groups, and they often present a greater threat to the nation. The public is their preferred target, and explosives tend to be their primary weapon of choice (COT, 2007). Firearms are their second weapon of choice. In fact, in the United States, lone wolves are much more likely to use firearms than lone wolves in other parts of the world (Spaaij, 2010). The targets most often selected by lone wolves in the United States are civilians, followed by medical staffs (Spaaij, 2010). It is very rare that medical staffs are targeted outside the United States. This difference can be explained in part by the preferred targets selected by antiabortion extremists, who comprise a significant proportion of lone wolf terrorists. There are exceptions, of course. Theodore Kaczynski directed his attacks at a wide variety of targets, including university professors, airline executives, and airliners—which resulted in his being called the UNAbomber (UNiversity and Airline). Kaczynski's motivations were to draw attention to his personal list of societal problems, and he desired a worldwide revolution against the effects of the industrial-technological system that he perceived was destroying the world.

The attacks of the lone wolf are generally premeditated, carefully planned, and self-financed. Lone wolves are usually not suicidal in their attacks, and they plan to escape arrest. Many lone wolves exhibit poor interpersonal and social skills, often resulting in a social isolationist attitude. Kaczynski was able to carry out 16 mail bombings over a 17-year period that resulted in 3 deaths and 23 serious injuries. His bombings were well-planned and sophisticated, and he often left false clues in the bombs to mislead investigators. He also frequently left tree branches and bark in the bombs as his signature. He was a highly educated person with a Harvard degree who withdrew from society and lived alone with bare necessities in an isolated cabin in the Montana wilderness for nearly 25 years. Despite the fact that his lawyers and his family believed he was mentally ill, Kaczynski refused to plead not guilty by reason of insanity. He did plead guilty to bombings in order to avoid the death penalty and remains imprisoned today.

Another example of a lone wolf terrorist is Timothy McVeigh, the Oklahoma City Bomber. Although another associate provided some tactical support, McVeigh apparently did all the planning, target selection, and decision making in the truck bombing and total destruction of the Alfred P. Murrah Federal Building in Oklahoma City in 1995. The blast killed 168 people, including many children, and injured over 500 others. The Oklahoma City bombing represented the deadliest terrorist attack in the United States prior to September 11, 2001. McVeigh's primary motive was to send the U.S. government a message concerning what he perceived as "bullying." A decorated Army veteran, he was described by those who know him as socially withdrawn and interpersonally inadequate.

Another frequently cited example of a lone wolf terrorist is Eric Rudolph, who was responsible for a series of bombings in Georgia and Alabama. His most significant bombing was at Olympic Park in Atlanta in 1996, which killed 1 person and wounded at least 111. He was also responsible for bombings of clinics that provided abortion services and nightclubs frequented by gays and lesbians. He planned and carried out the bombings on his own, although some religious extremists sympathized with his motives. Rudolph apparently identified with both antiabortion activist groups and those groups strongly opposed to equal rights regardless of sexual orientation. His activities landed him on the FBI's Ten Most Wanted list, and he spent more than 5 years in the Appalachian wilderness as a survivalist while on the run.

Another prominent lone wolf terrorist was the anthrax killer. On October 9, 2001, letters containing weapons-grade anthrax were sent to Senate Judiciary Committee Chairman Patrick Leahy and Senate Majority Leader Tom Daschle in their Washington, D.C., offices, although neither senator was hurt. However, by November of that year, 22 cases of anthrax had been reported, presumably associated with the mailing of letters. Anthrax in these cases refers to the spores that can be used as a biological weapon. Infection can be fatal. Five persons died from the 2001 attacks, and 15 others became quite ill. The FBI suspected that the perpetrator of the attacks was Bruce Ivins, a senior biodefense researcher employed by the U.S. government. If Ivins was the culprit, all the evidence indicates he committed his attacks as a lone wolf. In 2008, he committed suicide by an overdose of acetaminophen. In 2010, the FBI formally closed its investigation of the anthrax attacks, but doubt still lingers as to whether Ivins truly was the perpetrator. It should be mentioned that these attacks promoted a rash of anthrax hoaxes throughout the country, which mostly involved harmless talcum powder sent through the mail.

SUMMARY

In sum, lone wolf terrorists may present more of a challenge to profile than members of terrorist groups, although both are extremely difficult. Lone wolf terrorists often do not reveal their intentions to anyone, and they remain secluded before and after their attacks. Although many demonstrate impaired interpersonal and social skills and embrace an isolationist attitude, these features are hardly useful for profiling. A large segment of the general population displays these characteristics. Although a vast majority of terrorists who are affiliated with a terrorist organization are expected to have behavioral patterns of emotional stability, the rate of psychological problems appears to be significantly higher among lone wolf terrorists (COT, 2007; Hewitt, 2003). Again, this information is only marginally useful for profiling. Profiling based on the "personality" of the terrorists has been a failure. Terrorism is too diversified and complex to be easily subsumed into a simplified profile of its participants based on personality traits, socioeconomic class, and age. It is more effective for profiling and prediction of terrorist behavior to concentrate on how individuals behave, rather than on intrinsic characteristics (Clutterbuck & Warnes, 2011).

Lone wolf terrorists and organization-based terrorists—those affiliated with a group—are usually arrested as a result of good police work, investigative technology, and errors committed by the perpetrator. In their research on Jihad terrorist cells in the United Kingdom, Clutterbuck and Warnes (2011) discovered certain distinctive behavior characteristics of terrorists as a result of their activities in planning, preparing, and implementing their acts of terrorism. "These individuals exhibited a variety of common behaviours in their general lifestyle, both before they joined the conspiracy and during it" (p. 49).

As emphasized by Clutterbuck and Warnes (2011), terrorists, regardless of their motivations, must plan and prepare for their act of terrorism. They must acquire materials and construct explosives and a detonator, and they must also devise and develop a means of initiating the explosion. If they are unable to purchase or steal the necessary materials, they must use their ingenuity to build an explosive device from legitimately available supplies. Furthermore, in order to carry out these tasks, the terrorists must find premises where their activities do not arouse suspicion. After accomplishing these requirements, they must attain comprehensive knowledge and data for selecting a suitable target as well as planning the attack. They may require forged or fraudulent documents to gain access to security areas and weapons to complete the mission and protect themselves. There are a number of other requirements that well-planned terrorist attacks demand, but suspicious behavioral patterns may be detected at any level or any combination of the above stages of planning and preparation. Lone wolf terrorists will also need to go through the above stages, but they may be more difficult to detect before attacks because they usually work in isolation from others.

Clutterbuck and Warnes (2011) assert that the planning and preparation stages are most likely to provide the best opportunities to identify any pre-attack indicators and also represent the best chance to disrupt or prevent the attack. The researchers further emphasize that lone wolves follow similar paths and can be detected in the same manner. At this point in our knowledge, more research should be directed at establishing the validity of pre-attack indicators, but focusing on behavioral patterns appears to be a much more promising endeavor than trying to develop a terrorist profile based on previous members of terrorist groups.

In his testimony before the U.S. House Subcommittee on Terrorism and Unconventional Threats and Capabilities, Seth Jones (2008) stated that terrorist organizations have similar modus operandi that are ultimately detectable at various stages of operation. "Like other groups, [their] members need to communicate with each other, raise funds, build a support network, plan and execute attacks, and establish a base (or bases) of operations" (p. 9). Most of these stages, Jones posits, are vulnerable to penetration by police and intelligence agencies. He further noted that, historically, most terrorist groups were stopped by policing and intelligence, especially those terrorist groups based on religious motivations.

Passenger Profiling

Airline-related crimes (e.g., skyjacking, passenger assaults, terrorist activities) have made many of us uneasy since the Pan Am Flight 103 explosion over Lockerbie, Scotland; the 9/11 attacks; as well as failed attempts to bring airliners down in recent years. Never in skyjacking history have more innocent lives been lost than on September 11, 2001, when 19 men from the Islamist terrorist group al-Qaeda violently took control of four transcontinental passenger jets. Their intentions were to use the Boeing 767s, which were loaded with over 11,000 gallons of jet fuel, as large guided missiles to strike prominent symbols of U.S. power in the world. The skyjackers intentionally crashed two of the airliners into the Twin Towers of the World Trade Center in New York City, and another into the Pentagon in Arlington, Virginia. The fourth plane never made it to its destination, because passengers overpowered the terrorists and crashed the plane into a field near Shanksville, Pennsylvania, killing all on board.

After the 9/11 attacks and with the heightened threat of more terrorism, psychologists and behavioral scientists were asked to develop profiles that would help security personnel identify potential terrorists from passenger lists. Some obliged, and their suspect-based profiles usually took into consideration the clothes the passenger was wearing, the person's nationality, travel history, behavioral patterns while at the airport, and even the book that he or she may have just purchased at the airport bookstore. To improve their ability to identify potential terrorists, profile researchers examined the buying habits, dress patterns, and cultural and social backgrounds of previous airline terrorists, including not only 9/11 hijackers but also those sole hijackers of airliners in the 1970s.

EARLY ATTEMPTS AT PASSENGER PROFILING IN THE 1970s

The first U.S. Congressional action on airline antiterrorism began with passage of the Federal Aviation Act of 1958 (Fiske, 2010). This act created the Federal Aviation Administration (FAA), empowered the agency to set policies and regulations central to airline safety, and encouraged it to monitor and detect persons who may have malicious intent. However, during its earliest years, the FAA focused primarily on regulating prices and routes and was not particularly concerned with terrorism.

Between the years 1968 and 1978, an epidemic of skyjackings took place, most of them involving Cubans forcing airliners to Cuba. Some skyjackers were homesick Cubans, some claimed to be political activists, but most apparently desired to become significant and newsworthy. Very few were considered terrorists, however. In the late 1970s, the United States began to clamp down on these skyjackers. In 1972, the FAA issued a directive that all U.S. carriers had to either search or deny boarding to those who fit a certain profile (Dailey & Pickrel, 1975a). These profiles—intended to identify skyjackers—were subsequently adapted to identify terrorists. Ticket agents and other airline personnel were trained to apply a suspect-based behavioral profile to passengers at check-in counters. The profile, developed by FAA psychologists, warned that skyjackers were different from the usual air traveler in such aspects as socioeconomic class and mannerisms in the airport terminal. More specifically, the typical skyjacker was generally an unsuccessful member of society, inadequate socially and occupationally, lacking in resourcefulness, appeared to have substantial indicators of helplessness and hopelessness, and perhaps was suicidal. Apparently, these individuals viewed skyjacking as a way of improving their situation and gaining some control and significance in the world.

In explaining how a passenger profile is developed, John Dailey and Evan Pickrel (1975b), both Federal Aviation Administration psychologists, wrote,

> To create a hijacker profile, the information on hijackers is compared to similar information on normal air travelers. Items that clearly separate the groups are combined to form boarding-gate profiles which contain no dress or ethnic-group-type elements, do not violate the individual's constitutional rights, and have been tested in the courts. (p. 163)

When the FAA first started developing a profile, they posed the following questions:

- What kinds of people do the hijacking?
- Why do they do it?
- How do they go about it?
- What might be done to prevent their doing it?

Personal information gathered about the hijacker included age, gender, education, residential situation at the time of ticket purchase, appearance, mannerisms, occupational status, and work history. In addition, information was gathered about the hijacking event itself, including descriptions of the airports where the event took place, descriptions of aircraft operations and maintenance, weather conditions, and personnel interactions with hijackers. Supplementary information included the destination and origin of the flight, type of aircraft, day and time of the flight, number of passengers on the flight, weapons used and method of concealment, and hand and checked baggage characteristics.

A statistical analysis revealed that 87% of the hijackers would have been stopped at the boarding gate if available screening procedures had been used. Also, the original behavioral profile was able to identify members of a high-risk group in a ratio of 1 out of 100,000 travelers (Dailey & Pickrel, 1975b). Although the skyjacker profile was somewhat helpful at first, it quickly proved inadequate and incomplete because cultural, social, political, and economic forces are always changing. It should also be mentioned that many of the potential skyjackings were deterred or stopped due to two physical security approaches: the magnetometer scans and searches of passengers and their carry-on luggage. As far as the suspect-based behavioral profile, it was concluded that the most useful passenger profiles must be continually evaluated, researched, and updated with new information.

At this point, no *specific* profile has been developed that distinguishes potential skyjackers, just as there is none distinguishing terrorists from non-terrorists. The head of the Department of Homeland Security (DHS), Secretary Janet Napolitano, has continually emphasized that intelligence information shows there is no specific terrorist profile (e.g., Napolitano, 2010, 2011). However, this does not mean that suspect-based profiling of terrorists is worthless or unattainable. What is most necessary is the development of suspect-based profiling based on behavioral patterns rather than based on physical appearance, national origin, race, or ethnicity.

Suspect-Based Profiling Based on Behavioral Patterns

The planning for the 9/11 attacks took over 7 years and involved numerous meetings by the terrorists and their leaders at various locations throughout the world (9/11 Commission, 2004). The operation required enormous operational support and preparation, including the identification of and intelligence on meaningful targets, experimenting with different strategies for getting through security checks, preparing fraudulent identity documents, pilot training, substantial sums of money, and an assortment of travel plans. Osama bin Laden, the now-deceased head of al-Qaeda, provided leadership and considerable financial support for the operation, and also was involved in selecting the participants.

As we continue to gather more information about the attacks, it is apparent that there were many behavioral indicators or warnings. The terrorists who were first designated to fly the aircraft took flying lessons in the United States, with the stated intent of being trained as commercial airline pilots. They told the flight instructors they were interested in only flying jets—Boeing aircraft in particular—and during their training, they concentrated on learning to control the aircraft while in flight. The instructors noticed that they exhibited no interest in learning how to take off or land the aircraft. Ultimately, they were deemed incompetent as potential pilots, and bin Laden replaced them with individuals who spoke English, were educated, and could blend into the American culture more effectively. One recruit selected already had a commercial pilot's license he received while in Arizona in 1999. Three other recruits took pilot training in South Florida during mid- to late 2000 and soon received their pilot licenses for commercial aircraft. The four pilots left the United States 17 times during and after their training (Eldridge, Ginsberg, Hempel, Kephart, & Moore, 2004). Several of the terrorists carried fraudulent passports and other false identification documents in order to move in and out of the country and to board flights. More than half of the 19 terrorists were flagged by the Federal Aviation Administration's screening system for further inspection when they arrived for their fateful flights. At the Portland (Maine) International Airport, for example, two bought $2,500 first class, one-way tickets and were considered suspicious by airport officials. However, since their bags were inspected and were found to contain nothing incriminating, the terrorists were allowed to continue on their way.

There were so many behavioral indicators of an impending terrorist attack during the planning and preparation stages of the 9/11 attack that a traditional, appearance-based profile would have been unnecessary. Despite this fact, since 9/11, ethnic and racial minorities who fit the assumed "profile" of international terrorists (such as persons of Middle Eastern descent or origin) have been subjected to more extensive security screenings at airports and at customs checkpoints. Although air passenger profiling is a highly controversial topic, it continues to be used in some form at all major airports around the world. Some experts strongly believe that some sort of passenger profile that includes race, nationality, or ethnicity should be utilized as part of aviation security. Other experts, especially those concerned about human rights, disagree. For example, passenger profiles that rely on physical appearance are likely to be inaccurate and misleading. Furthermore, inaccurate or misguided profiles can become counterproductive because they may misdirect investigators to false leads, and may dismiss further investigations of those individuals who have malicious intent.

Furthermore, terrorist groups are often aware of the racial, ethnic, or nationality factors that are used in developing some profile strategies, and they are very likely to recruit those individuals who do not follow those characteristics as lead cells for important missions or as red herrings, distracting officials from their "real" plans. For example, Richard Reid, known as the Shoe Bomber; Umar Farouk Abdulmutallab, known as the Underwear Bomber; and Colleen LaRose, known as Jihad Jane, all represent members with ties to organized terrorist groups who are very different in appearance, racial background, and national origin. The Shoe Bomber was a British citizen, a self-admitted al-Qaeda member who pled guilty in U.S. Federal Court to eight criminal counts of terrorism, stemming from his attempt to detonate explosives hidden in his shoes while onboard an airliner in flight. The Underwear Bomber was a tall, Nigerian black man, the son of a wealthy banker, who attempted to detonate plastic explosives hidden in his underwear while onboard an American airliner en route from Amsterdam to Detroit. Jihad Jane was an American blond, blue-eyed woman from Pennsylvania who did not conform to the traditional profile of Middle Eastern terrorists in any way. She was accused of actively trying to recruit Islamic terrorists to wage a violent jihad as well as plotting to murder. On February 2, 2011, LaRose pled guilty to four federal charges, including conspiracy to murder a foreign agent, conspiracy to support terrorists, and lying to the FBI.

CAPPS and CAPPS II

As emphasized throughout this section, the evidence indicates that passenger profiling that focuses on behavioral patterns of terrorists is likely to be a more effective approach than one focusing on demographics. That is, it is more important to focus on how people act rather than who they are. Moreover, this approach is generally less objectionable to the public, although it, too, has been criticized, as we will discuss shortly.

The screening of all passengers in airports has been a reality for many years, even before September 11, 2001. At the end of the 20th century, as part of the "war on drugs," airline passengers went through metal detectors at most major airports, and their luggage was X-rayed, and sometimes opened and searched. After 9/11, the screening became more intense and sophisticated in the face of possible terrorist threats. Shortly after Umar Farouk Abdulmutallab, the Underwear Bomber, tried to detonate an incendiary device, major airports across the globe installed Advanced Imaging Technology (AIT) scanners, also known as full-body scanners, to screen all passengers. (See Photo 7.1 for a depiction of the TSA's controversial full-body image screening.)

In the United States, even before 9/11, major airlines also tried using a system largely based on behavioral patterns, called Computer Assisted Passenger Prescreening **(CAPPS)** (Armstrong & Pereira, 2001). CAPPS, first implemented in the 1990s, used basic data disclosed by passengers when they reserve and buy tickets—such as their names, addresses, and how they paid for their tickets. For example, passengers who purchase one-way tickets, pay in cash, travel alone, and buy tickets for passengers with different last names on the same credit card are targeted for further investigation or closer surveillance (Armstrong & Pereira, 2001). CAPPS had a number of serious flaws, however, as 9/11 highlighted. The system

Photo 7.1: An airline passenger being subjected to a full-body image screening at an international airport. The full-body scans are used in a number of airports, and in some, passengers are given the option to submit to an expansive pat-down search by a TSA agent instead of the full-body scan.

was highly dependent on passengers providing their true name and legitimate identi-fication. Skillfully produced fake identification cards or documents could easily beat the system.

In 2003, the TSA proposed an expanded version of CAPPS known as **CAPPS II**, which was designed to confirm passenger identities; perform criminal and intelligence database and credit card checks; and locate residence, home ownership, income, and patterns of travel and purchases. With this information, CAPPS would then determine a threat rating for each passenger. Those passengers who received an elevated rating would be detained and searched. However, the TSA quickly terminated that program before fully implementing the screening, partly because of invasion of privacy and other constitutional concerns (Ravich, 2007). For example, the system would have allowed the government unlimited access to financial and transactional data as well as access to other proprietary and public sources of information (C. J. Bennett, 2008).

SECURE FLIGHT

The TSA has continually attempted to develop a passenger screening system that is both sensitive to ethnic and racial concerns and improves the accuracy of identifying persons who may have malicious intent. After CAPPS and CAPPS II, in 2008, the TSA introduced another, supposedly less invasive prescreening program, called Secure Flight. The TSA's Office of Threat Assessment and Credentialing was assigned to lead the program. The program requires each airline to enter into the computer system the full name, date of birth, gender, passport information (if available), traveler number (if available), and redress number (if available) for each passenger. The redress number is a unique number that the individual may use in future correspondence with the Department of Homeland Security or when making future travel reservations. Secure Flight's basic goal is to identify those passengers who are a match on the "no-fly" or "selectee" list compiled by various intelligence agencies. The data was particularly compared against the existing Terrorist Screening Database, maintained by the Terrorist Screening Center. These lists, however, are very controversial, and there are numerous anecdotes about individuals—including young children—whose names mistakenly appeared on the no-fly list.

In 2006, another system, called the Automated Targeting System (ATS), was discov-ered by the public when it was briefly mentioned in the *Federal Register*, which is an official daily publication of rules, proposed rules, and notices of the U.S. government. The ATS was implemented during the early 1990s to screen cargo coming into the United States, but it was greatly expanded to screen and track travelers shortly after the 9/11 attacks without the public's knowledge. The ATS, a highly classified DHS comput-erized system, screens every person (citizen or noncitizen) crossing the U.S. borders, automatically examines a large volume of data related to that person, and assigns him or her a threat risk rating. According to the DHS (2006), the Customs and Border Protection Division uses "ATS to improve the collection, use, analysis, and dissemina-tion of information that is gathered for the primary purpose of targeting, identifying, and preventing potential terrorists and terrorist weapons from entering the United

States" (p. 2). The risk assessments on every traveler are intended to be retained for 40 years. The only way a traveler can avoid being assigned a threat risk assessment rating is to refrain from traveling to, through, or over the United States by airline. In addition, the threat assessment rating is not subject to access by the person under the Privacy Act, since this may compromise the means and methods of how the rating is determined. Among other things, the ATS considers the person's country of origin, how the travel was funded, records from secondary referrals, suspect and violator indices (criminal records and previous arrests), the traveler's no-show history, and even the individual's driving record.

Canada has a similar version of ATS, called Passenger Protect, implemented in June 2007 (C. J. Bennett, 2008). The Canadian program, although not as stringent as the U.S. program, is designed to identify passengers who may pose a threat to aviation security and disrupt their ability to cause harm or threaten aviation by taking action, such as preventing them from boarding the plane. The program is somewhat narrower than the U.S. program in terms of screening procedures in that the no-fly list is confined to those who pose an *immediate* threat to aviation security (C. J. Bennett, 2008). The ATS, on the other hand, assesses threat levels for all passengers for the long term.

TERRORIST SCREENING DATABASE (TSDB)

The **terrorist screening database,** which began its operations in 2003, is gathered by the FBI's Terrorist Screening Center (TSC) and used by multiple agencies to compile their own specific screening watch list. For example, the Department of Homeland Security uses the list to develop its no-fly list. Every day, the TSC provides an updated list of known and suspected terrorists to law enforcement and other authorities. To date, the TSC works closely with six other nations for information gathering on terrorist activities.

The TSC staff includes personnel from U.S. Customs and Border Protection, Immigration and Customs Enforcement, Secret Service, Coast Guard, Department of Justice, FBI, and the Drug Enforcement Administration. Although the U.S. Justice Department Office of the Inspector General has criticized the list for frequent errors and slow response to complaints, there is a serious attempt to make sure the information on the TSDB is timely, accurate, and maintained in a manner consistent with constitutional protections of privacy and civil liberties ensured to American citizens. The Terrorist Screening Center makes between 1,200 and 1,500 additions, modifications, or deletions to the TSDB every day (Wyllie, 2010).

However, terrorist groups can discover through "test flights" which of their members are selected by the computer systems for secondary screening and which members are not identified (Martonosi & Barnett, 2006). During their actual missions, those members not selected by the system and considered low-risk threats could take the lead roles. In addition, periodic undercover tests have found that many airport security personnel are inadequately trained, there are many weaknesses in the screening equipment and technology, and there is poor management and supervision of security employees (Martonosi & Barnett, 2006).

Despite the shortcomings of screening procedures and attempts at suspect profiling, the number of successful skyjackings or destruction of commercial aircraft in flight has decreased dramatically over the past four decades. This suggests that some of the probing, airport screening procedures, and suspect profiles based on behavioral indicators have worked and served as deterrents to a large extent. Still, there is much room for improvements, as pointed out above. In the next section, we discuss still another expansion of suspect-based profiling, one that relies more on human observation than on information obtained from large databases.

Behavioral Observation Techniques to Detect Suspicious Passengers

In recent years, passenger profiling has taken a different turn. Although there is no specific terrorist profile, officials believe they can at least identify persons who exhibit behavioral characteristics of fear, stress, or attempts to deceive. These characteristics would not for the most part be evident from the databases covered above.

SCREENING OF PASSENGER BY OBSERVATION TECHNIQUE (SPOT)

Screening of Passenger by Observation Technique, or SPOT, is a TSA behavioral observation method loosely based on an Israeli program derived from that country's direct experiences with terrorists. The U.S. program, which was pretested shortly after 2001 and implemented in earnest in 2007, is intended to provide the TSA **behavior detection officers** (BDOs) with a means of identifying individuals who pose or may pose transportation security risks by focusing on behaviors indicative of high levels of stress, fear, or deception (U.S. Department of Homeland Security, 2008). Instead of focusing on guns, bombs, or knives—these are items for the screening detectors to uncover—the BDOs look for behavioral patterns and facial expressions that may reveal deception and malicious intent. The BDOs "walk the line" of individuals waiting to check their baggage or stand and observe them as they go through airport screening (see Photo 7.2).They use memorized checklist indicators with corresponding values and thresholds that are designed to assess potentially problematic passengers. Individuals who exhibit behaviors or appearance that exceeds a predetermined threshold are referred for additional screening and questioning. BDOs themselves are not law enforcement officers; they do not conduct investigations, carry weapons, or make arrests.

As of March 2010, there were about 3,000 of these officers working at 161 airports across the United States (GAO, 2010). According to the Department of Homeland Security, SPOT is a derivative of other behavioral analysis programs that have been successful employed by law enforcement and security personnel in the United States and around the world.

Photo 7.2: A TSA behavior detection officer, top center, observes passengers in line at a security checkpoint in 2008. Approximately 3,000 BDOs have been trained and assigned to U.S. airports since 2004.

Through its SPOT program, the TSA collects two categories of information. First, observations made by the BDOs are entered into the SPOT database and may reveal trends across airports or over time within a single airport. Second, as noted above, persons whose behavior exceeds a threshold of behavioral indicators may be referred for additional screening. In this latter category, TSA agents may collect personally identifiable information to check the individual's identity against intelligence, terrorist, and law enforcement databases. Although the program was initially established to detect terrorist threats, it has recently been broadened to include the identification of behaviors indicative of criminal activity.

The premise of SPOT is partly based on the work of Paul Ekman (2009), a professor emeritus of psychology at the University of California Medical School in San Francisco. Ekman's work has focused on the Facial Action Coding System for analyzing human facial expressions. According to Ekman, microfacial expressions, such as tensing of the lips or the raising of the brow, reveal subtle emotions that may be linked to deception. He claims that a properly trained observer using these facial cues alone can detect deception with 70% accuracy, and can be up to 100% accurate by taking into consideration gestures and body movements (cited in Weinberger, 2010). Ekman reports that, to date, he has taught about one thousand TSA screeners. It should be mentioned that Ekman's claims are controversial, and his research is difficult to replicate (Vrij, 2011). In addition, he admits that 9 out of every 10 persons displaying "suspicious" behavior have perfectly innocent reasons for this (cited in Bradshaw, 2008). As Bradshaw observes, "Many travelers may be subjected to undue attention simply because they have a fear of flying, feel intimidated by being scrutinized by uniformed screeners or are carrying items that cause them shame, such as legal but erotic literature" (p. 10).

The TSA's relatively new SPOT program itself has been lauded and criticized. On the one hand, proponents say that it reduces, if not eliminates, reliance on racial, ethnic, or religious cues. BDOs observe behaviors, not inappropriate characteristics, although it should be noted that "appearance" is a relevant criterion. Critics question its cost as well as the ability of even trained observers to predict problematic activity based on facial or body cues. Since the program's inception, very few terrorist suspects have been detected, and the great majority of arrests have been those of illegal immigrants with no indications of ties to terrorism (GAO, 2010). In addition, the broad scientific community has urged caution against developing enthusiasm for the program without scientific validation (National Research Council, 2008).

In May 2010, the U.S. Government Accountability Office—an independent, nonpartisan agency—issued a report that analyzed (1) the extent to which TSA validated the

SPOT program before deployment, (2) implementation challenges, and (3) the extent to which TSA measures SPOT's effect on aviation security. The GAO concluded that the TSA deployed SPOT nationwide without first validating the scientific basis for identifying suspicious passengers in an airport environment. In addition, the GAO noted that no scientific consensus exists on whether behavior detection principles can be reliably used for counterterrorism purposes. The GAO further found that the TSA was experiencing problems fully utilizing the resources it had available to systematically collect and analyze the information obtained by BDOs on passengers who may pose a threat to the aviation system. In other words, the TSA was not properly collecting a database on passengers they detained, nor were they using other intelligence databases that were available to them. Finally, the TSA had not implemented any evaluation procedures to determine the effectiveness of the SPOT program to identify potential terrorists. In fairness to the TSA, there was a national sense of urgency after the 9/11 attacks that led to reliance on untested procedures and questionable methods in the screening of airline passengers.

We should note, as well, that the GAO did not recommend that the SPOT system be shut down. Rather, it offered suggestions for improving the system and emphasized the need for continuing research on its effectiveness. Nonetheless, questions remain about the efficiency, wisdom, and effectiveness of using BDOs to aid in assuring airport security.

It should be mentioned that Canada has embarked on a similar behavior observation program. In a 6-month experimental program conducted at the Vancouver, B.C., airport, 20 officers of the Canadian Air Transport Security Authority roamed the airport looking for suspicious actions, such as a traveler wearing heavy clothes on a hot day, paying unusual attention to the screening process, or sweating profusely (Bronskill, 2011; Saint-Cyr, 2011). These officers were in uniform and not only roamed the airport but made careful observations of passenger behavior at the checkpoint areas. However, at this writing, many experts are not convinced of the program's effectiveness, and at this point it seems susceptible to the same criticisms as SPOT. One of the major fears is that the program will be introduced without any valid scientific basis. Transport Canada, however, maintains that the program is based on decades of research that demonstrates there are certain involuntary, subconscious actions that can be indicative of deception (Saint-Cyr, 2011).

FUTURE ATTRIBUTE SCREENING TECHNOLOGY (FAST)

In 2008, news broke that DHS had begun testing a new "mind-reading" device, yet another approach to passenger screening. FAST (Future Attribute Screening Technology), also known as MALINTENT, is still in its developmental stages. According to DHS, FAST seeks to improve the screening of passengers by developing behavioral-based procedures that will provide additional indicators to screeners to enable them to make more informed decisions. If implemented, it would be used with individuals who had been singled out for additional scrutiny based on behavioral indicators like those described above. As you will see, FAST is more intrusive and will likely face vociferous opposition from individuals and groups concerned about civil liberties and invasions of privacy. The program is based on the assumption that "behavioral scientists hypothesize that someone with malintent may act strangely, show mannerisms out of the norm, or experience extreme physiological reactions based on the extent, time, and consequences of the event" (DHS, 2008, p. 2). Moreover, the program focuses on identifying intent, or pre-criminal behavior.

FAST is a sensor-based program that reads body reactions indicative of hostile intention and uses these reactions to develop stronger algorithmic predictions as to who should be singled out for additional screening and investigation. FAST operates somewhat on the same psychophysiological principles as the polygraph, but it is designed to collect its initial data from remote cameras and sensors, outside the awareness of passengers. It examines respiration factors, skin temperature, cardiac rate, and electrical resistance of the skin as the person is questioned by a TSA agent. The program is in an experimental stage at this point, so its effectiveness is still unknown. However, FAST completed the first stage of testing in March 2011 in an undisclosed location in the northeast.

According to DHS (2008, p. 4), FAST researchers are working on the following five sensor systems that can detect these cues:

1. A remote cardiovascular and respiratory sensor to measure heart rate, heart rate variability, respiration rates, and respiratory sinus arrhythmia (variation in heart rate during a breathing cycle).

2. A remote eye tracker, which uses a camera and processing software to track the position and gaze of the eyes (and, in some instances, the entire head) of a subject. Most eye trackers will also provide measurement of the pupil diameter.

3. Thermal cameras that provide detailed information on the changes in the thermal properties of the skin of the face, which will help assess electrodermal activity and measure respiration and eye movements. This will be discussed in more detail in the next section on new approaches to detecting deception.

4. A high-resolution video that allows for highly detailed images of the face and body to be taken so that image analysis can determine facial features and expressions and body movements, and an audio system for analyzing human voice for pitch change.

5. Other sensor types such as for pheromones detection are also under consideration.

A DHS science spokesperson claimed that preliminary testing of FAST has demonstrated 78% accuracy in detecting malicious intent and 80% in detecting deception (cited in Nikolas, 2011). However, the data collection was based on sensor information on 140 volunteers who were instructed to deceive. Whether the data will be similar on passengers passing through busy airport or transportation centers remains to be seen. At this point, it will be helpful to turn our attention to current research on deception in general, and specifically as it applies to suspect-based profiling.

Detecting Deception

A critical task associated with suspect-based profiling is the detection of deception. Specifically, once a suspect has been detained, either briefly or in a controlled environment, how can one tell whether he or she is telling the truth? The profiler—or behavioral analyst—should ideally be able to offer guidelines for detecting deception. Personnel in law enforcement, the military, and the intelligence community regularly deal with individuals who deceive them. During police and investigative interviews and interrogations, officers and agents want to know whether a suspect is lying when he or she denies participation or involvement in criminal activity or whether the suspect is planning terrorism activity. One of the most important tasks of intelligence officers during their time in Iraq and Afghanistan was to determine who was telling the truth and who could be trusted, among all the people with whom they came in contact (National Research Council, 2010). "These are potentially questions of life and death" (p. 6).

Deception is behavior that is intended to conceal, misrepresent, or distort truth or information for the purpose of misleading others. In light of all the situations in which truthfulness is a critical variable, we must ask whether people really are able to detect deception in others. Detecting deception about future intentions is especially important in the area of national security. Had government officials detected deception in just 1 of the 19 terrorists of the September 11, 2001, attack on the United States, the horror that followed may have been avoided. All 19 terrorists told lies to government officials on at least three different occasions (Honts, Hartwig, Kleinman, & Meissner, 2009): once when they applied for a visa for entry into the United States, a second time when they entered the United States, and a third time when they boarded the doomed flights. However, should these officials have been able to tell they were lying?

The quick answer is no—very, very few people, professionals or laypersons, are able to detect deception with much accuracy or consistency. This includes behavioral analysts. "What the research has shown is that people are not good at detecting lies" (Loftus, 2011, p. 538). Nevertheless, people (especially professionals) firmly believe they can. While our society is replete with folklore concerning how to tell whether someone is lying, the empirical research over the past 30 years cogently demonstrates that the human ability to identify liars from truth tellers is abysmally poor. One reason that people are not good at detecting deception is because they rely on behaviors that are not useful or, worse, on behaviors and cues that lead them astray (Loftus, 2011). For example, some people think that liars will avert their gaze or fidget excessively. Unfortunately, these cues are highly unreliable in detecting deception. Furthermore, some cultures and ethnic groups differ widely in their nonverbal behavioral patterns, with gaze aversion being considered more of a sign of respect under certain circumstances.

Another problem with detecting deception is that, in today's society, lying is commonplace. It is a fact of daily life, and not an extraordinary event (DePaulo et al., 2003). According to DePaulo et al., "People frequently lie to make themselves (and sometimes others) look better or feel better; they try to appear to be the kind of person they only wish they could truthfully claim to be" (p. 101). Therefore, because lying is so ubiquitous—even those who are "lie detectors" themselves do not always tell the truth—it is "normal" and does not stand out as unusual behavior. Another problem is that some liars begin to believe that their deceptions are actually true (Merckelbach, Jelicic, & Pieters, 2011), and therefore they may not display "signs" of not telling the truth. They often rehearse their stories, and sometimes begin to live by them to the point that the lies become embedded into their frame of reference.

Research does show that observers can detect *emotion* using verbal, nonverbal, and microfacial expressions. In other words, we can tell if someone is embarrassed, or uncomfortable, or bored. However, the assumption that observers can detect *deception* simply through emotions such as stressful reactions is unwarranted. With regard to airport security, for example, there are a host of reasons why passengers tend to be stressed before and after boarding a plane. However, there is very little evidence that supports the claims that trained BDOs or TSA agents can detect individuals who may pose a threat to aviation security based on their demeanor or their responses. It is possible that as the number of databases as well as the information within them increase and additional research evidence accumulates, we will make progress in this regard, but we are not there yet.

POLICE INVESTIGATORS' ABILITY TO DETECT DECEPTION

Police academies and other law enforcement training facilities often provide some instruction in deception detection, most often using the Inbau (Inbau, Reid, Buckley, & Jayne, 2001) method called *behavior analysis interviewing*. As noted by Aldert Vrij (2008), most instruction in the training of police investigators focuses on nonverbal behavior as being more diagnostic of deceit than speech content. In addition, one key assumption in the Inbau et al. approach is that, compared to liars, "truth tellers expected to be exonerated and therefore should be inclined to offer helpful information" (Vrij, Mann, Kristen, & Fisher, 2007, p. 501). However, there is no empirical evidence to support these claims. Vrij (2005) discovered, for example, that truthful and innocent suspects tended to be *less* cooperative than deceptive suspects. Why? Perhaps because they understood the reality that they could be accused of and charged with something they did not do. Most researchers report that the instruction on deception detection given at many police academies is misguided and not consonant with research findings (e.g., Leo, 2008; Meissner & Kassin, 2002).

PROMISING APPROACHES TO DETECTING DECEPTION

Fortunately, all is not hopeless when it comes to detecting deception. Interviewing approaches that focus on gathering information appear to be more effective in detecting deception compared to accusing someone of wrongdoing. The accusatory approach confronts the suspect, such as with questions like, "It appears you are hiding something," or "You weren't home when you said you were, were you?" In contrast, in this information-gathering approach, suspects are asked open-ended questions about their activities, such as, "Can you tell me what you were doing yesterday morning?"

Furthermore, the more words there are in the response, the more verbal cues there should be to discriminate between liars and truth tellers (Vrij et al., 2007). As pointed out by Loftus (2011), "the information-gathering approach is superior in that it leads to a larger body of information that can be used later to compare with other evidence or to check inconsistencies" (p. 538). By contrast, if the interview is accusatory in focus, the suspect will typically make short denials and consequently provide the fewest verbal cues to deceit (Vrij et al., 2007). Some training manuals recommend that the investigator should start by confronting the suspect with the existing evidence (Hartwig, Granhag, Strömwall, & Vrij, 2005). Research has shown that approaching the suspect with an accusatory tone in this way at the beginning of an interview or interrogation has a detrimental effect on lie detection accuracy (Hartwig et al., 2005).

Another effective approach is to ask questions that are not anticipated by the suspect. The assumption is that when liars are asked unexpected questions, they are forced to fabricate their answers on the spot, which is a difficult task (Vrij et al., 2009). This difficult task is referred to as "cognitive load," and the mental demand usually is characterized by longer time to answer and many more pauses than normal. It is also characterized by an increase in arousal, as the individual is afraid of not being believed. Consequently, spontaneous lies tend to contain more cues to deceit than planned lies (DePaulo et al., 2003).

Interestingly, as Vrij and his colleagues note, research has demonstrated that many **speech-related cues** are more diagnostic of deception than **nonverbal cues** (Vrij & Granhag, 2007). Nonverbal cues to deception are inconsistent, unreliable, and extremely difficult to discern, even by well-trained investigators knowledgeable about contemporary research. Behavioral analysts, then, might encourage investigators to be aware of speech patterns more than nonverbal cues. To use one illustration, spontaneous lies usually occur after longer-than-normal time to respond to a question (Boltz, Dyer, & Miller, 2010). This is because the person must first decide whether the truth or deception is more beneficial to him or her. ("Should I say I was home that night even though I wasn't?") If deception is considered more beneficial, then the lie has to be constructed and in a compelling way, which takes time. ("They'll want to know what I was doing, whether I watched a show, who can confirm this, etc.") If the lie has been prepared beforehand, presumably the response will be quicker. However, a delayed response may be a lie, but it is not necessarily an indication of guilt. Many an innocent suspect has lied to police for understandable reasons.

Another tactic is to ask questions that are unlikely to be anticipated by the suspect. Loftus (2011) gives the example of when a suspect claims to have been eating dinner with a friend at some critical point in time. In this case, the interviewer might ask, "Who finished his meal first, you or your friend?" Liars are less likely to respond with "I don't know" to this unanticipated question, for fear that a failure to offer some answer would look suspicious. Yet it is likely that most of us would have trouble answering that question and would display some hesitation before answering it.

In general, the research to date suggests that investigators who just pay attention to nonverbal cues are less accurate in identifying deception than those who take speech content and timing into account. Although most police investigators take some aspects of speech into consideration, the overall tendency is to rely on nonverbal behavioral patterns. Part of the problem is that when lying is expected, investigators may have little interest in words of denial and may prefer to look at bodily signs to detect deceit. However, liars consciously monitor their nonverbal behavior in an attempt to avoid detection and manage the impressions they convey to others (Boltz et al., 2010; DePaulo et al., 2003). For instance, rather than avert their gaze, they may stare into the eyes of the person they are talking to. However, they tend to be more careless in their self-regulation of other forms of communication, such as speech patterns.

In an often-cited and well-designed study, Paul Ekman and Maureen O'Sullivan (1991) compared laypersons and a wide assortment of "professional liar catchers" on the ability to detect deception. Their ambitious project included members of the U.S. Secret Service, Central Intelligence Agency, FBI, National Security Agency, Drug Enforcement Agency, California law enforcement judges, psychiatrists, college students, and working adults. Only *one* group was able to detect deception beyond chance: agents of the U.S. Secret Service. Even so, the 34 Secret Service agents were not impressive in their ability to identify deception (64% in overall accuracy), but none of them performed below average, and some (29%) achieved accuracy scores of 80% or more. Another important finding was that the accurate "lie catchers" reported using nonverbal cues (especially subtle facial expressions) *as well as* verbal cues to identify deceit. In other words, the accurate lie catchers used multiple clues rather than relying on any particular single indicator.

Frank and Ekman (1997) also examined some other aspects of deception detection. Because much of the previous research had looked at low-stakes, laboratory-produced lies, Frank and Ekman focused on high-stakes, "real-world" deception, that is, lies that occur in situations where the stakes are high and emotions are intense, as would be encountered in police interrogations and courtrooms, or—more relevant to this chapter—questioning by federal agents. The researchers found some support that the strong emotions generated in high-stakes situations tend to "leak" good cues for deception detection, and that these cues are apparent across other high-stakes situations. For example, Frank and Ekman discovered, under high-stakes situations, strong negative emotions (e.g., a scowl or frown) in the facial expressions of 90% of the liars. On the other hand, rarely did they find similar negative emotions in the facial expressions of truth tellers. In low-stakes situations, such as would be found in everyday, low-emotional lying, the observer needs to rely more on "thinking" cues, such as words, factual descriptions, pauses, long speech latencies, and speech errors, to detect deception. Low-stakes lying appears to be more situation-specific and probably lends itself to more inaccuracy by observers.

This leads us to another finding from the Frank and Ekman (1997) study. Although there are individual differences in the ability to detect deception, some people can be trained to identify deceivers at a better-than-chance level. Studies have demonstrated modest but statistically significant improvements in accuracy after such training, usually in the range of 5% to 10%. Valid, evidence-based training might even improve the accuracy further. In the Frank-Ekman research, those persons who were able to detect deception without much training seemed to improve the most with research-based training. Likewise, Porter, Woodworth, and Birt (2000) discovered that parole officers improved their scores at detecting deception after 2 days of such training. Kassin and Fong (1999), however, found that *traditional* police training on deception (the **Reid Technique of interrogation** that includes analysis of verbal and nonverbal behavior) actually *decreased* the officers' ability to detect deception. It is possible that the training that many law enforcement officers and detectives receive may contribute to their inaccuracy and perhaps even provide unwarranted confidence in their ability. The research has been consistent in pointing out that the more confident the officers, the worse their accuracy (Ekman & O'Sullivan, 1991; Kassin & Fong, 1999; Porter et al., 2000).

DETECTION OF INTENT

A vast majority of the research on deception has concentrated on detecting lying about past actions or events. However, it is far more important that suspect-based profiling be based on future intentions. It is critical, for instance, that airport security be able to distinguish between trustworthiness and deception about a suspect's intentions once he or she boards the aircraft. "The societal value of an increased accuracy in detecting criminal intentions (i.e., illegal actions planned, but not yet committed) can hardly be overstated" (Granhag & Knieps, 2011, p. 274). Usually, these intentions come with strong commitment and some amount of planning (Granhag & Knieps, 2011). Unfortunately, very little research has examined this area in any detail.

Vrij, Leal, Mann, and Granhag (2011) reported on two studies examining the ability of participants to detect dishonesty. The first study, conducted in an international airport, revealed that passengers being dishonest about their intentions (what they were going to do when arriving at their final destinations) provided less plausible statements compared to passengers who were truthful about their intentions. The study also showed that the two interviewers asking the questions could discriminate between lies and truths with 70% accuracy.

In the second study, Vrij et al. (2011) used military personnel and police officers as participants, primarily because they are more accustomed to deception scenarios than typical subjects such as college students. The participants were told they were to play roles as undercover agents, as if they were on a mission to identify hostile or friendly agents. The role required that each participant lie to two agents (to one about past actions and to the other about future actions), and tell the truth to two other agents (to one about past actions and to the other about future actions). The researchers discovered that the recall of true intentions is different from that of false intentions. Specifically, the participants were more accurate in distinguishing truth from dishonesty in the intention (future actions) scenarios than they were for the past action scenarios (70% accuracy vs. 55% accuracy, respectively). Basically, the results suggested that detecting true and false *intent* was easier than detecting truthful and deceptive *recall* of past activities. The intention questions came as a surprise to these professionals playing the role of interviewees, whereas the past activities questions did not. This indicates that suspects in real-life situations are better prepared for questions about past activities than questions about their intentions. For example, dishonest passengers being interviewed at an airport are likely to expect certain questions about their past activities, but may have considerable difficulty describing their plans for the future if they have malicious intent. These results were strongly supported in another study conducted by Granhag and Knieps (2011).

New Approaches to Detecting Deception

THERMAL IMAGING

Thermal imaging is a technique whereby changes in facial temperature patterns (which are due to changes in blood flow) are detected through special cameras (Warmelink et al., 2011). It is one of several techniques being developed by FAST, discussed above. Thermal imaging was initially proposed as a remote and rapid screening device for detecting deception. The device requires no skilled staff, and the subjects are unaware that their facial temperature is even being measured (Pavlidis, Eberhardt, & Levine, 2002). Hence, the instrument could be used in airport screening "where the facial thermal patterns of every passenger could be measured non-intrusively, thereby revealing instantaneously the identity of terrorists and other wrongdoers" (Warmelink et al., 2011, p. 40). The application of thermal imaging as a lie detection device is controversial, however, because the changes in facial temperatures occur for reasons other than deception as well. Airports are full of passengers who are anxious and aroused for a number of reasons, including excitement about going on vacation or visiting family members over the holidays.

Warmelink et al. (2011) tested the accuracy of thermal imaging as a lie detection instrument in air passenger screening. In the study, a researcher approached passengers at a large international airport and said he or she was seeking volunteers to talk about their travel plans. If they volunteered, passengers were asked the following two questions: (1) Where are you flying to today? (2) How would you describe the main purpose of your trip? The researcher wrote the comments down, and then said, "My colleague will ask you a few questions about your forthcoming trip. Some people will be asked to tell the truth, whereas others will be asked to lie during these interviews" (p. 42).

In the study, passengers were allocated randomly to either a truth or lie condition. Two researchers, who did not know which passenger was assigned to the truth-telling or lying condition, were randomly assigned to interview the passengers. During the interview, passenger facial temperatures were recorded with a thermal imaging camera located 10 meters away. Warmelink et al. (2011) found that thermal imaging *by itself* was not effective in discriminating liars from truth tellers. That is, thermal imaging, when used strictly as a remote and rapid screening device, has very limited ability to distinguish individuals with malicious intent from those individuals without malicious intent. However, Warmelink et al. did find that thermal imaging may have potential as a lie detection tool if passengers are actually interviewed. Liars' facial temperature rose significantly during the interview, while the truth tellers' temperature remained the same. On the basis of these facial patterns, 64% of truth tellers and 69% of liars were classified correctly. The interviewers outperformed the thermal recordings. They were able to classify correctly 72% of truth tellers and 77% of liars, even though they had no access to thermal imaging data. Speech and demeanor characteristics revealed more information about deceit than skin temperature. Warmelink et al. concluded, however, that these accuracy rates were still rather low for screening purposes at airports. "A lie detection tool at airports should be virtually flawless in identifying those truth tellers to be of practical use" (p. 45). Thermal imaging will classify too many non-deceptive passengers as having malicious intent who may be anxious for non-deceptive reasons. Passengers falsely accused of lying may be excluded from flying and are likely to undergo a more intensive interrogation or even detention.

Physiological measures of deception or even malicious intent are unlikely to be successful. The scientific community has yet to discover an identifiable physiological signature that is uniquely and directly associated with lying or malicious intent. If anything, physiological detection devices at airports are likely to produce an enormous number of false positives by tagging many innocent passengers as potential terrorists. Moreover, a system that produces a large number of false positives is unworkable at large, busy airports characterized by long lines passing through security checks. There may not be any physical security device that can flawlessly identify individuals with intentions to bring down an airplane unless we can, as noted by Brian Jenkins (2002), develop a device that can X-ray people's souls.

VOICE STRESS TECHNOLOGIES

It is assumed that each individual has a unique, personal style of speaking due to anatomical, structural differences in the speech mechanism and the manner in which the tongue, lips, and teeth are used. **Voiceprints** are oscillographic representations of speech that identify these unique elements of vocalization. Proponents argue that a deceptive speaker's voice changes under stress and that these stress-related changes are reflected through minute vibrations, or microtremors. These changes in the voice may not be audible to the human ear, but the claim is that they can be ascertained accurately and reliably by using sophisticated instruments specifically designed for this purpose. However, there are a host of reasons—in addition to lying—why a person's voice may be under stress while speaking. The value of voiceprints as discriminators between deception and truth has yet to be accepted by the scientific community.

Nevertheless, a number of commercial firms have marketed various pieces of hardware claimed to detect stress, and ultimately lying, from live or recorded segments of speech. In 1971, Dektor Counterintelligence and Security Corporation developed the Psychological Stress Evaluator (PSE), for example, which is specifically designed to measure deception-induced stress in the human voice. It is still on the market today, although it has gone through several modifications. While several other companies have developed similar instruments, the PSE has been the most extensively marketed. In the marketing literature, Dektor claims that the PSE is 95 to 99%

accurate in discriminating liars from truth tellers. Other **voice stress technologies** include the Computer Voice Stress Analyzer (CVSA), Diogenes Digital Voice Stress Analyzer, and the Vericator and Truster Pro.

Sujeeta Bhatt and Susan Brandon (2008) of the Defense Intelligence Agency reviewed 24 empirical studies on voice stress analysis that were conducted over a period of more than 30 years. They concluded that there was no supportive evidence for the effectiveness of voice stress analysis–based technologies for detection of deception in individuals. The National Research Council (2010) further concluded that "a person flipping a coin would be equally good at detecting deception" (p. 11). Furthermore, the hypothesis underlying the use of voice deception detection has been shown to be false (National Research Council, 2010). Research has discovered no microtremors, either in the muscles of the vocal tract or in the voice itself. "So the basic idea underlying voice stress technologies—that stress causes the normal microtremors in the voice to be suppressed—is not supported by the evidence" (p. 11). Currently, the intelligence community has apparently stayed away from voice stress technologies because of the absence of research evidence to support their accuracy. However, law enforcement agencies across the United States and other countries continue to use voice stress technologies. Many police investigators remain convinced that they are useful in interviews and interrogations. One reason for the continued use—despite the research evidence—is based on the assumption of many police investigators who believe that suspects will tell the truth if they can be convinced that a machine can detect lying.

With voice stress technologies called into question, the intelligence community continued to be convinced it needed some way of detecting deception. The Defense Academy for Credibility Assessment's headquarters organization, the Counterintelligence Field Activity, was given the job to find something that would do a better job than voice stress analyzers (National Research Council, 2010). Johns Hopkins University was contracted to develop such an instrument. The instrument under development is called the Credibility Assessment Screening System. It consists of three sensors and is very similar to a polygraph. Two sensors measure electrical conductivity of the skin, and one measures changes in blood flow through a finger. This instrument, like the voice stress analyzers, is controversial, and its effectiveness has yet to be firmly established.

Summary and Conclusions

Suspect-based profiling refers to the process of identifying possible perpetrators of crimes based on demographic and behavioral features gathered on known offenders. It is a controversial enterprise because, as practiced, it has often focused on race, ethnicity, and national origin, which has come to be called racial profiling. In this chapter, we have addressed the use of suspect-based profiling with respect to drug trafficking and terrorism, two areas against which law enforcement has dramatically expanded its efforts. In recent years, laws in a number of states that encourage the targeting of undocumented immigrants also raise concerns about racial profiling as well as the prerogative of states to engage in activities traditionally left to the federal government.

Worldwide concerns about terrorism have brought suspect-based profiling into the forefront of activities of government at all levels. Considerable effort has been directed at attempting to identify potential terrorists and to place them in typologies for better understanding. Several typologies have been offered, including the rationally motivated, psychologically motivated, and culturally motivated classifications discussed in this chapter. It is clear that an approach based on demographics alone is ineffective, and it is also clear that misconceptions about terrorists abound. Many are well educated and few are mentally disordered, although their views of the world do not correspond with the views of individuals who are not terrorists. With the exception of the events of 9/11, actions by lone wolf terrorists—those acting alone—have cost more lives than those of individuals associated with terrorist groups. Lone wolf terrorists also are more likely to be mentally disordered, whereas those affiliated with terrorist groups are unlikely to be so. They also lend themselves the best to profiling in that they often have specific targets, display social isolation, exhibit poor interpersonal skills, and often leave signatures. However, if they carry out only one attack—such as the Oklahoma City bombing—it is difficult to detect them before-the-fact unless police are alerted to suspicious activity on their part.

The U.S. government—particularly as represented in the TSA—has engaged in airline passenger profiling at least since the skyjackings that occurred during the last half of the 20th century. These skyjackers were not considered terrorists, but many of the same approaches were used to attempt to profile terrorists in later years. No specific profile has emerged, but the government is increasingly going in the direction of behaviorally based observation. In addition to the routine screening (e.g., no-fly list, body scans, pat-downs) that airline passengers now experience, behavioral detection officers walk the line in many airports, observing passenger behavior and facial expression, and selecting suspicious individuals for more intensive screening.

Once a suspect has been detained, either temporarily or in a more controlled setting, the detection of deception is a crucial task for the investigator. Research-based behavioral analysts have studied deception for many years, and today's profilers should be aware of their findings. Nevertheless, deception is not easily detected. For many years, it was assumed that "nonverbal cues" were good indicators of deception; these include such behaviors as avoiding eye contact, fidgeting, playing with one's jewelry, or shaking one's leg uncontrollably. More recent research indicates that none of these cues, by itself, indicates that a person is lying. Many do indicate stress, but even that cannot be assumed; in some cultures, for example, persons are taught to avoid eye contact as a sign of respect. However, even if stress is involved, there are numerous reasons other than lying for persons being questioned—particularly questioned by official figures—to be under stress.

Current research suggests that a combination of nonverbal cues and content cues are promising indicators of deception. Untruthful persons are less able to control their answers when they have little time to prepare a lie—thus, they are more likely to take their time to answer a question. Direct confrontation, or accusation, is less likely to elicit truth than an open-ended question; moreover, an open-ended question will encourage a person to reveal more information that can subsequently be verified or refuted. Recently developed physiological measures, such as voice stress analyzers or thermal imagery facial stress detectors, have not been empirically supported for detecting deception. Researchers have demonstrated, however, that individuals can be trained to detect deception to a reasonable extent—though never with absolute certitude—by paying attention to a combination of nonverbal and content cues.

KEY CONCEPTS

Behavior detection officers

CAPPS and CAPPS-II

Culturally motivated terrorist

FAST

Lone wolves

Nonverbal cues

Psychologically motivated terrorist

Rationally motivated terrorist

Reid technique of interrogation

Speech-related cues

SPOT program

Terrorist Screening Database (TSDB)

Thermal imaging

Voice stress technologies

Voiceprints

8

Reconstructive Psychological Evaluation

The Psychological Autopsy

During a routine firing exercise off the coast of Puerto Rico on April 19, 1989, a rapid series of three powerful explosions ripped through the center gun of Turret II on board the battleship USS *Iowa*, resulting in the death of 47 naval personnel. Investigations of the tragedy discovered that five 94-pound bags of propellant ignited while they were being jammed into the open breech of the huge 16-inch gun. The catastrophic mishap represented one of the worst disasters for the U.S. Navy during peacetime. Immediately, a Judge Advocate General's Manual investigation was convened. In this investigation, every conceivable source of ignition and every aspect of the USS *Iowa*'s condition and shipboard routine that may have contributed to the incident was evaluated (see Photo 8.1).

The tragic incident led to a request for a psychological autopsy, the apparent sullying of the reputation of a sailor aboard the ship, and a congressional investigation into the validity of the psychological autopsy itself—also called **equivocal death analysis (EDA)**, or reconstructive psychological evaluation. As mentioned in Chapter 1, the EDA is conducted on a dead person for the purpose of determining not the cause, but

Photo 8.1: Exploding turrets on the USS *Iowa* in 1989.

the mode and motivation of the death. We begin this chapter with a detailed discussion of the USS *Iowa* case, because it illustrates so well the many pitfalls that face profilers in their attempts to conduct these investigations.

The USS *Iowa* Case

As noted above, the office of the Judge Advocate General (JAG) was called upon to conduct an investigation of the disaster at sea. At one point, investigators received a letter from the sister of one of the dead crewmembers, asking who would receive the $100,000 insurance money; this raised suspicion of a possible deliberate initiation of the explosion. Consequently, the Naval Investigative Service (NIS) was directed to conduct a thorough investigation into the backgrounds and recent behavior of center gun room personnel as well as other crewmembers on the USS *Iowa*. (The NIS became the NCIS—the Naval Criminal Investigative Service—in 1992.) The Navy also requested an EDA from the FBI's National Center for the Analysis of Violent Crime (see Focus 2.1 in Chapter 2 for a description of the NCAVC). The FBI agents conducting the EDA were provided with most of the information generated by the NIS.

At the suggestion of the NIS, the FBI investigation centered on Gunner's Mate Clayton Hartwig. It is important to note that the FBI conducted the EDA without benefit of its own interviews, relying almost exclusively on the information that had been collected by the NIS. The investigation of Hartwig's background revealed that he had experimented with explosive devices and detonators in the past, and that he had a fascination with ship disasters. Inquiry into his personal life showed that he had recently had a falling out with a close friend. It was also discovered that Hartwig had attempted suicide while in high school and had talked about suicide in the weeks before the explosion. Perhaps more revealing, he had indicated he preferred to die as a result of an explosion.

The FBI's analysis concluded that Clayton Hartwig had intentionally caused the explosion of the USS *Iowa*, acting alone. Essentially, the FBI concluded that Hartwig had committed suicide, taking 46 other naval personnel with him. In fact, "The FBI report was the primary piece of evidence in support of the navy's attribution of responsibility for the incident to Clayton Hartwig" (Poythress, Otto, Darkes, & Starr, 1993, p. 8).

A memo from the Chief of Naval Operations (1989) further concluded, after examining the reports, that

> The combination of these factors leads me reluctantly to the conclusion that the most likely cause of the explosion was a detonation device, deliberately introduced between powders bags that were being rammed into the breech of the center gun. . . . I further concur with the investigating officers and the subsequent endorsers that the preponderance of evidence supports the theory that the most likely person to have introduced the detonation device was GMG2 Hartwig. (p. 83)

U.S. Congressional committees also carefully investigated the incident. The U.S. Senate Committee on Armed Services first heard on November 16, 1989, from Rear Admiral Richard Milligan, the Navy's investigating officer, and from other Navy witnesses who had assisted in the investigative effort. The Committee also heard from the commanding officer of the USS *Iowa* (see Photo 8.2) and other military personnel who had been aboard the ship. Three special agents from the NCAVC who had conducted the equivocal death analysis also testified. We have met or cited the agents in earlier chapters of the book: Ault, Hazelwood, and Reboussin; each has had a long career with the FBI and throughout their professional lives remained advocates of profiling as a general concept.

Senators, however, were generally skeptical of the FBI's overall conclusion. At several points during the senate testimony, three senators (Senators William Cohen of Maine, John Warner of Virginia, and Alan Dixon of Illinois) asked about the validity of the equivocal death analysis. At one point, Special Agent Ault replied, "Our product . . . is strictly opinion based upon the expertise

Photo 8.2: The commanding officer of the USS *Iowa*, Fred Moosally, testifying before the Senate Armed Services Committee in Washington, D.C., on December 12, 1989. Moosally neither agreed nor disagreed that Clayton Hartwig likely caused the explosion.

that we have acquired over the years of doing this and our own backgrounds. We give opinions" (Committee on Armed Services, 1990, p. 202).

The U.S. House of Representatives Armed Services Committee (HASC) also closely scrutinized the reports from the Navy and the FBI. The HASC was so skeptical of the conclusions that they enlisted the assistance of the American Psychological Association (APA) to independently review and evaluate the FBI's report and the Navy's conclusions (Poythress et al., 1993). A 12-member panel of experts (10 psychologists and 2 psychiatrists) rejected the conclusions of the FBI behavioral analysis that portrayed Clayton Hartwig as suicidal and responsible for the explosion. The House was also skeptical of the FBI's equivocal death analysis as a scientifically reliable and valid investigative method (Poythress et al., 1993), despite Agent Hazelwood's assertion that he could recall only 3 out 45 cases in which he was unable to arrive at a conclusive opinion when conducting an EDA. Poythress et al. posit that the FBI agents' conclusions were offered with absolute certainty rather than offered with a probabilistic statement. More importantly, 10 of the 12 experts consulted by the HASC considered the FBI analysis invalid. They felt the evidence gathered did not support the FBI's conclusion that Hartwig was suicidal. Even those experts who believed the analysis might be somewhat credible were critical of the procedures, methodology, and validity of the FBI's EDA. Furthermore, the panel and several of the congresspersons expressed strong reservations about the absolute certainty with which the FBI agents presented their conclusions (Moses, 1990). The HASC concluded that the Navy's investigation was "an investigative failure" (*U.S.S. Iowa Tragedy,* 1990).

In a subsequent letter to the APA journal *American Psychologist,* the FBI agents reiterated that the EDA is "a professional opinion based on years of law enforcement experience with indirect assessment and violent death" (Ault, Hazelwood, & Reboussin, 1994, p. 73). The agents further stated that EDA validity is essentially unattainable because the subject of the analysis is deceased, and the entire truth may never be known. Critics of the EDA process maintain that the FBI agents were "advocating opinions based merely on previous experience without any scientific support for those opinions, or even any possibility for demonstrating that hypotheses alternative to their opinions had been available for test" (Canter, 1999, p. 141).

In still another inquiry into the incident, the U.S. General Accounting Office (GAO, 1991) hired Sandia National Laboratories in New Mexico to examine and assess the Navy's first technical investigation. (The name of the General Accounting Office was changed to Government Accountability Office in 2004, to better reflect its role of overseeing government expenditures.) Among other specific questions, the then General Accounting Office wanted to know whether there was evidence of an intentional introduction of a foreign object or device into the breech. When Sandia investigators found evidence that the blast may have been an accident, the Navy reopened its probe of the *Iowa* explosion. It did not, though, reopen the psychological aspects of the case, maintaining it still believed the blast was caused by Hartwig.

Investigations by the GAO and Sandia National Laboratories concluded that the explosion was likely due to high-speed over-ramming of the explosive powder into the breech, with no evidence of a chemical or ignition device being *intentionally* placed there. The over-ramming meant there was no space between the powder bags and the 2,700-pound projectile. The rammer, under the direction of the gun captain's hand signals, rapidly pushed the powder 42 inches into the breech, 21 inches past the normal powder ram position, subsequently causing the detonation. Basically, there was no evidence that Clayton Hartwig was responsible for the explosion.

The *Iowa* incident brought considerable attention to the FBI's equivocal death analysis, which until then was virtually unknown in the psychological-behavioral sciences community (Poythress et al., 1993). FBI Agents Ault and Hazelwood, during their testimony before the HASC, indicated that the EDA is an extension of and is conceptually related to crime scene profiling (*Review of Navy Investigation,* 1990, p. 234). The EDA was traditionally conducted by law enforcement officials, particularly those associated with the FBI, who primarily examined material from the crime scene and other information directly available to the police (Canter, 1999). Today, as this method has attracted more attention, psychologists are more likely to be involved. The preferred and common term in the scientific and clinical communities is psychological autopsy, a term we will use throughout the chapter.

The Psychological Autopsy

For our purposes, the **psychological autopsy** represents the fifth category of profiling. It refers to a procedure that is done following a person's death in order to determine his or her mental state and circumstances prior to death. The psychological autopsy is a form of profiling because it involves the discovery and reconstruction of a deceased person's life based on the evidence left behind by that person. It entails revisiting the person's lifestyle, cognitive processes, and recent emotional and behavioral patterns prior to his or her death. A psychological autopsy can be valuable in various situations and circumstances, including insurance benefit determinations, worker's compensation cases, testamentary capacity cases, product liability determinations, malpractice cases, and criminal investigations. It should be clear, then, that it is not limited to criminal investigations.

The psychological autopsy was originally devised to assist certifying officials in clarifying deaths that were initially ambiguous, uncertain, or equivocal as to the *manner* of death (Shneidman, 1994). The method was first used in 1958, when the Los Angeles medical examiner/coroner Theodore J. Murphy consulted Edwin S. Shneidman, director of the L.A. Suicide Prevention Center, for assistance in determining the cause of an unusually high number of equivocal, or unexplained, deaths. Shneidman is generally credited with coining the term "psychological autopsy." Bruce Ebert (1987) later provided the first guidelines on how to conduct a psychological autopsy.

Although cause of death may be mentioned in the autopsy report, the psychological autopsy is not as concerned with the cause of death as with the mode or manner of death. The *cause of death* refers to the physiological system or structure that directly triggered the death, such as a gunshot wound to the brain, lack of oxygen to the brain, or a massive heart attack. This determination is usually the role of the medical examiner. The *mode of death,* on the other hand, falls into one of five categories. According to the United States Standard Certificate of Death, the modes of death include (1) suicide, (2) homicide, (3) accident, (4) natural cause, or (5) undetermined. For example, determining whether a death is accidental or the result of suicide can be especially important for parents and other family members and friends. In other cases, family may seek confirmation that their loved one was the victim of a homicide—as emotionally difficult as that may be—rather than a suicide.

Psychological autopsies often come into play when the death appears to be equivocal—that is, when the manner of death is unknown or undetermined. It is estimated that about 5 to 20% of all deaths are considered equivocal (Shneidman, 1981; Young, 1992). As a matter of practice, most medical examiners and coroners call an equivocal death a natural death until proven otherwise. In an equivocal case, it is difficult to evaluate the deceased's intentions, either because the factual circumstances of the death are incompletely known, or because the deceased's intentions were ambivalent, partial, inconsistent, or not clear. The term *manner* has special significance in any death investigation. Basically, "the manner of death refers to specific circumstances by which a death results" (La Fon, 2008, p. 420).

Today, the psychological autopsy is primarily undertaken in an effort to make a reasonable determination of what may have been in the mind of the deceased person leading up to and at the time of death (see Focus 8.1). La Fon (2008) identifies two basic types of psychological autopsies: suicide psychological autopsy (SPA) and equivocal death psychological autopsy (EDPA). SPA occurs when there is no question that the victim died at his or her own hand; its goal is to identify and understand the psychosocial factors that contributed to the suicide. The goal of the EDPA, on the other hand, is to clarify the mode of death and to determine the reasons for the death. Although the cause of death is generally clear, the manner (or mode) is often unclear. For example, Young (1992) gives the example of a parachutist who falls to the ground from an altitude of 5,000 feet and dies as the result of multiple injuries. The medical examiner can quickly determine that the cause of death was due to massive trauma to the vital organs. However, the examiner cannot establish whether it was accident, suicide, or even a homicide. That is, the examiner cannot immediately ascertain whether the parachute malfunctioned (accident), or whether the parachutist intentionally jumped with a parachute that he or she had rigged to malfunction (suicide). Alternately, the parachute may have been tampered with by someone else (homicide), or the parachutist may have suffered a heart attack during the jump (natural). In many cases of this nature, a professional may be called in to conduct a psychological autopsy.

Focus 8.1

Vincent Walker Foster Jr. Case: Death Near the Capitol

On July 20, 1993, police and the Fairfax County Fire and Rescue Department were called to Fort Marcy Park in North Virginia, maintained by the National Park Service. A male body had been found with a gunshot wound to the head and a gun in his right hand. There were no signs of a struggle and no evidence the body had been moved. The body was identified as Vincent Walker Foster Jr., a high-ranking White House lawyer in the Clinton Administration. The U.S. Park Police, along with the FBI, investigated and concluded, based on the evidence, that the death was a suicide.

However, rumors began to circulate that the conclusion that Foster had committed suicide was a White House cover-up for something far worse. The incident occurred during the time of the Whitewater probe, an investigation into real estate ventures associated with President Clinton and First Lady Hillary Rodham Clinton, dating back to their days in Arkansas. Skeptics, including some Republican members of Congress, believed that Foster—a long-time friend of the Clintons—was murdered because of what he knew about President Clinton and the First Lady's real estate ventures under the auspices of the Whitewater Development Company. Suspicions were increased with the discovery of Whitewater-related documents in Foster's White House office at the time of his death.

To stem increasing skepticism swirling around Washington, President Clinton asked Attorney General Janet Reno to appoint an independent counsel to investigate the allegations of possible foul play surrounding Foster's death. Robert B. Fiske was appointed as independent counsel; he immediately appointed a panel of distinguished and experienced forensic experts to conduct a thorough investigation of the cause and situation leading up to Foster's death. After receiving considerable evidence on the case, Independent Counsel Fiske concluded that Foster had committed suicide. Still, even after two carefully conducted investigations, conspiracy theories that Foster had been murdered persisted. A third investigation of the Whitewater real estate venture, led by another Independent Counsel, Kenneth Starr, also concluded after a 3-year study that Foster had indeed committed suicide. Two additional investigations by the U.S. Congress also examined the Foster suicide. One of the congressional investigations focused on whether White House officials had properly handled Foster's office papers after the suicide.

At least two of the above investigations required psychological autopsies conducted by forensic experts to carefully examine Foster's state of mind and activities before his death. Evidence from these examinations revealed Foster had indicated to several friends and family members 4 days before his death that he was very depressed, primarily because of the heavy workload, his discomfort at being in the public spotlight, and the overall pressure of working in the Capitol. Foster was also the target of several hostile *Wall Street Journal* editorials, suggesting incompetence, if not malfeasance. Foster mentioned to several people that he was seriously considering resigning from his position, and this desire seemed to increase shortly before his death. He contacted a physician the day before his death and stated he was under increasing levels of stress. The physician, a long-time family friend, prescribed antidepressant medication, but later said he did not think Foster was significantly depressed. Foster apparently did not leave a suicide note, but Dr. Alan Berman, a forensic suicide expert conducting one of the psychological autopsies, stated that this was not unusual because the great majority of persons committing suicide do not leave a note. Foster was, according to Dr. Berman, too self-focused at the time, overwhelmed, and out of control to leave a note.

Nevertheless, in spite of a series of psychological autopsies and official investigations that confirmed a suicide, some questions were left unanswered. Witnesses who saw Foster's body reported seeing different things; some did not see a gun in Foster's hand. The bullet from the gun was apparently never found, carpet threads on his clothes were never explained, and there were questions about which documents were removed from his office on the day of his death. None of this indicates that the death was *not* a suicide—explanations could easily be offered. In essence, in spite of the official, conclusive results, a legion of conspiracy theories continues to exist as to how and why Foster died that July day in 1993.

Occasionally, what appears to be a suicide might actually turn out to be a homicide. Examples of this can be found in court cases, some of which will be discussed in the next chapter. Burton and Dalby (2011) discuss a case in which a psychological autopsy was conducted to understand the mental state of a deceased 27-year-old woman who, over the course of a 3-year period, had given undisclosed birth to three babies. None of the infants—whose decaying bodies were found in garbage bags in her home—appeared to have survived beyond their first day. The most recent birth had occurred approximately 2 weeks before the death of the mother herself. She was found lying face down in her bedroom, naked and unresponsive, by her common-law husband. The woman's body showed no signs of trauma, and toxicology tests were negative.

A physical autopsy indicated that the mother probably had died of complications from the birth of her last child. However, physical autopsies of the infants could not establish the cause of the death for any of them, so investigators decided that a psychological autopsy was necessary to assist in investigating what could be a crime scene. The infants could have been killed by the woman, her husband, or a third party. In conducting the psychological autopsy, two qualified forensic psychologists reviewed the mother's diaries, interviews with friends and family, the death scene police report, and the medical examiner's report. It was revealed that the mother's pregnancies were not known to her friends or family, and she apparently made significant efforts to conceal them. In addition, there were no suicidal gestures or threats known to friends and family, and only brief spells of depression were reported in her diary. The psychological autopsy provided strong indications that the infants were killed by the mother immediately after she gave birth.

Purposes of Psychological Autopsies

Psychological autopsies are conducted for three primary purposes: (1) research, (2) clinical practice applications, and (3) litigation (Ogloff & Otto, 1993). We discuss each of these briefly below.

RESEARCH WITH PSYCHOLOGICAL AUTOPSIES

Researchers involved in the study of suicide conduct psychological autopsies to identify and understand the mental states and circumstances that contribute to an individual taking his or her own life. The knowledge gained from the research is used to improve suicide prevention programs and therapeutic interventions. For example, research indicates that a majority of suicide victims communicate their intentions to at least one person before killing themselves, although very often it is not directed to loved ones or close family members. Many victims also leave suicide notes that provide important research and investigative data for discovering why the person was driven toward self-destruction. We discuss these notes in more detail shortly.

It is important to stress that ethical issues often arise in the context of suicide. Many believe that some individuals should not be discouraged from taking their own lives if they plan to do so rationally and not as a result of being in a depressive state. For example, those who advocate "death with dignity" laws, whereby people with a terminal illness can end their lives without stigma, argue that prevention or intervention in these cases is inappropriate. Suicide researchers conducting psychological autopsies in these cases are advised to draw distinctions between those who exercised a planned, deliberate move to hasten their own deaths and those who would not have died had alternative options been available to them.

CLINICAL PRACTICE APPLICATIONS
OF PSYCHOLOGICAL AUTOPSIES

Some professionals indicate that the knowledge gained from a psychological autopsy also can be therapeutic to the family and friends of the deceased. For example, discovering the reasons for the suicide often diminishes the anger, shame, and guilt that many survivors experience. Survivors also begin to understand more fully the factors that prompted the suicide, instead of blaming themselves.

Psychological autopsies are often conducted by clinicians in mental health facilities when patients in treatment commit suicide. In these situations, the purpose of the psychological autopsy is to ascertain what treatment approaches or practices might have prevented or even might have contributed to the suicide, with the goal of improving clinical practice for future patients. In some cases, the findings of these psychological autopsies may also be used in legal proceedings when suicide-malpractice questions arise.

PSYCHOLOGICAL AUTOPSIES IN LEGAL CASES

Psychological autopsies are often used in forensic decision making, particularly in civil cases. In a majority of these cases, the question to be answered revolves around whether the decedent's death was the product of an accident, foul play, or suicide. This is a question frequently asked by insurance companies. Although some insurance policies do compensate the family if the death is determined to be suicide, many policies do not. Consequently, if the manner of death is equivocal, it is in the best financial interest of the insurance company to hire a professional to do a complete psychological autopsy to determine whether the death was likely the result of suicide or some other cause.

In other civil litigations, psychological autopsies are presented as evidence when a decedent's testamentary capacity is questioned. In these instances, a will is contested on the grounds that the deceased lacked the capacity to execute or change a will at some point before his or her death, or was unduly influenced by another person (Ogloff & Otto, 1993). In such cases, a mental health professional may be asked to perform a psychological autopsy and offer an opinion concerning the mental status and capacity of the deceased at the time the will was signed.

In legal contexts, the psychological autopsy also is frequently conducted to reconstruct the possible reasons for a suicide and ultimately to establish legal culpability on the part of other persons or organizations. For example, if a police officer shoots himself on the steps of the state capitol building, the message he was trying to send to all those concerned may be unclear. Family members of the deceased, convinced the department had poor stress management techniques or nonexistent early detection procedures for identifying emotional problems in its officers, may sue the department for emotional and financial damages. Under these conditions, a mental health professional may be retained to do a reconstruction of the victim's mental state during and before the incident.

Psychological autopsies have also been part of civil proceedings in the private sector, where it was necessary to ascertain whether certain events on the job—such as various kinds of harassment by fellow workers or supervisors—affected the person who ultimately committed suicide. Failure of the company or organization to have adequate policies and procedures in place for handling problems of this sort may be sufficient reason to find the company liable.

Another legal situation where psychological autopsies are valuable is that of cases involving worker's compensation. Over the past three decades, worker's compensation laws have increasingly been interpreted to include mental harms as well as physical harms caused by a work-related injury (Biffl, 1996). The psychological autopsy evaluates how certain events and circumstances may have influenced the deceased to commit suicide or resulted in death by other means. In these cases, the mental health professional may be commissioned by the plaintiffs in the worker's compensation proceedings to strengthen their claims that stressful work conditions led to the employee's suicide.

Psychological autopsies are used more in civil than criminal cases, but there are noteworthy criminal cases in which they have been sought. Of key interest in these cases is whether the death was a suicide or a homicide, specifically one staged to look like a suicide. In the following chapter, we will discuss a few cases in which courts addressed the question of the validity of psychological autopsies in criminal cases.

PSYCHOLOGICAL AUTOPSIES AND THE MILITARY

According to La Fon (2008), the U.S. military is one of the major consumers of psychological autopsies. "Each branch of the Armed Forces including the Navy, Army, and Air Force, have the task of conducting an EDPA for every equivocal death that occurs either on base property or to military personnel" (p. 422). In fact, before 2001, a psychological autopsy was required on every suicide committed in the Army (Ritchie, Benedek, Malone, & Carr-Malone, 2006). These investigations were intended to gather information from the soldier's units and their families that might prove important in preventing future suicides. After 2001, a psychological autopsy was required only if the death was equivocal. The new requirement also dictated that those personnel who did psychological autopsies must have received comprehensive training on how to do them. "The additional training covers basics of crime scene investigation, physical autopsy procedures, toxicology, and understanding of suicidal behavior and determinants" (Ritchie et al., 2006, p. 704).

In 2008, the Department of Defense launched the DoD Suicide Event Report (DoDSER) across the services (Air Force, Army, Marine Corps, and Navy) to support its suicide prevention program. The DoDSER uses a variety of suicide information, including successful suicides, suicide attempts, and other suicide-related behavior. It does not, however, report on the number and nature of psychological autopsies that are done each year. In the most recent DoDSER (Department of Defense, 2010), the most significant stressors associated with suicide in the military are failed marital/ intimate relationships (51%), other failed relationship (non-intimate) (14%), history of Article 15 proceedings (which refers to non-judicial punishment) (15%), and civil legal problems (13%). Thirty-six percent of the suicide victims had been diagnosed with a mental disorder, but post-traumatic stress disorder (PTSD) as a contributing factor was relatively rare (4%).

Both civilian and military psychologists conduct psychological autopsies, and they are performed both in cases of equivocal death and suspected suicide. As noted above, psychological autopsies are apparently not conducted in cases of a "known" suicide. In most cases, the beneficiaries of the deceased military personnel receive remuneration regardless of the cause of death. Interestingly, suicide rates among military personnel during the wars in Iraq and Afghanistan were higher than during any other war or occupation and have risen in recent years (Department of Defense, 2010). Nevertheless, for some families, the cause of death is never firmly established, even when an official finding has been released.

SUICIDE BY COP

In the 1990s, researchers became aware of another type of suicide associated with law enforcement, one in which the suicide victim actually uses the police officer to achieve his or her own death. **Suicide by cop,** generally abbreviated SbC, refers to "incidents in which individuals, bent on self-destruction, engage in life-threatening and criminal behavior to force the police to kill them" (Geberth, 1993, p. 105). Pinizzotto, Davis, and Miller (2005) define the incident as "an act motivated in whole or in part by the offender's desire to commit suicide that results in a justifiable homicide by a law enforcement officer" (p. 10). T. F. Monahan (2001) defines the phenomenon similarly: "SbC occurs when an individual bent on self-destruction opts to provoke a deadly force reaction from a law enforcement officer rather than commit suicide by his or her own hand" (p. 638).

According to some researchers and experts, approximately 10 to 13% of all police deadly force cases are a result of SbC incidents (Homant & Kennedy, 2001; V. B. Lord, 2000; Pinizzotto et al., 2005; Scoville, 1998). Some data suggest it may be even higher, approximately 25% (Oyster, 2001). However, it should be emphasized that in many cases, it is difficult to firmly establish that the SbC victim fully intended to be killed by a police officer. In these cases, a psychological autopsy is clearly necessary, as no single behavior or piece of physical evidence is enough to conclude that the shooting was an SbC incident.

In a comprehensive study of SbC, Hutson and his colleagues (1998) examined all officer-involved shootings investigated by the Los Angeles County Sheriff's Department from 1987 to 1997. To qualify as an SbC incident, the case had to have included the following: (1) evidence of the individual's suicide intent, (2) evidence that the victim specifically wanted officers to shoot him or her, (3) evidence the SbC victim possessed a lethal weapon or what seemed to be a lethal weapon, and (4) evidence that the individual intentionally escalated the encounter and provoked officers to shoot him or her. The researchers discovered that SbC accounted for 11% of all officer-involved shootings in Los Angeles County during that 10-year period. Ages of the SbC victims ranged from 18 to 54, and 98% were male. Nearly 50% of the victims had firearms on them, and another 17% possessed replica firearms. Comparable studies in Oregon and Florida have discovered similar findings (Wilson, Davis, Bloom, Batten, & Kamara, 1998). Interestingly, all deaths in these studies were classified by the coroner's office as homicides, as opposed to suicides, because the policy is that a violent death at the hand of another is legally a homicide. A death certificate that would list "suicide by cop" remains a controversial alternative among medical examiners and coroners (Neitzel & Gill, 2011).

Additional research evidence suggests that many of the SbC victims had a history of mental disorders, and many were under the influence of alcohol or hard drugs, such as cocaine, at the time of the incident (Lord, 2000; Slatkin, 2003). A majority possessed either a gun (73%) or knife (22%) at the time of the SbC (V. B. Lord, 2000). In a majority of the shootings, the victims, by statements or actions, clearly indicated their intentions to die at the hands of the police. For example, SbC victims refuse to drop the weapon and often approach the officer in a threatening manner (Lindsay, 2001). Not surprisingly, SbC victims with guns were more likely to be fatally shot by officers (93%) than those with knives (V. B. Lord, 2000).

Most SbC victims had no criminal record, but those who did most often had a record of domestic violence or drug-related offenses. Many SbC victims are believed to have committed suicide because they could not bring themselves to take their own life because of religious beliefs, for fear they would botch the job, or for other personal reasons (Klinger, 2001).

AUTOEROTIC ASPHYXIA

Autoerotic asphyxia (AEA) refers to obtaining sexual excitement from hypoxia (lack of oxygen), usually accomplished through near strangulation or suffocation while masturbating. The euphoria produced by the hypoxia is believed to enhance masturbatory sensations and orgasm intensity. Participants use a variety of methods to deprive themselves of oxygen (also called **hypoxyphilia** by mental health professionals), including ligature hanging, near suffocation or smothering by plastic bags or duct tape, inhalation of noxious chemicals (such as butane or nitrous oxide), or submersion underwater. Unfortunately, most of what is known about this practice comes from studies of fatalities (Hucker, 2008). **Autoerotic death** refers to an unanticipated death that results while the participant is engaged in solo or accompanied sexual activity "and the arousal-enhancing device designed to rescue the participant fails" (Schields, Hunsaker, & Hunsaker, 2005, p. 45).

Death due to suspected autoerotic asphyxiation is divided into two broad categories: typical and atypical. **Typical autoerotic asphyxiation** denotes ligature asphyxiation due to some binding around the neck, such as a dog collar, belts, or bungee cords. It is believed to be the most common autoerotic method practiced. Unfortunately, it also has a high potential to be fatal when things go wrong. When practiced as a solo sexual activity, the presence of a distinct release mechanism may confirm to forensic investigators that the fatality was accidental (Schields, Hunsaker, Hunsaker, Wetli, et al., 2005). A release mechanism refers to an escape strategy the victim has devised for releasing the neck ligature or bindings before losing consciousness, such as quick-release devices, slipknots, or readily available physical supports (feet touching the floor). Sometimes, however, lack of oxygen to the brain results in unintended loss of consciousness, causing accidental death. In many cases, practitioners employ protective padding about the neck to prevent telltale ligature marks. It should be mentioned, however, that in rare cases the practitioner intended to commit suicide from the outset (Hucker & Blanchard, 1992). Such cases may require a psychological autopsy to determine the motivations of the participant.

Unlike typical cases, **atypical autoerotic asphyxiation** does not involve ligature binding around the neck. In other words, practitioners deprive themselves of oxygen but do not use ligatures. Instead, they achieve sexual gratification by other means, such as plastic bags covering the head or the entire body (Behrendt, Buhl, & Seidl, 2002; Shields, Hunsaker, Hunsaker, Wetli, et al., 2005); face masks (Janssen, Koops, Anders, Kuhn, & Püschel, 2005); experimentation with electricity (Klintschar, Grabuschnigg, & Beham, 1998; Schott, Davis, & Hunsaker, 2003); or compression of the chest or abdomen (Schields, Hunsaker, Hunsacker, Wetli, et al., 2005).

It is estimated that there may be as many as 250 to 1,200 AEA deaths in North America each year (Cowell, 2009). Estimates are almost certainly inaccurate, however, since there are no centralized data sources and most of AEA deaths probably go unreported. Distressed family members who discover the victim in a "compromised" condition may feel compelled to alter the situation (e.g., by dressing the victim or hiding paraphernalia), perhaps to make it appear as either a homicide or a suicide. Distinguishing AEA cases from suicide is difficult in some instances.

In North America and Germany, the primary victims of known autoerotic deaths are white, young, middle-class, unmarried males. Approximately 30% of the male victims are found nude, and approximately 25% are found wearing women's clothing (Breitmeier et al., 2003; Douglas & Munn, 1992a). Often, pornographic materials and sexual aids are present. Females engage in AEA, but apparently in much smaller numbers than males (Behrendt et al., 2002; Gosink & Jumbelic, 2000). However, a 7-year retrospective study by Sauvageau (2008) suggests a lower incidence of autoerotic deaths and a higher percentage of female and atypical autoerotic fatalities than previously reported in U.S. studies. One of the most disturbing phenomena in recent years is the apparent increase in deaths of children playing "the choking game," described below, although this is not necessarily autoerotic in nature.

In a comprehensive review of the research on autoerotic deaths between 1954 and 2004, Sauvageau and Racette (2006) found an overall male-to-female ratio of 21:7. A majority of known female victims were found naked, and most died from a single ligature around the neck. Although the evidence of sexual props is rarely found in female AES deaths, there are exceptions. Behrendt et al. (2002) studied the accidental autoerotic deaths of four women, all of whom were found immobilized by self-tied ropes, string, or handcuffs. Overall, the four cases closely mirrored findings from scenes of males with various paraphernalia and props.

The Choking Game

The **choking game** is an activity, mainly involving adolescents, where the participant obstructs the normal flow of blood to the brain to achieve a brief euphoric state caused by a cerebral hypoxia or low oxygen in the brain. Although the practice involves a lack of oxygen to the brain, it is not usually done for autoerotic purposes but primarily for the euphoria that accompanies the procedure. This practice often results in a loss of consciousness, followed by a rush of blood flow to the brain when the obstruction is removed, and occasionally death. In these latter instances, the deceased individual was not intending to die. These "games" are given various names, including black hole, suffocation roulette, space cowboy, California high, blackout, airplaning, sleeperhold, rising sun, flatlining, funky chicken, and space monkey.

According to a 2008 report from the Centers for Disease Control and Prevention, at least 82 choking game deaths among youths aged 6 to 19 occurred between 1995 and 2007 in the United States. In many cases, a psychological autopsy is conducted, especially if the victims were adolescents (Giggie, 2010). The usual age range is between 9 and 15 years with a male-to-female ratio of about 2:1 (Andrew & Fallon, 2007). Le and Macnab (2001) investigated four deaths and one near death due to strangulation by hanging from cloth towels in dispensers located in Canadian schools. The participants, all males ages 7 to 12, were playing the choking game by pulling down a loop of the cloth towel, wrapping the towel around their necks, and hanging from it until they lost consciousness.

In a recent study by Linkletter, Gordon, and Dooley (2011), 65 videos of the choking game were found on YouTube over a 2-week period in 2007. As noted by the authors, YouTube has enabled millions of young people to see videos of the choking game and other dangerous activities. Hypoxic seizures (loss of consciousness) were seen in 55% of the YouTube videos, and they occurred in 88% of the videos that employed the "sleeper hold" technique. The sleeper hold is where another child, called a "choker," stands behind the participant, wraps his or her forearm around the neck of the participant, and applies pressure to the neck until consciousness is lost. The researchers found that these YouTube videos were very popular and were viewed 279,240 times during a 3-week period, with an average of 4,296 times for each video. Linkletter et al. noted that when the young people regained consciousness, those who were not confused afterward verbalized euphoric sensations, including "That was the coolest thing I've ever done," "I felt wicked," "That was amazing," and "What a rush" (p. 276).

A survey involving 2,504 questionnaires completed by students in middle and high schools in Texas and Ontario revealed that 68% of the students had heard about the choking game, 45% knew someone who had tried it, and 6.6% had tried it themselves (Macnab, Deevska, Gagnon, Cannon, & Andrew, 2009). Asphyxial games appear to represent a form of unsafe play that is not apparently recognized by parents, teachers, coroners, or doctors. A recent survey of pediatricians and family physicians revealed that one third of these medical professionals were completely unaware of the choking game engaged in by children and adolescents (McClave, Russell, Lyren, O'Riordan, & Bass, 2010).

How Psychological Autopsies Are Performed

As described in previous sections of the chapter, the psychological autopsy is a reconstructive process designed to identify and evaluate the behavior, thoughts, moods, and events that led up to and may have contributed to a person's death. Each autopsy is unique, and informational sources and available resources will be different for each case (see Focus 8.2 for a list of factors that may be taken into account). Nevertheless, if the psychological autopsy is to gain credibility as a scientific approach, many professionals assert that there should be an established procedure to be followed by those who conduct them. Although significant strides have been made in achieving a standardized process, more work is needed in this regard. We will return to this point shortly, after first describing how the typical autopsy is conducted.

Focus 8.2

Operational Criteria for Classification of Suicide

The following criteria were developed by the U.S. Army to provide a standard definition of suicide for purposes of conducting a psychological autopsy. In addition, the Army stipulates that the psychological autopsy must be conducted by a mental health professional, defined as a psychiatrist, psychologist, psychiatric nurse, or social worker.

(A) *Self-inflicted*. There is evidence that death was self-inflicted. Pathological (autopsy), toxicological, investigatory, and psychological evidence, and statements of the decedent or witnesses may be used for this determination.

(B) *Intent*. There is evidence (explicit and/or implicit) that at the time of injury the decedent intended to kill self or wished to die and that decedent understood the probable consequences of his or her actions. The following are taken into account:

(1) Explicit verbal or nonverbal expressions of intent to kill self.

(2) Implicit or indirect evidence of intent to die such as the following:

(a) Preparations for death, inappropriate to or unexpected in the context of a decedent's life.
(b) Expressions of farewell or desire to die, or acknowledgment of impending death.
(c) Expressions of hopelessness.
(d) Efforts to procure or learn about means of death or rehearse fatal behavior.
(e) Precautions to avoid rescue.
(f) Evidence that decedent recognized high potential lethality of means of death.
(g) Previous suicide attempt.
(h) Previous suicide threat.
(i) Stressful events or significant losses (actual or threatened).
(j) Serious depression or mental disorder.

Source: Department of the Army (1988), p. 6.

In general, the information gathered is largely from third-party sources: interviews with significant others and records of various types. The investigation usually requires interviews with close family members, relatives, friends, acquaintances, supervisors, teachers, health care providers, and coworkers. The investigator also must rely heavily on archival information, both recent and remote (Ogloff & Otto, 1993). Hospital, mental health, medical, and school records; as well as letters, diaries, emails, Facebook postings, websites visited, and material downloaded by the deceased may provide information that will be helpful in evaluating the person's mental state at a particular point in time. Psychological/psychiatric, educational, military, and employment histories are scrutinized. Records pertaining to mental health treatment and medical care may provide information relating to a possible history of depression or other psychiatric difficulties, previous suicide attempts, and a history of physical or sexual abuse. If available, the coroner's report, the police report (including death scene sketches and photographs), and laboratory results (e.g., toxicological profiles) are also utilized. The investigator also researches the history of any known alcohol or substance abuse, mood or emotional changes, and potential psychological stressors. Pharmacy printouts of previous drug prescriptions also may be helpful.

It is important for the investigator to consider the individual's behavior and mental state over the previous 24, 48, and 72 hours before the suicide (see Focus 8.3). Pre-death behaviors—such as paying up insurance policies, giving away important possessions, and making arrangements for family and pets—are especially significant. The quality and nature of relationships are probably most important to the assessment process, especially relationships with spouse, children, and other intimates in the person's life. Records from social service and law enforcement agencies as well as financial information, including bank and billing statements, a credit check, and financial counseling center records, are all important, suggesting any stressors that may have recently been introduced into the life of the deceased.

Focus 8.3

Classification of Suicides by Intent

One classification system that incorporates the notion of degree of intention and that may be used in the autopsy is as follows:

1. First-degree suicide: Deliberate, planned, premeditated.
2. Second-degree suicide: Impulsive, unplanned, under great provocation or compromising circumstances.
3. Third-degree suicide: Victim placed his or her life in jeopardy by voluntary self-injury, but we infer the intention to die was relatively low because the method of self-injury was relatively harmless, or because provisions for rescue were made. The victim was "unlucky" enough to die.

The following are two other categories of self-inflicted death that are not typically classified as suicide because the intention to die cannot be established.

1. Self-destruction when the victim was psychotic or highly intoxicated from the effects of drugs or alcohol. These circumstances suggest impaired capacity for intention.
2. Self-destruction due to self-negligence. This last category of death has been described as subintentioned death. A subintentioned death is a death in which the decedent plays some partial, covert, or unconscious role in his or her own demise. Evidence for this ambivalence toward life may be found in a history of poor judgment, excessive risk-taking, abuse of alcohol, misuse of drugs, neglect

of self, a self-destructive life-style, a disregard of prescribed life-saving medication, and in other actions where the individual fosters, facilitates, exacerbates, or hastens the process of his or her dying. In terms of the traditional classification of modes of death (natural, accident, suicide, and homicide), some instances of all four types can be subsumed under this category, depending on the particular details of each case.

Source: Department of the Army (1988), p. 6.

A trip to the decedent's home and/or place of work is essential. As pointed out by Samuel Gosling and his associates (Gosling, 2008; Gosling, Ko, Mannarelli, & Morris, 2002), people spend most of their daily lives in their personal living and work environments, and they often decorate these places with the objects and symbols reflecting their personal tastes. "To make these spaces their own, individuals may adorn them with self-directed identity claims—symbolic statements made by the occupants for their own benefit, intended to reinforce their self-views" (Gosling et al., 2002, p. 380). In large part, the décor and symbols in a person's living space represent how the person wants others to see him or her. These items may include pictures, awards, posters, inspirational messages, college degrees, and mementos collected from places travelled. These objects are referred to as "identity claims," and they say, "This is who I am" (Gosling, 2008). A second group of symbolic clues about a person's life and personality are called "feeling regulators," and include such items as family photos, keepsakes, music, and books. Anything intended to alter the environment or mood of a person is a feeling regulator. However, there are also physical aspects that are left behind inadvertently in the living space, called behavioral residue. **Behavioral residue** refers to the physical traces left in the living space by our everyday actions, such as receipts, trash, and wine stains. It does not simply reflect a single unreliable act, but a whole pattern of consistent acts. Another type of behavioral residue is the amount of neatness or organization in a living or work space, such as a garage or bedroom. Books or CDs in alphabetical order, tools placed in neat order, or clothes strewn around the bedroom provide additional information about a decedent. A messy room, for instance, could—but does not necessarily—indicate that a person was overwhelmed with other responsibilities.

The investigator should also examine the location where the death took place to discover if there was evidence of rescuability or evidence that the victim took precautions against being rescued. (In an episode of a popular television series, for example, a physician concluded that her mother wanted to be rescued because the mother—a prominent surgeon—slit *across* her wrist rather than lengthwise, following the path of her veins. As a surgeon, the mother would have known that a lengthwise slit would inevitably cause death.) The investigator also would want to know whether there was evidence of planning or rehearsal of the incident. What books did the decedent read, and do they somehow relate to the individual's manner of death?

Interviews conducted with close family members and significant others should be completed within weeks of the decedent's death. Waiting longer than 6 months is likely to reduce the accuracy of memory, but a timely investigation should also be done with great sensitivity to the requests of the survivors. It is very important that investigators approach informants in an empathic and cautious manner. Doing a psychological autopsy demands a high level of sensitivity and judgment while carrying out the investigation. Ethical considerations include securing informed consent from the participants, establishing mutual respect, and ensuring confidentiality of the information (Murthy, 2010).

The investigator (usually a forensic psychologist or mental health professional) is expected to write a comprehensive report dealing with the relevant factors and significant events prior to the death, and render a professional opinion as to the manner of death: natural, suicide, accident, homicide, or undetermined. By gathering information that concentrates on the individual's psychological state, a professional opinion can be offered as to whether the death was intentional, or whether it resulted from entirely unforeseeable consequences, such as an accident. Typical equivocal deaths may be single-vehicle accidents where the car leaves no skid marks or hangings where there is the possibility of the death having resulted from an autoerotic accident. Knowledge of statistical databases is important, providing information about the likelihood of certain kinds of deaths occurring in a particular manner.

THE INVESTIGATIVE VALUE OF SUICIDE NOTES

The suicide note is often one of the most valuable pieces of information in the investigation of equivocal deaths. About one third of those individuals who commit suicide leave a suicide note (Haines, Williams, & Lester, 2011). Some cases may require very careful examination of the note to establish whether it was written in the decedent's handwriting (Canter, 2005b). Canter provides an interesting narrative describing a case in which he was asked to do a psychological autopsy. The dead woman was found hanging, and nearby was a suicide note in her handwriting. This evidence was taken as a clear indication that it was suicide, and no further investigation or evidence was collected. But questions were raised about the case, including the hypothesis that her husband may have forced her to write the note and then tricked her into hanging herself, making the entire incident look like a suicide. Canter's psychological autopsy, however, indicated that the wife did voluntarily take her own life. Interestingly, as we will show in Chapter 9, the husband in this case (R. v. Guilfoyle, 2001) was charged with murder, but the court did not allow Canter's psychological autopsy to be admitted into evidence. The man was ultimately convicted of murder, and the appellate court upheld the conviction, observing that the present academic state of psychological autopsies did not permit their use in the courtroom.

Canter (1999) makes the important point that not all close family members know of the intentions of suicide victims, and they are often shocked when they learn of the suicide of their loved ones. In many cases, especially concerning the suicide of adolescents, it is not unusual for family members and friends to insist that they had no prior clues that the person was suicidal. When an unexpected suicide occurs and the decedent leaves no suicide note, suspicions of foul play might be anticipated. A systematic psychological autopsy of the victim might enable an investigation to reach a more convincing and timely conclusion. "In other cases it would help those touched by the death to come to terms more fully with the events surrounding it" (Canter, 1999, pp. 145–146).

Determining the authenticity of suicide notes is sometimes extremely difficult and often hinges on the subjectivity of human judgment, especially in suspected homicide investigations (Bennell, Jones, & Taylor, 2011). Research demonstrates that there are at least two sets of factors that are helpful in determining their authenticity. One set of factors involves language structure, such as the average sentence length, percentage of nouns, and the percentage of action verbs. The other set is concerned with content-related aspects of the note, such as the total number of words, presence of instructions to survivors, expression of positive affect, and the presentation of explanations of the suicide. Research indicates the genuine notes are significantly longer but contain many short sentence fragments (N. J. Jones & Bennell, 2007). In addition, genuine suicide notes, compared to fake suicide notes, have significantly more instructions to survivors and greater expression of positive affect, as illustrated in the form of affection, gratitude, or concern toward survivors. These notes also have a higher frequency of endearment terms, such as "love," "dear," and "sweetheart." According to Bennell et al. (2011), these positive emotions tend to be interspersed throughout the backdrop of despair in the authentic suicide note. "Thus, although an individual may have achieved the cognitive resolution to engage in the suicidal act, the associated emotional state may nonetheless be characterized as ambivalent" (p. 670).

Evaluating the Psychological Autopsy

Although some progress has been made on determining the reliability and validity of the psychological autopsy, much work still needs to be done, and even psychologists who conduct these autopsies are concerned about establishing their reliability and validity (Snider, Hane, & Berman, 2006). Recent research indicates that the psychological autopsy shows considerable promise for determining suicide intentions of the deceased (Portzky, Audenaert, & van Heeringen, 2009). Of course, the quality of the psychological autopsy will depend significantly on the training, knowledge, experience, and clinical acumen of the investigator (Knoll, 2008). Poythress et al. (1993) further warn that

> persons who conduct reconstructive psychological evaluations should not assert categorical conclusions about the precise mental state or actions suspected of the actor at the time of his or her demise. The conclusions and inferences drawn in psychological reconstructions are, at best, informed speculations or theoretical formulations and should be labeled as such. (p. 12)

Selkin (1994) argues that clear, definitive procedures for carrying out psychological autopsies have yet to be developed, and investigators have a long way to go before standardized methods for conducting the psychological autopsy are established. Others agree with the statement that no definitive standards have been developed but do feel that progress is being made toward a standardized procedure (Knoll, 2008, 2009; Snider et al., 2006). Nevertheless, as we will discuss in the next chapter, before psychological autopsy reports become widely accepted as evidence in courts, those who conduct them must make greater gains in developing such procedures in order for them to achieve a greater scientific status.

Poythress et al. (1993) make three recommendations for forensic psychologists to follow when doing psychological autopsies or equivocal death analyses. First, the use of these procedures and techniques should not be extended to non-death situations (such as burglary or kidnapping), at least until the reliability and validity of the methods are clearly established. Second, in legal and quasi-legal contexts, psychologists who conduct reconstructive psychological evaluations should not make conclusions about the *precise* mental state or actions suspected of the actor at the time of his or her demise. Third, psychologists, mental health professionals, and social scientists should be careful not to mislead consumers about the accuracy of conclusions drawn from these psychological reconstructions, unless the research data support such conclusions. Currently, the research data are inconclusive about the accuracy of such methods, and clearly more well-executed research needs to be undertaken before firm conclusions about the validity of psychological autopsies can be made.

As we will discuss in Chapter 9, it is widely recognized that the lack of standardization and the unsolved issues of establishing its reliability and validity pose significant problems when the psychological autopsy is brought into legal cases where it may be deemed inadmissible by court standards (Snider et al., 2006). Basically, it is crucial to realize that psychological autopsies are subject to the same judicial scrutiny as other scientific methods and information. It is important, therefore, that we go over each of these concepts and where the scientific community stands on each.

STANDARDIZATION

The vast majority of psychological autopsies have been done in the United States (Canter, 1999). Forensic psychologists who develop psychological autopsies usually do their own interviews, conduct background investigations, and examine other pertinent information that they believe will contribute to a meaningful forensic report. Recall that almost two decades ago, Selkin (1994) noted that clear, definitive procedures for carrying out the psychological autopsy had not been developed and that investigators still had a long way to go before standardized methods for conducting the psychological autopsy are established. A few years later, Ritchie and Gelles (2002) agreed and discussed standardization problems as they relate to conducting military psychological autopsies. Shneidman (1976) tried to develop an outline for conducting a psychological autopsy back in the 1970s, which consisted of a 16-point checklist. As noted by Canter (1999), Shneidman's checklist is not that dissimilar to what you might find in a medical history questionnaire from a doctor's office. The major departure from the typical medical history lies in Shneidman's focus on what is known about the behavioral patterns, relationships, reactions to stress, thought processes, and mood states prior to the person's death.

Standardization should include structured or semi-structured interviews and checklists that systematically address each area relevant to death analysis, as well as provide guidelines for interpreting responses and information gathered. Currently, "There is just a set of ideas and recommendations that provide guidelines on what may be considered" (Canter, 2005b, p. 321). Without evidence-based standardization, however, the analysis of an equivocal death is strongly influenced by the skills, experience, training, and sensitivities of the investigator (Werlang & Botega, 2003). And, as occurred in the USS *Iowa* case, one expert's opinion often differs from another expert's opinion, because opinions are not based on a standardized approach.

Not only is there no standard for conducting a psychological autopsy, but there are no standards for training or quality assurance. Consequently, it is not unusual for the results of some psychological autopsies to be disallowed in court proceedings.

RELIABILITY AND VALIDITY

Reliability refers to consistency. An instrument or procedure is reliable if it yields the same results over and over again. For example, if a scale measuring weight gives significantly different readings each time you step on it—even within 2 minutes' time—it is unreliable. If a procedure produces the same results when interpreted by different professionals or investigators who are provided with the same information and comparable training, it is said to be high in interjudge or interrater reliability. *Interrater reliability* refers to the degree to which different mental health professionals or experts classify the equivocal death into the same category: suicide, accident, homicide, natural cause, or undetermined. Interrater reliability would improve significantly if the psychological autopsy was standardized with well-researched procedures and protocol.

Validity answers the question, does an instrument or procedure measure what it is supposed to measure? Does the psychological autopsy *accurately* determine whether the equivocal death was a suicide, accident, or homicide? It should be emphasized that a procedure must be reliable before it can be tested for validity. The validity question is more difficult to answer than reliability, because it is hard to find a fully acceptable standard for accuracy. In an equivocal death situation, for example, the decedent is obviously not available to confirm his or her intentions or precisely what happened at the time of death. In addition, information gathered from family, friends, significant others, coworkers, and supervisors may be biased and distorted (Maris, Berman, & Silverman, 2000). People with close relationships with the decedent are likely to offer biased opinions for fear their statements might be leaked to media, especially those heavily publicized cases (Snider et al., 2006). Moreover, family members and intimates may also give distorted views of the deceased due to feelings of guilt and shame (Gelles, 1995). This bias is detrimental to the establishment of reliability and validity of the psychological autopsy.

Summary and Conclusions

The psychological autopsy is one form of profiling that can be distinguished from all other forms in that, as its name indicates, it is conducted on a dead person. In addition, as is the case for the psychological profile discussed in Chapter 6, it is conducted on a known individual. Like most other forms of profiling, however, there is no "gold standard" or widely accepted procedure for conducting such a profile; for that reason, it may be regarded with suspicion, particularly in legal contexts. As we saw in this chapter, congressional representatives were highly skeptical of the psychological autopsy conducted on

Clayton Hartwig during the investigation of the USS *Iowa* tragedy. In Chapter 9, we will provide examples of a similar skepticism displayed by the judicial system.

Psychological autopsies—also referred to as equivalent death analyses (EDAs)—are useful for research purposes, clinical applications, and for resolving some legal issues. In the research context, they contribute to the knowledge base on various causes and manners of death, as well as the effects of self-inflicted death on the survivors. In the context of clinical practice, a psychological autopsy has implications for the treatment of survivors as well as future patients. By far the greatest number of psychological autopsies occurs in the legal context, in both civil and criminal cases. The cause of death is often at issue in civil litigation, and in the criminal context, the results of such an autopsy can either question or lend credence to the claim that an individual did not commit suicide, but rather was the victim of a homicide, or vice versa.

In some senses, the psychological autopsy resembles the work of an investigative reporter. The person conducting the autopsy reviews available documents, including official death investigation reports, and interviews a variety of individuals who knew the decedent. Such autopsies are often requested when the person has apparently committed suicide, but there is possibility of foul play; or, in the opposite case, when a person was the apparent victim of a homicide, but there is a possibility of suicide. Knowledge of what occurred in the months and weeks prior to the death is crucial. Therefore, any writings, verbalizations, actions, or events in the person's life can be relevant to the investigation.

Various branches of the military have been prime consumers of psychological autopsies, but this has lessened somewhat over the last decade, perhaps in light of budgetary restrictions. Whereas psychological autopsies were formerly required in all cases of suicide, they are now required only if the death was equivocal—that is, if there was question as to whether the individual did indeed take his or her own life. Psychological autopsies also may be particularly useful in homicide investigations and alleged instances of suicide by cop and autoerotic death. In all of these cases, survivors may seek evidence that the individual did not intend to kill himself or herself. The person conducting the autopsy—who should be independent of any "side" of the issue—may confirm their suspicions or may find evidence that suicide was indeed the decedent's intent. If there was a suicide note in the case, determining its authenticity becomes an important component of the psychological autopsy.

There are many benefits to a comprehensive psychological autopsy, but scholars are guarded about extending its use beyond research or clinical practice. Although some believe that it is a standard, reliable, and valid tool, others argue that it is still in its infancy and requires far more empirical support before its scientific basis is established.

KEY CONCEPTS

Atypical autoerotic asphyxiation	Behavioral residue	Psychological autopsy
	Choking game	Suicide by cop (SbC)
Autoerotic asphyxia (AEA)	Equivocal death analysis (EDA)	Typical autoerotic asphyxiation
Autoerotic death	Hypoxyphilia	

9

Profiling in Court

Throughout this book, profiling has been defined as an enterprise that is either art or science, depending upon one's perspective. Some "profilers" are highly respected researchers or practitioners, careful not to make outlandish claims or predictions; unfortunately, others are not so cautious. Some forms of profiling have garnered supportive evidence; others are faltering or are accompanied by little research. The same can be said of the typologies that may be used in profiling reports; for example, typologies of pedophiles appear to have more empirical support than typologies of terrorists. Put another way, pedophiles as a group have distinguishing characteristics, but even pedophiles are not all alike.

In criminal courts, it is not uncommon for prosecutors—and sometimes defense attorneys—to want to introduce profiling evidence in the form of expert testimony. A profiler on the witness stand, testifying that a crime scene was disorganized, that a defendant's unique signature was found at the crime scene, or that the defendant did not possess characteristics of a sexual sadist, can be extremely persuasive to a jury. In this chapter, we focus directly on the issue of whether such profiling evidence is, as well as should be, admitted into trial courts and, if so, what type of profiling evidence is, as well as should be, admitted? As we will see, courts are more accepting of profiling when it is used as an investigative tool to help police in solving a crime, and less accepting when a behavioral consultant wants to testify in the courtroom that a defendant "fits the profile" of those who commit a particular crime. This is usually considered inadmissible character evidence.

Profiling evidence also may be introduced in *civil* courts, such as when a family is seeking damages as the result of an accident or crime victimization. For example, the psychological autopsy—the form of profiling discussed in Chapter 8—may be introduced to support a family's claim that the death of their loved one was not a suicide and that they are thus entitled to insurance benefits. In an interesting civil case (*Schieber et al. v. City of Philadelphia*, 2001), the family of a rape-murder victim sued police, arguing among other things that police training was inadequate and that police had ignored previous warnings from the FBI that a serial rapist might be on the loose. To bolster their case, attorneys for the family tried to introduce a profile report prepared by an FBI agent. In its opinion, the court made positive comments about criminal profiling, seeming to support its scientific status. But the court also noted that the agent who prepared the report, Frederick Kingston, stated explicitly that it was speculative and was provided exclusively for the police department's investigative use. Placing considerable emphasis on these cautious statements, the court ruled that the report could not be admitted into evidence in this civil proceeding.

At this point in time, most of the commentary about profiling in the courts is focused on criminal courts, and this is where we direct our attention as well. The great majority of cases to be discussed in this chapter involve crimes rather than civil actions.

Courts across the globe have grappled with whether to allow profiling evidence, as well as what type to allow. The answer often depends upon how that evidence is described. In some courts, "behavioral analysis" is looked at more favorably than "profiling." As Risinger and Loop (2002) have observed, "Though courts have generally rejected testimony concerning profiling frankly so offered, they have often bent over backwards to admit profiling-based testimony, or testimony by profilers, when it could be labeled differently" (sect. IC, para. 254). Also relevant are the credentials of the expert and the type of evidence: Is it crime scene analysis, which would involve such concepts as signature, modus operandi, and organized or disorganized crime scenes; linkage analysis; a psychological autopsy; or testimony about whether a given individual fits the profile of, say, a sexual sadist? Each of these falls under the very broad umbrella of "profile evidence" that has been considered by courts, and each will be discussed separately in the chapter.

Paths to Admission of Evidence

Alison et al. (2004) observed that attempts to introduce profiling in court have taken two different paths. In one path, attorneys for either side try to introduce the original report prepared by the profiler to illustrate or suggest to a jury that the defendant matches or does not match it. The prosecution, of course, claims that the profile matches the defendant. When the defense attorney introduces a profile, it is to argue that the profile does *not* match his or her client. Canter et al. (2004) refer to this path as **profile-defendant correspondence (P–DC).** In an interesting twist, during a recent trial, a psychologist called by the defense testified that the alleged *victim* fit the classic profile of both a sociopath and a psychopath, supporting the defense's argument that the victim was lying about being sexually assaulted. The psychologist had not interviewed the victim. Although the evidence was allowed by the trial judge, the defendant was convicted of the crime. In the process, one could argue that the victim's reputation was tarnished.

Although many trial courts are guarded about this issue, others routinely accept profiling evidence and testimony, particularly if the expert does not directly compare the defendant to a particular profile (Bosco, Zappala, & Santtila, 2010; George, 2008). For example, testimony that a defendant fits or does not fit the profile of a sexual sadist or a child molester is more likely to be rejected by the courts than testimony about typical characteristics of such offenders as a group. We will illustrate this as we discuss some of these cases below.

In the second path identified by Canter et al. (2004), **profile–crime correspondence (P–CC)**, profilers report the similarity between two or more *crimes*, which would indicate that the same individual has committed them. This also has been referred to as case linkage or similarity analysis. Alison et al. (2004) report that P–DC is more controversial than P–CC because of its prejudicial effect, in that "[it] necessitates direct commentary about the defendant, whereas [P–CC] considers the similarity between offenses" (p. 79). Recall from Chapter 2, though, that criticism about linkage analysis appears regularly in the legal and social science literature (e.g., Bennell et al., 2012; Risinger & Loop, 2002; Snook, Luther, House, Bennell, & Taylor, 2012), and that even elaborate databases designed to facilitate linking crimes (e.g., ViCLAS; ViCAP) have not reached the stage of development whereby their reliability and validity can be firmly established.

Although the above paths—P–DC and P–CC—are the two main ones, we should note that there are divergences. For example, when police seek an arrest warrant or a search warrant from a judicial officer, it is profile–*suspect* correspondence, not profile–defendant correspondence. At least one case (*State v. Pennell*, 1989) involved a psychological profile that police used in support of obtaining a search warrant. In addition, police have been allowed to arrest individuals based on their correspondence with certain profiles, including the "drug courier" profile (*U.S. v. Sokolow*, 1989). However, the U.S. Supreme Court also ruled that evidence showing that a defendant fit a drug courier profile could not be admitted at trial. Put another way, police are entitled to stop someone who "fit the drug courier profile," but this information would not be allowed at trial to prove the defendant's guilt. However, if the defendant were allowed to introduce the profile to say he did *not* fit the profile, the prosecution could rebut that with testimony that he did.

In general, commentators have fewer problems with allowing profiling—regardless of the path—to be part of the *investigation process*. For example, most behavioral scientists would probably agree with Australian psychologist Richard Kocsis (2009), who expressed the following:

> *Although modest*, scientific evidence is beginning to emerge to support the basic concept that suitably skilled experts can demonstrate a comparatively superior degree of insight when seeking to accurately predict the *likely* characteristics of a perpetrator to a crime, based on an assessment of the exhibited criminal behaviors. (p. 258, emphasis added)

Even in the investigative context there are pitfalls, however, as we discuss later in the chapter.

Researchers and scholars are far more skeptical about profiling testimony in the courtroom. According to Kocsis (2009), "it is prudent to avoid the use of profiling *in the courtroom* and to instead confine its application to its more traditional investigative context" (2009, p. 258, emphasis added). In addition, Kocsis and others (e.g., Risinger & Loop, 2002) recommend that, if they do allow profiling testimony, courts exercise extreme caution in admitting the evidence, considering profiling's early stage of scientific development.

Standards for Admission of Expert Testimony

In trial courts, judges and juries are the triers of fact. They hear and weigh evidence and decide whether there is sufficient evidence to (depending on the context) proceed with a case, convict someone of a crime, or find a defendant negligent in a civil court. Because neither judges nor jurors are omniscient or all knowing, they sometimes benefit from the knowledge that may be imparted by an **expert witness.** Today, as indicated above, many trial courts—especially in the United States—do admit profiling evidence of various types, and this seems to occur particularly when such evidence is offered by the prosecution (George, 2008). Nevertheless, appellate courts sometimes reverse these decisions, ruling that the evidence should not have been admitted. It is by no means certain that this will happen, however. In fact, after a comprehensive review of legal cases involving profiling testimony in the United States, George found that profiling evidence was alive and well in U.S. courtrooms, even after review by appellate courts. Courts in other countries are more cautious (Canadian Human Rights Commission, 2011; Meyer, 2010; Youngs, 2009).

Under the law, expert witnesses are used to provide knowledge that is "beyond the ken" of the average layperson. Scientific knowledge clearly fits into this category; most people are not knowledgeable of the intricacies of blood analysis, the effects of environmental contaminants, chemical reactions, medical procedures, or myriad other topics that are the province of the natural and physical sciences. Do the social and behavioral sciences come under the same umbrella? The quick answer to that is "yes," but social and behavioral scientists often have more hurdles to overcome if they wish to testify in court than the "hard" scientists. With reference to profiling evidence, a key question becomes, "Is it scientific?" As we shall see shortly, though, some courts have placed more weight on the credentials and experience of the experts than on the scientific validity of their methods and techniques. That is, the evidence is accepted less because it is scientific and more because it is offered by individuals with long-standing experience in criminal investigative procedures.

In deciding whether to admit expert testimony, judges are guided by standards or criteria that have been set by legal rules of evidence and, in some cases, by appellate courts, including the U.S. Supreme Court. In other countries, standards may differ slightly, but most have similarities to U.S. criteria, including acceptance by the scientific community and relevance to the issue being litigated. We review briefly some of these standards below. (See Table 9.1 for a summary; see also Figures 9.1 and 9.2 for illustrative charts of the federal and state court systems.)

THE FRYE GENERAL ACCEPTANCE RULE

The earliest standard for evaluating expert testimony was offered by a federal court in the oft-cited case *Frye v. United States* (1923)—a case involving a rudimentary form of the polygraph test—and is still applied in many U.S. courts today. Standards very

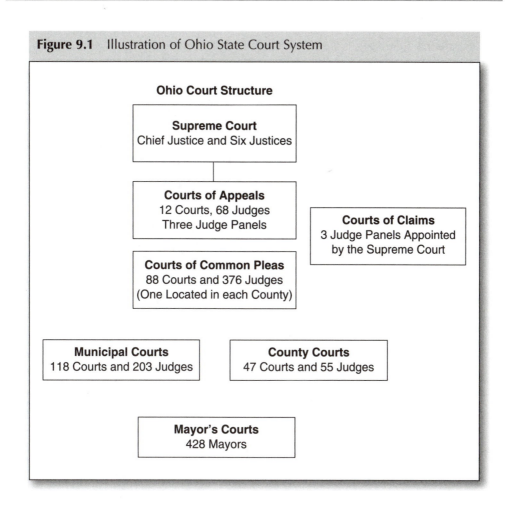

Figure 9.1 Illustration of Ohio State Court System

Ohio Court Structure

Supreme Court
Chief Justice and Six Justices

Courts of Appeals
12 Courts, 68 Judges
Three Judge Panels

Courts of Claims
3 Judge Panels Appointed
by the Supreme Court

Courts of Common Pleas
88 Courts and 376 Judges
(One Located in each County)

Municipal Courts
118 Courts and 203 Judges

County Courts
47 Courts and 55 Judges

Mayor's Courts
428 Mayors

similar to the **Frye standard** are also used in the United Kingdom, Australia, and Canada. The court in *Frye* said that, even if the credentials of the expert were flawless, the scientific knowledge had to have been gathered using scientific techniques that had gained general acceptance in the field. Over the years, this has been referred to as the "general acceptance standard." At the time, the systolic blood pressure detection test that was the precursor of the modern polygraph had not gained general acceptance. With the federal court's ruling, general acceptance remained the sole criterion until the end of the 20th century, when the U.S. Supreme Court weighed in on the matter, attempting to give more direction to judges regarding the admission of expert scientific testimony. In the process, the Supreme Court placed more emphasis on the relevance, reliability, and validity of research findings and required that judges evaluate scientific evidence much more carefully than they had under the *Frye* standard. Together, three important cases decided by the U.S. Supreme Court were seen as a major shift in the law, because they urged judges to take a far more active role in assessing evidence—some called it a gatekeeper role.

Figure 9.2   Illustration of Federal Court System, United States

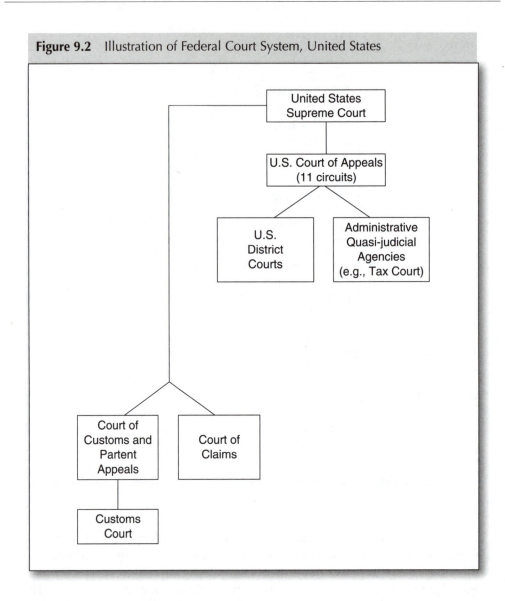

THE DAUBERT TRILOGY

The three cases, all decided in the 1990s, were *Daubert v. Merrell Dow Pharmaceuticals* (1993), *General Electric Co. v. Joiner* (1997), and *Kumho Tire v. Carmichael* (1999). They are often referred to as the "*Daubert* trilogy," and most commentators refer simply to *Daubert* or the **Daubert standard.** Together, the three cases outline the federal standard, although not necessarily standards set in various state courts. Nonetheless, by the end of the 20th century, 30 states had adopted a standard identical to or closely related to *Daubert* (Parry & Drogan, 2000).

Daubert v. Merrell Dow Pharmaceuticals (1993) was a civil case that involved neither psychology nor profiling. Families sued the pharmaceutical giant, alleging that its product, Bendectin, which was taken by mothers during pregnancy as an antinausea

Table 9.1   Frye and Daubert Summary

Frye v. United States (1923)	Content must be beyond the knowledge of the average layperson.Scientific information, methods, techniques must have general acceptance from the scientific community.
Daubert v. Merrell Dow (1993)	Content must be beyond the knowledge of the average layperson.Witness must have established expert credentials.Content must be relevant to the case.Reliability/validity should be assessed (consider falsifiability, known or potential error rate; peer review and publication; general acceptance in scientific community).
General Electric Co. v. Joiner (1997)	Reinforces all of the above; in addition, if trial judge carefully evaluated the information offered, appeals courts should not second-guess the decision of the trial judge.
Kumho v. Carmichael (1999)	*Daubert* standard applies to scientific, technical, and other specialized knowledge.

drug, caused birth defects in their children. Merrell Dow submitted research evidence that the drug was not harmful, but the plaintiffs wanted to introduce new evidence from other medical researchers who had conducted new studies and had reanalyzed the previous research. Lower federal courts rejected the new evidence, saying it did not meet the *Frye* standard of general acceptability. The families then appealed this decision to the U.S. Supreme Court.

In deciding the case, the Supreme Court offered the following guidelines for determining the reliability of expert evidence, once the credentials of the expert himself or herself had been established: (a) **falsifiability,** (b) the known or potential **error rate**, (c) whether the research cited has been subjected to peer review and publication, and (d) general acceptance in the scientific community. Note that *Frye*'s emphasis on general acceptance did not disappear; however, by itself it was not considered a sufficient criterion. The Court also emphasized that the evidence to be offered must have **relevance** to the case at hand. The *Daubert* standard, while demanding more scrutiny from the trial court judge, also provided for some flexibility. The Court did not indicate, for example, how much weight to place on each of these criteria. Note also that the credentials of the expert are to be taken into consideration. Faigman and Monahan (2009) offer a useful appraisal:

> At its most basic, Daubert requires the proponent of expert testimony to bear the burden of proof to show that his or her expert is qualified, that the proffered testimony is relevant to a fact in dispute, and that the basis for the expert's opinion is reliable and valid. (p. 9)

In *General Electric Co. v. Joiner* (1997), a trial judge had apparently performed the role of carefully evaluating the evidence that was required by the *Daubert* case.

Robert Joiner, a nonsmoker, had lung cancer; he had worked as an electrician for more than 18 years and argued that exposure to harmful chemicals caused his cancer. The district (trial) court refused to allow the testimony of four scientists who supported Joiner's beliefs, but the intermediate appellate court ruled that this decision was in error. The U.S. Supreme Court upheld the trial judge's decision, stating that it was not up to appellate courts to second-guess the decisions of trial judges when they had performed a careful scrutiny of the evidence. Scholars uncomfortable with the results of that case have suggested that the evidence that was offered by the experts may have been "good science," but the problem was either that the judge did not understand it or that the scientists themselves should have done a better job of explaining it (Blanck & Berven, 1999). Nevertheless, the trial court's role as gatekeeper was confirmed in this case.

Until *Kumho Tire Co. v. Carmichael* (1999), it was not clear that the *Daubert* standard need apply to *psychological* knowledge, because psychology was not part of either the *Daubert* or the *Joiner* case. Neither was it a part of the *Kumho* case, which involved the role a defective tire played in causing an auto accident. However, *Kumho* is an important case for behavioral and social scientists because the Court ruled that the *Daubert* standard applied to scientific, technical, and *other specialized knowledge*—a wide mantle that clearly embraces psychology. Thus, it became clear that psychological knowledge would also be subject to scrutiny before being admitted into courts.

Shortly after *Daubert* was announced, many researchers began to explore the effects of the case on the decision making of judges (see, generally, Skeem, Douglas, & Lilienfeld, 2009). Although studies found that judges were aware of *Daubert* and somewhat more careful in the degree to which they allowed expert testimony to be introduced, the weight of the research suggests that *Daubert* did not dramatically change the way the courts operate. Courts seem to be relatively comfortable scrutinizing an expert's qualifications or considering whether a procedure has "general acceptance by the scientific community"—the *Frye* test. Researchers also have found that judges are less comfortable dealing with error rates and falsifiability. The *error rate* refers to the proportion of data that is wrong or at least potentially wrong. For example, in what percentage of cases is an individual predicted to be dangerous but does not become dangerous (reflecting a false positive prediction)? Falsifiability, as discussed in Chapter 3, refers to the possibility that the statements made by an expert are so clear and specific that they can be shown to be incorrect through systematic observation or empirical study.

Gatowski et al. (2001), surveying 400 state trial court judges, found that only about 5% of them understood these two concepts—error rates and falsifiability. Dahir et al. (2005) found a similar lack of understanding in these areas. These researchers contacted 260 trial court judges and inquired about their willingness to admit profiling and syndrome evidence; they found high rates of admissibility. They also asked which of the various criteria that emerged from the *Daubert* case were most influential in this decision. The most determinative factor was the expert's qualifications, followed by relevance to the case, general acceptance by the scientific community, and general reliability. Only one judge specifically mentioned error rate, and two mentioned falsifiability. Dahir et al. concluded that trial court judges are more comfortable with the less scientific criteria in deciding whether to admit expert testimony into court proceedings.

Even when evidence meets the test of scientific admissibility, it will not necessarily be accepted in court. All rules of evidence require that its **probative value** outweigh its prejudicial value. Evidence is probative if it tends to prove an issue. If the scientific information is considered too prejudicial against the defendant, it might not be admitted. Moreover, when an appellate court reviews a case involving expert testimony, it is sometimes asked to decide whether the trial judge sufficiently weighed the probative and prejudicial values. As one appeals court stated in a case that involved profiling,

> a review of the record reveals the trial court was aware of the potential danger of unfair prejudice to the defendant and was careful to give a proper instruction limiting the jury's consideration of the evidence solely to the basis for the experts' opinions. (*Simmons v. State*, 2000)

With the above review as a backdrop, we now can examine more specifically how profiling has fared in court proceedings.

Profiling as Expert Evidence

Despite the fact that profiling evidence is admitted in many courts, there is considerable debate in the legal and psychological literature as to whether it should be. Some argue that profiles may be helpful as investigatory tools but should not be allowed in the courts (e.g., George, 2008; Kocsis, 2009; Meyer, 2010; Risinger & Loop, 2002). Still others are in favor of admitting profiling evidence (e.g., Ingram, 1998; Woskett, Coyle, & Lincoln, 2007). Arguments against profiling typically include the undue influence of the expert, particularly if testifying for the prosecution; lack of validity of the techniques used; and the prejudicial nature of the information provided. Some critics note that, even if the expert does not indicate directly that a person "fits a profile," the jury may be led to that conclusion quite naturally.

Perhaps because of the influence of the FBI and its training programs, profiling is far more accepted in U.S. courts than in other countries. As George (2008) points out, many profilers either work for the FBI or are past agents; consequently, they are more likely to testify for the prosecution. He even cites an example of a profiler being pressured by a colleague *not* to testify on behalf of the defense. In Australia, profiling evidence is generally not accepted. "(M)ore caution has been exercised over its admissibility especially regarding the expertise of its practitioners" (Woskett et al., 2007, p. 306). In Canada, several recent cases—to be discussed shortly—suggest that the scientific reliability of the behavioral aspects of profiling has not been sufficiently established to be accepted in the courtroom. This led the Canadian Human Rights Commission (2011) to issue several recommendations for developing performance criteria and to undertake research on the effectiveness of behavioral profiling.

In England, a prominent case—*R. v. Stagg*—is said to have dealt a blow to criminal or offender profiling in court (see Focus 9.1). The presiding judge in that case said offender profiling was not generally accepted by the psychological profession, and he did not allow the profiler to take the stand to bolster the prosecution's case. While acknowledging that a profile could be used in developing lines of inquiry and helping police in investigation, it should not be used to identify a suspect, the judge stated. Interestingly, though, he expressed doubt about the usefulness of offender profiles *even during the investigation process* (Ormerod & Sturman, 2005). Nevertheless, as we noted in earlier chapters and as emphasized by Ormerod and Sturman, police can exercise broad discretion over their investigative methods, and consulting a profiler is but one path to take in solving a crime. In the *Stagg* case, however, investigators appear to have given undue weight to the opinions of the profiler, and the profiler in turn seems to have perceived himself as part of the prosecution team (Ormerod & Sturman, 2005).

Focus 9.1

Rachel Nickell's Case: "The Bane of Our Lives"

In July of 1992, Rachel Nickell was stabbed 49 times while walking with her 2-year-old son on Wimbledon Common, in southwest London. She was 23 years old. The murder precipitated a lengthy police undercover operation, influenced substantially by a profiler, and it culminated in charges being dismissed against the only suspect on whom police focused, Colin Stagg. The case also proved to be an embarrassment for behavioral scientists who give assistance to police seeking to solve violent crimes.

Beginning in the mid-1980s, psychologist Paul Britton had apparently helped police in some investigations, almost all involving sex murders. According to one news article, he was "riding high" during these years, appeared in a television documentary, and helped in the creation of an Offender Profiling Research Unit within the Home Office (Ronson, 2010). As we learned in Chapter 3, David Canter and his associates subsequently brought more respectability to the field of behavioral analysis by their careful research and data collection methods. At a recent conference, Canter is said to have referred to what happened in the Nickell case as "the bane of our lives" (quoted in Ronson, 2010).

Shortly after Rachel Nickell's murder, Britton was asked to draw up an offender profile. In his own memoirs, Britton (1997) describes his technique as trying to visualize the crimes, similar to the method of James Brussel, who was discussed in Chapter 1. He told police the murderer would be a single man who lived at home with his parents within walking distance of the Wimbledon Common, and who owned a collection of pornography. He would have had a prior but minor sexual offense, but his deviancy would likely escalate. Colin Stagg lived a short distance from the Common. He had apparently been cautioned by police for sunbathing naked on the Common and had also written an obscene letter to a woman whose name he obtained from a lonely hearts page in a magazine. He was also walking his dog on the Common on the day of the murder. When police questioned him, he admitted to owning porno-graphic magazines but denied killing the victim.

Police, convinced that Stagg was guilty, asked Britton for advice on how to elicit a confession. Britton recommended an undercover operation whereby a female police officer would attempt to lure Stagg into a confession. In police parlance, she was to set up a "honeytrap." The officer contacted Stagg, telling him she had received his name from the woman he had initially contacted via the lonely hearts page. Stagg began corresponding with the undercover officer, asking her if he could send her his sexual fantasies. She answered yes, and he did. The first fantasies were innocuous, so the officer—with Britton's blessing—encouraged him not to hold back. She indicated that she was broad-minded and had an affinity with violence. Stagg introduced vio-lent content, adding that he was not really a violent man (Ronson, 2010). Britton, meanwhile, told police there were elements of sadism in Stagg's letters. The officer eventually met with Stagg in the park and again attempted to elicit comments that would indicate his knowledge of facts about the Nickell case or a direct admission that he had killed the young woman. The relationship continued for weeks, during which time Stagg sent increasingly violent letters at the officer's urging. Britton told police that the chances of having two men with such highly deviant fantasies were very slim, and police arrested Stagg.

Although British media indicated that Stagg had confessed, he vehemently denied doing so. He was detained for 14 months before a judge freed him on the first day of his trial. In the process, the judge made the following statements about profiling: "The notion of psychological profiling in any circumstances as proof of identity is redolent of considerable danger." The judge continued, "I don't wish to give encour-agement to investigating or prosecuting authorities to seek to construct or supple-ment a case on this kind of basis."

Rachel Nickell's real murderer—Robert Napper—was charged with her murder in 1997 and confessed to it in 1998. In the interim between the investigation of Stagg and Napper's arrest, Napper killed another mother and her 4-year-old daughter. The undercover police officer successfully sued for the psychological damage she had suf-fered as a result of what she claimed was a negligent investigation (Ormerod & Sturman, 2005). In December of 2008, the Metropolitan Police apologized to Stagg, acknowledging that he had been wrongly accused.

In the following pages, we provide illustrations of other cases in which profile evidence was accepted or rejected in courts, for a variety of different reasons. Although the focus will be on U.S. cases, those from other countries will be intro-duced as well, usually for comparison purposes. This is by no means a comprehensive review, and—because this is not a legal textbook—it is not intended to be the definitive word on the issues discussed. Nevertheless, when possible we try to address trends or directions that the courts seem to be taking. Furthermore, each case dis-cussed is complex and comprises many issues that are not addressed here. Rather, the cases provide examples of the work done by profilers and the issues that have been discussed throughout earlier chapters. (Focus 9.2 contains summary notes on many of the cases discussed in this chapter.)

Focus 9.2

Profiling-Related Criminal Cases

The following provides a very brief overview of criminal cases discussed in this chapter, listed by defendant name. Note that the *ultimate decision* refers to the final disposition of the case; it may not reflect the decision of the trial court. *Type of testimony* refers to profiling-related issues; in most cases, other issues were litigated as well.

Defendant in Case	Expert and Side	Type of Testimony or Issue	Ultimate Decision
Simmons	Neer (P)	Motivation	Allowed
Masters	Meloy (P)	Motivation	Allowed
Sorabella	Lanning (P)	Child sex offender profile	Allowed
Pennell	Douglas (P)	Linkage analysis	Allowed, but profiling questioned
Jackson	Jacobs (D)	Psychological autopsy	Allowed
Sysyn	Ryan(D)	Psychological autopsy	Not allowed
Armstrong	—— (D)	Rapist profile	Not allowed
Drake	Walter, Richard (P)	Profiling credentials	Credentials questioned No prosecutor error
Wallace	Ressler, Burgess (D)	OD dichotomy; murder	Allowed; prosecutor used testimony to advantage
Fortin	Hazelwood (P)	Linkage analysis	Not allowed; other testimony allowed
Haynes	Walter, Robert (P)	Murder classification Ultimate issue	Not allowed Not allowed
Lowe	Douglas (P)	General profiling; sexual murder	Not allowed
Hillier	Longford (P)	Bail issue/ dangerousness	Not allowed
Klymchuk	Brantley (P)	Motivation Staging	Not allowed
Guilfoyle	Canter (D)	Psychological autopsy	Not allowed
Mohan	Hill (D)	Psychosexual profile	Not allowed

Defendant in Case	Expert and Side	Type of Testimony or Issue	Ultimate Decision
Ranger	Lines (P)	Staging; motivation	Allowed Not allowed
Stagg	Britton (P)	General profiling	Not allowed
Meeks	Ray (P)	Motivation	Allowed
St. Jean	Grant (P)	Psychological autopsy	Allowed

PROFILING CREDENTIALS

A number of court cases have revolved around the credentials of the expert being called to testify. As noted in previous chapters, there is as yet no accrediting group for profilers, and many behavioral experts resist that moniker, now preferring titles like "behavioral analyst" or "criminal investigative analyst." There is also no standard way to prepare a profile report, although some researchers and practitioners have presented a variety of helpful protocols (e.g., see profile report highlighted in Focus 3.3). In addition, the training of profilers is somewhat scattered.

Although in the United States, anyone can call himself or herself a profiler, not anyone can claim the credentials of a trained analyst. Nevertheless, the lack of standardization and the paucity of empirical research on the techniques used—even by those with specific training—are major reasons why caution is urged with respect to legal proceedings. Recall that in the previous chapter, we noted that the psychological autopsy was resisted in some professional quarters because there is no established procedure for conducting one.

With few exceptions, in the United States, FBI-trained crime scene analysts, or those now trained under the ICIAF described in Chapter 2, are accepted as experts in that field. However, their testimony may be limited to certain aspects, as will be noted again below. Many courts are not amenable to allowing *law enforcement agents* to testify about someone's personality or motivation for committing a crime, referred to as **motivational analysis.** Even here there are exceptions, however, as in the *Simmons* case (2000). In that case, at the trial level, an agent associated with the FBI's Behavioral Analysis Unit was allowed to testify that a brutal murder involving the multiple stabbing and disemboweling of a 65-year-old woman was motivated by sexual gratification, which made the offender eligible for the death penalty. The investigators in the case had found its details too gruesome to call in psychologists or psychiatrists—they said that even experienced clinical professionals did not have the expertise to deal with the deviant conduct that was evident from the crime scene. The BAU agent, Thomas Neer, presented testimony based on his analysis of physical evidence at the scene, and he was careful not to say he was providing a psychological profile of the defendant, Clarence Simmons. Nevertheless, he was allowed to say that the crime was motivated by sexual gratification, which was necessary to make

Simmons eligible for the death penalty. Simmons was convicted and sentenced to death. The appellate court upheld Simmons' conviction (*Simmons v. State,* 2000). In general, though, courts are reluctant to allow law enforcement agents to offer motivational analysis.

Courts are, however, more accepting of testimony directly related to crime scene analysis, or features of the crime scene such as staging or organized and disorganized crime scenes. This is probably because this is seen as directly within their area of expertise. In fact, in a military case, *United States v. Meeks* (1992), **crime scene analysis** itself was recognized as a body of specialized knowledge beyond the ken of the average person, thus allowing the expert to help the fact finder in arriving at a decision. The expert, FBI profiler Judson Ray, was allowed to testify on psychological aspects as well, such as that the offender went to the crime scene with sex and killing on his mind (George, 2008). And, in *State v. Pennell* (1989, 1991), an FBI agent's testimony did not even have to meet the test of scientific acceptability because his own experience in criminal investigation was sufficient to make him an expert. The agent in the case was John Douglas, who was introduced in Chapter 2 and has been mentioned in other chapters throughout the book. Douglas is, of course, one of the most well-known FBI profilers in U.S. history, but as we will see shortly, his testimony is not invariably allowed. Since these cases, analysts trained by the FBI have had little difficulty getting accepted into court proceedings, at least at the lower-court level. When cases reach appellate courts, they sometimes—but not always—become more problematic.

There have been cases in which even highly credentialed agents have had their testimony rejected by trial courts, however. At least part of this is due to the *Daubert* decision. For example, soon after *Daubert,* a trial court in an Ohio case (*State v. Lowe,* 1991) did not allow the testimony of Agent Douglas. The appellate court upheld this exclusion, stating that the "purported scientific analytic processes [used by Douglas] ... are based on intuitiveness honed by his considerable experience in the field of homicide investigation." However, they did not amount to sufficient evidence of reliability, the court said. As required by *Daubert,* the trial judge seems to have taken a closer look at the reliability of expert testimony.

Some profilers have attained a certain celebrity status, have written books based on their experiences, and have made themselves available for media interviews relative to high-profile cases. Some, but not all, are FBI trained: The names of John Douglas, Robert (Roy) Hazelwood, Thomas Neer, Greg McCrary, Mary Ellen O'Toole, Richard Walter, Park Dietz, Robert Ressler, and Kenneth Lanning, among others, have often appeared in court cases. Douglas is, without doubt, the most well known. A consulting firm, Academy Group, Inc., is composed of retired FBI, Secret Service, and Virginia State Police special agents, all of whom were formerly psychological profilers or behavioral analysts for their respective agencies. They offer criminal investigation and behavioral analyses to the public sector. For example, retired agent Hazelwood provided service to prosecutors in a highly cited New Jersey case to be discussed below. Greg McCrary consulted with lawyers for the state of Ohio in the case involving the estate of Dr. Samuel Sheppard, the case that refused to go away for almost 50 years (see Focus 9.3).

Focus 9.3

Consultant vs. Consultant: The Sheppard Case

Estate of Sam Sheppard v. State of Ohio

The story of Samuel Sheppard, the Ohio physician convicted of the murder of his wife in 1954 and acquitted 12 years later, is familiar to many for a variety of reasons. It was a sensational case, involving a wealthy, pregnant victim whose husband was having an extramarital affair. It drew extensive pretrial publicity, which was the main reason Sheppard was freed from prison and granted a new trial after having served 12 years of a sentence of life imprisonment (*Sheppard v. Maxwell*, 1966). The new trial, in which he was represented by defense lawyer F. Lee Bailey, ended in an acquittal. The high-profile case produced a television series and later a film, *The Fugitive*, in which the main character escaped from police custody and searched obsessively for the one-armed bandit he had encountered in his home. In real life, Sheppard experienced additional tragedies: His mother committed suicide shortly after he was sentenced to life imprisonment, and his father died of a bleeding ulcer 11 days later. After his release from prison, Sheppard got married again, to a woman with whom he had corresponded while in prison. Later he divorced, became a professional wrestler, drank alcohol excessively, and eventually died in 1970 at the age of 46.

Over the years, there were many unanswered questions about the case. Some people never believed in Sheppard's innocence, while others believed the real murderer was never found. Samuel Reese Sheppard—who was 7 at the time of the murder—insisted his father had been wrongfully convicted and imprisoned. Nearly 50 years after the crime, he sued the state for the wrongful imprisonment of his father. In *The Estate of Sam Sheppard v. State of Ohio* numerous witnesses were called, and lawyers for both sides sought help from experts knowledgeable about profiling.

Greg McCrary, a former FBI profiler, prepared a report for the state in December 1999 and gave a deposition after reviewing a multitude of photographs and written documents. Like other well-known profilers we have mentioned (e.g., Brussel, Douglas, Britton), he wrote about and granted media interviews about his involvement in the case. McCrary concluded that the crime was indeed a domestic murder, but it was staged to look like a burglary. He saw evidence of "overkill" in the crime scene—that is, more force against the victim than would have been needed had this been a murder accompanying a burglary. He also believed the items stolen were inappropriate for a burglary—they did not fit that crime.

The lawyer for Sheppard consulted Brent Turvey and asked for his assessment of the report prepared by McCrary. In his affidavit submitted to the court, Turvey (2002) outlined the many reasons he believed McCrary's report was flawed and his testimony

(Continued)

(Continued)

should be limited. Turvey first emphasized that the report qualified as a "criminal profile"—despite McCrary's preferred terminology of "criminal investigative analysis report." Turvey then stated that criminal profiling was not scientific, in accordance with criteria established in the *Daubert* trilogy, although there was a body of knowledge relating to it. Turvey also asserted that McCrary uncritically accepted the initial investigation prepared by law enforcement and did not address the weaknesses or limitations of their efforts. "This is not a legitimate forensic practice" (n.p.), he stated. He listed several other approaches that were not legitimate, in his view, and concluded by stating that McCrary had overstated the confidence of his theories by a wide margin.

Samuel Reese Sheppard lost his civil suit, with a jury ruling that there was insufficient evidence to hold that the state had falsely imprisoned his father. Later, an appeals court ruled that the son did not have standing to sue the state, that only the individual who was himself imprisoned had that standing. The senior Sheppard, of course, was long dead. Thus, the final legal word on the case is that Sam Sheppard was not guilty beyond a reasonable doubt of his wife's murder, and that—nonetheless—the State of Ohio did not imprison him wrongfully.

Other self-described profilers, some with few academic credentials, became involved in high-interest cases, like those of the Beltway Snipers, JonBenet Ramsey, Caylee Anthony, and Madeleine McCann. Each of these nationally followed cases saw profilers emerge to make appearances on cable networks, and some were willing to testify in courts. John Douglas was at one point hired independently by the parents of JonBenet. It is important to emphasize that consulting with law enforcement *during the investigative phase* of a case does not require sterling credentials or experience. Standards for testifying in court as an expert, however, are more demanding. Even practitioners, researchers, and scholars with solid credentials can run into problems.

One of the most sobering cases relating to credentials, *People v. Drake*, dates back to the mid-1980s and was revisited almost 20 years later in *Drake v. Portuondo* (2003). This was a double-murder case in which the prosecution called Richard Walter, who had some FBI training and was associated with the Michigan Department of Corrections. During the expert certification process, Walter embellished both his experiential and his academic background. His testimony—which centered around a diagnosis of the defendant without having examined him—was allowed in court, and the defendant was convicted. It should be noted that Walter did not possess academic credentials beyond a master's degree in psychology—but this is not unlike many other profilers or behavioral analysts. Drake, the convicted felon, appealed his conviction from his prison cell. He was eventually given a second trial, but was again convicted. (See Box 9.4 for more details about this case.)

Focus 9.4

From the Prison Cell: The Drake Case

State v. Drake, Drake v. Portuondo

In 1982, Robie J. Drake was tried and convicted of the murder of two teenagers whose bodies were found in a parked car, one with a number of bite marks. During the trial, the prosecution called Richard Walter, a self-described profiler who testified, among other things, that Drake suffered from "picquerism," a questionable diagnosis. Walter also exaggerated his credentials, suggesting that he had conducted thousands of profiles while working in the Los Angeles County Medical Examiner's Office; he referred to himself as an adjunct professor at a university, though he had actually only guest lectured.

Drake was convicted. For the next 20 years, from his prison cell, he continued to make the case that he had not been given a fair trial based on a number of factors, including admission of Walter's testimony. With respect to Walter, the appeal focused primarily on his credentials and allegedly false statements; Drake asserted that the prosecutor knew about the falsehoods and should not have called him to the stand.

In 2003, the 2nd Circuit Court of Appeals ruled that Walter's testimony *was* false in some respects and could be considered perjurious. It remanded the case to the district court to decide whether the testimony was indeed perjurious and the prosecutor was at fault in allowing it. The district court refused to fault the prosecutor, and said that even if the expert's testimony was questionable, there was sufficient evidence against the defendant that it was reasonable to believe that a jury would have convicted Drake regardless. The district court also said that though it was "dismayed at the cavalier attitude displayed by Walter," the responses he gave were at best misleading, and not necessarily perjurious. Thus, the worst that could be said was that the expert's information misled the jury. Nevertheless, this would not have affected the jury's ultimate decision, the court said. In a follow-up appeal, the 2nd Circuit Court in 2009 granted Drake a new trial based on prosecutorial misconduct (Prohaska, 2010). Drake was tried, convicted, and sentenced to two consecutive life terms, with eligibility for parole in approximately 2031. He remains in prison, proclaims his innocence, and vows to pursue further appeals (Prohaska, 2010).

It is important to emphasize that Walter was investigated by the American Academy for Forensic Sciences because of this incident, but he was cleared of wrongdoing. Nevertheless, the facts of the case led many commentators to question the degree to which individuals can tout credentials without more verification (e.g., Turvey, 2008). As noted throughout the chapter, both self-proclaimed and trained profilers testify in many courts, and academic credentials are not necessarily revered by the courts over experience, even after *Daubert*.

Walter, who holds no academic credentials beyond a master's degree, remains actively involved in criminal investigations in a rather unusual way. Together with other former law enforcement officers, including FBI agents, he formed the Vidocq Society, which was recently the subject of a sympathetic book, *The Murder Room*, which Walter wrote with the journalist Michael Capuzzo. In the preface, the journalist notes that his publisher investigated the facts of the *Drake* case and concluded that Walter had been unfairly depicted in various commentaries.

As suggested above, courts outside of the United States have been more guarded about accepting credentials of profilers or finding their testimony persuasive (Youngs, 2009). In Australia, for example, only psychologists or psychiatrists can offer profiling evidence in court (Woskett et al., 2007). This was apparently made the rule following a key case (*R. v. Hillier*, 2003) in which a man was accused of killing his estranged wife. The evidence was circumstantial, and there were no witnesses. The state wanted bail denied on the basis that Hillier was a danger to his children. A self-described "behavioral consultant" who had studied profiling in the United States gave the opinion, based on photos of the crime scene and information obtained from police, that Hillier might try to kill his children. Others, including social service workers and a psychiatrist, disagreed. The court did not discount the possibility that the consultant's credentials might enable him to draw tentative conclusions that could help police investigating a crime. However, it found no support for denying bail, and it issued a stern warning to behavioral consultants and police:

> the fact that profiling may sometimes prove to be a valid investigative tool does not justify a conclusion that its exponents may leap majestically over the limitations of modern psychology and psychiatry and give expert evidence as to the personality and conduct of a particular person. (p. 105, para. 21–23)

And, cogently, the court stated, "Amongst the many factors which may lead an expert witness into error is a malady which, if encountered in a new car salesperson, might be described as gross product enthusiasm" (p. 105, para. 21–23). Hillier was ultimately convicted and appealed his conviction based on DNA evidence. The Supreme Court of Australia ruled that there were reasonable grounds to believe someone else committed the crime.

In England and Wales, commentators have been concerned about the misuse of profiling by police or in courts, particularly after the facts of the Nickell case (*R v. Stagg*, 1994) came to light (see Focus 9.1). Courts in the UK in general have been extremely skeptical of profiling, both as to whether it is widely accepted and as to whether it is scientific. Gudjonsson and Copson (1997) studied 90 trials and found that only two individual profilers were admitted as experts. In effect, profiling has made little headway into British courts (Meyer, 2010). If it is to survive in the legal system, Ormerod and Sturman (2005) recommend that constraints be placed on the techniques used by profilers, that they be "accredited by the Home Office on strict criteria and that the bases of accreditation should be transparent and publicly available" (p. 176). They also recommend standards for monitoring individual profilers and subjecting them to periodic review.

In Canada, where the standards for admissibility of expert testimony are similar though not identical to those outlined in *Daubert*, many courts also have expressed skepticism about various profiling evidence. In a recent case (*R. v. Klymchuk*, 2005), a Canadian appellate court seemed particularly concerned that the testimony of a behavioral analyst trained by the FBI would have undue influence over the jury, which was likely to regard profiling as scientific and infallible as a result of its extensive coverage in the popular media. We will discuss this and other key Canadian decisions below; together they suggest that the bar is high for the admission of such evidence.

Crime Scene Profiling in the Courtroom

It is well established that investigators and other experts in the courtroom can discuss the facts of the crime scene, including what they observed, the modus operandi, presence of a signature, and possible staging. When investigators conclude that a homicide has been staged to look like a burglary, for example, this testimony is usually allowed. However, when they cross a line and provide evidence on motives or lead a jury to draw inferences about guilt, they are on shakier ground.

Agents and researchers associated with the FBI have often testified that crime scenes were organized, disorganized, or mixed. In one such case—*State v. Wallace*, 2000, a North Carolina case—the *defense* lawyer called the profilers, but the prosecutor turned the testimony to his advantage during cross-examination. Wallace, the defendant, was charged with and ultimately convicted of nine murders, and consequently was given nine death sentences. At his trial, his defense lawyer called Robert Ressler and Anne Burgess (both discussed in Chapter 2), who were acknowledged as experts in criminology, the psychology of serial offending, crime classification, and—in Dr. Burgess's case—mental illness. The defense was seeking to document that Wallace was not responsible by virtue of a mental illness, or at the very least had diminished capacity for understanding the nature of the offenses. Interestingly, Ressler classified Wallace as a "mixed" offender, because his crimes displayed elements of both the organized and disorganized type. The defense attorney highlighted the disorganized aspects of the crimes. However, the prosecutor, on cross-examination, focused on the organized aspects and argued that organization pointed to a lack of mental illness. Despite the defendant's attempts to challenge this cross-examination, the appeals court of North Carolina allowed the conviction to stand.

LINKAGE ANALYSIS IN THE COURTROOM

In a rudimentary sense, **linkage analysis** is basic to the process of criminal investigation. Law enforcement officials have always looked for similarities in methods of perpetrating crimes in the event that several were committed by the same individual. Did the burglar gain access through a basement window in several different cases? What kinds of items were left behind? Were various victims' bodies posed in a crude fashion? In recent years, with the help of sophisticated investigative technology and computerized databases, linkage analysis has become even more firmly entrenched in police procedures. However, the questions remain: How reliable is it, and does it meet the test of scientific acceptance in court?

The Pennell Case

One of the first noteworthy court cases dealing with linkage analysis was *State v. Pennell* (1989, 1991), the Delaware case referred to briefly above. It involved the torture and killings of three women. Early in the investigative stage, police had obtained a profile that helped them to obtain a search warrant and make an arrest. Two of the crimes were clearly linked to the defendant by physical evidence alone. The third crime occurred sometime after details of the first two cases were reported in the media, and thus could have been a "copycat" killing. Prosecutors wanted to convict Pennell of all three crimes. FBI agent John Douglas made the link at the trial stage, by noting what he believed were common signatures found at the scene. Pennell was convicted. He appealed his conviction, arguing among other things that linkage analysis was not generally acceptable in the scientific community. (Note that this was before *Daubert*, at a time when the *Frye* general acceptance standard dominated.)

The Delaware Supreme Court, however, allowed the testimony about the common signature (which essentially supported linkage analysis) on the basis of John Douglas's many years of experience as an FBI analyst. As noted above, his years of experience were sufficient to qualify him as an expert, so the Court seemed to assume that his knowledge was reliable. However, the Court indicated that it was strongly opposed to *profile evidence*, which it said was extremely prejudicial. Interestingly, George (2008) suggests that Douglas and his colleagues in the FBI "created a new application of profiling called 'linkage analysis' with the explicit goal of gaining admission as expert witnesses" (p. 231). As we noted at the beginning of the chapter, the terminology used in presenting the evidence is what makes the difference to some courts: To the Delaware court, "signature" and "linkage" testimony were acceptable; "profiling" testimony would not have been.

A more recent and widely cited New Jersey case—*State v. Fortin* (2000, 2007)—also addresses the issue of linkage analysis, and here the technique received less favorable review. We discuss the Fortin case in detail because it is often cited in the legal literature and reflects the uncertain state of linkage analysis in criminal courts.

The Fortin Case

Melissa Padilla was brutally attacked and killed in August of 1994, her body mutilated and left half naked in a culvert (see introduction to Chapter 2). She had been living in a motel in Woodbridge, New Jersey, with her four children and her boyfriend and had gone out to buy pizza at a convenience store. The area in which they lived was downtrodden and known to be populated by a variety of transients. Padilla and her boyfriend were unemployed and apparently survived partly by dealing dope out of their room (Risinger & Loop, 2002). Because of these factors, there were many possible suspects; a lengthy investigation followed, but there was no evidence persuasive enough to charge anyone with the crime. Steven Fortin (who was not the boyfriend) lived in the area and moved to Maine shortly thereafter.

Eight months later, in April 1995, a Maine State Trooper was sexually assaulted and mutilated in a similar manner to Padilla, but the trooper survived. The off-duty officer was driving a marked State Police cruiser, with permission, when she noticed a car stopped in the breakdown lane on Interstate 95. It was pointing in the wrong direction, its lights facing oncoming traffic, so she stopped to investigate. The driver was Steven Fortin. He had no license or valid registration, and the trooper detected the odor of alcohol on his breath. She radioed in the traffic stop and was waiting for on-duty officers to arrive to drive Fortin in for processing when he knocked her unconscious and assaulted her. He later pled guilty to this offense and was immediately imprisoned.

Meanwhile, however, because he gave New Jersey as his latest place of residence, police in Maine had contacted their counterparts in Woodbridge for more information. New Jersey police noted similarities to the Padilla murder, Fortin's girlfriend placed him within 200 yards of the Padilla murder scene just an hour before the young woman was killed, and Fortin was charged with her murder. There were many similarities between the two offenses, including clothing left partly on, digital penetration, bite marks, young women victims, and where the victim was found. However, scholars who are cautious about linkage analysis have noted that there were many dissimilarities and vague links as well (Ebisike, 2008; Risinger & Loop, 2002).

Fortin had quickly entered into a plea agreement in the Maine case, but he refused to admit to the Padilla murder. He was indicted in New Jersey in early September of 1995 but was not tried until almost 2 years later. Meanwhile, he remained incarcerated in Maine. At Fortin's New Jersey trial, Robert (Roy) Hazelwood, the former FBI profiler, was allowed to testify as to a possible motive, the modus operandi, and the ritualistic nature of the crime. The prosecutor was allowed to bring in the facts of the Maine case, and Hazelwood was allowed to testify that the Maine and New Jersey cases were so unique that only one person could have committed both—in other words, he was providing linkage analysis.

When the case reached the New Jersey Supreme Court, that court issued a ruling that was inimical to linkage analysis, though observers note that it was a narrow ruling. The Court ruled that—based on his many years of experience as an FBI investigator—Hazelwood could testify on criminal investigative techniques, but not on whether the two crimes were committed by the same person. *With respect to linkage analysis, the court considered the area too esoteric and untested by peers—thereby not meeting the criterion for general acceptance.* This is the argument that is made by critics of this form of profiling, who maintain that there is very little means of evaluating the accuracy of this approach (e.g., Risinger & Loop, 2002; Snook et al., 2012). Fortin was eventually retried, without the linkage analysis testimony. At one point in this very complex case, prosecutors also attempted to introduce data from the ViCAP database, but were again rebuffed by the courts (Ebisike, 2008). Nonetheless, Steven Fortin was ultimately convicted of the murder of Melissa Padilla and remains on death row in New Jersey.

As observed by Risinger and Loop (2002), the New Jersey Supreme Court in its opinion manifested a "kind of split personality altogether too common when courts deal with issues of expert reliability in criminal cases" (para. 276). Thus, while it rejected "linkage analysis" because of its lack of scientific reliability, it did allow Hazelwood to assist the court by describing the similarities between the two crimes, as long as he did not give the opinion that the defendant committed both. It is very difficult to discern the distinction here.

In a commentary critical of the usage of linkage analysis in courts, Risinger and Loop (2002) make the important point that linkage analysis after the fact is quite different from profiling during the investigative phase of a case. During the investigative phase, profiling can be seen as a helpful skill in describing perpetrators from observing the details of their crimes. Linkage analysis, they say,

> appears to have been developed, not as an investigatory aid, but primarily as a means of obtaining either the admission of other crimes, *evidence which might not otherwise be admitted*, or a means to convince the jury that the other crime's evidence was more meaningful than they otherwise might believe, or both. In sum, it was not a way to identify known perpetrators, but a tool to help build a case against defendants already believed to be guilty. (sect. 254, emphasis added)

Risinger and Loop argue succinctly that, because this is such a powerful weapon in the prosecutor's armory, the fact that it is so lacking in scientific validity should make it unacceptable to the courts.

MOTIVATIONS OF OFFENDERS
AND PSYCHOLOGICAL CHARACTERISTICS

Investigators and other experts can discuss the facts of the crime scene, including what they observed, the modus operandi, presence of signature, and possible staging, as the cases above illustrate. They are on somewhat shakier ground with linkage analysis. However, when they tread on peripheral territory such as the possible motivation of the perpetrator, the criminal mind, or the psychological characteristics of defendants, they are even more likely to be challenged.

This is particularly true in Canada, where "the unanimous position of Canadian courts on the behavioural aspects of profiling is that its scientificity is not so established as to meet requirements of admissibility" (Bourque et al., 2009, p. 4). We begin this subsection with several Canadian cases that illustrate this well.

R. v. Mohan (1994), the key case, directly addressed the validity and reliability of a psychological profile sought to be introduced into evidence. In this case, a pediatrician was charged with sexual assault of four female patients between the ages of 13 and 16. The defense wanted to call a psychiatrist who would offer evidence on common psychosexual profiles, including those of pedophiles and sexual psychopaths, and who would testify that the defendant did not possess the characteristics associated with those profiles. The trial judge excluded the evidence, and the Supreme Court of Canada upheld that exclusion, suggesting that the profile was based on *novel science*, and that the scientific community had not developed a standard for the offender who committed this type of crime.

R. v. Ranger (2003) involved the murders of two teenaged sisters who were stabbed to death in their home. Rohan Ranger was subsequently tried and convicted; his cousin, Adrian Kindade, was tried separately and also convicted. Detective Inspector Kathryn Lines, identified as the manager of the Behavioural Sciences Section of the Ontario Provincial Police, was allowed to testify that, based on her review of photographs and videotape as well as her own attendance at the crime scene, the crime was staged to look like a break-in. Interestingly, the court even permitted Detective Lines to read a passage from the *Crime Classification Manual*, discussed in Chapter 2. This testimony is in keeping with the general principle that experienced investigators are well equipped for crime scene analysis.

However, Detective Lines' testimony also included her own conclusion about the perpetrator's *motive* for staging the scene, as well as her belief that the most likely suspect would be someone who had a particular interest in one of the two sisters. The appeals court in the case ruled that the testimony regarding *staging* was admissible as crime scene evidence, but the opinions regarding *motivation* and the characteristics of the likely perpetrator were not. The court also expressed concern that this testimony would be perceived by the jury as having more weight than it deserved, because of Lines' status as an expert witness. Recall that standards for admissibility of expert testimony include a weighing of the probative versus prejudicial value. In this case, the appeals court believed her testimony had undue influence over the jury.

Significantly, the court in the *Ranger* case concluded the following about criminal profiling:

> Criminal profiling is a novel field of scientific evidence, the reliability of which was not demonstrated at trial. To the contrary, it would appear from her limited testimony about the available verification of opinions in her field of work that her opinions amounted to no more than educated guesses. (*R. v. Ranger*, sect. II, para. 82)

In *R. v. Klymchuk* (2005), the Ontario Court of Appeal again expressed discomfort about behavioral analysis in the courts and dealt a blow to motivation-based testimony. Ivan Klymchuk was convicted of the murder of his wife. There was no forensic evidence to implicate him, but he had been having an affair when the crime occurred. Prosecutors maintained that the murder was staged to look like a burglary, and they brought in an FBI agent, Allan Brantley, to make that case. Brantley was also allowed to testify at trial as to the killer's motive. The court of appeals overturned Klymchuk's conviction, ruling that Brantley's testimony could not be subjected to rigorous scientific scrutiny. "Current popular culture ascribes to criminalists like Agent Brantley a level of knowledge and objectivity that all but demands acceptance of their opinions" (para. 37).

In the United States, expert testimony on the psychological characteristics of criminal defendants has been admitted with less difficulty, depending on how it is cloaked. Individuals with impressive credentials get considerable leeway as well, particularly at the trial stage. In one interesting case, however, when the case reached the court of appeals, that court ruled that the profiler's testimony should not have been admitted (*State v. Haynes*, 1988). Richard Haynes was charged with murder and grand theft auto. At his trial, criminal profiler Robert Walter (not to be confused with Richard Walter, discussed earlier in the chapter) testified that, based on his examination of the crime scene reports, this was an "anger-retaliatory" murder. The court of appeals ruled that Walter's offender profiling testimony was not scientific, could not be considered reliable, and should not have been admitted. It also indicated that the expert testimony given by Walter was more prejudicial than probative, and that it amounted to inadmissible **character evidence** as well. Walter had testified at length about the traits and characteristics of anger-retaliatory murderers, leading the jury to conclude that Richard Haynes matched these criteria.

However, in a case that has disturbing repercussions even to this day, psychologist J. Reid Meloy was allowed to testify about the characteristics of sexual murder and about events that might trigger it (*People v. Masters,* 2001; *Masters v. People,* 2002). Meloy's resume includes many years as a researcher and consultant to law enforcement. Because of its troubling facts and its implications for expert testimony in criminal courts, we discuss this below in some detail.

The Masters Case

Timothy Masters was arrested and charged with rape and murder in 1998, more than 10 years after the victim's body was found. At the time of the crime, Masters—then a 15-year-old who lived nearby and had apparently walked by the woman's body without reporting it to police—was questioned in the case, but all evidence against him was circumstantial and police were unable to muster a strong case for the prosecution.

In 1998, with this "cold case" in their files, police contacted Reid Meloy and provided him with materials they had obtained in their earlier investigation. The materials included short stories with violent content that Masters had written as a teenager and drawings and doodles that were thought to suggest a hatred of women. Meloy never spoke with Masters, but after reviewing the files provided by police, he became convinced that Masters had committed the crime (Franklin, 2008). Prosecutors felt they had marshaled sufficient evidence, and Masters was arrested.

Reid Meloy testified in pretrial hearings and at the trial. His written report and testimony included phrases such as "a boiling kettle of latent violence," and indicated that the drawings and stories represented a retreat into a "compensatory narcissistic fantasy world, replete with sexuality and violence." Masters was convicted and appealed his conviction, but the Supreme Court of Colorado ruled against him (*Masters v. People,* 2002), saying that the trial court had not abused its discretion by allowing Meloy to testify.

The case did not end there. In 2008, Masters' conviction was overturned after new DNA evidence was revealed, and he was released from prison, having served nearly a decade behind bars. In 2011, a grand jury dismissed all charges against him, validating his innocence in the minds of his supporters. In the same year, Meloy announced that he would be willing to testify against the police officers in the original case, stating that they had withheld crucial evidence from him and that he would probably not have testified the way he did if the police had provided him with complete information. J. Reid Meloy is a well-known forensic psychologist who has conducted extensive research on adolescent crime, stalking, and violence, and mentioning this case is not meant to impugn his reputation. Nevertheless, the facts of the *Masters* case are a stark reminder that expert testimony often is of significant consequence in someone's life.

In sum, information about the psychological characteristics of an individual is closely related to fitting a person to a profile or to a typology. There is great reluctance on the part of some courts to allow such testimony and even more reluctance to allow someone to be classified in a given way. Courts struggle with this, though, as evidenced by a Connecticut case (*State v. Sorabella*, 2006), involving multiple charges of attempts to commit sexual assault, importing child pornography, and enticing a minor over the Internet. Former FBI agent Kenneth Lanning, who had considerable experience with cases involving sex offenses against children, was allowed to testify on the psychological and behavioral characteristics of sex offenders, specifically what he referred to as "preferential sex offenders" as compared with "situational sex offenders." The trial judge specifically instructed him not to say that Sorabella fit the profile of either one, however. The intermediate court of appeals said this testimony should not have been admitted because it was too prejudicial. Nevertheless, the Connecticut Supreme Court, in the final ruling on this case, allowed Lanning's testimony, saying that it was helpful to the jury, the trial judge properly limited the testimony, and that its prejudicial effect did not outweigh its probative value.

THE PSYCHOLOGICAL AUTOPSY

As we noted in Chapter 8, equivocal death analyses—also referred to as psychological autopsies—are very common but also very complex. Unfortunately, they are also unstandardized, with little agreement on precisely how they should be conducted. Not surprisingly, courts have been very cautious about allowing them into evidence. Recall the skepticism expressed about the psychological autopsy in the USS *Iowa* case. In that case, FBI profilers during the congressional investigation stated that validity was unattainable, a comment that would seem to strike the death knell for scientific admissibility. Others, however, do not agree. Many lawyers have argued, for example, that—particularly in insurance cases where suspected suicides are in question—a psychological autopsy is important. "It is a tool which has application in many legal contexts but which is critical in defending a life insurance coverage case on the basis of the suicide provision" (Canadian Human Rights Commission, 2011, n.p.).

However, a case out of England, *R. v. Guilfoyle* (2001), illustrates very well the tenuous scientific state of the psychological autopsy. Recall that we discussed this briefly in Chapter 8. Guilfoyle was charged with the murder of his pregnant wife, who was found hanging in their garage. A note was found on the scene, and the death was initially believed to be a suicide. In the weeks following the death, though, police heard from relatives and friends that Paula Guilfoyle had been ecstatic about the birth of her first child, that she had not given any sign of being depressed, and—perhaps most damningly—that her husband had had an extramarital affair. They subsequently charged Guilfoyle with her death, suggesting that he had, among other things, tricked her into writing a suicide note and even into placing her own neck in a noose. Guilfoyle was convicted and remains imprisoned to this day.

In appealing the conviction, Guilfoyle's attorney tried to introduce new evidence in the form of a psychological autopsy completed by David Canter, as we mentioned in the previous chapter. Canter had examined the wife's diaries, other papers, and various post-mortem reports, but was not given access to neighbors, relatives, or witnesses at the time of these events. However, Canter concluded that Paula Guilfoyle had written the note and had, indeed, committed suicide.

The court of appeal ruled that the psychologist's opinion was *inadmissible*, partly because there was no way of testing the reliability of the testimony—for example, there was no substantial body of academic writing approving the methodology. In addition, the court noted that Canter had not up to that point conducted psychological autopsies, although this in itself would not be a bar to presenting evidence if it were otherwise reliable. As the court noted, "the present academic status of psychological autopsies is not, in our judgment, such as to permit them to be admitted as a basis for expert opinion before a jury" (*R. v. Guilfoyle*, 2001, n. 25).

Writing about this case later, Canter (2005b) admits to being somewhat naïve at the time about how much could be gleaned on the basis of his restricted access to information. Nevertheless, he has since had the opportunity to speak with friends and relatives of Paula Guilfoyle, and he remains of the opinion that she did indeed commit suicide, and that her husband was wrongly convicted. Canter cites extensive research on suicide that dispels myths that everyone who commits suicide somehow reveals their intention prior to the act. In addition, he notes that—as mentioned earlier in the book—when potential suicides do inform someone of their intentions, it is often not those close to them.

Although the psychological autopsy is suspect in many court cases, it is occasionally allowed. In *Jackson v. State* (1989), a Florida woman was charged with mental child abuse after her 17-year-old daughter, a nude dancer, shot herself. The mother had forged the girl's birth certificate to make it appear to the club that she was old enough, and had apparently forced her daughter to take this job. A psychiatrist had conducted a psychological autopsy on the girl, with results that were very incriminating against the mother. To establish the scientific nature of the autopsy, the psychiatrist told the court that psychological autopsies have been accepted in the field of psychiatry and that hospitals often require them in the case of suicides. The mother was convicted of mental child abuse but appealed her conviction. Her attorney argued that the psychiatrist's testimony should not have been allowed because the autopsy was not reliable— being based on testimony about the state of mind of someone the psychiatrist had never met. The appellate court sided with the state, affirmed the conviction, and indicated that the autopsy testimony by the psychiatrist was no different than expert testimony in testamentary capacity cases, where clinicians had also not interviewed the subjects of their reports.

In *Sysyn v. State* (2000), another Florida case, the trial court had *not* allowed psychological autopsy evidence. The defendant in the case was charged with killing an individual whom she believed to be purposefully goading her into killing her (the victim and the defendant were both female). The defendant believed that the victim was a prostitute and a drug addict and may have had AIDS. While driving a vehicle in which the victim was the passenger, the defendant said she felt a sharp object in her arm, presumably a dirty needle. At this point, the defendant took a handgun from the victim and shot her in the head. A psychologist was ready to testify, based on a psychological autopsy, that the victim was indeed suicidal, but the trial court did not allow this; on appeal, the appeals court ruled that the lower court had not abused its discretion and therefore had not second-guessed the decision not to allow the evidence.

In still another case, a defense attorney challenging the admission of a psychological autopsy did not win the argument. The court in *United States v. St. Jean* (1995) ruled that an expert providing information derived from a psychological autopsy had testimony that was helpful to the trier of fact. The judge also ruled that the procedure was accepted in the mental health community.

As the above cases indicate, and as we have seen in other profiling instances, prosecutors have more success than defense attorneys when it comes to admitting profile evidence. It is likely, as well, that psychological autopsies are admitted in civil courts more than they are in criminal cases.

ULTIMATE ISSUE TESTIMONY

Many critics of profiling evidence in the courts are concerned, not only about its scientific status, but also about its association with the "ultimate issue." Expert witnesses traditionally have been prohibited from giving an opinion on the **ultimate issue**—which refers to the final decision that must be reached in a court—although some jurisdictions have abolished this rule (Ebisike, 2008). The ultimate issue would be, for example, was this person insane? Is this person competent to stand trial? Should this person be given the death penalty? It is well known, though, that even in jurisdictions where the ultimate issue prohibition exists, it is not unusual for some judges to press for a final opinion and for experts to deliver it in a way that is deemed acceptable. For example, rather than saying, "Yes, this person is not competent to stand trial," an expert would say, "The results of my evaluation would support a finding that the defendant is not competent to stand trial."

Nevertheless, opponents of profiling testimony argue that, even though an outright ultimate opinion is not asked for—or provided—profiling testimony opens the door to jurors drawing foregone conclusions based upon the information provided by the expert. Thus, J. Reid Meloy's testimony regarding the juvenile drawings of Timothy Masters, undoubtedly expressed with great confidence and aplomb on the witness stand, led the jury to conclude that these drawings connected Masters to the victim's death.

According to George (2008),

> A prosecutor's expert educates the jury about crime scene classification, including behavioral characteristics such as organization and disorganization, and discusses how these features relate to an offender's motivation, personality, and general behavior. *The prosecutor then submits evidence about the defendant that reflects the characteristics described by the profilers, thus inviting the jury to conclude that the defendant meets the profile of a typical offender.* (p. 242, emphasis added)

Moreover, according to Ebisike (2008), "ultimate issue is in-built in all forms of offender profiling evidence. . . . Offender profile testimony and its derivatives are generally geared towards one thing—pointing to the accused's guilt or innocence." George further adds that when these decisions are appealed, appellate courts are more likely than not to rule in accordance with the trial courts.

Trial courts themselves do not speak with one voice on this matter, however. In many instances, in cases where commentators might argue that the ultimate issue question was pertinent, the phrase is never uttered in a court opinion. In some instances, however, courts specifically reject testimony on this very basis. In *State v. Armstrong* (1991), for example, a case involving the rape of an 8-year-old girl, the *defense* wanted to introduce evidence from a clinical psychologist who maintained that the defendant's psychological dynamics "would not support the view of him being a child sexual perpetrator." The prosecution argued that this opinion essentially expressed an ultimate view of the defendant's innocence, and the court agreed. The 4th Circuit Court of Appeals ruled that excluding this testimony was not an error on the part of the trial court. (Note that this was a defense attempt to introduce profiling evidence.) And, in *State v. Haynes* (1988), the case discussed above, courts ruled that profile evidence represented opinion testimony on an ultimate issue and was inadmissible. As can be seen by reviewing just these few cases, courts differ in their approach to this type of testimony.

Summary and Conclusions

Profiling—whether referred to as criminal or offender profiling, crime scene profiling, behavioral analysis, or behavioral investigative analysis—routinely accompanies the *investigation* of crime, particularly serious and serial offenses. Although not all law enforcement agencies consult profilers, many do. With increasingly more training of behavioral analysts by the FBI and similar entities across the globe, it is likely that this consultation will continue. Questions raised in this chapter relate to whether profiling should be restricted to this investigative phase or should be admitted into court proceedings as evidence beyond the ken of the average person, thus requiring the help of an expert witness. As we have seen, the answer to these questions depends upon a number of factors, and there is considerable variation in court decisions.

As a backdrop to the cases and issues discussed in the chapter, we reviewed the standards for the evaluation of expert testimony, established by U.S. courts first in *Frye v. United States* and later in the *Daubert* trilogy. Since the 1993 *Daubert* decision, federal courts have been bound by these standards, and most states have adopted them directly or have used similar versions. It is important to emphasize that the Supreme Court, in *Daubert*, did not tell courts how much weight to place on the various criteria it outlined (e.g., general acceptance, error rate, etc.); as we learned in the chapter, research indicates that courts tend to rely very heavily on the credentials of the expert and on general acceptance of the evidence within the scientific community. Few courts consider error rate. Courts in other countries have adopted different standards, but most have embraced the need for some general acceptance in the field.

Particularly after the *Daubert* decision, trial courts have nevertheless been more aware of their gatekeeper role and have made efforts to scrutinize more carefully the scientific status of the profiler's testimony, and they have been more likely to reject evidence that was not scientifically based. There is little consistency in these court decisions, though, and observers note that—at least in the United States—profiling evidence still makes its way into both criminal and civil courts. In addition, we do not know what goes on in most trial courts; their decisions usually do not come to light unless publicized or appealed. On the basis of the research evidence that is available, there do appear to be two trends among appellate courts: (1) If the trial court was careful to conduct a *Daubert*-like review of the testimony, the appellate court tends not to second-guess the trial court; and (2) appellate courts have overruled trial courts when nonscientific evidence was too readily admitted.

The credentials and the training of the profilers themselves also must be taken into consideration. Traditionally, profilers trained by the FBI have had few problems being accepted as experts, particularly as experts in criminal analysis. Testimony on their observations about the crime scene, staging, trophy taking, and MO, for example, has usually been allowed. However, when these profilers cross over to give opinions about motivations or psychological characteristics of defendants, they are on shakier ground.

Linkage analysis, the process of trying to tie separate cases to the same offender, is widely employed in the investigatory process, but its status as reliable, scientific information has yet to be firmly established. We covered in detail the *Fortin* case, where the Court rejected linkage analysis as a method too new and untested to be admitted *as such*; however, the same court also allowed the agent to testify about similarities between two crimes. In many respects, the terminology used to describe the evidence being offered can make the difference as to whether it will be accepted by the presiding judge. Similar conclusions can be drawn about psychological autopsies, which have been admitted by some courts and regarded with suspicion by others. In civil courts—which we hardly touched in this chapter—psychological autopsies may be regarded more favorably.

Expert witnesses are generally not allowed to give opinions on ultimate legal issues—the ultimate decision is for the triers of fact, the judge or jurors, to make. However, allowing expert testimony on certain aspects of profiling—such as characteristics associated with certain types of sex offenders—invites jurors to assume that the defendant belongs to this classification. Those who are cautious about allowing profilers to testify believe jurors are too strongly influenced by the expert testimony, and that its prejudicial effect far outweighs its probative value.

The above comments relate primarily to U.S. courts. As we have seen, there are substantial differences in profiling as it is viewed by courts in other countries. Profiling in general has been dealt severe blows in courts in Australia, Canada, and the United Kingdom, for example. Skepticism about profiles even in the investigative phase has been expressed, often sarcastically. One court, as we noted, offered the analogy to a new car salesman's gross product enthusiasm. Although we have not focused on these international differences, it is important to realize that they exist, and that behavioral analysis as a whole has a way to go before being universally accepted.

Supporters of profiling (or behavioral analysis, or investigative analysis) emphasize that the behavioral sciences have much to offer the courts, as long as their techniques are carefully standardized and their practitioners are well trained, certified, and cautious in expressing their opinions. There is near universal agreement that "profilers" should not assert the guilt of a particular individual and should not state definitively that an individual fits the profile—or does not fit the profile—of a particular offender.

There is less agreement over whether the profiler should discuss general characteristics or classifications of offenders; again, this type of testimony leads jurors too closely to making inferences that are based on nonscientific data. The training of investigative analysts, such as that offered by Canter and his associates in England and the IACS program discussed in Chapter 3, is likely to increase the respectability of these endeavors in the eyes of the judicial system. At this time, however, it appears premature to elevate them to the status of expert knowledge.

KEY CONCEPTS

Character evidence	Falsifiability	Profile–crime correspondence (P–CC)
Crime scene analysis	Frye standard	
Daubert standard	Linkage analysis	Profile–defendant correspondence (P–DC)
Error rate	Motivational analysis	Relevance
Expert witness	Probative value	Ultimate issue

References

Abrahamsen, D. (1960). *The psychology of crime*. New York: Columbia University Press.

Abrams, K. M., & Robinson, G. E. (2002). Occupational effects of stalking. *Canadian Journal of Psychiatry, 47*, 468–472.

Aggarwal, N. (2009). Rethinking suicide bombing. *Crisis, 30*, 94–97.

Alison, L. (2005). From trait-based profiling to psychological contributions to apprehension methods. In L. Alison (Ed.), *The forensic psychologist's casebook: Psychological profiling and criminal investigation* (pp. 3–22). Portland, OR: Willan.

Alison, L. J., & Canter, D. V. (1999a). Professional, legal and ethical issues in offender profiling. In D. V. Canter & L. J. Alison (Eds.), *Profiling in policy and practice* (pp. 23–54). Aldershot, UK: Ashgate.

Alison, L. J., & Canter, D. V. (1999b). Profiling in policy and practice. In D. V. Canter & L. J. Alison (Eds.), *Profiling in policy and practice* (pp. 3–19). Aldershot, UK: Ashgate.

Alison, L. J., Goodwill, A., & Alison, E. (2005). In L. Alison (Ed.), *The forensic psychologist's casebook: Psychological profiling and criminal investigation* (pp. 235–277). Devon, UK: Willan.

Alison, L. J., Goodwill, A., Almond, L., van den Heuvel, C., & Winter, J. (2011). Pragmatic solutions to offender profiling and behavioural investigative advice. In L. Alison & L. Rainbow (Eds.), *Professionalizing offender profiling* (pp. 51–71). London: Routledge.

Alison, L. J., Smith, M. D., Eastman, O., & Rainbow, L. (2003). Toulmin's philosophy of argument and its relevance to offending profiling. *Psychology, Crime & Law, 9*, 173–183.

Alison, L. J., Smith, M. D., & Morgan, K. (2003). Interpreting the accuracy of offender profiles. *Psychology, Crime & Law, 9*, 185–195.

Alison, L. J., West, A., & Goodwill, A. (2004). The academic and the practitioner: Pragmatists' views of offender profiling. *Psychology, Public Policy, and Law, 10*, 71–101.

American Psychiatric Association. (2000). *Diagnostic and statistical manual of mental disorders—revised (DSM-IV-R)*. Washington, DC: Author.

Andrew, T. A., & Fallon, K. K. (2007). Asphyxial games in children and adolescents. *American Journal of Forensic Medicine and Pathology, 28*, 303–307.

Andrews, D. A., & Bonta, J. (1998). *The psychology of criminal conduct* (2nd ed.). Cincinnati, OH: Anderson.

Andrews, D. A., Bonta, J., & Hoge, P. D. (1990). Classification for effective rehabilitation: Rediscovering psychology. *Criminal Justice and Behavior, 17*, 19–52.

Anselin, L., Syabri, I., & Kho, Y. (2006). GeoDa: An introduction to spatial data analysis. *Geographical Analysis, 38*, 5–22.

Arizona v. United States, 11-182 (2012).

Armstrong, D., & Pereira, J. (2001, October 23). Nation's airlines adopt aggressive measures for passenger profiling. *Wall Street Journal*, p. A12.

Ash, I. K. (2009). Surprise, memory, and retrospective judgment making: Testing cognitive reconstruction theories of the hindsight bias effect. *Journal of Experimental Psychology: Learning, Memory, and Cognition, 35*, 916–933.

Ask, K., & Granhag, P. A. (2005). Motivational sources of confirmation bias in criminal investigations: The need for cognitive closure. *Journal of Investigative Psychology and Offender Profiling, 2*, 43–63.

Ault, R. L., Hazelwood, R. R., & Reboussin, R. (1994). Epistemological status of equivocal death analysis. *American Psychologist, 49*, 72–73.

Ault, R., & Reese, J. T. (1980, March). A psychological assessment of crime profiling. *FBI Law Enforcement Bulletin, 49*(3), 22–25.

Australian Bureau of Criminal Intelligence. (1997, February). *Tracking violent crime*. Paper presented to the Australian Institute of Criminology, Second National Outlook Symposium.

Barling, J. (1996). The prediction, experience, and consequences of workplace violence. In G. R. VanderBos & E. Q. Bulatao (Eds.), *Violence on the job: Identifying risks and developing solutions* (pp. 29–40). Washington, DC: American Psychological Association.

Baron, R. A., & Byrne, D. (2000). *Social psychology* (9th ed.). Boston: Allyn & Bacon.

Bartol, C. R., & Bartol, A. M. (2012). *Introduction to forensic psychology: Research and application* (3rd ed.). Thousand Oaks, CA: Sage.

Bateman, A. L., & Salfati, C. G. (2007). An examination of behavioral consistency using individual behaviors or groups of behaviors in serial homicide. *Behavioral Sciences & the Law, 25*, 527–544.

Beccaria, C. (1767). *An essay on crimes and punishments*. London: Almon.

Behavioral Trace Investigations. (2009). *Forensic behavioural profiling*. North Sydney, Australia: Author.

Behrendt, N., Buhl, N., & Seidl, S. (2002). The lethal paraphiliac syndrome: Accidental autoerotic deaths in four women and a review of the literature. *International Journal of Legal Medicine, 116*, 148–152.

Belknap, J. (2010). Rape: Too hard to report and too easy to discredit victims. *Violence Against Women, 16*, 1335–1344.

Bell, B. G., & Grubin, D. (2010). Functional magnetic resonance imaging may promote theoretical understanding of the polygraph test. *Journal of Forensic Psychiatry & Psychology, 21*, 52–65.

Bennell, C. (2008). An introduction to the special issue on criminal profiling. *Journal of Police and Criminal Psychology, 23*, 49–50.

Bennell, C., & Canter, D. V. (2002). Linking commercial burglaries by modus operandi: Tests using regression and ROC analysis. *Science and Justice, 42*, 153–162.

Bennell, C., & Jones, N. J. (2005). Between a ROC and a hard place: A method for linking serial burglaries using an offender's modus operandi. *Journal of Investigative Psychology and Offender Profiling, 2*, 23–41.

Bennell, C., Jones, N. J., & Taylor, A. (2011). Determining the authenticity of suicide notes: Can training improve human judgment? *Criminal Justice and Behavior, 38*, 669–689.

Bennell, C., Snook, B., MacDonald, S., House, J. C., & Taylor, P. J. (2012). Computerized crime linkage systems: A critical review and research agenda. *Criminal Justice and Behavior, 39*, 620–634.

Bennell, C., Snook, B., Taylor, P. J., Corey, S., & Keyton, J. (2007). It's no riddle, choose the middle: The effect of number of crimes and topographical detail on police officer predictions of serial burglars' home locations. *Criminal Justice and Behavior, 34*, 119–132.

Bennett, C. J. (2008). Unsafe at any altitude: The comparative politics of no-fly lists in the United States and Canada. In M. B. Salter & P. Adey (Eds.), *Politics at the airport* (pp. 51–76). Minneapolis: University of Minnesota Press.

Bennett, T., & Wright, R. (1984). *Burglars on burglary: Prevention and the offender.* Brookfield, VT: Gower.

Bentham, J. (1823). Punishment and utility. In J. G. Murphy (Ed.), *Punishment and rehabilitation.* Belmont, CA: Wordsworth.

Berger, M. (1957, January 25). Twisted course of "Mad Bomber" vengeance traced in a deeply complex personality. *New York Times*, p. 1.

Bernasco, W. (2008). Them again? Same-offender involvement in repeat and near repeat burglaries. *European Journal of Criminology, 5*, 411–431.

Beyer, K. R., & Beasley, J. O. (2003). Nonfamily child abductors who murder their victims: Offender demographics from interviews with incarcerated offenders. *Journal of Interpersonal Violence, 18*, 1167–1188.

Bhatt, S., & Brandon, S. E. (2008, December 12). *Review of voice stress–based technologies for the detection of deception.* Washington, DC: U.S. Department of Defense.

Biffl, E. (1996). Psychological autopsies: Do they belong in the courtroom? *American Journal of Criminal Law, 24*, 123–145.

Bijleveld, C., & Smit, P. (2006). Homicide in The Netherlands: On the structuring of homicide typologies. *Homicide Studies, 10*, 195–219.

Blanck, P. D., & Berven, H. M. (1999). Evidence of disability after *Daubert. Psychology, Public Policy, and Law, 5*, 16–40.

Block, R., & Bernasco, W. (2009). Finding a serial burglar's home using distance decay and conditional origin-destination patterns: A test of empirical Bayes journey-to-crime estimation in The Hague. *Journal of Investigative Psychology and Offender Profiling, 6*, 187–211.

Block, R., Galary, A., & Brice, D. (2007). The journey to crime: Victims and offenders converge in violence index offenses in Chicago. *Security Journal, 20*, 123–137.

Boba, R. (2009). *Crime analysis with crime mapping.* Thousand Oaks, CA: Sage.

Boltz, M. G., Dyer, R. L., & Miller, A. R. (2010). Are you lying to me? Temporal cues for deception. *Journal of Language and Social Psychology, 29*, 458–466.

Borum, R., Cornell, D. G., Modzeleski, W., & Jimerson, S. R. (2010). What can be done about school shootings? A review of the evidence. *Educational Researcher, 39*, 27–37.

Borum, R., Fein, R., Vossekuil, B., & Berglund, J. (1999). Threat assessment: Defining an approach for evaluating risk of targeted violence. *Behavioral Sciences & the Law, 17*, 323–337.

Borum, R., Lodewijks, H., Bartel, P. S., & Forth, A. E. (2010). Structured Assessment of Violence Risk in Youth (SAVRY). In R. I. Otto & K. S. Douglas (Eds.), *Handbook of violence risk assessment: International perspectives on forensic mental health* (pp. 63–79). New York: Routledge/Taylor & Francis.

Bosco, D., Zappala, A., & Santtila, P. (2010). The admissibility of offender profiling in courtroom: A review of legal issues and court opinions. *International Journal of Law and Psychiatry, 33*, 184–191.

Boudreaux, M. C., Lord, W. D., & Etter, S. E. (2000). Child abduction: An overview of current and historical perspectives. *Child Maltreatment, 5*, 63–71.

Bourque, J., LeBlanc, S., Utzschneider, A., & Wright, C. (2009, March). *The effectiveness of profiling from a national security perspective.* Ottawa, ON: Canadian Human Rights Commission.

Bowers, K. J., & Johnson, S. D. (2005). Domestic burglary repeats and space-time clusters: The dimensions of risk. *European Journal of Criminology, 2*, 67–92.

Bradsaw, J. (2008, July/August). Behavioral detectives patrol airports. *The National Psychologist*, p. 10.

Brandon, S. E. (2011). Impacts of psychological science on national security agencies post-9/11. *American Psychologist, 66,* 495–506.

Brantingham, P. (2004, December). Commentary. In T. Rich & M. Shively (Eds), *A methodology for evaluating geographic profiling software* (pp. 37–48). Cambridge, MA: Abt Associates.

Brantingham, P. J., & Brantingham, P. L. (1984). *Patterns in crime.* New York: Macmillan.

Brantingham, P. J., & Brantingham, P. L. (1991). Notes on the geometry of crime. In P. J. Brantingham & P. L. Brantingham (Eds.), *Environmental criminology* (pp. 27–54). Prospect Heights, IL: Waveland Press. (Originally published in 1981)

Brantingham, P. J., & Brantingham, P. L. (1993). Environment, routine, and situation: Toward a pattern theory of crime. In R. V. Clarke & M. Felson (Eds.), *Routine activity and rational choice* (pp. 222–257). New Brunswick, NJ: Transaction.

Brantley, A. G., & Kosky, R. H., Jr. (2005, January). Serial murder in the Netherlands: A look at motivation, behavior, and characteristics. *FBI Law Enforcement Bulletin,* 26–32.

Breitmeier, D., Mansouri, F., Albrecht, K., Böhm, U., Tröger, H. D., & Kleemann, W. J. (2003). Accidental autoerotic deaths between 1978 and 1997. Institute of Legal Medicine, Medical School Hannover. *Forensic Science International, 137,* 41–44.

Brent, D. A. (1989). The psychological autopsy: Methodological issues for the study of adolescent suicide. *Suicide and Life-Threatening Behavior, 19,* 43–57.

Brett, A. (2004). "Kindling theory" in arson: How dangerous are firesetters? *Australian and New Zealand Journal of Psychiatry, 38,* 419–425.

Briggs, C. M., & Cutright, P. (1994). Structural and cultural determinants of child homicide: A cross-national analysis. *Violence and Victims, 9,* 3–16.

Britton, P. (1997). *The jigsaw man.* London: Bantam Press.

Bronskill, J. (2011, August 30). Air passenger observation plan post 9-11 raises red flag for privacy watchdog. *The Canadian Press.* Available at http://www.globalnews.ca/air+passenger+observation+plan+post+911+raises+red+flag+for+privacy+watchdog/6442472237/story.html

Brown, B. B., & Harris, P. B. (1989). Residential burglary victimization: Reactions to the invasion of a primary territory. *Journal of Environmental Psychology, 9,* 119–132.

Brussel, J. A. (1968). *Casebook of a crime psychiatrist.* New York: Bernard Geis Associates.

Bryan, R. E. (2006). *Men's double breasted suits USA.* Available at http://www.ahfashion.com/mens_double_breasted_suits/index.htm

Buhs, E. S., & Ladd, G. W. (2001). Peer rejection as an antecedent of young children's school adjustment: An examination of mediating processes. *Developmental Psychology, 37,* 550–560.

Bureau of Alcohol, Tobacco, Firearms and Explosives. (n.d.). *Criminal investigative analysis.* Available at http://www.atf.gov/explosives/programs/criminal-investigative-analysis/

Bureau of Labor Statistics. (2010, July 14). *Workplace violence fact sheet.* Washington, DC: Author.

Burgess, A., Hartman, C., Ressler, R. K., Douglas, J. E., & McCormick A. (1986). Sexual homicide: A motivational model. *Journal of Interpersonal Violence, 1,* 251–272.

Burgess, E. W., & Bogue, D. J. (1967). The delinquency research of Clifford R. Shaw and Henry D. McKay and associates. In E. W. Burgess & D. J. Bogue (Eds.), *Urban sociology* (pp. 230–257). Chicago: University of Chicago Press.

Burton, S., & Dalby, J. T. (2012). Psychological autopsy in the investigation of serial neonaticides. *Journal of Forensic Sciences, 57,* 270–272.

Calhoun, F. S., & Weston, S. W. (2003). *Contemporary threat assessment: A practical guide for identifying, assessing, and managing individuals of violent intent.* San Diego, CA: Specialized Training Service.

California Division of Occupational Safety and Health. (1995). *Guidelines for workplace security.* San Francisco: California Department of Industrial Relations.

Canadian Centre for Justice Statistics. (2005). *Family violence in Canada: A statistical profile.* Ottawa, ON: Author.

Canadian Human Rights Commission. (2011). *Behavioural profiling.* Available at http://www .chrc-ccdp.ca/research_program_recherche/profiling_profilage/page4-eng.aspx

Canning, K. E., Hilts, M. A., & Muirhead, Y. E. (2011). False allegation of child abduction. *Journal of Forensic Sciences, 56,* 794–802.

Canter, D. V. (1994). *Criminal shadows:* London: HarperCollins.

Canter, D. V. (1999). Equivocal death. In D. Canter & L. Alison (Eds.), *Profiling in policy and practice* (pp. 125–156). Aldershot, UK: Ashgate.

Canter, D. V. (2000a). *Criminal shadows: The inner narratives of evil.* Irving, TX: Authorlink Press.

Canter, D. V. (2000b). Offender profiling and criminal differentiation. *Legal and Criminological Psychology, 5,* 23–46.

Canter, D. V. (2003). *Mapping murder: The secrets of geographical profiling.* London: Virgin Publishing.

Canter, D. V. (2004). Offender profiling and investigative psychology. *Journal of Investigative Psychology and Offender Profiling,* 4–6.

Canter, D. V. (2005a). Confusing operational predicaments and cognitive explorations: Comments on Rossmo and Snook et al. *Applied Cognitive Psychology, 19,* 663–668.

Canter, D. V. (2005b). Suicide or murder? Implicit narratives in the Eddie Gilfoyle case. In L. Alison (Ed.), *The forensic psychologist's casebook: Psychological profiling and criminal investigation* (pp. 315–333). Portland, OR: Willan.

Canter, D. V. (2009). Developments in geographical offending profiling: Commentary on Bayesian journey-to-crime modeling. *Journal of Investigative Psychology and Offender Profiling, 6,* 161–166.

Canter, D. V., & Alison, L. J. (2000). Profiling property crimes. In D. Canter & L. Alison (Eds.), *Profiling property crimes.* Burlington, VT: Ashgate.

Canter, D. V., Alison, L. J., Alison, E., & Wentink, N. (2004). The organized/disorganized typology of serial murder: Myth or model? *Psychology, Public Policy, and Law, 10,* 293–320.

Canter, D. V., Bennell, C., Alison, L. J., & Reddy, S. (2003). Differentiating sex offences: A behaviorally based thematic classification of stranger rapes. *Behavioral Sciences & the Law, 21,* 157–174.

Canter, D. V., Coffey, T., Huntley, M., & Missen, C. (2000). Predicting serial killers' home base using a decision support system. *Journal of Quantitative Criminology, 16,* 457–478.

Canter, D. V., & Fritzon, K. (1998). Differentiating arsonists: A model of firesetting actions and characteristics. *Legal and Criminological Psychology, 3,* 73–96.

Canter, D. V., & Gregory, A. (1994). Identifying the residential location of rapists. *Journal of the Forensic Science Society, 34,* 169–175.

Canter, D. V., & Hammond, L. (2006). A comparison of the efficacy of different decay functions in geographical profiling for a sample of U.S. serial killers. *Journal of Investigative Psychology and Offender Profiling, 3,* 91–103.

Canter, D. V., & Heritage, R. (1990). A multivariate model of sexual offence behavior: Developments in "offender profiling." *Journal of Forensic Psychiatry, 1,* 185–212.

Canter, D. V., & Hodge, S. (2008). Criminals' mental maps. In D. V. Canter & D. Youngs (Eds.), *Principles of geographical offender profiling* (pp. 249–258). Burlington, VT: Ashgate.

Canter, D. V., & Larkin, P. (1993). The environmental range of serial rapists. *Journal of Environmental Psychology, 13,* 63–69.

Canter, D. V., Missen, C., & Hodge, S. (1996). Are serial killers special? *Policing Today, 2,* 1–12.

Canter, D. V., & Wentink, N. (2004). An empirical test of Holmes and Holmes's serial murder typology. *Criminal Justice and Behavior, 31,* 489–515.

Canter, D. V., & Youngs, D. (2003). Beyond offender profiling: The need for an investigative psychology. In R. Bull & D. Carson (Eds.), *Handbook of psychology in legal contexts* (2nd ed., pp. 171–206). Chichester, UK: Wiley.

Canter, D. V., & Youngs, D. (2008). Geographical offender profiling: Origins and principles. In D. Canter & D. Youngs (Eds.), *Principles of geographical offender profiling* (pp. 1–20). Burlington, VT: Ashgate.

Canter, D. V., & Youngs, D. (2009). *Investigative psychology: Offender profiling and the analysis of criminal action.* Chichester, UK: Wiley.

Capone, D. L., & Nichols, W. (1975). Crime and distance: An analysis of offender behaviour in space. *Proceedings of the Association of American Geographers, 7,* 45–49.

Carson, D. (2011). Investigative psychology and law: Towards collaboration by focusing on evidence and inferential reasoning. *Journal of Investigative Psychology and Offender Profiling, 8,* 74–89.

Catalano, R. (2010, September). *National Crime Victimization Survey: Victimization during household burglary.* Washington, DC: U.S. Department of Justice, Bureau of Justice Statistics.

Catalano, R., Haggerty, K., Oesterle, S., Fleming, C., & Hawkins, J. D. (2004). The importance of bonding to school for healthy development: Findings from the Social Development Research Group. *Journal of School Health, 74,* 252–261.

CBC News. (2007, May 27). *Police stop more blacks, Ontario study finds.* Available at http://www.cbc.ca/Canada/story/2005/05/26/race 050526.html

Centers for Disease Control and Prevention. (2008). Unintentional strangulation deaths from the "choking game" among youths aged 6–19 years—United States, 1995–2007. *Morbidity and Mortality Weekly Report, 57,* 141–144.

Chenoune, F. (1993). *A history of men's fashion.* Paris: Flammarion.

Chief of Naval Operations. (1989, August 31). *Investigation to inquire into the explosion in number two turret on board USS Iowa (BB 61) which occurred in the vicinity of the Puerto Rico operating area on or about 19 April 1989.* Washington, DC: Author.

Cleckley, H. (1941). *The mask of sanity.* St. Louis, MO: C. V. Mosby.

Clutterbuck, L., & Warnes, R. (2011). *Exploring patterns of behaviour in violent Jihadist terrorists: An analysis of six significant terrorist conspiracies in the UK.* Santa Monica, CA: RAND Corporation.

Cohen, L. E., & Felson, M. (1979). Social change and crime rate trends: A routine activity approach. *American Sociological Review, 44,* 588–608.

Coie, J. D., & Miller-Johnson, S. (2001). Peer factors and interventions. In R. Loeber & D. P. Farrington (Eds.), *Child delinquents: Development, intervention, and service needs* (pp. 191–210). Thousand Oaks, CA: Sage.

Collins, P. I., Johnson, G. F., Choy, A., Davidson, K. T., & Mackay, R. E. (1998). Advances in violent crime analysis and law enforcement: The Canadian Violent Crime Linkage Analysis System. *Journal of Government Information, 25,* 277–284.

Committee on Armed Services. (1990, May 25). *Review of the Department of the Navy's investigation into the gun turret explosion aboard the U.S.S. "Iowa."* Committee on Armed Services, United States Senate, 101st Congress, First Session.

Connecticut v. Sorabella, 277 Connecticut 155, 169, 891, A.2d, cert denied, 549 U.S. 821, 127 S. Ct. 131, 166, L. Ed, 2d 36 (2006).

Considine, B. (1957, April 7). How they caught the Mad Bomber. *American Weekly,* pp. 5, 23–25.

Copson, G. (1995). *Coals to Newcastle? Part I: A study of offender profiling.* London: Home Office, Police Research Group.

Copson, G., Badcock, R., Boon, J., & Britton, P. (1997). Articulating a systematic approach to clinical crime profiling. *Criminal Behaviour and Mental Health, 7,* 13–17.

Cornell, D. G., & Allen, K. (2011). Development, evaluation, and future directions of the Virginia Student Threat Assessment Guidelines. *Journal of School Violence, 10*, 88–106.

Cornell, D. G., Gregory, A., & Fan, X. (2011). Reductions in long-term suspensions following adoption of the Virginia Student Threat Assessment Guidelines. *NASSP Bulletin, 95*(3), 175–194.

Cornell, D. G., & Sheras, P. (2006). *Guidelines for responding to student threats of violence.* Longmont, CO: Sopris West.

Cornell, D. G., Sheras, P. L., Kaplan, S., McConville, D., Douglass, J., Elkon, A., et al. (2004). Guidelines for student threat assessment: Field-test findings. *School Psychology Review, 33*, 527–546.

Cornish, D. B., & Clark, R. V. (1986). *The reasoning criminal: Rational choice perspectives on offending.* New York: Springer Verlag.

COT. (2007, June 7). *Lone-wolf terrorism.* The Hague, Netherlands: COT, Instituut voor Veiligheidsen Crisismanagement.

Cowan, P. A., & Cowan, C. P. (2004). From family relationships to peer rejection to antisocial behavior in middle childhood. In J. B. Kupersmidt & K. A. Dodge (Eds.), *Children's peer relations: From development to intervention* (pp. 159–178). Washington, DC: American Psychological Association.

Cowell, D. D. (2009). Autoerotic asphyxiation: Secret pleasure—lethal outcome? *Pediatrics, 124*, 1319–1324.

Cox, T., & Leather, P. (1994). The prevention of violence at work: Application of a cognitive behavioral theory. *International Review of Industrial and Organizational Psychology, 9*, 213–246.

Critical Incident Response Group. (2001). *Workplace violence: Issues in response.* Quantico, VA: National Center for the Analysis of Violent Crime.

Dahir, V. B., Richardson, J. T., Ginsburg, G. P., Gatowski, S. I., Dobbin, S. A., & Merlino, M. L. (2005). Judicial application of *Daubert* to psychological syndrome and profile evidence: A research note. *Psychology, Public Policy, and Law, 11*, 62–82.

Dahlberg, L. L., & Potter, L. B. (2001). Youth violence: Developmental pathways and prevention challenges. *American Journal of Preventive Medicine, 20*(1s), 3–14.

Dailey, J. T., & Pickrel, E. W. (1975a, April). Federal Aviation Administration's behavioral research program for the defense against hijacking. *Aviation, Space and Environmental Medicine, 46*(4), 423–427.

Dailey, J. T., & Pickrel, E. W. (1975b). Some psychological contributions to defenses against hijackers. *American Psychologist, 30*, 161–175.

Dale, A., Davies, A., & Wei, L. (1997). Developing a typology of rapists' speech. *Journal of Pragmatics, 27*, 653–669.

Daniels, J. A., Volungis, A., Pshenishny, E., Gandhi, P., Winkler, A., Cramer, D. P., et al. (2010). A qualitative investigation of averted school shooting rampages. *Counseling Psychologist, 38*, 69–95.

Daubert v. Merrell Dow Pharmaceuticals, Inc., 509 U.S. 579, 113 S. Ct. 2786 (1993).

Definitions, C.F.R. 18 U.S. C§ 2331.

DeLisi, M., & Scherer, A. M. (2006). Multiple homicide offenders: Offense characteristics, social correlates, and criminal careers. *Criminal Justice and Behavior, 33*, 367–391.

Del Bove, G., & Mackay, S. (2011). An empirically derived classification system for juvenile firesetters. *Criminal Justice and Behavior, 38*, 796–817.

Demir, B., Broussard, B., Goulding, S. M., & Compton, M. T. (2009). Beliefs about causes of schizophrenia among police officers before and after crisis intervention team training. *Community Mental Health, 45*, 385–392.

Demme, J. (Director). (1991). *The silence of the lambs.* [Motion picture]. United States: Strong Heart/Demme Production & Orion Pictures Corporation.

Department of Defense. (2010, September). *Suicide event report: Annual report.* Washington, DC: Author.

Department of Homeland Security. (2006, November 22). *Privacy impact assessment for the Automated Targeting System.* Washington, DC: Author.

Department of Homeland Security. (2008a, July 24). *Implementing privacy protections in government data mining.* Washington, DC: Author. Available at http://www.dhs.gov/xlibrary/assets/privacy/privacy_datamining_July24_2008_minutes.pdf

Department of Homeland Security. (2008b, December 15). *Privacy impact assessment for the Future Attribute Screening Technology (FAST) project.* Washington, DC: Author.

Department of the Army. (1988, September 30). *Suicide prevention and psychological autopsy.* Washington, DC: Author.

DePaulo, B. M., Lindsay, J. J., Malone, B. E., Muhlenbruck, L., Charlton, K., & Cooper, H. (2003). Cues to deception. *Psychological Bulletin, 129,* 74–118.

Dern, H., Dern, C., Horn, A., & Horn, U. (2009). The fire behind the smoke: A reply to Snook and colleagues. *Criminal Justice and Behavior, 36,* 1085–1090.

Deslauriers-Varin, N., & Beauregard, E. (2010). Victims' routine activities and sex offenders' target selection scripts: A latent class analysis. *Sexual Abuse: A Journal of Research and Treatment, 22,* 315–342.

Devery, C. (2010). Criminal profiling and criminal investigation. *Journal of Contemporary Criminal Justice, 26,* 393–409.

Dickens, G., Sugarman, P., Edgar, S., Hofberg, K., Tewari, S., & Ahmad, F. (2009). Recidivism and dangerousness in arsonists. *Journal of Forensic Psychiatry & Psychology, 20,* 621–639.

Dietz, A. S. (2000). Toward the development of a roles framework for police psychology. *Journal of Police and Criminal Psychology, 15,* 1–4.

Dietz, P. E. (1985). Sex offender profiling by the FBI: A preliminary conceptual model. In M. H. Ben-Aron, S. J. Hucker, & C. D. Webster (Eds.), *Clinical criminology: The assessment and treatment of criminal behavior* (pp. 207–219). Toronto, ON: Clarke Institute of Psychiatry.

Ditzler, T. G. (2004). Malevolent minds: The teleology of terrorism. In F. M. Moghaddam & A. J. Marsella (Eds.), *Understanding terrorism: Psychosocial roots, consequences, and interventions* (pp. 187–206). Washington, DC: American Psychological Association.

Dodge, K. A. (2003). Do social information-processing patterns mediate aggressive behavior? In B. B. Lahey, T. E. Moffitt, & A. Caspi (Eds.), *Causes of conduct disorder and juvenile delinquency* (pp. 254-276). New York: Guilford Press.

Dodge, K. A., Landsford, J. E., Burks, V. S., Bates, J. E., Pettit, G. S., Fontaine, R., et al. (2003). Peer rejection and social information-processing factors in the development of aggressive behavior problems in children. *Child Development, 74,* 374–393.

Dodge, K. A., & Pettit, G. S. (2003). A biopsychological model of the development of chronic conduct problems in adolescence. *Developmental Psychology, 39,* 349–371.

Doley, R. (2003). Pyromania: Fact or fiction. *British Journal of Criminology, 43,* 797–807.

Douglas, A.-J. (2011, August). Child abductions: Known relationships are the greater danger. *FBI Law Enforcement Bulletin, 80*(8), 8–9.

Douglas, J. E. (2007, Spring). Inside the mind of the mind hunter. *Annals of the American Psychotherapy Association,* 8–11.

Douglas, J. E., Burgess, A. W., Burgess, A. G., & Ressler, R. K. (1992). *Crime classification manual: A standard system for investigating and classifying violent crimes.* New York: Lexington Books.

Douglas, J. E., Burgess, A. W., Burgess, A. G., & Ressler, R. K. (2006). *Crime classification manual: A standard system for investigating and classifying violent crimes* (2nd ed.). San Francisco: Jossey-Bass.

Douglas, J. E., & Munn, C. (1992a). The detection of staging and personation at the crime scene. In J. E. Douglas, A. W. Burgess, A. G. Burgess, & R. K. Ressler (Eds.), *Crime classification manual* (pp. 249–258). New York: Lexington Books.

Douglas, J. E., & Munn, C. (1992b). Modus operandi and the signature aspects of violent crime. In J. E. Douglas, A. W. Burgess, A. G. Burgess, & R. K. Ressler (Eds.), *Crime classification manual* (pp. 259–268). New York: Lexington Books.

Douglas, J. E., & Munn, C. (1992c, February). Violent crime scene analysis. *FBI Law Enforcement Bulletin*, 1–10.

Douglas, J. E., & Olshaker, M. (1995). *Mind hunter: Inside the FBI's elite serial crime unit.* New York: Pocket Books.

Douglas, J. E., & Olshaker, M. (1999). *The anatomy of motive.* New York: Scribner.

Douglas, J. E., & Olshaker, M. (2000). *The cases that haunt us.* New York: Pocket Books.

Douglas, J. E., Ressler, R. K., Burgess, A. W., & Hartman, C. R. (1986). Criminal profiling from crime scene analysis. *Behavioral Sciences & the Law, 4,* 401–421.

Douglas, K. S., & Ogloff, J. R. P. (2003). The impact of confidence on the accuracy of structured professional and actuarial violence risk judgments in a sample of forensic psychiatric patients. *Law and Human Behavior, 27,* 573–587.

Drake v. Portuondo, 321 F. 3d 338 (2003).

Ducat, L., & Ogloff, J. R. P. (2011). Understanding and preventing bushfire-setting: A psychological perspective. *Psychiatry, Psychology and Law, 18,* 341–356.

Dupré, K. E., Barling, J., Turner, N., & Stride, C. B. (2010). Comparing perceived injustices from supervisors and romantic partners as predictors of aggression. *Journal of Occupational Health Psychology, 15,* 359–370.

Duwe, G., Donnay, W., & Tewksbury, R. (2008). Does residential proximity matter? A geographic analysis of sex offense recidivism. *Criminal Justice and Behavior, 35,* 484–504.

Dvorak, J. A. (2000, December 21). Kansas launches racial profiling study. *Kansas City Star,* pp. 1, 11.

Dwyer, K., Osher, D., & Warger, C. (1998). *Early warning, timely response: A guide to safe schools.* Washington, DC: U.S. Department of Education.

Ebert, B. W. (1987). Guide to conducting a psychological autopsy. *Professional Psychology: Research and Practice, 18,* 52–56.

Ebisike, N. (2008). *Offender profiling in the courtroom: The use and abuse of expert witness testimony.* Westport, CT: Praeger.

Eke, A. W., Hilton, N. Z., Meloy, J. R., Mohandie, K., & Williams, J. (2011). Predictors of recidivism by stalkers: A nine-year follow-up of police contacts. *Behavioral Sciences & the Law, 29,* 271–283.

Ekman, P. (2009). *Telling lies: Clues to deceit in the marketplace, politics, and marriage.* New York: Norton.

Ekman, P., & O'Sullivan, M. (1991). Who can catch a liar? *American Psychologist, 46,* 913–920.

Ekman, P., O'Sullivan, M., Friesen, W. V., & Scherer, K. (1991). *Journal of Nonverbal Behavior, 15,* 123–135.

Eldridge, J. D., & Jones, J. P. (1991). Warped space: A geography of distance decay. *Professional Geographer, 43,* 500–511.

Eldridge, T. R., Ginsburg, S., Hempel, W. T., II, Kephart, J. L., & Moore, K. (2004, August 21). *9/11 and terrorist travel: Staff Report of the National Commission on Terrorists Attacks upon the United States.* Washington, DC: U.S. Government Printing Office.

Faigman, D. L., & Monahan, J. (2009). Standards of legal admissibility and their implications for psychological science. In J. L. Skeem, K. S. Douglas, & S. O. Lilienfeld (Eds.), *Psychological science in the courtroom: Consensus and controversy* (pp. 3–25). New York: Guilford Press.

Fanetti, M., & Boles, R. (2004). Forensic interviewing and assessment issues with children. In W. T. O'Donohue & E. R. Levensky (Eds.), *Handbook of forensic psychology: Resource for mental health professionals and legal professionals* (pp. 245–265). Amsterdam: Elsevier.

Federal Bureau of Investigation. (1985, August). Crime scene and profile characteristics of organized and disorganized murders. *FBI Law Enforcement Bulletin, 54,* 18–25.

Federal Bureau of Investigation. (2005). *Crime in the United States 2004: Uniform Crime Reports.* Washington, DC: U.S. Department of Justice.

Federal Bureau of Investigation. (2010a). *Crime in the United States 2009: Uniform Crime Reports.* Washington, DC: U.S. Department of Justice.

Federal Bureau of Investigation. (2010b, August 7). *NCIC missing persons and unidentified person statistics for 2007.* Washington, DC: Federal Bureau of Investigation, National Crime Information Center.

Federal Bureau of Investigation. (2011a, May 9). *Behavioral interview program: Attempting to understand violent offenders.* Available at http://www.fbi.gov/news/stories/2011/may/bau_050911/bau_050911

Federal Bureau of Investigation. (2011b). *Crime in the United States 2010: Uniform Crime Reports.* Washington, DC: U.S. Department of Justice.

Federal Bureau of Investigation. (2011c, March 23). *Non-family abductions.* Washington, DC: U.S. Department of Justice.

Fein, R. A., & Vossekuil, B. (1998, July). *Protective intelligence and threat assessment investigations: A guide for state and local law enforcement officials.* Washington, DC: U.S. Department of Justice and U.S. Secret Service.

Fein, R. A., Vossekuil, B., & Holden, G. A. (1995, July). *Threat assessment: An approach to prevent targeted violence.* Washington, DC: U.S. Department of Justice, National Institute of Justice.

Filbert, K. (2008, February). Targeting crime in hot spots and hot places. *Geography & Public Safety, 1*(1), 4–7.

Fingar, T. (2011). Analysis in the U.S. intelligence community: Missions, masters, and methods. In B. Fishschhoff & C. Chauvin (Eds.), *Intelligence analysis: Behavioral and social scientific foundations* (pp. 3–27). Washington, DC: National Academies Press.

Finkelhor, D., Hammer, H., & Sedlak, A. J. (2002, October). *Nonfamily abducted children: National estimates and characteristics.* Washington, DC: U.S. Department of Justice.

Finkelhor, D., Hotaling, G. T., & Sedlack, A. J. (1992). The abduction of children by strangers and nonfamily members: Estimating the incidence using multiple methods. *Journal of Interpersonal Violence, 7,* 226–243.

Finkelhor, D., Ormrod, R., Turner, H., & Hamby, S. L. (2005). The victimization of children and youth: A comprehensive, national survey. *Child Maltreatment, 10,* 5–25.

Finn, R. (2008). Criminal profiler shares some secrets. *Psychiatry News, 36*(5), 36.

Firestone, P., Bradford, J. M., Greenberg, D. M., & Larose, M. R. (1998). Homicidal sex offenders: Psychological, phallometric, and diagnostic features. *Journal of the American Academy of Psychology and Law, 26,* 537–552.

Fisher, B. S., Cullen, F. T., & Turner, M. G. (2000). *Sexual victimization of college women.* Washington, DC: U.S. Department of Justice, National Institute of Justice.

Fiske, I. D. (2010). Failure to secure the skies: Why America has struggled to protect itself and how it can change. *Virginia Journal of Law & Technology, 15,* 173–197.

Fontaine, N., Carbonneau, R., Vitaro, F., Barker, E. D., & Tremblay, R. E. (2009). Research review: A critical review of studies on the developmental trajectories of antisocial behavior in females. *Journal of Child Psychology and Psychiatry, 50,* 363–385.

Foster, D. (2000). *Author unknown: On the trail of the anonymous.* New York: Henry Holt.

Fox, J. A., & Levin, J. (1998). Multiple murder: Patterns of serial and mass murder. In M. Tonry (Ed.), *Crime and justice: A review of the research* (pp. 407–455). Chicago: University of Chicago Press.

Fox, J. A., & Levin, J. (2003). Mass murder: An analysis of extreme violence. *Journal of Applied Psychoanalytic Studies, 5*, 47–64.

Fox, J. A., & Levin, J. (2005). *Extreme killing: Understanding serial and mass murder.* Thousand Oaks, CA: Sage.

Frank, M. G., & Ekman, P. (1997). The ability to detect deceit generalizes across different types of high-stake lies. *Journal of Personality and Social Psychology, 72*, 1429–1439.

Franklin, K. (2008). The Tim Masters case: Chasing Reid Meloy. *In the News.* Available at http://forensicpsychologist.blogspot.com/2008/02/tim-masters-case-chasing-reid-meloy.html

Fritzon, K. (2001). An examination of the relationship between distance travelled and motivational aspects of arson. *Journal of Environmental Psychology, 21*, 45–60.

Fritzon, K., Canter, D., & Wilton, Z. (2001). The application of an action system mode to destructive behaviour: The examples of arson and terrorism. *Behavioral Sciences & the Law, 19*, 657–690.

Fritzon, K., & Ridgway, J. (2001). Near-death experience: The role of victim reaction in attempted homicide. *Journal of Interpersonal Violence, 16*, 679–696.

Frye v. United States, 293 F. 1013 (D.C. Cir. 1923).

Gatowski, S., Dobbin, S., Richardson, J. T., Ginsburg, G., Merlino, M., & Dahir, V. (2001). Asking the gatekeepers: A national survey of judges on judging expert evidence in a post-Daubert world. *Law and Human Behavior, 25*, 433–458.

Geberth, V. J. (1993, July). Suicide-by-cop: Inviting death from the hands of a police officer. *Law and Order*, 105–106.

Geberth, V. J. (2004). An equivocal death and staged crime scene: Making a homicide appear to be a suicide. *Law and Order, 52*(11), 7–14.

Gekoski, A., & Gray, J. M. (2011). "It may be true, but how's it helping?" UK police detectives' views of the operational usefulness of offender profiling. *International Journal of Police Science and Management, 13*, 103–116.

Gelles, M. G. (1995). The psychological autopsy: An investigative aid. In M. I. Kurke & E. M. Scrivner (Eds.), *Police psychology into the 21st century* (pp. 337–355). Hillsdale, NJ: Erlbaum.

General Electric Co. v. Joiner, 522 U.S. 136 118 S. Ct. 512 (1997).

Gentile, S. R., Asamen, J. K., Harmell, P. H., & Weathers, R. (2002). The stalking of psychologists by their clients. *Professional Psychology: Research and Practice, 33*, 490–494.

George, J. A. (2008). Offender profiling and expert testimony: Scientifically valid or glorified results? *Vanderbilt Law Review, 61*(1), 221–260.

Gerler, E. R., Jr. (2007). What the Amish taught us. *Journal of School Violence, 6*, 1–2.

Gier, V. S., Kreiner, D. S., & Hudnell, W. J. (2012). AMBER alerts: Are school-type photographs the best choice for identifying missing children? *Journal of Police and Criminal Psychology, 27*, 9–23.

Giggie, M. A. (2010). Psychological autopsy in children and adolescents. In E. G. Benedek, P. Ash, & C. L. Scott (Eds.), *Principles and practice of child and adolescent mental health* (pp. 431–442). Arlington, VA: American Psychiatric Publishing.

Ginges, J., Atran, S., Sachdeva, S., & Medin, D. (2011). Psychology out of the laboratory: The challenge of violent extremism. *American Psychologist, 66*, 507–519.

Gladwell, M. (2005). *Blink: The power of thinking without thinking.* New York: Little, Brown.

Gladwell, M. (2009). Dangerous minds: Criminal profiling made easy. In M. Gladwell (Ed.), *What the dog saw* (pp. 336–356). New York: Little, Brown.

Godwin, G. M. (2000). *Hunting serial predators: A multivariate classification approach to profiling violent behavior.* Boca Raton, FL: CRC Press.

Godwin, M., & Canter, D. (1997). Encounter and death: The spatial behavior of U.S. serial killers. *Policing: An International Journal of Police Strategy and Management, 20*, 24–38.

Goodman, N. (1978). *Ways of worldmaking.* Indianapolis, IN: Hackett.

Goodwill, A. M., & Alison, L. J. (2006). The development of a filter model for prioritizing suspects in burglary offences. *Psychology, Crime and Law, 12*, 395–416.

Gordon, M. E., Kleiman, L. S., & Hanie, C. A. (1978). Industrial-organization psychology: Open thy ears O house of Israel. *American Psychologist, 33*, 893–905.

Gosink, P., & Jumbelic, M. I. (2000). Autoerotic asphyxiation in a female. *American Journal of Forensic Medicine and Pathology, 21*, 114–118.

Gosling, S. D. (2008). *Snoop: What your stuff says about you.* New York: Basic Books.

Gosling, S. D., Ko, S. J., Mannarelli, T., & Morris, M. E. (2002). A room with a cue: Personality judgments based on offices and bedrooms. *Journal of Personality and Social Psychology, 82*, 370–398.

Gottfredson, G. D., Gottfredson, D. C., Payne, A. A., & Gottfredson, N. C. (2005). School climate predictors of school disorder: Results from a national study of delinquency prevention in schools. *Journal of Research in Crime and Delinquency, 42*, 412–444.

Granhag, P. A., & Knieps, M. (2011). Episodic future thought: Illuminating the trademarks of forming true and false intentions. *Applied Cognitive Psychology, 25*, 274–280.

Greenberg, L., & Barling, J. (1999). Predicting employee aggression against coworkers, subordinates and supervisors: The roles of person behaviors and perceived workplace factors. *Journal of Organizational Behavior, 20*, 897–913.

Greenburg, M. M. (2011). *The Mad Bomber of New York: The extraordinary true story of the manhunt that paralyzed a city.* New York: Union Square Press.

Gregorie, T. (2000). Workplace violence. In G. Coleman, M. Gaboury, M. Murray, & A. Seymour (Eds.), *1999 National Victim Assistance Academy* (pp. 1–27). Washington, DC: U.S. Department of Justice.

Gretton, H. M., McBride, M., Hare, R. D., O'Shaughnessy, R., & Kumka, G. (2001). Psychopathy and recidivism in adolescence sex offenders. *Criminal Justice and Behavior, 28*, 427–449.

Griffin, T., & Miller, M. K. (2008). Child abduction, AMBER Alert, and crime control theater. *Criminal Justice Review, 33*, 159–176.

Griffin, T., Miller, M. K., Hoppe, J., Rebideaux, A., & Hammack, R. (2007). A preliminary examination of AMBER Alert's effects. *Criminal Justice Policy Review, 18*, 378–394.

Groth, A. N. (1979a). *Men who rape: The psychology of the offender.* New York: Plenum.

Groth, A. N. (1979b). Sexual trauma in the life histories of rapists and child molesters. *Victimology, 4*, 10–16.

Grove, W. M., & Meehl, P. E. (1996). Comparative efficiency of informal (subjective, impressionistic) and formal (mechanical, algorithmic) prediction procedures: The clinical-statistical controversy. *Psychology, Public Policy, and Law, 2*, 293–323.

Grubin, D. (2002). The potential use of polygraph in forensic psychiatry. *Criminal Behaviour and Mental Health, 12*, 45–55.

Grubin, D. (2008). The case for polygraph testing of sex offenders. *Legal and Criminological Psychology, 13*, 177–189.

Grubin, D., Kelly, P., & Brunsdon, C. (2001). *Linking serious sexual assaults through behaviour.* London: Home Office.

Gudjonsson, G. H., & Copson, G. (1997). The role of the expert in criminal investigation. In J. L. Jackson & D. A. Bekerian (Eds.), *Offender profiling: Theory, research and practice* (pp. 61–76). Chichester, UK: Wiley.

Guerette, R. T. (2002). Geographical profiling. In D. Levinson (Ed.), *Encyclopedia of crime and punishment* (Vol. 2, pp. 780–784). Thousand Oaks, CA: Sage.

Haines, J., Williams, C. L., & Lester, D. (2011). The characteristics of those who do and do not leave suicide notes: Is the method valid? *Omega: Journal of Death & Dying, 63,* 79–94.

Häkkänen, H., Hurme, K., & Liukkonen, M. (2007). Distance patterns and disposal sites in rural area homicides committed in Finland. *Journal of Investigative Psychology and Offender Profiling, 4,* 181–197.

Häkkänen, H., Linhlöf, P., & Santtila, P. (2004). Crime scene actions and offender characteristics in a sample of Finnish stranger rapes. *Journal of Investigative Psychology and Offender Profiling, 1,* 17–32.

Häkkänen, H., Puolakka, P., & Santtila, P. (2004). Crime scene actions and offender characteristics in arsons. *Legal and Criminological Psychology, 9,* 197–214.

Hallett, B. (2004). Dishonest crimes, dishonest language: An argument about terrorism. In F. M. Moghaddam & A. J. Marsella (Eds.), *Understanding terrorism: Psychosocial roots, consequences, and intervention* (pp. 49–68). Washington, DC: American Psychological Association.

Hanfland, K. A., Keppel, R. D., & Weis, J. G. (1997, May). *Case management for missing children homicide investigation.* Washington, DC: U.S. Department of Justice, Office of Justice Programs.

Hanson, R. K. (2005). Twenty years of progress in violence risk assessment. *Journal of Interpersonal Violence, 20,* 212–217.

Hanson, R. K. (2009). The psychological assessment of risk for crime and violence. *Canadian Psychology, 50,* 172–182.

Hanson, R. K., & Harris, A. J. R. (2000). Where should we intervene? Dynamic predictors of sexual offense recidivism. *Criminal Justice and Behavior, 27,* 6–35.

Harbort, S., & Mokros, A. (2001). Serial murders in Germany from 1945 to 1995: A descriptive study. *Homicide Studies, 5,* 311–334.

Harcourt, B. E. (2003). The shaping of chance: Actuarial models and criminal profiling at the turn of the twenty-first century. *University of Chicago Law Review, 70,* 105–128.

Harcourt, B. E. (2007). *Against prediction: Profiling, policing, and punishing in an actuarial age.* Chicago: University of Chicago Press.

Hare, R. D. (1980). A research scale for the assessment of psychopathy in criminal populations. *Personality and Individual Differences, 1,* 111–119.

Hare, R. D. (1991). *The Hare Psychopathy Checklist–Revised.* Toronto, ON: Multi-Health Systems.

Hare, R. D. (1996). Psychopathy: A clinical construct whose time has come. *Criminal Justice and Behavior, 23,* 25–54.

Hare, R. D. (1998). Psychopathy, affect, and behavior. In D. Cooke, A. Forth, & R. Hare (Eds.), *Psychopathy: Theory, research, and implications for society* (pp. 105–138). Dordrecht, The Netherlands: Kluwer.

Hare, R. D., Clark, D., Grann, M., & Thornton, D. (2000). Psychopathy and the predictive validity of the PCL-R: An international perspective. *Behavioral Sciences & the Law, 18,* 623–645.

Harries, K., & LeBeau, J. (2007). Issues in the geographic profiling of crime: Review and commentary. *Police Practice and Research, 8,* 321–333.

Harris, A. J. R., & Hanson, R. K. (2004). *Sex offender recidivism: A simple question.* Ottawa, ON: Public Safety and Emergency Preparedness Canada.

Harris, D. A. (1999, June). *Driving while black: Racial profiling on our nation's highways.* New York: American Civil Liberties Union. Available at http://www.aclu.org/profiling/report/index.html

Harris, D. A., Smallbone, S., Dennison, S., & Knight, R. (2009). Specialization and versatility in sexual offenders referred for civil treatment. *Journal of Criminal Justice, 37,* 33–37.

Harris, G. T., & Rice, M. E. (1996). A typology of mentally disordered firesetters. *Journal of Interpersonal Violence, 11,* 351–363.

Hart, S. D., & Dempster, R. J. (1997). Impulsivity and psychopathy. In C. D. Webster & M. A. Jackson (Eds.), *Impulsivity: Theory, assessment, and treatment* (pp. 212–232). New York: Guilford Press.

Hartup, W. W. (2005). The development of aggression: Where do you stand? In R. E. Tremblay, W. W. Hartup, & J. Archer (Eds.), *Developmental origins of aggression* (pp. 3–25). New York: Guilford Press.

Hartwig, M., Granhag, P. A., Strömwall, L. A. & Vrij, A. (2005). Detecting deception via strategic disclosure of evidence. *Law and Human Behavior, 29,* 469–484.

Hatch-Maillette, M. A., & Scalora, M. J. (2002). Gender, sexual harassment, workplace violence, and risk assessment: Convergence around psychiatric staff's perceptions of personal safety. *Aggression and Violence, 7,* 271–291.

Hayes, A., Outten, W. N., & Steer, R. L. (2000). Workplace violence: Prediction and prevention. *Pace Law Review,* Paper 471. Available at http://digitalcommons.pace.edu/lawrev/471

Hazelwood, R., & Burgess, A. (1995). *Practical aspects of rape investigation: A multidisciplinary approach* (2nd ed.). Boca Raton, FL: CRC Press.

Hazelwood, R., & Douglas, J. (1980, April). The lust murderer. *FBI Law Enforcement Bulletin, 49*(2), 18–24.

Hazelwood, R., Ressler, R. K., Depue, R. L., & Douglas, J. E. (1995). Criminal investigative analysis: An overview. In R. R. Hazelwood & A. W. Burgess (Eds.), *Practical aspects of rape investigation: A multidisciplinary approach* (2nd ed., pp. 115–126). Boca Raton, FL: CRC Press.

Hazelwood, R. R., & Warren, J. (2003). Linkage analysis: Modus operandi, ritual, and signature in serial sexual crime. *Aggression and Violent Behavior, 8,* 587–598.

Heil, P., Ahlmeyer, S., & Simons, D. (2003). Crossover sexual offenses. *Sexual Abuse: A Journal of Research and Treatment, 15,* 221–236.

Heilbrun, K., Dvoskin, J., & Heilbrun, A. (2009). Toward preventing future tragedies: Mass killings on college campuses, public health, and threat/risk assessment. *Psychological Injury and Law, 2,* 93–99.

Heilbrun, K., Marczyk, G. R., & DeMatteo, D. (2002). *Forensic mental health assessments: A casebook.* New York: Oxford University Press.

Heuer, R. J., Jr. (1999). *Psychology of intelligence analysis.* Washington, DC: Center for the Study of Intelligence, Central Intelligence Agency.

Hewitt, C. (2003). *Understanding terrorism in America: From the Klan to al Qaeda.* New York: Routledge.

Hickey, E. W. (1997). *Serial murderers and their victims* (2nd ed). Belmont, CA: Wadsworth.

Hickey, E. W. (2010). *Serial murderers and their victims* (5th ed.). Belmont, CA: Wadsworth.

Hicks, S. J., & Sales, B. D. (2006). *Criminal profiling: Developing an effective science and practice.* Washington, DC: American Psychological Association.

Hilton, N. Z., Harris, G. T., & Rice, M. E. (Eds.). (2010). *Risk assessment for domestically violent men: Tools for criminal justice, offender intervention, and victim services.* Washington, DC: American Psychological Association.

Hoffman, B. (1993). *"Holy terror": The implication of terrorism motivated by a religious imperative* (RAND Research Paper P-7834). Santa Monica, CA: RAND.

Holmes, R. M., & DeBurger, J. T. (1985). Profiles in terror: The serial murderer. In R. M. Holmes & S. T. Holmes (Eds.), *Contemporary perspectives on serial murder* (pp. 5–16). Thousand Oaks, CA: Sage.

Holmes, R. M., & DeBurger, J. (1988). *Serial murder.* Newbury Park, CA: Sage.

Holmes, R. M., & Holmes, S. T. (1998). *Serial murder* (2nd ed.). Thousand Oaks, CA: Sage.

Holmes, R. M., & Holmes, S. T. (2002a). *Profiling violent crimes: An investigative tool* (3rd ed.). Thousand Oaks, CA: Sage.

Holmes, R. M., & Holmes, S. T. (2009). *Profiling violent crimes: An investigative tool* (4th ed.). Thousand Oaks, CA: Sage.

Holmes, S. T., Hickey, E., & Holmes, R. M. (1991). Female serial murderesses: Constructing differentiating typologies. *Journal of Contemporary Criminal Justice, 7,* 245–256.

Holmes, S. T., & Holmes, R. M. (2002). *Sex crimes: Patterns and behavior* (2nd ed.). Thousand Oaks, CA: Sage.

Homant, R. J., & Kennedy, D. B. (1998). Psychological aspects of crime scene profiling: Validity research. *Criminal Justice and Behavior, 25,* 319–343.

Homant, R. J., & Kennedy, D. B. (2001). A typology of suicide of police incidents. In D. C. Sheehan & J. T. Warren (Eds.), *Suicide and law enforcement* (pp. 577–586). Washington, DC: U.S. Department of Justice, FBI Behavioral Science Unit.

Honts, C. R., Hartwig, M., Kleinman, S. M., & Meissner, C. A. (2009, April 17). *Credibility assessment at portals. Portals Committee Report.* Available at http://truth.boisestate.edu/eyesonly/Portals?PortalsCommitteReport.pdf

Hucker, S. J. (2008). Sexual masochism: Psychopathology and theory. In D. R. Laws & W. T. O'Donohue (Eds.), *Sexual deviance: Theory, assessment, and treatment* (2nd ed., pp. 250–263). New York: Guilford.

Hucker, S. J., & Blanchard, R. (1992). Death scene characteristics in 118 fatal cases of autoerotic asphyxia compared with suicidal asphyxia. *Behavioral Sciences & the Law, 10,* 509–523.

Hudson, R. A. (1999, September). *The sociology and psychology of terrorism: Who becomes a terrorist and why?* Washington, DC: Library of Congress, Federal Research Division.

Hutson, H. R., Anglin, D., Yarborough, J., Hardaway, K., Russell, M., Strote, J., et al. (1998). Suicide by cop. *Annals of Emergency Medicine, 32,* 665–669.

Icove, D. J., & Estepp, M. H. (1987, April). Motive-based offender profiles of arson and fire-related crime. *FBI Law Enforcement Bulletin,* 17–23.

Inbau, F. E., Reid, J. E., Buckley, J. P., & Jayne, B. C. (2001). *Criminal interrogation and confessions* (4th ed.). Gaithersburg, MD: Aspen Publishers.

Ingram, S. (1998). If the profile fits: Admitting criminal psychological profiles into evidence in criminal trials. *Journal of Urban and Contemporary Law, 54,* 239–267.

Jackson v. Indiana, 406 U.S. 715 (1972).

Jackson v. State, 553 So.2d 719 (1989).

Jackson, J. L., van Koppen, P. J., & Herbrink, J. C. M. (1993). *Does the service meet the needs? An evaluation of consumer satisfaction profile analysis and investigative advice offered by the Scientific Research Advisory Unit of the National Criminal Intelligence Division (CRI)—The Netherlands.* Leiden: Netherlands Institute for the Study of Criminality and Law Enforcement.

Jaffe, G. (2011, August 12). Army suicides set record in July. *The Washington Post,* National section, p. 1.

James, D. V., & Farnham, F. R. (2003). Stalking and serious violence. *Journal of the American Academy of Psychiatry and the Law, 31,* 432–439.

Janssen, W., Koops, E., Anders, S., Kuhn, S., & Püschel, K. (2005). Forensic aspects of 40 accidental autoerotic deaths in northern Germany. *Forensic Science International, 147S,* S61–S64.

Jeffreys-Jones, R. (2007). *The FBI: A history.* New Haven, CT: Yale University Press.

Jenkins, B. M. (2002, July 25). Get use to it: Our airports are vulnerable to terrorism. *Los Angeles Times.* Available at http://articles.latimes.com/2002/jul/25/opinion/oe-jenkins25

Jenkins, P. (1988). Serial murder in England 1940–1985. *Journal of Criminal Justice, 16,* 1–15.

Jenkins, P. (1993). Chance or choice: The selection of serial murder victims. In A. V. Wilson (Ed.), *Homicide: The victim/offender connection* (pp. 461–478). Cincinnati, OH: Anderson.

Johnson, S. D. (2008). Repeat burglary victimization: A tale of two theories. *Journal of Experimental Criminology, 4,* 215–240.

Johnson, S. D., Bowers, K., & Hirschfield, A. (1997). New insights in the spatial and temporal distribution of repeat victimisation. *British Journal of Criminology, 37*, 224–241.

Jones, N. J., & Bennell, C. (2007). The development and validation of statistical prediction rules for discrimination between genuine and simulated suicide notes. *Archives of Suicide Research, 11*, 219–233.

Jones, S. G. (2008, September 18). *Defeating terrorist groups: Testimony presented before the House Armed Services Committee, Subcommittee on Terrorism and Unconventional Threats and Capabilities.* Santa Monica, CA: RAND Corporation.

Kahneman, D., & Tversky, A. (1973). On the psychology of prediction. *Psychological Review, 80*, 237–251.

Kanin, E. J. (1994). False rape allegations. *Archives of Sexual Behavior, 23*, 81–92.

Kassin, S. M., Drizin, S. A., Grisso, T., Gudjonsson, G. H., Leo, R. A., & Redlich, A. D. (2010). Police induced confessions: Risk factors and recommendations. *Law and Human Behavior, 34*, 3–38.

Kassin, S. M., & Fong, C. T. (1999). "I'm innocent!": Effects of training on judgment of truth and deception in the interrogation room. *Law and Human Behavior, 23*, 499–516.

Kelly, G. A. (1963). *A theory of personality: The psychology of personal constructs.* New York: Norton.

Kendall, D., McElroy, H., & Dale, A. (1999). Developments in offending profiling: The analysis of rapists' speech. *Police Research and Management, 3*, 1–24.

Keppel, R. D., & Birnes, W. J. (2003). *The psychology of serial killer investigations: The grisly business unit.* San Diego, CA: Academic Press.

Keppel, R. D., Weis, J. G., Brown, K. M., & Welch, K. (2005). The Jack the Ripper murders: A modus operandi and signature analysis of the 1888–1991 Whitechapel murders. *Journal of Investigative Psychology and Offender Profiling, 2*, 1–21.

Kerlinger, F. N. (1973). *Foundations of behavioral research* (2nd ed.). New York: Holt.

Kessler, R. (2002). *The bureau: The secret history of the FBI.* New York: St. Martin's Press.

Kiilakoski, T., & Oksanen, A. (2011). Soundtrack of the school shootings: Cultural script, music and male rage. *Young, 19*(3), 247–249.

Kind, S. S. (1987). Navigational ideas and the Yorkshire Ripper investigation. *Journal of Navigation, 40*, 385–393.

Kitchin, R. M. (1994). Cognitive maps: What are they and why study them? *Journal of Environmental Psychology, 14*, 1–19.

Klinger, D. A. (2001). Suicidal intent in victim-precipitated homicide: Insights from the study of "suicide-by-cop." *Homicide Studies, 5*, 206–226.

Klintschar, M., Grabuschnigg, P., & Beham, A. (1998). Death from electrocution during autoerotic practice: Case report and review of the literature. *American Journal of Forensic Medicine and Pathology, 19*, 190–193.

Knabe-Nicol, S., & Alison, L. (2011). The cognitive expertise of geographic profilers. In L. Alison & L. Rainbow (Eds.), *Professionalizing offender profiling: Forensic and investigative psychology in practice* (pp. 126–159). London: Routledge.

Knight, R. A., & Prentky, R. A. (1987). The developmental antecedents and adult adaptations of rapist subtypes. *Criminal Justice and Behavior, 14*, 403–426.

Knight, R. A., & Prentky, R. A. (1990). Classifying sexual offenders: The development and corroboration of taxonomic models. In W. L. Marshall, D. R. Laws, & H. E. Barbaree (Eds.), *The handbook of sexual assault: Issues, theories, and treatments of the offender* (pp. 23–52). New York: Plenum.

Knight, R. A., Warren, J. I., Reboussin, R., & Soley, B. J. (1998). Predicting rapist type from crime-scene variables. *Criminal Justice and Behavior, 25*, 46–80.

Knoll, J. L. (2008). The psychological autopsy, Part I: Applications and methods. *Journal of Psychiatric Practice, 14*, 393–397.

Knoll, J. L. (2009). The psychological autopsy, Part II: Toward a standardized protocol. *Journal of Psychiatric Practice, 15*, 52–59.

Kocsis, R. N. (1997). Criminal profiling the residence location of serial rape and arson offenders. *Australian Police Journal, 51*, 250–253.

Kocsis, R. N. (2009). Criminal profiling: Facts, fiction, and courtroom admissibility. In J. L. Skeem, K. S. Douglas, & C. O. Lilienfeld (Eds.), *Psychological science in the courtroom: Consensus and controversy* (pp. 246–262). New York. Guilford.

Kocsis, R. N. (2010). *Criminal profiling: Principles and practice*. Totowa, NJ: Humana Press.

Kocsis, R. N., Cooksey, R. W., & Irwin, H. J. (2002). Psychological profiling of offender characteristics from crime behaviors in serial rape offenses. *International Journal of Offender Therapy and Comparative Criminology, 46*, 144–169.

Kocsis, R. N., & Irwin, H. J. (1997). An analysis of spatial patterns in serial rape, arson, and burglary: The utility of the circle theory of environmental range for psychological profiling. *Psychiatry, Psychology, and the Law, 4*, 195–206.

Kocsis, R. N., Irwin, H. J., Hayes, A. F., & Nunn, R. (2000). Expertise in psychological profiling: A comparative assessment. *Journal of Interpersonal Violence, 15*, 311–331.

Korem, D. (1997). *The art of profiling: Reading people right the first time*. Richardson, TX: International Focus Press.

Kraemer, G. W., Lord, W. D., & Heilbrun, K. (2004). Comparing single and serial homicide offenses. *Behavioral Sciences & the Law, 22*, 325–343.

Kropp, P. R., Hart, S. D., & Lyon, D. R. (2008). Risk assessment of public figure stalkers. In J. R. Meloy, L. Sheridan, & J. Hoffmann (Eds.), *Stalking, threatening, and attacking public figures: A psychological and behavioral analysis* (pp. 343–361). New York: Oxford University Press.

Kropp, P. R., Hart, S. D., Lyon, D. R., & Storey, J. E. (2011). The development and validation of the Guidelines for Stalking Assessment and Management. *Behavioral Sciences & the Law, 29*, 302–316.

Kumho Tire Co. v. Carmichael, 199 S. Ct. 1167 (1999).

La Fon, D. S. (2002). The psychological autopsy. In B. E. Turvey (Ed.), *Criminal profiling: An introduction to behavioral evidence analysis* (2nd ed., pp. 157–167). San Diego, CA: Academic Press.

La Fon, D. S. (2008). The psychological autopsy. In B. E. Turvey (Ed.), *Criminal profiling: An introduction to behavioral evidence analysis* (3rd ed., pp. 419–429). Amsterdam: Elsevier/Academic Press.

Laird, R. D., Jordan, K. Y., Dodge, K. A., Pettit, G. S., & Bates, J. E. (2001). Peer rejection in childhood, involvement with antisocial peers in early adolescence, and the development of externalizing behavior problems. *Development and Psychopathology, 13*, 337–354.

Lambie, I., & Randell, I. (2011). Creating a firestorm: A review of children who deliberately light fires. *Clinical Psychology Review, 31*, 307–327.

Langan, P. A., Schmitt, E. C., & Durose, M. R. (2003, November). *Recidivism of sex offenders released from prison in 1994*. Washington, DC: U.S. Department of Justice, Office of Justice Programs.

Langer, W. C. (1943). *The mind of Adolf Hitler: The secret wartime report*. New York: Basic Books.

Langman, P. (2009). Rampage school shooters: A typology. *Aggression and Violent Behavior, 14*, 79–86.

Larkin, R. W. (2009). The Columbine legacy: Rampage shootings as political acts. *American Behavioral Scientist, 52*, 1309–1326.

Laukkanen, M., & Santtila, P. (2006). Predicting the residential location of a serial commercial robber. *Forensic Science International, 157*, 71–82.

Laukkanen, M., Santtila, P., Jern, P., & Sandnabba, K. (2008). Predicting offender home location in urban burglary series. *Forensic Science International, 176,* 224–233.

Le, D., & Macnab, A. J. (2001). Self strangulation by hanging from cloth towel dispensers in Canadian schools. *Injury Prevention, 7,* 231–233.

Leary, M. R., Kowalski, R. M., Smith, L., & Phillips, S. (2003). Teasing, rejection, and violence: Case studies of the school shootings. *Aggressive Behavior, 29,* 202–214.

LeBlanc, M. M., & Barling, J. (2005). Understanding the many faces of workplace violence. In S. Fox & P. E. Spector (Eds.), *Counterproductive work behavior: Investigations of actors and targets* (pp. 41–63). Washington, DC: American Psychological Association.

LeBlanc, M. M., & Kelloway, E. K. (2002). Predictors and outcomes of workplace violence and aggression. *Journal of Applied Psychology, 87,* 444–453.

Leclerc, B., Wortley, R., & Smallbone, S. (2010). Investigating mobility patterns for repetitive sexual contact in adult child sex offending. *Journal of Criminal Justice, 38,* 648–656.

Leitner, M., & Kent, J. (2009). Bayesian journey-to-crime modeling of single and multiple crime-type series in Baltimore County, MD. *Journal of Investigative Psychology and Offender Profiling, 6,* 213–236.

Leo, R. A. (2008). *Police interrogation and American justice.* Cambridge, MA: Harvard University Press.

Levine, N. (2000). *CrimeStat: A spatial statistics program for the analysis of crime incident locations.* Annandale, VA: Ned Levine & Associates.

Levine, N. (2002). *CrimeStat II: A spatial statistics program for the analysis of crime incident locations.* Houston, TX: Ned Levine & Associates.

Levine, N. (2009). Introduction to the special issue on Bayesian journey-to-crime estimation. *Journal of Investigative Psychology and Offender Profiling, 6,* 167–185.

Lewin, T. (2001, January 1). New state laws tackle familiar national issues. *New York Times.* Available at http://www.nytimes.com/2001/01/01/us/new-state-laws-tackle-familiar-national-issues.html

Lilienfeld, S. O., & Landfield, K. (2008). Science and pseudoscience in law enforcement: A user-friendly primer. *Criminal Justice and Behavior, 35,* 1215–1230.

Lindsay, M. S. (2001). Identifying the dynamics of suicide by cop. In D. C. Sheehan & J. T. Warren (Eds.), *Suicide and law enforcement* (pp. 599–606). Washington, DC: U.S. Department of Justice, Behavioral Science Unit.

Linkletter, M., Gordon, K., & Dooley, J. (2011). The choking game and YouTube: A dangerous combination. *Clinical Pediatrics, 49,* 274–279.

Lisak, D., Conklin, A., Hopper, J., Miller, P. M., Altschuler, L., & Smith, B. M. (2000). The Abuse-Perpetration Inventory: Development of a valid assessment instrument for research on the cycle of violence. *Family Violence & Sexual Assault Bulletin, 16*(1), 21–30.

Lisak D., Gardinier, L., Nicksa, S. C., & Cote, A. M. (2010). False allegations of sexual assault: An analysis of ten years of reported cases. *Violence Against Women, 16,* 1318–1334.

Lisak, D., & Miller, P. M. (2002). Repeat rape and multiple offending among undetected rapists. *Violence and Victims, 17,* 73–84.

Loftus, E. F. (2011). Intelligence gathering post-9/11. *American Psychologist, 66,* 532–541.

Lonsway, K. A. (2010). Trying to move the elephant in the living room: Responding to the challenge of false rape reports. *Violence Against Women, 16,* 1356–1371.

Lord, V. B. (2000). Law enforcement–assisted suicide. *Criminal Justice and Behavior, 27,* 401–419.

Lord, W. D., Boudreaux, M. C., & Lanning, K. V. (2001, April). Investigating potential child abduction cases: A developmental perspective. *FBI Law Enforcement Bulletin,* 1–10.

Lundrigan, S., & Canter, D. V. (2001). A multivariate analysis of serial murderers' disposal site location choice. *Journal of Environmental Psychology, 21,* 423–431.

Lundrigan, S., & Czarnomski, S. (2006). Spatial characteristics of serial sexual assault in New Zealand. *Australian and New Zealand Journal of Criminology, 39,* 218–231.

MacKenzie, R. D., McEwan, T. E., Pathé, M., James, D. V., Ogloff, J. R. P., & Mullen, P. E. (2009). *Stalking Risk Profile: Guidelines for the assessment and management of stalkers.* Melbourne, Australia: Centre for Forensic Behavioural Science.

Macnab, A. J., Deevska, M., Gagnon, F., Cannon, W. G., & Andrew, T. (2009). Asphyxial games or "the choking game": A potentially fatal risk behavior. *Injury Prevention, 15,* 45–49.

Maikovich, A. K. (2005). A new understanding of terrorism using cognitive dissonance principles. *Journal for the Theory of Social Behaviour, 35,* 373–397.

Mamalian, C. A., & LaVigne, N. G. (1999, January). *The use of computerized crime mapping by law enforcement: Survey results.* Washington, DC: U.S. Department of Justice, National Institute of Justice.

Maris, R. W., Berman, A. L., & Silverman, M. M. (2000). *Comprehensive textbook of suicidology.* New York: Guilford.

Markson, L., Woodhams, J., & Bond, J. W. (2010). Linking serial residential burglary: Comparing the utility of modus operandi behaviours, geographical proximity, and temporal proximity. *Journal of Investigative Psychology and Offender Profiling, 7,* 91–107.

Marshall, B. C., & Alison, L. J. (2007). Stereotyping, congruence and presentation order: Interpretative biases in utilizing offender profiles. *Psychology, Crime & Law, 13,* 285–303.

Martineau, M. M., & Corey, S. (2008). Investigating the reliability of the Violent Crime Linkage System (ViCLAS) crime report. *Journal of Police and Criminal Psychology, 23,* 51–60.

Martonosi, S. E., & Barnett, A. (2006). How effective is security screening of airline passengers? *Interfaces, 36,* 545–552.

Masters v. People, 58 P.3d 979, 983 (Colo. 2002).

Mazzoni, G., & Vannucci, M. (2007). Hindsight bias, the misinformation effect, and false autobiographical memories. *Social Cognition, 25,* 203–220.

McClave, J. L., Russell, P. J., Lyren, A., O'Riordan, M. A., & Bass, N. E. (2010). The choking game: Physician perspectives. *Pediatrics, 125,* 82–87.

McCue, C. (2011, March). Proactive policing: Using geographic analysis to fight crime. *Geography & Public Safety, 2*(4), 3–5.

McEwan, T. E., Mullen, P. E., & Purcell, R. (2007). Identifying risk factors in stalking: A review of current research. *International Journal of Law and Psychiatry, 30,* 1–9.

McEwan, T. E., Pathé, M., & Ogloff, J. R. P. (2011). Advances in stalking risk assessment. *Behavioral Sciences & the Law, 29,* 180–201.

McGee, J., & DeBernardo, C. (1999). The classroom avenger: A behavioral profile of school-based shootings. *Forensic Examiner, 8,* 16–18.

McGowan, M. R., Horn, R. A., & Mellott, R. N. (2011). The predictive validity of the Structured Assessment of Violence Risk in youth in secondary educational settings. *Psychological Assessment, 23,* 478–486.

McWhorter, S. K., Stander, V. A., Merrill, L. L., Thomsen, C. J., & Milner, J. S. (2009). Reports of rape reperpetration by newly enlisted male Navy personnel. *Violence and Victims, 24,* 204–218.

Meadows, S. (2006, July 17). Murder on their minds. *Newsweek,* pp. 28–29.

Meagher, P. J. (1956, December 25). 16-year search for madman. *New York Times,* pp. 1, 31.

Meehl, P. E. (1954). *Clinical versus statistical prediction: A theoretical analysis and a review of the evidence.* Minneapolis: University of Minnesota Press.

Meissner, C. A., Hartwig, M., & Russano, M. B. (2010). The need for a positive psychological approach and collaborative effort for improving practice in the interrogation room. *Law and Human Behavior, 34,* 43–45.

Meissner, C. A., & Kassin, S. M. (2002). "He's guilty!": Investigation bias in judgments of truth and deception. *Law and Human Behavior, 26*, 469–480.

Meissner, C. A., & Lassiter, G. D. (2010). Conclusion: What have we learned? Implications for practice, policy, and future research. In G. D. Lassiter & C. A. Meissner (Eds.), *Police interrogations and false confessions: Current research, practice, and policy recommendations*. Washington, DC: American Psychological Association.

Meloy, J. R., & Felthouse, A. (2011). Introduction to this issue: International perspectives on stalking. *Behavioral Sciences & the Law, 29*, 139–140.

Melton, G. B., Petrila, J., Poythress, N. G., & Slobogin, C. (2007). *Psychological evaluations for the courts: A handbook for mental health professionals and lawyers*. New York: Guilford.

Merckelbach, H., Jelicic, M., & Pieters, M. (2011). The residual effect of feigning: How intentional faking may evolve into a less conscious form of symptom reporting. *Journal of Clinical and Experimental Neuropsychology, 33*, 131–139.

Merry, S., & Harsent, L. (2000). Intruders, pilferers, raiders and invaders: The interpersonal dimension of burglary. In D. Canter & L. Alison (Eds.), *Profiling property crimes* (pp. 31–56). Burlington, VT: Ashgate.

Meyer, C. B. (2010). Criminal profiling as expert evidence? An international case law perspective. In R. N. Kocsis (Ed.), *Criminal profiling: International theory, research, and practice* (pp. 207–247). Totowa, NJ: Humana Press.

Mischel, W. (1968). *Personality and assessment*. New York: Wiley.

Mischel, W., & Peake, P. K. (1982). Beyond déjà vu in the search for cross-sectional consistency. *Psychological Review, 89*, 730–735.

Moffitt, T. E. (1993a). Adolescent-limited and life-course persistent antisocial behavior: A developmental taxonomy. *Psychological Review, 100*, 674–701.

Moffitt, T. E. (1993b). The neuropsychology of conduct disorder. *Development and Psychopathology, 5*, 135–151.

Moffit, T. E. (2003). The new look of behavior genetics in developmental psychopathology: Gene–environmental interplay in antisocial behavior. *Psychological Bulletin, 131*, 533–554.

Moffitt, T. E. (2006). Life-course-persistent versus adolescent-limited antisocial behavior. In D. Cicchetti & D. J. Cohen (Eds.), *Developmental psychopathology. Vol. 3: Risk, disorder, and adaptation* (2nd ed., pp. 570–598). Hoboken, NJ: Wiley.

Moffitt, T. E., Caspi, A., Harrington, H., & Milne, B. J. (2002). Males on the life-course-persistent and adolescence-limited antisocial pathways: Follow-up at age 26 years. *Development and Psychopathology, 14*, 179–207.

Moghaddam, F. M. (2004). Cultural preconditions for potential terrorist groups: Terrorism and societal change. In F. M. Moghaddam & A. J. Marsella (Eds.), *Understanding terrorism: Psychosocial roots, consequences, and interventions* (pp. 103–117). Washington, DC: American Psychological Association.

Mohandie, K. (2004). Stalking behavior and crisis negotiations. *International Journal of Police Crisis Negotiations, 4*, 23–44.

Mohandie, K., Meloy, J. R., McGowan, M. G., & Williams, J. (2006). The RECON typology of stalking: Reliability and validity based upon a large sample of North American stalkers. *Journal of Forensic Sciences, 51*, 147–155.

Monahan, J. (1981). *The clinical prediction of violent behavior*. Rockville, MD: National Institute of Mental Health.

Monahan, J. (1996). Violence prediction: The past twenty years and the next twenty years. *Criminal Justice and Behavior, 23*, 107–120.

Monahan, J., Steadman, H. J., Silver, E., Appelbaum, P. S., Robbins, P. C., Mulvey, E. P., et al. (2001). *Rethinking risk assessment: The MacArthur Study of Mental Disorder and Violence.* New York: Oxford University Press.

Monahan, K. C., Steinberg, L., & Cauffman, E. (2009). Affiliation with antisocial peers, susceptibility to peer influence, and antisocial behavior during the transition to adulthood. *Developmental Psychology, 45,* 1520–1530.

Monahan, T. F. (2001). Suicide by cop: Strategies for crisis negotiations and first responders. In D. C. Sheehan & J. T. Warren (Eds.), *Suicide and law enforcement* (pp. 637–646). Washington, DC: U.S. Department of Justice, FBI Behavioral Science Unit.

Montet, L. (2008). The observations of the French judiciary: A critique of the French Ministry of Justice policy report into criminal analysis. In R. N. Kocsis (Ed.), *Criminal profiling: International theory, research, and practice* (pp. 289–302). Totowa, NJ: Humana Press.

Moore, W. H., Petrie, C. V., Braga, A. A., & McLaughlin, B. L. (2003). *Deadly lessons: Understanding lethal school violence.* Washington, DC: National Academies Press.

Morgan, F. (2001). Repeat burglary in a Perth suburb: Indicator of short-term or long-term risk? In G. Farrell & K. Pease (Eds.), *Repeat victimization* (pp. 83–118). Monsey, NY: Criminal Justice Press.

Morris, N., & Miller, M. (1985). Predictions of dangerousness. In M. Tonry & N. Morris (Eds.), *Crime and justice: An annual review of research* (Vol. 6, pp. 1–50). Chicago: University of Chicago Press.

Morris, T. P. (1957). *The criminal area: A study in social ecology.* London: Routledge and Kegan Paul.

Morton, R. J., & Hilts, M. A. (Eds.). (2005). *Serial murder: Multidisciplinary perspectives for investigators.* Washington, DC: U.S. Department of Justice, Federal Bureau of Investigation.

Moses, S. (1990). Psychologists criticize probe of blast on Iowa. *APA Monitor, 21*(2), 20.

Mullen, P. E., MacKenzie, R., Ogloff, J. R. P., Pathé, M., McEwan, T., & Purcell, R. (2006). Assessing and managing risk in the stalking situation. *Journal of the American Academy of Psychiatry and Law, 34,* 439–450.

Mullen, P. E., Pathé, M., & Purcell, R. (2000). *Stalkers and their victims.* Cambridge, UK: Cambridge University Press.

Mullen, P. E., Pathé, M., & Purcell, R. (2001). Stalking: New constructions of human behaviour. *Australian and New Zealand Journal of Psychiatry, 35,* 9–16.

Mullen, P. E., Pathé, M., & Purcell, R. (2009). *Stalkers and their victims* (2nd ed.). Cambridge, UK: Cambridge University Press.

Mullen, P. E., Pathé, P. E., Purcell, R., & Stuart, G. W. (1999). Study of stalkers. *American Journal of Psychiatry, 156,* 1244–1249.

Muller, D. A. (2000). Criminal profiling: Real science or just wishful thinking? *Homicide Studies, 4,* 234–264.

Murray, H. A. (1943). Analysis of the personality of Adolf Hitler: With predictions of his future behavior and suggestions for dealing with him now and after Germany's surrender. Washington, DC: Office of Strategic Services.

Murthy, V. (2010). Psychological autopsy: A review. *Al Ameen Journal of Medical Science, 3,* 177–181.

Musch, J., & Wagner, T. (2007). Did everyone know it all along? A review of individual differences in hindsight bias. *Social Cognition, 25,* 64–82.

Muschert, G. W. (2002). *Media and massacre: The social construction of the Columbine story.* Boulder: University of Colorado Press.

Myers, W. C. (2004). Serial murder by children and adolescents. *Behavioral Sciences & the Law, 22,* 357–374.

Nader, K., & Mello, C. (2002). Shootings, hostage takings, and children. In A. M. La Greca, W. K. Silverman, E. M. Vernberg, & M. C. Roberts (Eds.), *Helping children cope with disasters and terrorism* (pp. 301–326). Washington, DC: American Psychological Association.

Nagayama-Hall, G. (1992, November/December). Inside the mind of the rapist. *Psychology Today*, 25, p. 12.

Nagin, D. (2007). Moving choice to center stage in criminological research and theory. *Criminology, 45*, 259–272.

Napolitano, J. (2010, September 22). *Statement of Secretary Janet Napolitano before the United States Senate Committee on Homeland Security and Government Affairs: Nine years after 9/11: Confronting the terrorist threat to the homeland.* Available at http://www.dhs.gov/ynews/testimony/testimony_1285168556484.shtm

Napolitano, J. (2011, August 8). How DHS is countering violent extremism. *The Blog@Homeland Security*. Available at http://blog.dhs.gov/2011/08/how–dhs–is–countering–violent–extremism.html

National Center for Missing & Exploited Children. (2010). 2009 *AMBER Alert Report*. Alexandria, VA: Author.

National Institute of Justice. (2011). *Special report: Making sense of DNA backlogs, 2010—Myths vs. reality*. Washington, DC: Author.

National Research Council. (2003). *The polygraph and lie detection*. Committee to Review the Scientific Evidence on the Polygraph. Washington, DC: National Academies Press.

National Research Council. (2008). *Protecting individual privacy in the struggle against terrorists: A framework for assessment*. Washington, DC: National Academies Press.

National Research Council. (2010). *Field evaluation in the intelligence and counterintelligence context*. Washington, DC: National Academies Press.

Neitzel, A. R., & Gill, J. R. (2011). Death certification of "suicide by cop." *Journal of Forensic Sciences, 56*, 1657–1660.

Nesbo, J. (2010). *The snowman* (D. Bartlett, Trans.). New York: Knopf.

Nestler, S. (2010). Belief perseverance: The role of accessible content and accessibility experiences. *Social Psychology, 41*, 35–41.

Neuman, J. H., & Baron, R. A. (1998). Workplace violence and workplace aggression: Evidence concerning specific forms, potential causes, and preferred targets. *Journal of Management, 24*, 391–419.

Newman, D. W., & Brown, N.-Q. D. (2009). Historical overview and perceptions of racial and terrorist profiling in an era of Homeland Security. *Criminal Justice Policy Review, 20*, 359–374.

Nickerson, R. S. (2011). Role of human factors and ergonomics in meeting the challenge of terrorism. *American Psychologist, 66*, 555–566.

Nikolas, K. (2011, October 17). DHS tests Future Attribute Screening Technology. *Digital Journal*. Available at http://www.digitaljournal.com/article/312942

9/11 Commission. (2004, September 9). *The 9/11 Commission Report*. Washington, DC: U.S. Government Printing Office.

Nolan, C. (2011, April 29). Men's fashions of the 1930s. *Encyclopedia.com*.

Ogloff, J. R. P., & Otto, R. K. (1993). Psychological autopsy: Clinical and legal perspectives. *Saint Louis University Law Journal, 37*, 607–644.

Omestad, T. (1994, Summer). Psychology and the CIA: Leaders on the couch. *Foreign Policy, 94*, 104–122.

Ormerod, D., & Sturman, J. (2005). Working with the courts: Advice for expert witnesses. In L. Alison (Ed.), *The forensic psychologist's casebook: Psychological profiling and criminal investigation* (pp. 170–193). Portland, OR: Willan.

O'Toole, M. E. (1999, February). Criminal profiling: The FBI uses criminal investigative analysis to solve crimes. *Corrections Today*, 44–46.

O'Toole, M. E. (2000). *The school shooter: A threat assessment perspective.* Quantico, VA: Critical Incident Response Group, National Center for the Analysis of Violent Crime.

Otto, R. K., Poythress, N., Starr, L., & Darkes, J. (1993). An empirical study of reports of the APA's peer review panel in the congressional review of the U.S.S. *Iowa* incident. *Journal of Personality Assessment, 61,* 425–442.

Oyster, C. K. (2001). Police reactions to suicide by cop. In D. C. Sheehan & J. T. Warren (Eds.), *Suicide and law enforcement* (pp. 647–652). Washington, DC: U.S. Department of Justice, FBI Behavioral Science Unit.

Palerea, R., Zona, M. A., Lane, J. C., & Langhinrichsen-Rohling, J. (1999). The dangerous nature of intimate relationship stalking: Threats, violence, and associated risk factors. *Behavioral Science & the Law, 17,* 269–283.

Pardini, D., & Loeber, R. (2008). Interpersonal callousness trajectories across adolescence: Early social influences and adult outcomes. *Criminal Justice and Behavior, 35,* 173–196.

Parry, J., & Drogan, E. Y. (2000). *Criminal law handbook on psychiatric and psychological evidence and testimony.* Washington, DC: American Bar Association.

Passenger profiling important to aviation security, experts say. (2002, February 28). *Aviation Daily, 347*(40), p. 3.

Patterson, G. R. (1982). *Coercive family processes.* Eugene, OR: Castalia Press.

Paulsen, D. (2006). Connecting the dots: Assessing the accuracy of geographic profiling software. *Policing: An International Journal of Police Strategies & Management, 29,* 306–334.

Paulsen, D. (2007). Improving geographic profiling through commuter/marauder prediction. *Police Practice and Research, 8,* 347–357.

Pavlidis, J., Eberhardt, N. L., & Levine, J. A. (2002). Seeing through the face of deception. *Nature, 415,* 35.

Pearsall, B. (2010, June). Predictive policing: The future of law enforcement? *NIJ Journal, 266,* 16–19.

People v. Drake, 129 A. D. 2d 963, 514 N.Y.S 2d 280 (1987).

People v. Masters, 33 P.3d 1191 (Colo. App. 2001).

Petherick, W. (Ed.). (2006). *Serial crime: Theoretical and practical issues in behavioral profiling.* Amsterdam: Elsevier/Academic Press.

Pinizzotto, A. J. (1984). Forensic psychology: Criminal personality profiling. *Journal of Police Science and Administration, 12,* 32–40.

Pinizzotto, A. J., Davis, E. F., & Miller, C. E. (2005, February). Suicide by cop: Defining a devastating dilemma. *FBI Law Enforcement,* 8–20.

Pinizzotto, A. J., & Finkel, N. J. (1990). Criminal personality profiling: An outcome and process study. *Law and Human Behavior, 14,* 215–234.

Piquero, A. R., Brame, R., Fagan, J., & Moffitt, T. E. (2005, May). *Assessing the offending activity of criminal domestic violence suspects: Offense specialization, escalation, and de-escalation evidence from the Spouse Assault Replication Program.* Washington, DC: U.S. Department of Justice, National Criminal Justice Reference Service.

Piquero, A. R., Farrington, D. P., Nagin, D. S., & Moffitt, T. E. (2010). Trajectories of offending and their relation to life failure in late middle age: Findings from the Cambridge Study in Delinquent Development. *Journal of Research in Crime and Delinquency, 47,* 151–173.

Police Services Act. (2010, July 5, 2010). *Violent Crime Linkage Analysis System Reports.* Ontario Regulation 265/10. Available at http://www.canlii.org/en/on/laws/regu/o-reg-550-96/latest/

Pollock, W., Joo, H.-J., & Lawton, B. (2010). Juvenile arrest rates for burglary: A routine activities approach. *Journal of Criminal Justice, 38,* 572–579.

Popper, K. (1968). *The logic of scientific discovery.* New York: Harper & Row.

Porter, S., Fairweather, D., Drugge, J., Herve, H., Birt, A. R., & Boer, D. (2000). Profiles of psychopathy in incarcerated sexual offenders. *Criminal Justice and Behavior, 27*, 216–233.

Porter, S., Woodworth, M., & Birt, A. R. (2000). Truth, lies and videotape: An investigation of the ability of federal probation officers to detect deception. *Law and Human Behavior, 24*, 643–658.

Porter, S., Woodworth, M., Earle, J., Drugge, J., & Boer, D. (2003). Characteristics of sexual homicides committed by psychopathic and nonpsychopathic offenders. *Law and Human Behavior, 27*, 459–480.

Portzky, G., Audenaert, K., & van Heeringen, K. (2009). Psychological and psychiatric factors associated with adolescent suicide: A case–control psychological autopsy study. *Journal of Adolescence, 32*, 849–862.

Post, J. M., & Gold, S. N. (2002). The psychology of the terrorist: An interview with Jerrold M. Post. *Journal of Trauma Practice, 1*, 83–100.

Poythress, N. G., Otto, R. K., Darkes, J., & Starr, L. (1993). APA's expert panel in the congressional review of the USS *Iowa* incident. *American Psychologist, 48*, 8–15.

Prentky, R. A., & Knight, R. A. (1991). Identifying critical dimensions for discriminating among rapists. *Journal of Consulting and Clinical Psychology, 59*, 643–661.

Pritchard, T. (2001, February 4). Inside the hunt for a serial rapist. *The Observer*. Available at http://www.guardian.co.uk/uk/2001/feb/04/theobserver.uknews1

Prohaska, T. J. (2010, May 27). Murder sentence longer, 50 to life, in Drake retrial. *BuffaloNews.com*.

Quinet, K. (2007). The missing missing: Toward a quantification of serial murder victimization in the United States. *Homicide Studies, 11*, 319–339.

R. v. Guilfoyle (2001). 2 Cr. App. Rep 57.

R. v. Hillier (2003). ACTSC 50, 25 June 2003 (Australia).

R. v. Klymchuck (2005). 203 C.C.C. 3d 341 (Ont. C.A.).

R. v. Mohan (1994). 89 C.C.C. 3d 402; 114 D.L.R. 4th 419.

R. v. Ranger (2003). 178 C.C.C. 3d 375.

R. v. Stagg (1994). 9 Arch News, 4.

Racial Profiling Data Collection Resource Center. (2011). *Legislation and litigation*. Boston: Northeastern University. Available at http://www.racialprofilinganalysis.neu.edu/legislation/

Rainbow, L. (2011). Taming the beast: The UK approach to the management of behavioural investigative advice. In L. Alison & L. Rainbow (Eds.), *Professionalizing offender profiling* (pp. 5–17). London: Routledge.

Rainbow, L., Almond, L., & Alison, L. (2011). BIA support to investigative decision making. In L. Alison & L. Rainbow (Eds.), *Professionalizing offender profiling* (pp. 35–50). London: Routledge.

Rainbow, L., & Gregory, A. (2011). What behavioural investigative advisers actually do. In L. Alison & L. Rainbow (Eds.), *Professionalizing offender profiling* (pp. 18–34). London: Routledge.

Ramirez, D. A., Hoopes, J., & Quinlan, T. L. (2003). Defining racial profiling in a post–September 11 world. *American Criminal Law Review, 40*, 1195–1239.

Ramirez, D. A., McDevitt, J., & Farrell, A. (2000, November). *A resource guide on racial profiling data collection systems: Promising practices and lessons learned*. Boston: Northeastern University Press. Available at http://www.usdoj.gov

Ramsland, K. (2009, Spring). James A. Brussel: The "Sherlock Holmes of the couch." *Forensic Examiner, 18*(1), 29–33.

Ravich, T. M. (2007). Is airline passenger profiling necessary? *University of Miami Law Review, 62*, 1–52.

Regina v. Stagg. (1994). CCC 14th September.

Reiser, M. (1972). *The police department psychologist.* Springfield, IL: Charles C Thomas.

Rengert, G. F., & Groff, E. (2011). *Residential burglary: How the urban environment and our lifestyles play a contributing role* (3rd ed.), Springfield, IL: Charles C Thomas.

Ressler, R. K., Burgess, A. W., Douglas, J. E., Hartman, C. R., & D'Agostino, R. B. (1986). Sexual killers and their victims: Identifying patterns through crime scene analysis. *Journal of Interpersonal Violence, 1,* 288–308.

Ressler, R. K., Burgess, A. W., Hartman, C. R., Douglas, J. E., & McCormack, A. (1986). Murderers who rape and mutilate. *Journal of Interpersonal Violence, 1,* 273–283.

Review of Navy Investigation of U.S.S. Iowa Explosion. (1990). Joint Hearings before the Investigations Subcommittee and the Defense Policy Panel of the Committee on Armed Services, House of Representatives, 101st Congress, 1st Session (HASC No. 101–41). Washington, DC: U.S. Government Printing Office.

Rhodes, W. M., & Conley, C. (2008). Crime and mobility: An empirical study. In D. Canter & D. Youngs (Eds.), *Principles of geographical offender profiling* (pp. 127–148). Burlington, VT: Ashgate.

Rich, T., & Shively, M. (2004, December). *A methodology for evaluating geographic profiling software.* Cambridge, MA: Abt Associates.

Risinger, D. M., & Loop, J. L. (2002). Three card monte, Monty Hall, modus operandi and "offender profiling": Some lessons of modern cognitive science for the law of evidence. *Cardozo Law Review, 24,* 193–211.

Ritchie, E. C., Benedek, D., Malone, R., & Carr-Malone, R. (2006). Psychiatry and the military. *Psychiatric Clinics of North America, 29,* 695–707.

Ritchie, E. C., & Gelles, M. G. (2002). Psychological autopsy: The current Department of Defense effort to standardize training and quality assurance. *Journal of Forensic Sciences, 47,* 1370–1372.

Romans, J. S. C., Hays, J. R., & White, T. K. (1996). Stalking and related behaviors experienced by counseling center staff members from current and former clients. *Professional Psychology: Research and Practice, 27,* 595–599.

Ronson, J. (2010, May 14). Whodunnit? *The Guardian.* Available at http://www.guardian.co.uk/uk/2010/may/15/criminal-profiling-jon-ronson

Rosenfeld, B. (2004). Violence risk factors in stalking and obsessional harassment: A review and preliminary meta-analysis. *Criminal Justice and Behavior, 31,* 9–36.

Rosenfeld, B., Fava, J., & Galietta, M. (2009). Working with the stalking offender: Considerations for risk assessment and intervention. In D. J. Whitaker & J. R. Lutzer (Eds.), *Preventing partner violence: Research and evidence-based intervention strategies* (pp. 95–109). Washington, DC: American Psychological Association.

Rosenfeld, B., & Harmon, R. (2002). Factors associated with violence in stalking and obsessional harassment cases. *Criminal Justice and Behavior, 29,* 671–691.

Ross, M. P. (2000). Shame, blame, and community: Justice responses to violence against women. *American Psychologist, 55,* 1332–1343.

Ross, R., & Anderson, C. A. (1982). Shortcomings in the attribution process: On the origins and maintenance of erroneous social assessments. In D. Kahneman, S. P. Slovic, & A. Tversky (Eds.), *Judgments under uncertainty: Heuristic and biases* (pp. 129–152). Cambridge, UK: Cambridge University Press.

Rossi, D. (1982). Crime scene behavioral analysis: Another tool for the law enforcement investigator. *Police Chief, 18*(4), 152–155.

Rossmo, D. K. (1995). Place, space, and police investigations: Hunting serial violent criminals. In J. E. Eck & D. Weisburd (Eds.), *Crime and place* (pp. 217–235). New York: Criminal Justice Press.

Rossmo, D. K. (1997). Geographic profiling. In J. L. Jackson & D. A. Bekerian (Eds.), *Offender profiling: Theory, research and practice* (pp. 159–175). Chichester, UK: Wiley.

Rossmo, D. K. (2000). *Geographic profiling*. Boca Raton, FL: CRC Press.

Rothman, A. J., & Hardin, C. D. (1997). Differential use of the availability heuristic in social judgment. *Personality and Social Psychology Bulletin, 23*, 123–138.

Rubin, J. (2011, October 29). Police link 6 more slayings to Grim Sleeper suspect. *Los Angeles Times.* Available at http://articles.latimes.com/2011/oct/29/local/la-me-grim-sleeper-20111029.

Rubin, K. H., Bukowski, W., & Parker, J. G. (2006). Peer interactions, relationships, and groups. In N. Eisenberg (Ed.), *Handbook of child psychology, Vol. 3: Social, emotional, and personality development* (6th ed., pp. 571–601). Hoboken, NJ: Wiley.

Sagovsky, A., & Johnson, S. D. (2007). When does repeat burglary victimization occur? *Australian and New Zealand Journal of Criminology, 40*, 1–26.

Saint-Cyr, Y. (2011, September 1). Canadian Air Transport Security Authority to scrutinize travelers' behaviour at airports. *Slaw.* Available at http://slaw.practicesource.com/blog/tag/canadian-air-transport-security/

Salekin, R. T., Brannen, D. N., Zalot, A. A., Leistico, A.-M. & Neumann, C. S. (2006). Factor structure of psychopathy in youth: Testing the applicability of the new four-factor model. *Criminal Justice and Behavior, 33*, 133–157.

Salfati, C. G., & Bateman, A. L. (2005). Serial homicide: An investigation of behavioural consistency. *Journal of Investigative Psychology and Offender Profiling, 2*, 121–144.

Salfati, C. G., & Canter, D. V. (1999). Differentiating stranger murders: Profiling offending characteristics from behavioral styles. *Behavioral Sciences & the Law, 17*, 391–406.

Santtila, P., Häkkänen, H., Alison, L., & Whyte, C. (2003). Juvenile firesetters: Crime scene actions and offender characteristics. *Legal and Criminological Psychology, 8*, 1–20.

Santtila, P., Pakkanen, T., Zappalà, A., Bosco, D., Valkama, M., & Mokros, A. (2008). Behavioural crime linking in serial homicide. *Psychology, Crime & Law, 14*, 245–265.

Sarangi, S., & Alison, L. (2005). Life story accounts of left-wing terrorists in India. *Journal of Investigative Psychology and Offender Profiling, 2*, 69–86.

Sauvageau, A. (2008). Autoerotic deaths: A seven-year retrospective epidemiological study. *The Open Forensic Sciences Journal, 1*, 1–5.

Sauvageau, A., & Racette, S. (2006). Autoerotic deaths in the literature from 1954 to 2004: A review. *Journal of Forensic Sciences, 51*, 140–146.

Schieber et al. v. City of Philadelphia, 156 F.Supp.2d 451 (E.D. Pa. 2001).

Schields, L. B. E., Hunsaker, D. M., & Hunsaker, J. C. (2005). Autoerotic asphyxia. *American Journal of Forensic Medicine and Pathology, 26*, 45–52.

Schields, L. B. E., Hunsaker, D. M., Hunsaker, J. C., Wetli, C. V., Hutchins, K. D., & Holmes, R. M. (2005). Atypical autoerotic death: Part II. *American Journal of Forensic Medicine and Pathology, 26*, 53–62.

Schott, J. C., Davis, G. J., & Hunsaker, J. C., III. (2003). Accidental electrocution during autoeroticism: A shocking case. *American Journal of Forensic Medicine and Pathology, 24*, 92–95.

Schwartz-Watts, D. M. (2006). Commentary: Stalking Risk Profile. *Journal of the American Academy of Psychiatry and Law, 34*, 455–457.

Scott, E. S., & Steinberg, L. (2008). Adolescent development and regulation of youth crime. *The Future of Children, 18*, 15–33.

Scott, S. (2010, November 24). The threats and realities of airline security. *Homeline1.* Available at http://www.homeland1.com/air-traffic/articles/913564-The-threats-and-realities-of-airline-security/

Scoville, D. (1998, November). Getting you to pull the trigger. *Police*, 36–44.

Selkin, J. (1987). *Psychological autopsy in the courtroom.* Denver, CO: Author.

Selkin, J. (1994). Psychological autopsy: Scientific psychohistory or clinical intuition? *American Psychologist, 49,* 74–75.

Sellbom, M., Fischler, G. L., & Ben-Porath, Y. S. (2007). Identifying MMPI-2 predictors of police officer integrity and misconduct. *Criminal Justice and Behavior, 34,* 985–1004.

Sewell, K. W., & Mendelsohn, M. (2000). Profiling potentially violent youth: Statistical and conceptual problems. *Children's Services: Social Policy, Research, and Practice, 3,* 147–169.

Shaw, C. R., & McKay, H. D. (1969). *Juvenile delinquency and urban areas.* Chicago: University of Chicago Press.

Sheehan, M., & Butler, E. (1957, January 22). N.Y. "Mad Bomber" seized in state: Arrest made in Waterbury. *The Bridgeport Post,* pp. 1, 12.

Sheppard v. Maxwell, 384 U.S. 333 (1966).

Sheridan, L., & Roberts, K. (2011). Key questions to consider in stalking cases. *Behavioral Sciences & the Law, 29,* 255–270.

Sherman, C. (2003). *A rose for Mary: The hunt for the real Boston Strangler.* Boston: Northeastern University Press.

Shneidman, E. S. (1976). *Suicidology: Contemporary developments.* New York: Grune & Stratton.

Shneidman, E. S. (1981). The psychological autopsy. *Suicide and Life-Threatening Behavior, 11*(4), 325–340.

Shneidman, E. S. (1994). The psychological autopsy. *American Psychologist, 49,* 75–76.

Shye, S. (1985). *Facet theory approaches to social research.* New York: Springer Verlag.

Sicafuse, L. L., & Miller, M. K. (2010). Social psychological influences on the popularity of AMBER Alerts. *Criminal Justice and Behavior, 37,* 1237–1254.

Sickmund, M. (2010, February). *Juveniles in residential placement, 1997–2008.* Washington, DC: U.S. Department of Justice, Office of Juvenile Justice and Delinquency Prevention.

Silke, A. (2008). Holy warriors: Exploring the psychological processes of Jihadi radicalization. *European Journal of Criminology, 5,* 99–123.

Simmons v. State, 797 So.2d 1134 (Ala. Crim. App. 2000).

Simon, H. (1957). *Models of man: Social and rational.* Oxford, UK: Wiley.

Simonton, D. K. (1993). Putting the best leaders in the White House: Personality, policy, and performance. *Political Psychology, 14,* 537–557.

Skeem, J. L., Douglas, K. S., & Lilienfeld, S. O. (2009). *Psychological science in the courtroom: Consensus and controversy.* New York: Guilford.

Skeem, J. L., & Monahan, J. (2011). Current directions in risk assessment. *Current Directions in Psychological Science, 20,* 38–42.

Slatkin, A. A. (2003, April). Suicide risk and hostage/barricade situations involving older persons. *FBI Law Enforcement Bulletin,* 26–32.

Sloman, S. A., Over, D., Slovak, L., & Stibel, J. M. (2003). Frequencies illusion and other fallacies. *Organizational Behavior and Human Decision Processes, 91,* 296–309.

Snider, J. F., Hane, S., & Berman, A. L. (2006). Standardizing the psychological autopsy: Addressing the Daubert standard. *Suicide and Life-Threatening Behavior, 36,* 511–518.

Snook, B., Canter, D. V., & Bennell, C. (2002). Predicting the home location of serial offender: A preliminary comparison of the accuracy of human judges with a geographic profiling system: *Behavioral Sciences & the Law, 20,* 109–118.

Snook, B., Cullen, R. M., Bennell, C., Taylor, P. J., & Gendreau, P. (2008). The criminal profiling illusion: What's behind the smoke and mirrors? *Criminal Justice and Behavior, 35,* 1257–1276.

Snook, B., Cullen, R. M., Mokros, A., & Harbort, S. (2005). Serial murderers' spatial decisions: Factors that influence crime location choice. *Journal of Investigative Psychology and Offender Profiling, 2,* 147–161.

Snook, B., Eastwood, J., Gendreau, P., Goggin, C., & Cullen, R. M. (2007). Taking stock of criminal profiling: A narrative review and meta-analysis. *Criminal Justice and Behavior, 34,* 437–453.

Snook, B., Luther, K., House, J. C., Bennell, C., & Taylor, P. J. (2012). The Violent Crime Linkage Analysis System: A test of inter-rater reliability. *Criminal Justice and Behavior, 39,* 607–619.

Snook, B., Taylor, P. J., & Bennell, C. (2004). Geographic profiling: The fast, frugal, and accurate way. *Applied Cognitive Psychology, 18,* 105–121.

Snook, B., Taylor, P. J., & Bennell, C. (2005). Commentary: Shortcuts to geographic profiling success: A reply to Rossmo (2005). *Applied Cognitive Psychology, 19,* 655–661.

Snook, B., Taylor, P. J., Gendreau, P., & Bennell, C. (2009). On the need for scientific experimentation in the criminal profiling field: A reply to Dern and colleagues. *Criminal Justice and Behavior, 36,* 1091–1094.

Snook, B., Wright, M., House, J., & Alison, L. (2006). Searching for a needle in a needle stack: Combining criminal careers and journey-to-crime research for criminal suspect prioritization. *Police Practice and Research, 7,* 217–230.

Snyder, H. N. (2008, August). *Juvenile arrests 2005.* Washington, DC: U.S. Department of Justice, Office of Juvenile Justice and Delinquency Prevention.

Spaaij, R. (2010). The enigma of lone wolf terrorism: An assessment. *Studies in Conflict & Terrorism, 33,* 854–870.

Spitzberg, B. (2007). The state of the art of stalking: Taking stock of the emerging literature. *Aggression and Violent Behavior, 12,* 64–86.

Stambaugh, H., & Styron, H. (2003, January). *Special report: Firefighter arson.* Emmitsburg, MD: Department of Homeland Security, U.S. Fire Administration, National Fire Data Center.

State v. Armstrong, 587, So.2d 168 (La. Ct. Appl. 1991).

State v. Fortin, 162 N.J. 517 (2000).

State v. Fortin, 189 N.J. 579; 917 A.2d 746 (2007).

State v. Haynes, 1988 WL 99189 (Ohio Ct. App. Sept, 21, 1988).

State v. Lowe, 75 Ohio App. 3d 404, 599 N.E.2d 783 (Ohio Ct. App. 1991).

State v. Pennell, 584 A. 2d 513, Del. Super. Ct. (1989).

State v. Pennell, 602, A.2d 48 (Del. 1991).

State v. Sorabella, 277 Conn. 155, 891 A.2d 897 (2006).

State v. Wallace, 351 N.C. 481 (2000).

Stattin, H., Kerr, M., & Bergman, L. R. (2010). On the utility of Moffitt's typology trajectories in long-term perspective. *European Journal of Criminology, 7,* 521–545.

Steinberg, L. (2008). A social neuroscience perspective on adolescent risk taking. *Developmental Review, 28,* 78–106.

Steinberg, L. (2009). Should the science of adolescent brain development inform public policy? *American Psychologist, 11,* 739–750.

Steinberg, L. (2010). A dual systems model of adolescent risk-taking. *Developmental Psychobiology,* 216–224.

Steinberg, L., Graham, S., O'Brien, L., Woolard, J., Cauffman, E., & Banich, M. (2009). Age differences in future orientation and delay discounting. *Child Development, 80,* 28–44.

Steinberg, L., & Monahan, K. (2007). Age differences in resistance to peer influence. *Developmental Psychology, 43,* 1531–1543.

Stern, J. (2003). *Terror in the name of God: Why religious militants kill.* New York: HarperCollins.

Stevens, J. A. (1997). Standard investigatory tools and offender profiling. In J. L. Jackson & D. A. Bekerian (Eds.), *Offender profiling: Theory, research and practice* (pp. 77–91). Chichester, UK: Wiley.

Stouthamer-Loeber, M., Wei, E., Loeber, R., & Masten, A. S. (2004). Desistence from persistent serious delinquency in the transition to adulthood. *Development and Psychopathology, 16,* 897–918.

Suspect is held as "Mad Bomber"; he admits role. (1957, January 22). *New York Times*, pp. 1, 58.

Sysyn v. State, 756 So.2d 1058; 2000 Fla. App. Lexis 4238 (2000).

Ter Beek, M., van den Eshof, P., & Mali, B. (2009). Statistical modelling in the investigation of stranger rape. *Investigative Psychology and Offender Profiling, 7*, 31–47.

Terrazas, A. (2011, March). *Middle Eastern and North African immigrants in the United States.* Washington, DC: Migration Policy Institute.

Terrorism Research Center. (1997). *The basics: Combating terrorism.* Alexandria, VA: Author.

Thomas, P., Jones, L. A., & Gerstein, T. (2010, March 16). Special FBI team joins hunt for missing girl. *ABC News Nightline.* Available at http://abcnews.go.com/Nightline/TheLaw/lindsey-baum-missing-girl-fbi/story?id=10107104

Tjaden, P. (1997, November). The crime of stalking: How big is the problem? *NIJ Research Review.* Washington, DC: U.S. Department of Justice.

Tjaden, P., & Thoennes, N. (1998a). *Prevalence, incidence, and consequences of violence against women: Findings from the National Violence Against Women Survey.* Washington, DC: U.S. Department of Justice.

Tjaden, P., & Thoennes, N. (1998b, November). *Stalking in America: Findings from the National Violence Against Women Survey* (Research in brief). Washington, DC: U.S. Department of Justice.

Tonkin, M., Woodhams, J., Bull, R., Bond, J. W., & Palmer, E. J. (2011). Linking different types of crime using geographical and temporal proximity. *Criminal Justice and Behavior, 38*, 1069–1088.

Torres, A. N., Boccaccini, M. T., & Miller, H. A. (2006). Perceptions of the validity and utility of criminal profiling among forensic psychologists and psychiatrists. *Professional Psychology: Research and Practice, 37*, 51–58.

Travis, A. (2008, August 20). MI5 report challenges views on terrorism in Britain. *The Guardian.* Available at http://www.guardian.co.uk/uk/2008/aug/20/uksecurity.terrorism1/

Trentacosta, C. J., & Shaw, D. S. (2009). Emotional self-regulation, peer rejection, and antisocial behavior: Developmental associations from early childhood to early adolescence. *Journal of Applied Developmental Psychology, 30*, 356–365.

Turner, S. (1969). Delinquency and distance. In M. W. Wolfgang & T. Sellin (Eds.), *Delinquency: Selected studies* (pp. 11–26). New York: Wiley.

Turvey, B. E. (2000). *Affidavit filed in Estate of Sheppard v. State of Ohio, Case NO. 312322.* Available at http://www.corpus-delicti.com/sheppard.html

Turvey, B. E. (2002). Serial homicide. In B. E. Turvey (Ed.), *Criminal profiling: An introduction to behavioral evidence analysis* (2nd ed., pp. 513–528). San Diego, CA: Academic Press.

Turvey, B. E. (2008). *Criminal profiling: An introduction to behavioral evidence analysis* (3rd ed.). San Diego, CA: Elsevier.

Turvey, B. E. (2012). *Criminal profiling: An introduction to behavioral evidence analysis* (4th ed.). San Diego, CA: Elsevier.

Tversky, A., & Kahneman, D. (1973). Availability: A heuristic for judging frequency and probability. *Cognitive Psychology, 5*, 207–232.

Tversky, A., & Kahneman, D. (1974, September 27). Judgment under uncertainty: Heuristic and biases. *Science, 185*, 1124–1131.

Tversky, A., & Kahneman, D. (1982). Judgment under uncertainty: Heuristics and biases. In D. Kahneman, P. Slovic, & A. Tversky (Eds.), *Judgment under uncertainty* (pp. 3–20). New York: Cambridge University Press.

Uchida, C. D. (2011, March). A predictive policing symposium: A strategic discussion. *Geography & Public Safety, 3*(1), 2–3.

Ullman, S. E. (1997). Review and critique of empirical studies of rape avoidance. *Criminal Justice and Behavior, 24*, 177–204.

Ullman, S. E. (2007). A 10-year update of "review and critique of empirical studies of rape avoidance." *Criminal Justice and Behavior, 34,* 411–429.

Ullman, S. E., & Knight, R. (1995). Women's resistance strategies to different rapist types. *Criminal Justice and Behavior, 22,* 262–283.

United States v. Meeks, 35 M J. 64, 65 (C.M.A. 1992).

United States v. St. Jean, 1995 WL 106960. (1995).

United States v. Sokolow, 490 U.S. 1 (1989).

U.S. Department of Homeland Security. (2008, August 5). *Privacy impact assessment for the Screening of Passengers by Observation Techniques (SPOT) program.* Washington, DC: Author.

U.S. Department of Justice. (2000). *Terrorism in the United States—1998.* Washington, DC: Author.

U.S. Department of Justice. (2008). *Department of Justice Conference highlights AMBER Alert system success, finds way to enhance program.* Available at http://www.ojp.usdoj.gov/news room/pressreleases/2008/oaag09002.htm

U.S. Department of Justice, Office of the Inspector General. (2009, January). *Audit Report 09–08: The Federal Bureau of Investigation's effort to combat crimes against children.* Washington, DC: Author.

U.S. Department of Labor. (2011, March). *Workplace violence: Risk factors.* Washington, DC: Author.

U.S. Fire Administration. (March 11, 2011). *USFA announces the 2011 Arson Awareness Week theme.* Emmitsburg, MD: Author. Available at http://www.usfa.fema.gov/media/press/2011releases/033111.shtm

U.S. General Accounting Office. (1991, August). *U.S.S.* Iowa *explosion; Sandia National Laboratories' final technical report.* Washington, DC: Author.

U.S. Government Accountability Office. (2010, May). *Aviation security: Efforts to validate TSA's Passenger Screening Behavior Detection Program, but opportunities exist to strengthen validation and address operational challenges.* Washington, DC: Author. Available at http://www.gao.gov/new.items/d10763.pdf

U.S.S. Iowa *tragedy: An investigative failure: Report of the Investigations Subcommittee and the Defense Policy Panel of the Committee on Armed Services,* House of Representatives, 101st Congress, 2nd Session (1990).

VandenBos, G. R. (Ed.). (2007). *APA dictionary of psychology.* Washington, DC: American Psychological Association.

Van Koppen, P. J., & Jansen, W. J. (1998). The road to robbery: Travel patterns in commercial robberies. *British Journal of Criminology, 38,* 230–246.

Van Lier, P. A. C., Vitaro, F., Wanner, B., Vuijk, P., & Crijnen, A. A. M. (2005). Gender differences in developmental links among antisocial behavior, friends' antisocial behavior, and peer rejection in childhood: Results from two cultures. *Child Development, 76,* 841–855.

Van Lier, P. A. C., Vuijk, P., & Crijen, A. M. (2005). Understanding mechanisms of change in the development of antisocial behavior: The impact of a universal intervention. *Journal of Abnormal Psychology, 33,* 521–533.

Van Lier, P. A. C., Wanner, B., & Vitaro, F., (2007). Onset of antisocial behavior affiliation with deviant friends and childhood maladjustment: A text of the childhood- and adolescent-onset models. *Development and Psychopathology, 19,* 167–185.

Vaughn, M. G., Fun. Q., DeLisi, M., Wright, J. P., Beaver, K. M., Perron, B. E., & Howard, M. O. (2010). Prevalence and correlates of fire-setting in the United States: Results from the National Epidemiological Survey on Alcohol and Related Conditions. Comprehensive Psychiatry, *51,* 217–233.

Verlinden, S., Hersen, M., & Thomas, J. (2000). Risk factors in school shootings. *Clinical Psychology Review, 20,* 3–56.

Vitacco, M. J., Neumann, C. S., & Jackson, R. L. (2005). Testing a four-factor model of psychopathy and its association with ethnicity, gender intelligence, and violence. *Journal of Consulting and Clinical Psychology, 73,* 466–476.

Viteles, M. S. (1929). Psychological methods in the selection of patrolmen in Europe. *Annals of the American Academy, 146*, 160–165.

Vossekuil, B., Fein, R., Reddy, M., Borum, R., & Modzeleski, W. (2002). *The final report and findings of the Safe School Initiative: Implications for the prevention of school attacks in the United States*. Washington, DC: U.S. Secret Service and Department of Education.

Vrij, A. (2005). Cooperation of liars and truth tellers. *Applied Cognitive Psychology, 19*, 39–50.

Vrij, A. (2008). Nonverbal dominance versus verbal accuracy in lie detection: A plea to change police practice. *Criminal Justice and Behavior, 35*, 1323–1336.

Vrij, A. (2011). How I got started: From applied social psychology to applied cognitive psychology. *Applied Cognitive Psychology*. (DOI: 10.1002/acp.1841)

Vrij, A., & Granhag, P. A. (2007). Interviewing to detect deception. In S. A. Christianson (Ed.), *Offenders' memories of violent crimes* (pp. 279–304). Chichester, UK: Wiley.

Vrij, A., Leal, S., Granhag, P. A., Mann, S., Fisher, R. P., Hillman, J., & Sperry, K. (2009). Outsmarting the liars: The benefit of asking unanticipated questions. *Law and Human Behavior, 33*, 159–166.

Vrij, A., Leal, S., Mann, S. A., & Granhag, P. A. (2011). A comparison between lying about intentions and past activities: Verbal cues and detection accuracy. *Applied Cognitive Psychology, 25*, 212–218.

Vrij, A., Mann, S., Kristen, S., & Fisher, R. P. (2007). Cues to deception and ability to detect lies as a function of police interview styles. *Law and Human Behavior, 31*, 499–518.

Walsh, A. (2005). African Americans and serial killing in the media. *Homicide Studies, 9*, 271–291.

Walsh, D. (1980). *Break-ins: Burglary from private houses*. London: Constable.

Warmelink, L., Vrij, A., Mann, S., Leal, S., Forrester, D., & Fisher, R. P. (2011). Thermal imaging as a lie detection tool at airports. *Law and Human Behavior, 35*, 40–48.

Warren, J., Reboussin, R., Hazelwood, R., Cummings, A., Gibbs, N., & Trumbetta, S. (1998). Crime scene and distance correlates of serial rape. *Journal of Quantitative Criminology, 14*, 35–59.

Warren, L. J., Mullen, P. E., & Ogloff, J. R. P. (2011). A clinical study of those who utter threats to kill. *Behavioral Sciences & the Law, 29*, 141–154.

Webster, C. D., & Hucker, S. J. (2007). *Violence risk assessment and management*. West Sussex, UK: Wiley.

Weinberger, S. (2010, May 26). Airport security: Intent to deceive? *Nature, 465*, 412–415.

Weisbrot, D. M. (2008). Prelude to school shooting? Assessing threatening behaviors in childhood and adolescence. *Journal of the American Academy of Child & Adolescent Psychiatry, 47*, 847–852.

Werlang, B. G., & Botega, N. J. (2003). A semistructured interview for psychological autopsy: An inter-rater reliability study. *Suicide and Life-Threatening Behavior, 33*, 326–330.

Who gets "Mad Bomber" reward? Police or girl, or maybe, no one. (1957, January 23). *Ogden Standard-Examiner*, p. 2A.

Whren v. United States, 517 **U.S.** 806 (1996).

Wiesner, M., Kim, H. K., & Capaldi, D. M. (2005). Developmental trajectories of offending: Validation and prediction to young adult alcohol abuse, drug use, and depressive symptoms. *Development and Psychopathology, 17*, 251–270.

Wike, T. L., & Fraser, M. W. (2009). School shootings: Making sense of the senseless. *Aggression and Violent Behavior, 14*, 162–169.

Wilson, E. F., Davis, J. F., Bloom, J. D., Batten, P. J., & Kamara, S. G. (1998). Homicide or suicide: The killing of suicidal persons by law enforcement officers. *Journal of Forensic Sciences, 43*, 46–52.

Wilson, R. (2008, February). What is applied geography for the study of crime and public safety? *Geography & Public Safety, 1*(1), 1–3.

Winship, F. M. (1957, January 3). Wily mad bomber escapes all detection from police. *Fairbanks Daily News-Miner*, p. 9.

Wolf, B. C., & Lavezzi, W. A. (2007). Paths to destruction: The lives and crimes of two serial killers. *Journal of Forensic Science, 52*, 199–203.

Woodhams, J., Bull, R., & Hollin, C. R. (2010). Case linkage: Identifying crimes committed by the same offender. In R. N. Kocsis (Ed.), *Criminal profiling: International theory, research, and practice* (pp. 117–133). Totowa, NJ: Humana Press.

Woodhams, J., & Grant, T. (2006). Developing a categorization system for rapists' speech. *Psychology, Crime & Law, 12*, 245–260.

Woodhams, J., & Laubschagne, G. (2012). A test of case linkage principles with solved and unsolved serial rapes. *Journal of Police and Criminal Psychology, 27*, 85–98.

Woodhams, J., & Toye, K. (2007). An empirical test of the assumptions of case linkage and offender profiling with serial commercial robberies. *Psychology, Public Policy, and Law, 13*, 59–85.

Woodworth, M., & Porter, S. (2002). In cold blood: Characteristics of criminal homicides as a function of psychopathy. *Journal of Abnormal Psychology, 111*, 436–445.

Woskett, J., Coyle, I. R., & Lincoln, R. (2007). The probity of profiling: Opinions of Australian lawyers on the utility of criminal profiling in court. *Psychiatry, Psychology and Law, 14*, 306–314.

Wyllie, D. (2010, September 23). Terrorist Screening Center, database provide powerful tool in post-9/11 world. *Homeland, 1*, 1–4.

Yokota, K., & Canter, D. (2004). Burglars' specialisation: Development of a thematic approach in investigative psychology. *Behaviormetrika, 31*, 153–167.

Young, T. J. (1992). Procedures and problems in conducting a psychological autopsy. *International Journal of Offender Therapy and Comparative Criminology, 36*, 43–52.

Youngs, D. (2009). Investigative psychology in the courtroom: Beyond the offender profile. *Journal of Investigative Psychology and Offender Profiling, 6*, 1–9.

Youstin, T. J., Nobles, M. R., Ward, J. T., & Cook, C. L. (2011). Assessing the generalizability of the near repeat phenomenon. *Criminal Justice and Behavior, 38*, 1042–1063.

Zandbergen, P. A. (2008). Commentary on Duwe, Donnay, and Tewksbury (2008). "Does residential proximity matter? A geographic analysis of sex offenders recidivism." *Criminal Justice and Behavior, 35*, 1449–1451.

Photo Credits

Index

About the Authors

Curt R. Bartol was a college professor for more than 30 years, teaching a wide variety of both undergraduate and graduate courses, including Biopsychology, Criminal Behavior, Juvenile Delinquency, Introduction to Forensic Psychology, Social Psychology, and Psychology and Law. He earned his PhD in personality/social psychology from Northern Illinois University in 1972. He was instrumental in creating and launching Castleton State College's graduate program in forensic psychology and served as its director for 6 years. As a licensed clinical psychologist, he has been a consulting police psychologist to local, municipal, state, and federal law enforcement agencies for more than 30 years. In addition to this book, he has written *Criminal Behavior: A Psychosocial Approach* (now in its 10th edition). He also has coauthored *Juvenile Delinquency: A Systems Approach; Delinquency and Justice: A Psychosocial Approach* (2nd ed.); *Introduction to Forensic Psychology* (3rd ed.), and *Psychology and Law: Theory, Research, and Application* (3rd ed.). He also has been the long-time editor of the SAGE journal *Criminal Justice and Behavior*.

Anne M. Bartol earned an MA and a PhD in criminal justice from the State University of New York at Albany. She also holds an MA in journalism from the University of Wisconsin–Madison. She taught criminal justice, sociology, and journalism courses over a 20-year college teaching career, and has worked as a journalist and as a social worker in child and adolescent protective services. In addition to this book, she has coauthored *Introduction to Forensic Psychology; Juvenile Delinquency: A Systems Approach; Delinquency and Justice: A Psychosocial Approach; Psychology and Law: Theory, Research, and Application*; and *Criminal Behavior*. She has also served as book review editor and managing editor of *Criminal Justice and Behavior* and has published articles on women and criminal justice, rural courts, and the history of forensic psychology.

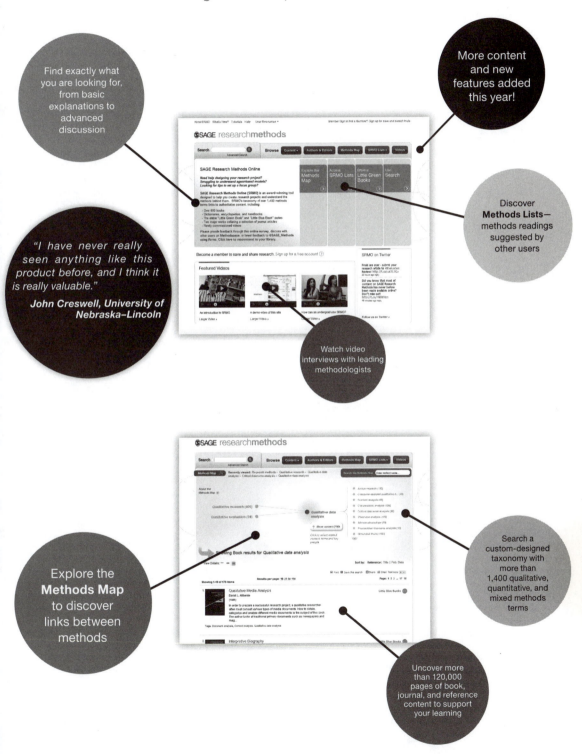

SAGE researchmethods

The essential online tool for researchers from the world's leading methods publisher

Find exactly what you are looking for, from basic explanations to advanced discussion

More content and new features added this year!

"I have never really seen anything like this product before, and I think it is really valuable."

John Creswell, University of Nebraska–Lincoln

Discover **Methods Lists**—methods readings suggested by other users

Watch video interviews with leading methodologists

Explore the **Methods Map** to discover links between methods

Search a custom-designed taxonomy with more than 1,400 qualitative, quantitative, and mixed methods terms

Uncover more than 120,000 pages of book, journal, and reference content to support your learning

Find out more at
www.sageresearchmethods.com